THE
ALPINE JOURNAL
2023

Tom Patey on the gabbro cliffs of Hirta near Dun channel, St Kilda. Mike Dixon's new biography of this legendary figure is reviewed on p301. *(John Cleare)*

THE
ALPINE JOURNAL
2023

The Journal of the Alpine Club

A record of mountain adventure
and scientific observation

Editor: Ed Douglas

Production: Nathan Ryder

Volume 127
Number 371

Supported by the
MOUNT EVEREST FOUNDATION

Published by
THE ALPINE CLUB

THE ALPINE JOURNAL 2023
Volume 127. Number 371

www.alpine-club.org.uk

Address all editorial communication to the Hon Editor:
Alpine Club, 55 Charlotte Rd, London EC2A 3QF

Address all sales and distribution communications to:
Cordee, 11 Jacknell Rd, Dodwells Bridge Ind Est, Hinckley LE10 3BS

Back numbers:
Apply to the Alpine Club, 55 Charlotte Rd, London EC2A 3QF or,
for 1969 to date, apply to Cordee, as above.

First published in 2023 by The Alpine Club
Typeset by Ryder Design – www.ryderdesign.studio
Printed and bound by Novoprint SA, Barcelona

A CIP catalogue record for this book is available from The British Library

ISBN 978-1-7399535-2-2

Front cover: Marek Holeček on his way down the 'never-ending' south-west ridge of Sura Peak (6764m) in Nepal's Honku valley, following the first ascent of *Simply Beautiful*, climbed with Matej Bernat, on the north-west face. *(Matěj Bernát)*

Endpapers
Front: The King Swing pendulum from Boot Flake on the Nose of El Capitan (VI, 5.8, A3), photographed by Glen Denny. Denny's life and highly regarded work are outlined in John Cleare's article on p97. 'An action image yet geometric in its simplicity, essentially three blank blocks of different texture are separated by the two vertical lines that outline the boot itself, the one a powerful black fissure, the other the fine peg crack that is used to surmount the flake.' *(Courtesy of Peggy Denny)*
Back: Charlie Raymond climbing *Moby Dick* in 1962, a short route on the lower south-west face of El Capitan (II, 5.9). 'In this carefully composed image,' Cleare writes, 'the climber, an interloper in this vertical wilderness of rock and roofs, of texture and shadow, fights his way up what appears to be the only possible line of weakness.' *(Courtesy of Peggy Denny)*

Foreword

A few years before the Great War, the Austrian-born philosopher Ludwig Wittgenstein spent a few weeks flying kites on Kinder Scout, research for a doctorate in the exciting new field of aeronautics.[1] He never completed his work. Solving engineering problems was replaced instead with ideas about how we think. Wittgenstein had a fascination for language and what he termed *Sprachspiel*, or 'language games', and thought a great deal about games in general. 'If there are no rules,' he once told his students at Cambridge, 'there is no game.'

Where does that leave alpinism? Our recent president Victor Saunders, whose valedictory speech appears in this year's *Alpine Journal*, tells me that alpinism must be a game because of the constant accusations of cheating. Yet even Wittgenstein wasn't sure that all games are played according to rules. Towards the end of his life he argued there are games we 'play aimlessly' or where we 'make up the rules as we go along.' There are also 'games with concealed rules', which players only discover after they start playing. That rings true for mountaineering. Then there are games that only pretend to be games. An obvious example, featuring on the radio comedy *I'm Sorry I Haven't A Clue*, is 'Mornington Crescent'. Perhaps climbing mountains is like Mornington Crescent?

One way to get round these questions is to say that mountaineering is more a question of style. A good example is the recent achievement realised by the Norwegian Sámi former cross-country skier Kristin Harila and her climbing guide Tenjen Sherpa. In a shade over three months these two climbed all 14 8,000m peaks, shattering the putative record of seven months held by Nimsdai Purja set in 2019. I say 'putative' because it became apparent that Purja had not actually been to the geographical summits of Manaslu and Dhaualgiri, omissions that he said were a consequence of ignorance and were later corrected. Trouble is, once you define your game as reaching the summit, then them's the rules.

Both Harila and Purja came to climbing comparatively late, both made extraordinary sacrifices to realise their ambition, selling or mortgaging their homes to meet the huge expense of their endeavours. Both used fixed ropes and oxygen and relied on helicopters to get them from one mountain to the next. Harila said she spent half a million dollars on her first 8,000er attempt in 2022, thwarted only by Chinese intransigence that denied her visas for Shishapangma and Cho Oyu. Goodness knows how much the successful round cost; it must be comfortable over a million. Both climbers, however, saw opportunities to recoup those costs. Purja has written a best-selling

1. His supervisor at the meteorological station above Glossop was Arthur Schuster, Ernest Rutherford's predecessor at Manchester and the older brother of Felix Schuster, a notable Alpine Club member and related to the Club president Claud Schuster.

account of his life and was the subject of a feature film. He is a social media star, earning a fortune from endorsing products.

Many will shake their heads at such profligacy and point out that jumaring ropes is not climbing. That may be true, but it's *something*. And if that 'something' isn't a game many alpinists admire, the public begs to differ. Although some commentators have detected a greater willingness to criticise the Norwegian woman than the Nepal-born man, which fits a well-established pattern in climbing of female ascents being marginalised for reasons that are overlooked when it comes to men, another subject that also features in this year's *Alpine Journal*. Purja climbed pretty much the same way as Harila but hasn't yet faced the same scrutiny.

The thing about style is that we have the tendency to turn it into a moral question rather then a kind of regulation. We speak of good style and bad style. It's not too much of a leap to start thinking of climbers who practice 'bad style' as being 'bad people'. They're not, or at least, not necessarily. (Bad style can lead to exploitation of high-altitude workers, even their deaths, like that of Mohammad Hassan on K2 during Harila's ascent.) They just play a different game. Perhaps it's better to think in terms of creativity. Jumaring ropes on a trashed route and flying away in a helicopter might be judged by some an achievement but it's not imaginative.

On the other hand, having deep experience, a sense of fun and a creative mind can, deep into the second century of alpinism, produce innovative ascents that just make you smile. There is a good example reported in this year's *Alpine Journal*, featuring the first ascent from Will Sim and Fabi Buhl of Gulmit Tower whose base they reached by paraglider, getting around the dangerous approach that would have put any porters they hired at risk. It didn't make the headlines, but it made my day.

After nine years as editor, to go with five more I served at the turn of the millennium, I am stepping down from the *Alpine Journal*, although I will be supporting the new editor Adam Butterworth in his first year as he settles into a job that has been for me an absolute pleasure. There are other changes too. Rod Smith, who has edited the Alpine Club Obituary since the 2018 edition, also steps down, to be replaced by Suzanne Strawther. Robin Campbell, who has researched the frontispiece artworks for much longer, has also chosen this moment to put down this task. William Mitchell has kindly agreed to take over.

I would like to thank them and all the other volunteers who work towards making the *Alpine Journal* what it is. No doubt it will evolve in the years to come and I very much look forward to seeing that.

Ed Douglas

Contents

continued …

This year's section frontispieces are drawn from the mountain prints and watercolours bequeathed in 1958 to the British Museum by Robert Wylie Lloyd (1868-1958). See also Robin Campbell's article on Lloyd and his collection on p126, in which he challenges persuasively the location of three of these works.

Climbs & Expeditions

'Jungfrau from near Unterseen', print after Johann Ludwig Aberli, made and published by Christian von Mechel, Basel, 1768, etching and aquatint with hand-colouring, 39cm × 29.2cm *(British Museum)*

MAREK HOLOČEK

The Gods Are Kind on Sura Peak

Sura Peak in Nepal's Hongu valley, close to Makalu. The first ascent was likely made in 1983 by Austrians Sepp Egarter and Volker Klammer via the south-west ridge, decades before the Nepali government put the peak on the approved list. In 2019, Pemba Ongchu Sherpa and the Japanese alpinist Hiroki Nakayama added a route up the north-east face. *(All photos courtesy of Marek Holeček)*

Matěj Bernát and Marek Holeček made the first ascent of the north-west face of Sura Peak (6764m) between 19 and 23 May 2023. They called their route Simply Beautiful and proposed a grade of M6 with an average slope of 70°, reaching 90° in some places. The route was 1,500m long with an elevation gain of 1,300m.

The Sura Peak story began with my expedition in 2021. That spring, the west face of Baruntse was the goal and after all kinds of setbacks the mountain finally gave way via the tough and tricky *Heavenly Trap* (see 'Heaven's Trap', *AJ* 2021 pp3-14). After a hard struggle, one of my dreams came true. One might think that the eyes can embrace only one beauty and

A foreshortened view of the north-west face of Sura Peak from the first bivouac.

focus on one goal at a time. Unfortunately, this is not the case because the eyes are restless and unfaithful. Even while acclimatising for Baruntse, I was eagerly observing the wider surroundings; the space was being created for something more.

For the past two years, the image of a nameless pyramid rising steeply above a glacier had been returning to me every now and then when I closed my eyes. In my mind I was picturing the possible line leading to the top. Nothing could be done about it. The thought had sprung to life and I burdened

A view of the face from base camp with the line of ascent and four bivouacs marked.

it with the reality of questions. And so I searched my archive for photos, browsed the internet and magazines, sent these questions to others. Then I processed all the information and subjected that to more questions. 'Who has already climbed there? When? Which route did they take?'

Is it possible to complete an idea that has been sketched out then fully realised without me taking a single actual step? And anyway, what's this pointy hill called? Here, I can see it: Sura Peak, an almost 7,000m-tall rascal. Well, I'm going for it. No wonder our return to the Baruntse region and the sandy shore that surrounds its glacial lake at more than 5,000m did not take long. This is the location of base camp. Behind it a wall of mountains rises. It is a fairy-tale corner of the Himalaya: terrifying and desolate.

However, before my path could lead me to that familiar place again, I had to cross off more items on my list. I had a clear idea of where I wanted to climb, and what, but there was still a question hanging in the air: with whom? I sent signals into the airwaves, addressing my fellow climbers but for whatever reasons, after two months of searching, the column headed 'Climbing Partner' remained empty. It was necessary to change the scope of my search. If there are no mature fish at the bottom of the pond, the fisherman must wade in shallower waters for young fry. And let's see, right at the very first attempt and after a few formal phone phrases, a young fish called Matěj Bernát is flipping about in the net.

Don't think I chose my climbing partner randomly or according to some alphabetical list. It was based on performance. That's how it's always been. At some point, your well-functioning machine seizes up and one has to try a different set of gear wheels. During almost 50 expeditions, I have shared my journey with many friends, each of them a bit crazy in their own way and focused on some goal of their own but it's always enriching, determined and great.

The afternoon of the first day's proper climbing, approaching the ice barrier.

The beauty of youth lies in the ability to make quick decisions. Youth gushes with energy and is not weighed down by bad experience or bound by the shackles of obligation.

'Okay, Matěj, we are leaving in May and we'll fine tune the rest in the meantime,' I told him before hanging up.

Originally, I intended to describe the entire course of events in a strictly technical way, devoid of feelings and romance. I wanted to keep myself in check. However, to cut down the whole concept of mountain climbing and moving in the mountains to a mere athletic-gymnastic 'positional change', i.e. from valley to summit, would be highly disrespectful, if not barbaric, to my philosophy of life. Mountain climbing is not a classically measurable sport and its purpose is not primarily to reach the top but to live the experience. I don't remember the summits but the strong, hard and beautiful moments along with my climbing partners who helped me look down from the peaks.

But to the point. Before Matěj and I reached base camp, we had been roaming in the central Himalaya for two weeks to train our lungs and legs. In other words, we had been strengthening the internal overload protection so we could face those moments when the body struggles with the lack of oxygen. We reached the cool place by the mountain lake on 13 May. Immediately after the porter dropped off the baggage I happily sent him back to Khare. It is a small village over 10 hours away in another valley, separated by a pass lying at an altitude of 5,500m. We were left all alone in a beautiful place surrounded by the mountains, waiting for the starting gun.

This was the right moment to take a closer look at what lay ahead. There was only a little snow and the reliefs of dark rock and deep blue ice peeked out from the surrounding mountain walls, as though I was looking at a herd

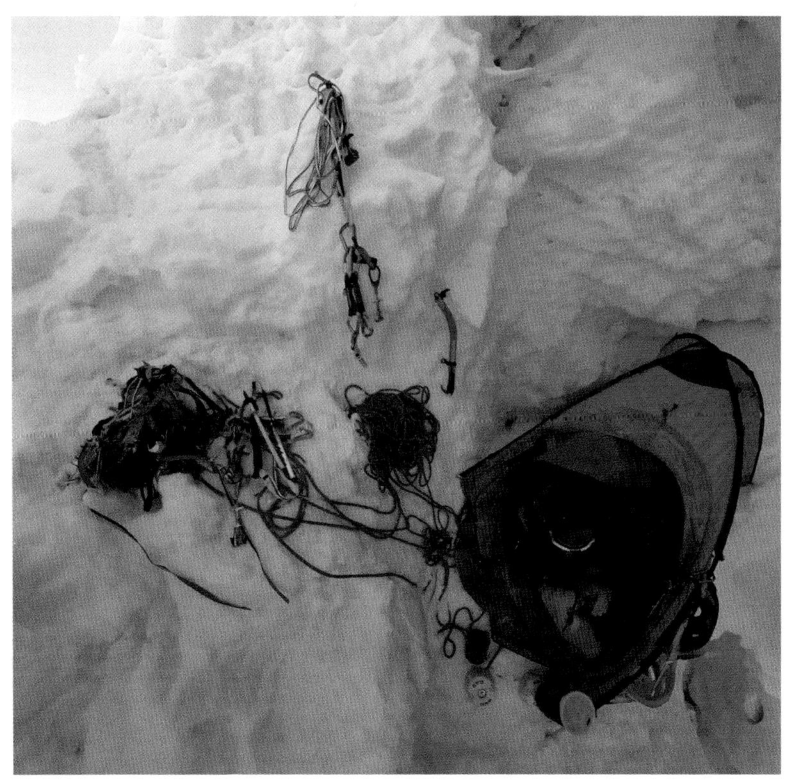

The second bivouac in a welcome ice cave.

of starving horses whose every bone was sticking out of their skin and whose ribs could be played like the strings of a harp. This year's monsoon didn't bring any salvation in the form of snow. There was another difference compared to previous years: perceptible all-day cold. Whether this was good for our climb or not remained to be seen. Reconciling with what you can't control is key and then trying to turn what you have into a miracle. With the help of the stars above, human imagination, skill and desire are gifted with such ability. You don't need anything else. All we had to do then was to wait for the auspicious moment foretold by our 'weather girl' Alena who delivered our daily portion of her meteorological news via satellite.

The launch date day didn't arrive until Friday 19 May. Matěj and I prepared our packs with gear and everything we might need for the following five days. Those five days should be enough for our way up and a safe return.

Day One

Our camp was located directly under the face on the glacier at 5,500m: a comfortable place to sleep, except for the view above us. From the foot of the mountain an icy slope rises at an angle of 50° in its lower part. This slope then steepens and in the upper part changes to vertical where a forked

Approaching the rock barrier during the morning after the ice cave.

serac grinned at us. Above the serac loomed an ominously overhanging and impenetrably dark rock face. So. Good night, sleep tight and don't let the bedbugs or dark nightmares bite.

Day Two

Conditions on the first section corresponded to our expectations. We didn't belay each other at the start; the rope served only as a silent connection of our destinies. We gained height quickly with every hour. Around 10am in the morning the sun's rays finally reached us. They were not aggressive but strong enough to slowly loosen the morning stiffness caused by frost. Shortly after noon we managed to reach the steepest part of the icy slide that breached the serac. The slope reached 80° and only in a few places steepened into a vertical wall of blue ice.

With the increasing strain our progress slowed and the afternoon sun quickly drifted westwards. We started feeling pain in the neck and shoulders as we constantly looked up, swinging axes into the ice. Our lungs could still catch up but they would have certainly voted for a break. During one diagonal traverse leading through a system of grooves that linked sections on our line, I chanced upon a cave. It must have been formed some time ago

Holeček in the rock barrier, where the rock was unreliable and rotten. The weather began to worsen during this section, forcing the climbers into a harsh bivouac.

The party's over. Matěj Bernát waking up after their hard night out.

when one part of the ice slid downwards, creating a terrain fault with a one-metre crack. Yay. It was the perfect place for a bivouac, just a bit above 6,000m. The cave must have been sent from heaven.

Day Three

The weather hadn't bothered us too much with wind and snow but now there was an unwelcome change. In the morning, the sun smiled at us but after that short joyful moment the clouds took over. We climbed another 150m of ice flutes leading from the bivouac to the point where a continuous rock barrier grew out of them. This was a long anticipated challenge. The very first metres proved the rock was like gingerbread sprinkled with loose snow sugar. We started to dance on our crampons and swing our ice axes barely able to find traction. It reminded me of cartoon characters trying to support themselves over an abyss with legs and arms spinning like propellers in the air.

After a lot of effort I climbed 70m up this manure pit. Belays were for psychological effect only. We couldn't rely on anything. Although Matěj fell off twice following and the belay stopped us flying down to the valley. I knew we wouldn't move an inch further that day. The weather was giving us strong hints we should find a place to sleep, and quickly. Icy falls of spindrift began sliding from above and the wind bit our bones through our clothes. Yet there was no platform in sight that would offer space for even a buttock. The terrain all around was hostilely slanted. We had no choice but to dig into the 70° slope but after 20 minutes of wild scrabbling we couldn't celebrate victory. Under the few centimetres of ice there was rock at the same angle. We were, to put it bluntly, in deep shit.

It was quite clear what to do next. We fixed the fabric of the tent to our hanging belay. It evoked a big garbage bag hung on a nail. We had to cram ourselves inside with our sleeping bags and all our gear and make sure that nothing fell down. There was no support from the tent so our bodies kept sliding down the slope. We were two marionettes tied by strings to the middle of an inhospitable mountain face. A night full of suffering unmatched by anything I'd experienced before took more than enough of our waning strength.

Now fully committed the team wove their way through the rock barrier.

Day Four

This was the key day of the entire ascent. Although we didn't know if we could succeed in climbing the following 80m of rock, it was crystal clear that if we didn't, we would be in big trouble. Descending the climbing we'd already done in the two previous days was hard to imagine. On the other hand, the rock section above our heads looked like one huge overhang.

Each time I am indecisive my inner voice whispers to me. 'Just give it a try. Give it a focused valid attempt. Then you'll see.' It took me long hours before I was able to overcome these two rope lengths, with my feet digging in the biscuity terrain. The abyss below our feet down to the foot of the glacier was about a kilometre. Yet the fear was gone. There wasn't any more space for fear. I only felt muscle fatigue that started an alarm buzzing in my head to warn me I was running out of gas. Our bodies were shivering from hypothermia and then it started snowing. Yet at last that damn rock was behind us and the way to the top opened up.

At that moment Matěj replaced me on lead and with great precision started to climb the next two icy pitches. At the end of the second rope length he found a crack I had picked out at our start. I had thought there might be a place for a bivy and so it was. In the middle of the 70° slope another kiss of luck. We set up the tent and boiled water to refresh our frozen and dried intestines. Then we hit the sack, which felt like a four-poster compared to our bed the previous evening.

A close-up topo of the route's critical section through the rock barrier.

Day Five

We were now heading for the cherry on top. Easy to say, but it proved harder to do. The ice resembled blue glass and every time my toes kicked into the unyielding slope, my nervous system lit up with shooting pain. We could feel the same spasms in our hands caused by thousands of blows of our ice axes. I was losing feeling in my shoulders from the straps of my backpack cutting painfully into my armpits. Yet less than two hours after leaving the bivouac we had climbed the last 140m of elevation to the top. There was nowhere further to climb. No applause, no standing ovation. We forced our faces to squeeze out smiles that expressed the relieved joy that we no longer had to take another step higher. We hugged each other with a pat on the back. We quickly took out our cameras.

I felt relieved but the day was far from over. I took one last look at the spiky world all around us, at that rigid frozen beauty, once again trying to inscribe it indelibly on my memory. The image never lasts long before it starts to fade and finally disappears completely. The only thing that remains captured in the colourful memories is the hardship, hard work and the climbing partner with whom you underwent the martyrdom. Our gaze falls on the nearest giants: Baruntse is within reach, directly connected by a ridge; Chamlang juts out from the other side. Suddenly, I feel a strong emotional impulse that overwhelms me. You are a nostalgic old fool, I tell myself as I wipe away the tears welling up in my eyes. Sure, you managed to make a great first ascent on this and that hill some years ago. Pull yourself together because this is no time to reminisce. Maybe it was also the realisation that my train was approaching its destination and I'd be disembarking in the coming years. 'Okay, thank you Himalaya.' My last boohoo and I go to hell.

The final bivouac, another hole in the ice but much welcomed.

Matěj took the lead on descent down the sharp ridge resembling the spine of the Loch Ness monster. I was glad because the footsteps in the snow indicate that someone has passed here and it is feasible. It's kind of a placebo effect and a connection with life. It doesn't matter that Matěj and I are tied to a rope 20m apart. We are moving in the same rhythm, leaving our protection in the hands of the Almighty. There's a kilometre of space on both sides and we have to drive in our ice axes and crampons with every

Holeček and Bernát on the summit. Holeček said: 'I was horrified at how old I am compared to Matěj.' The west face of Baruntse with Holeček's route Heavenly Trap appears behind.

step. Both of us are pretending we are secure. Our hands and legs slip a little each time before gaining stability in the loose snow. Hours pass and the valley approaches only reluctantly. We leave the snow cover behind us just before it gets dark. We look like rag dolls whose soft feet tread clumsily in a sea of stones. Every now and then the rocks come loose and roll down with a rumble into the approaching darkness.

The story of Sura Peak is coming to an end. Before 11pm we reach the 'teahouse' at Seto Pokhari, a stone enclosure covered with a rubberized fabric instead of a roof. Here, the porters and our friend Pavel are waiting for us. This is the peak of luxury and centre of civilisation for our exhausted bodies.

To sum up: the climb we called *Simply Beautiful* was pure alpinism. A beautiful untouched face. No posh base camp with staff. Only a few backup meals before we started, one battle tent, a pack full of gear, a rope like a umbilical cord, our plan and determination. Nothing useless. Then a battle for each step up the north-west face all the way up to the top and a rush back down to life.

My last words belong to Matěj. Thank you. And I wish also to thank the one or those up there for keeping a protective hand over us.

CALLUM JOHNSON

Barnaj II East

The view from advance base camp. Barnaj II east is the right hand of the two pointy peaks. *(Callum Johnson)*

In Autumn 2022 I went with four friends to the Kishtwar region of the Indian Himalaya, a valley full of unclimbed 6,000m peaks. After getting shut down on an attempt to climb a new route on an unclimbed mountain because of heavy snowfall we rested and re-focussed. The expedition culminated in the first ascent of Barnaj II East (6303m) via the north face.

The air hostess sees my bright red rucksack with yellow climbing helmet attached and asks, 'Are you going to climb Everest?' I smile and reply that I don't have that kind of money and what we're going to attempt hasn't been climbed before. My first expedition to the Greater Ranges has begun: the 'duffle shuffle' is in full swing. I am nervously excited for what the next month will hold in store. I meet the team in Delhi: Dave Sharpe, Will Harris, Matt Glenn and Tom Seccombe. The experience and strength of these guys gives me confidence that I will learn, be humbled and hopefully manage to climb something.

Delhi feels like a busy smelly sauna. We negotiate the chaotic roads, watching how rickshaws, bicycles and trucks don't collide as three lanes merge to one without warning. Our accommodation offers curry for breakfast, curry for lunch and curry for dinner. Love it or hate it, curry is what's on the menu. Visiting the Indian Mountaineering Federation to receive our permit to climb Barnaj II, formalities are completed with the exchange of thousands of dollars for seemingly nothing, not even a piece of paper. Yet all appears to be well and our expedition is allowed to continue.

A short flight takes us to the mountain town of Leh, the capital of Ladakh. At 3,500m the air is cool and clear and a couple of nights here feels like more useful acclimatisation than the humid heat of Delhi. Exploring the market stalls we buy dried fruit, peanut butter and pillows: base-camp comfort and mountain snacks. We bounce along dirt roads for 12 hours in the Force Traveller minibus, somehow, thankfully, maintaining contact with the road around countless switchback bends above precipitous drops. Crossing the Indus and then the Zanskar rivers, we travel south over several mountain passes to another watershed and are in the Kishtwar region. Impressive pointy peaks dominate every vista.

In the final small village of rustic houses, each with their own patch of arid land to work, we meet our horsemen. Loads are sized up and debated in what seems like a heated discussion in Ladakhi with everyone speaking at the same time until they are finally divided up for each shepherd to load onto their animal. We look on, letting them do their thing, amazed that things progress.

The procession of shepherds, yaks and donkeys is strung out along the trail. We round the hillside and get our first view up the Hagshu valley. A peak in the distance is striking: this is Chiring and it's unclimbed. Despite being at 4,400m our base camp is only a day's walk from the road: luxury for an expedition. The camp itself is tucked behind a moraine bank on a flat grassy area islanded by a small stream of clear mountain water. The train of animals with our bags trickles in and we gradually pitch camp, our home for the next three weeks.

Snow falls continuously overnight, laying 30cm at base camp by next morning, but spirits are still high. We need to acclimatise here for a day or two anyway. Gear is unpacked and checked, the expedition chess tournament kicks off and our cook, Naveen, and his helper Mangal deliver the first of many excellent feasts. Curry, of course.

Our mandatory acclimatisation – mandatory suffering – must commence, the inevitable slog uphill breathing hard with a heavy rucksack pulling you back. The warm sun is melting the snow, gradually turning it to a sticky slop.

On the approach to the face. *(Matt Glenn)*

We walk slowly, as a team, up to a 5,000m camp. I stay three nights, with gradual improvement in sleep each night. The weather is still good but for how long? There is a keenness and slight sense of urgency to start moving towards the main objective. On one of my days at the acclimatisation camp I manage to drag myself up to 5,600m. The views are staggering but brief before a squally afternoon snow shower comes in. I sit for a minute, head spinning, breathing heavily. I think my vision is going funny and I'm seeing stars before I realise it is snowflakes swirling on an updraft.

From our acclimatisation highpoint there was a view of the upper north face of Barnaj II, which gets Dave and Matt psyched. Will, Tom and myself have our sights set on the east face of Chiring, a mountain that caught my eye, intrigued and inspired me. Being visible from a long way down the valley I couldn't take my eyes off it so I was almost tripping over my own feet on the walk in. Being unclimbed and impressively steep, it has all the right ingredients. Setting off from base camp late in the morning, with bags packed for six days out, we stopped by the advance base that Tom and Matt had established the day before to pick up a few bits of gear, leave our trainers and put on our double boots.

The approach to Chiring, although fairly flat, seems to take forever as a team of three roped together to walk up the glacier, following a set of bear tracks. This was an unexpected novelty. I have heard stories of there being a Himalayan brown bear in the valley and it is still here, each paw print bigger than my size 43 boot. The tracks in the soft snow weave around impressive crevasses: this is one glacier-savvy bear. We continue until below what we called the Chiring icefall: a significant steepening in the glacier a few hundred metres below the east face. We make camp here and plan to tackle the icefall in the morning. The views of the east and north face of the mountain

Setting off up the ice runnel. *(Callum Johnson)*

from our camp are both inspiring and intimidating. Three of us top and tailing in a two-person mountain tent is a cramped sleeping arrangement. I end up in the middle which has the advantage of being warm but the disadvantage of being kicked or nudged whenever Will or Tom turn over.

Next morning we weave our way cautiously up the icefall, along the glacier and up the lower snow slopes of Chiring's east face. We spend a long time deliberating over what line to aim for and settle on a series of (hopefully) icy corners and snow ramps and ledges to gain the north-east arête higher

Topo of Barnaj II's north face with route *Seracnaphobia* (ED, M5, AI4, 1600m) shown. *(Matt Glenn)*

up where it is snowy. We cut a comfortable ledge for the tent; it's only 1pm but we are content that we have put ourselves in a good position for starting early tomorrow morning.

The afternoon turns cloudy, as it often has done, snow starts to fall and does not cease; we keep an eye on it and on the snow accumulating on the slope outside our tent. After dinner and nightfall we check the snow again, not happy with how much has fallen and with the angle of the slopes above us. We make the decision to move our camp down 200m to a col. It is a windy night in the tent, with snow being blown in through the air vents as it swirls around outside. We get a good soaking all round. The morning is bright and clear again but the east face of Chiring has been transformed. It looks to be in good Scottish winter nick but these are not 6,000m-peak conditions. There is another 30cm of fresh snow. The return to base camp with our bags still heavy is draining. Tom does an excellent job leading us back down the icefall, with our tracks and the crevasses now hidden under fresh snow. These are a nervy few hours. Matt and Dave have also turned around on their attempt to climb Barnaj II. Dave has been feeling unwell and struggling to breathe. So the whole team is back at base camp.

Whilst resting at base camp waiting for the latest snowfall to consolidate, I explore the huge granite boulders in the glacial moraine. The rock quality is excellent. This is some of the most idyllic bouldering I have ever done. It is a good escape from the head games of the mountains, and brought back a feeling of succeeding at something. It is nice to remind the fingers

Settling in at the bivy. *(Matt Glenn)*

how to pull on small holds too. I convince the others to go for a morning's bouldering the next day. We focus on hard moves close to the ground. With only a couple of sleeping mats in place of a bouldering mat, it's best not to fall awkwardly.

After much deliberation we decide that Matt, Tom and myself will attempt Barnaj II from the north while Will and Dave attempt it from the south. I welcome Matt's critique of what I'm packing. I hope to cut back on what I took on our Chiring attempt where my bag felt impossibly heavy. I had taken too much food and too many clothes. With all the gear laid out on a tarpaulin, each piece is questioned before being packed into the rucksack. Again we walk round to our advance base by the moraine-trapped lake, an idyllic location with intimidating views. This time our eyes are fixed on the north face of Barnaj II and its complex ridgeline.

I groan as the 1am alarm sounds but we shoulder our bags and stumble over the moraine bank and onto the glacier, the stars shining brightly and cold air nipping exposed skin. Matt breaks trail up the initial snow slope, following vague remnants of tracks from his previous attempt. The snow ramp steepens to a broad icy gully; we move together and get established on the north face.

As I reach the belay, Matt and Tom are already looking up at the next pitch. Clipping in, I slump onto the sling and breathe deeply, trying to suck some oxygen out of the thin air at 5,800m. My head falls forward against the ice and Tom puts a comforting hand on my shoulder whilst Matt racks the ice screws. We are nearing the end of our first day on the north face of Barnaj II and I'm knackered already: multiple bad nights of sleep, the altitude and a diet of oily carb-heavy curries is catching up on me. We finally find a suitable bivy spot for the night at 5,900m and after 15 hours on the go, the small icy ledge looks more inviting than it has any right to. In an attempt to make the ledge slope slightly less towards the precipitous drop, Tom chips

In the upper mixed section. *(Callum Johnson)*

Tom Seccombe arriving at the summit of Barnaj II East. *(Matt Glenn)*

away at the ice with the adze of his axe. I am determined to try and make up for my lack of leading during the day and contribute to the team, so I get the stove on quick and start melting snow. I fill water bottles and then cook freeze-dried meals for everyone.

The upper couloir yields slightly trickier climbing that we pitch with some short sections of moving together. Good icy steps of around Scottish V, before some mixed sections and then the the ridgeline at 6,100m. We decide to camp here, tired after yesterday's long day and keen to enjoy the morning sun from this position. Although a desirable location, the notable lack of any ledge bigger than one bum cheeks is concerning. We manage to dig out the most promising area slightly more and support the edge with some flakes of rock that had broken off. It's just enough but we regret not taking the snow hammock. We face a night sitting, three of us wrapped in the tent fabric, trying not to slide off the edge. I fill a dry bag with snow and it becomes a team effort to melt this without melting the tent and setting our sleeping bags on fire. Water doesn't boil so hot at 6,100m so our evening meals have a certain crunch to them.

The first rays of morning sun bring a comforting warmth that melts the verglas the cold moist wind whipped onto us in the night. We spend more time warming up and rehydrating, slowly tidying up our camp, but conscious of our weather window we keep it efficient. Matt takes on the breakfast pitches, several rope lengths of technical mixed climbing up the ridgeline, a refreshing change of styles from the previous couple of days. We traverse the ridgeline to a 6,303m forepeak that gives us a view of the north summit of Barnaj II and the complex ridgeline that separates us. We stop in our tracks. With the incoming bad weather, poor snow conditions and the commitment of the ridge ahead (we calculate two days climbing over the

Looking across to the summit of Barnaj II North. A poor forecast, snow conditions and committing ground dissuaded the team from continuing. *(Tom Seccombe)*

north and south summits of Barnaj II and one day descent down the south side) we decide to retrace our steps and descend the way we have climbed. We call our high point (the 6,303m peak) Barnaj II East as it's the highest peak on the east ridgeline leading towards the north summit.

We reverse the ridgeline and then descend entirely on abalakov threads. I cleverly manage to drop my belay plate on the second of 25 abseils, so descend the rest of the way using a faffy biner block. On the lower snow slopes we can rope up and down climb. Being the lightest in the team I move through to the sharp end to lead us through the icefall, weaving in the darkness through crevasses that could hide a house. We stumble back into advance base just before midnight. I'll spare you the details but my bowels are through with oily curries and half-cooked freeze-dried meals. Yet while I feel empty and drained of energy, I'm content to have climbed a new route up a big north face to an unclimbed peak with a strong team. I couldn't have done it without Matt and Tom. Thanks guys.

Acknowledgements

I would like to say many thanks to: Sandra Dekker and Hamish Frost for weather reports; Mick Fowler and Tom Livingstone for beta; all previous expeditions to the area for their trip reports and photos; Himalayan Run and Trek for in-country logistics; the Mount Everest Foundation, Alpine Club, British Mountaineering Council and the Neil Mackenzie Trust for grants; Basecamp food for discount on freeze-dried meals; Mountain Equipment, Scarpa, Grivel, Sea to Summit, Edelweiss, for equipment.

Left to right: Johnson, Seccombe and Glenn on the summit. *(Callum Johnson)*

Glenn on the descent. Advance base is near the top of the image photo on the opposite side of the glacier, some 1,000m below. *(Callum Johnson)*

NICHOLAS HURNDALL SMITH

Yawash Sar I

Nigel Bassam in new snow underneath Yawash Sar I at the end of the team's three attempts on the peak. *(All images courtesy of Nicholas Hurndall Smith)*

More than 1,400 people had died in Pakistan and millions forced from their homes due to terrible monsoon flooding: three times the usual rainfall. Under local advisement, it we decided our expedition to unclimbed peaks in the Ghujerab mountains could still go ahead. The post-monsoon season proved an excellent time to visit; in the main we had cloudless skies with little wind. Karim Hayat, our guide, had been before in September 2013 and also had good weather. The monsoon itself doesn't seem to affect this area much.

From Shimshal, we walked north for several days towards the Chinese border. Once past the 5,000m Boisum pass, we headed down (and occasionally up) through persistent snow and, after endless plodding, reached a shepherds'

The Yawash Sar I team, from left to right: Ross Bell, Nicholas Hurndall Smith, Nigel Bassam, Paul Winder, Karim Hayat and Waseem Shah.

hut where we stopped to regroup. Our differing pace had led to gaps in the procession and we felt a little out of touch in the clag. Squeezing inside the tiny hut with the porters, we ate hot food and talked to Jalal and Bulbul whilst they heated water for chai. Wakhi is their language, also spoken in Tajikistan and Afghanistan and Kashgar in Xinjiang.

'*Chiz hol he*? How are you?'

It was nerve-wracking to see one's bags carried for three days over mountain pass, river and snow. I saw my donkey refuse a number of times. On its back were all my diabetic supplies, bar my insulin, which I was carrying. The donkeys carry 40kg, which I'm told is a reasonable weight. Karim told me privately that he much preferred human porters as kit can so easily be damaged. But the porters prefer donkeys as they are paid for two loads. In fact we only had one real porter who carried 20kg.

Karim, now an AC member, had been a porter for Victor Saunders and Mick Fowler in 1992. He was also in the team that supported Tom Ballard in 2019 but, with forebodings about the conditions, he descended before Tom was tragically killed. He was later flown out to Turkey to take part in the film about Tom and his mother Alison Hargreaves. In June 2013 he had been at camp two on Nanga Parbat when terrorists gunned down 11 climbers. As he descended to base camp in the afternoon, the army were flying in and out. Later that year on a trip to the Ghujerab he soloed a 5,836m peak, which he named Umeed Sar. Umeed means 'hope': his response to the Nanga Parbat tragedy, which proved difficult for him personally. It was from there he took his photo of our current objective, Yawash Sar I, which sowed the seeds of this expedition.

A foreshortened close-up the of the south face of Yawash Sar I showing the team's high point.

Bulbul, our sirdar, had climbed K2 earlier in 2022. He had also been there in 2021 with Rick Allen and Jerry Gore, when Rick died. He had helped to bury Rick's body with Jerry. The mountaineering community is a small one.

Base camp was located near a cool clear river running down from the West Ghidims glacier. Our five climbers' tents quickly formed a clump amongst a series of side streams, closer to the centre of the valley. Speeches were made, tips paid and our trusty porters retreated. I spent the next few hours trying to put my tent into some semblance of organised chaos. We took turns to enjoy the 'shower'. Karim set up the toilet, complete with booby trap: a large rock intended to offer the chance to stand or crouch. A fortnight later this collapsed into the (now less deep) pit with me on it. Luckily I was switched on, and performed a dyno to safety.

Tom Bell, paramedic and AC member, went on for days about putting all our mountain food in a barrel to deter the mountain mice. I was sceptical. There was little wildlife up there besides yaks and a solitary eagle, alpine choughs, wagtails and the odd spider. Yet Tom was right. Soon there was evidence and then sightings of a 'mountain rat', as Karim called it, mostly in the mess tent. I spotted the culprit making its entrance and spontaneously grabbed it with no clue what to do with it. As I threw it outside, the scoundrel sank its teeth into my finger, drawing blood.

Some of us recovered sufficiently to do some exploratory climbing. And what a mountain we had above us! Our first task, once the weather and snow conditions improved, was to explore access to Yawash Sar I from the south.

Descending to advance base below the icefall.

We recced and then with heavy bags set up a camp at 5,200m. No one, as far as we knew, had ever stepped into this valley. Our high camp was on a moraine below and to one side of an icefall, which we then climbed in three easy pitches. Above was a huge bowl of pristine firm snow whose lower section was heavily crevassed. Our eyes were drawn by a snow gully on the left that led to a long and involved ridge. Karim was keen on attacking the south face front-on but the start looked steep. We returned to camp at dusk, happy to have got to a high point of 5,400m.

It was cold during the night. With the door open to avoid condensation, the temperature in the tent was about -6°C. Feeling parched, we drank as much hot water as possible and at 4.20am headed back up the icefall with the moon and stars ablaze. A steady pace kept the cold at bay and soon the sun rose, though we remained in shadow. Approaching the face and the steep ice leading to it, the route started to look more amenable. It was 8.30am when the sun hit us, just as I was about to lead the steep lower section of the south face.

The belay at the top of the ice slope that led to the first rock section was not pleasant or safe. When the first rays of the sun hit the face high above, rock and ice started to come loose and occasionally a real 'whizzer' went past, uncomfortably close. In my mind there was no sensible reason to continue. We called a halt at about 5,550m, feeling disappointed. Nigel Bassam, who had been the least keen on this route, now seemed the most frustrated. Having been hit in the face and chest by smaller missiles, I was glad to be out of the line of fire. We were back at our tents by 11.30am and Karim headed down to base camp, complaining of a bad headache.

The steep approach slope to the south-east ridge.

Sleep helped to raise morale. Everything in this valley was unclimbed apart from Karim's Umeed Sar and we hoped that with more climbers at the high camp, we could change that. Nigel and I left at 4.20am next morning for another summit bid. We took the same route to the upper glacier but this time turned right to climb over a bergschrund and up a steep snow and ice slope, hoping to get on to the south spur of the south-east ridge. It felt like classic north face climbing up several hundred metres, something neither of us were really in practice for. But we made steady progress moving together, huffing and puffing, with the altitude weighing heavily on us. As the angle eased, ice and névé turned to softer snow and I made a bucket seat to belay Nigel up to join me at the col just after 9am. After a short break, we crossed another bergschrund and finally reached rock.

From here I had planned to tackle the ridge direct, steeply at first, in the hope we would reach some easy ground. The ridge certainly looked flatter higher up. We had also hoped that stepping onto rock would be a pleasure. It was not. We had expected loose rock but this was dangerously so. Climbing the south ridge of the Strahlhorn three weeks earlier had been great training for this. We slowly and gingerly gained height to 6,000m, tiptoeing through the choss and my heart was in my mouth committing to steeper moves. Every hold was suspect. Where possible I tossed bread bin sized rocks far down onto the glacier to help clear the route for Nigel.

We soon had more problems. Light snow was falling and we had lost our good rhythm moving slowly up with 15m of rope between us. There was still no wind. I started to contemplate a night out; there was still so far to go.

The approach slop to the left of the photo and the south-east ridge with the team's highpoint marked.

I also looked down the other (eastern) side of the col and wondered if that might offer a good line of descent. As 1pm approached, we decided the dangers were too great, the ground we needed to cover too involved and our progress too slow. The best option was to back off and go down the way we had come, a much harder prospect than climbing it.

Nigel climbed down first, placing gear where possible, with me following. Solid gear placements were few and far between. We managed to set up two abseils lower down, the first from a block that looked large enough to stay glued to the mountain. It was a huge relief to get back to the steep snow. Even after this the descent was not plain sailing. After lowering Nigel from the top bucket seat, we made seven 60m abseils from abalakovs. It felt endlessly long and tense, as tiredness and dehydration set in.

Plodding slowly down, weaving our way through the snow-covered crevasse field, I was grateful for the tracks we had made there. We felt deflated yet happy to be on easier ground. Luckily it was cool again and the snow bridges felt solid. We reached camp just before dark at 5.40pm, welcomed by mugs of tea and cheery faces. It had been an intense and exhausting 14 hours.

On the first attempt, it was me who had made the decision to turn round, with Nigel wanting to continue. On the second, the opposite was the case. Both were the right decision. With two attempts behind us we were starting to appreciate the scale of the mountain. It was bitterly cold that night: -20°C outside the tent. The stars were shining and we had one more good day forecast before snow was due. I finally got warm wearing all the clothes I had inside my sleeping bag with my insulin stashed safely in my pocket.

Nigel Bassam at the team's highpoint.

A Nalgene hot water bottle by the toes was a game changer.

The weather held and sunshine hit our tent soon after 7am. I was suffering from mountaineer's foot, which Tilman describes as the inability at times to put one foot in front of another. We agreed to go down to base camp to rest and ponder our next move, arriving back in time for the most lavish lunch prepared by our outstanding cooks Abbas and Waseem: mutton korai cooked in milk cream and fresh tomatoes with chillies and spices, pasta, apples and coffee.

Snow did indeed come and the weather set in properly. The slopes were clagged in and snow flurries swept across camp. Paul Winder described it as 'a grim Tibetan wind'. I tried to keep us off the topic of what to do next for a day, so that all could have a proper breather. I knew I needed one.

We had time and a weather window ahead for one more attempt on Yawash Sar I. As we approached high camp once again we spotted Karim and Wasim descending after the first ascent of Peak 5742m, which they named Uncle and Nephew Peak. Karim and Wasim were over the moon. This was the first success for the team and I was delighted for them. Nigel and I puffed our way back up the icefall to drop some kit and make a plan. Hope and doubt seemed in balance. The weather was due to turn again soon so we had to make the most of the window. Back at high camp, we set the alarm for 1am and were in bed by 6pm.

Peak 6072m viewed from the south-east ridge with the team's highpoint marked.

The temperature inside the tent was -10°C when we woke and much colder out. These felt like conditions for frostbite. Putting on crampons that we'd left at the bottom of the icefall wasn't easy with cold hands. Once underway again we gradually felt better and began to move well. In fact, we moved so well we were in a position by 4am to start the steep ascent to the point where we'd turned back the previous week. Except we couldn't see the face and made the mistake of going too far left. I followed what I thought were our tracks, now rendered less clear by the previous day's sun, but they turned out to be the imprints of a falling boulder.

On the south-west ridge.

Sensing our position wasn't right, we hollowed out a seat with our axes to await the imminent dawn. I reached for my blood glucose sensor, switched it on, fumbled and dropped it. Down it went, its light visible in the darkness as it slid down over 100m onto the glacier below.

The first glimmers of dawn revealed the error of our ways: we had gone too far left and were at the foot of an inviting gully leading to the south-west ridge. We'd spied this as a potential option beforehand and now it seemed too arduous to traverse right over steep ice and snow to our original line. Next my insulin pump began its tell-tale squeal, indicating it had failed. This would continue for the next five hours until we reached easier ground, allowing me to intervene. I would have to rely on injections today, thanks to the back up insulin pen safely stowed in my inner pocket.

Up we went, moving well together over crisp névé and a lovely section of mixed ice and rock. When we were able to stop, we turned to admire the beautiful dawn colours, accompanied by the scream of my failed pump. As we gained height, conditions underfoot gradually worsened, definitely worse than the slope opposite that we'd climbed five days before. We also realised our line was threatened by a large cornice, so we opted for an even steeper line to the right. Névé gradually turned to powder and we found ourselves swimming and digging for placements. Our pace slackened and our calves burned. Then the sun hit our backs. That took the chill off but made the snow even worse.

I felt ready to give up but Nigel's encouragement kept me going. We finally reached the ridge at 8.30am and sat exhausted to warm ourselves on the sunny rocks at the bottom of a vertical but amenable looking wall. The view

Looking down the route of descent from the highpoint on Peak 6072m.

to the south-west was beautiful, with every peak for miles visible, so many unclimbed. And I now finally had the chance to remove my squealing insulin pump and silence it with my knife.

The continuation of the ridge was a series of rock towers many of which we hoped to bypass on snow and included a significant descent before the final steepening to the summit. We were close to 5,900m and even more aware of the vertical distance down to the glaciers either side of the ridge. Gearing up, I launched myself at the first steep pitch. The rock was sturdier and more inclined to stick to the mountain. I placed some good gear and arrived at a shelf of precariously balanced frisbee-sized rocks. Knees before crampons, in the hope of not braining Nigel, I made a belay to the side and Nigel followed.

We knew this was only a taste of what was to come and our fatigue suddenly felt all the greater. Hope was replaced with doubt and, after a short discussion, resignation. We had managed just one pitch on rock and given the hours it had taken us to get to this point, we both agreed it was game over. We cut some tat and abseiled from a solid block back to our pleasant rock perch above the cornice.

The descent became a trial. The ice was too rotten for abalakovs and the snow too loose for bollards. So I returned the ridge and descended further to find better ice. It soon became clear we would have to abseil down the rock to the left of the ridge below us. This became an adventure in itself. The ropes kept catching on loose rock so we looked for the steepest line of descent to make things easier. By the fifth abseil we'd reached steeper ground but one of the ropes got caught and as I tried to free it, the rope prised a

Critical rope damage.

block the size of a car wheel off. The air was filled with the reek of cordite and the rope was damaged, requiring some nimble but time-consuming rope work to tie it off and continue. I warned Nigel, while he was still in earshot that he would have to abseil past a knot.

Another three abseils with the same issues of falling rock and snagging ropes got us to the glacier and we returned to our small gear stash. Nigel, for whom nothing is too much trouble, ignored his fatigue in a vain search for the reader I had dropped earlier. I sat slumped on a solitary rock. Then we began the steady plod down to our high camp after a punishing 16-hour day.

I studied photos taken from the slopes opposite and realised how far we still had to go when we turned around. We were way too far left and had been better placed to attempt Peak 6027m (which I'm sure is higher). A harsher critic might have said we were on the wrong mountain. I was even more convinced that the best route up Yawash Sar I was up its south face, preferably with a higher camp below it and the ability to locate the start of the route in the dark. And perhaps a double helmet.

I woke at 6am to find light snow falling. Karim popped a cheerful face through the door to ask what our plans were. We decided to leave our camp in place, descend to base for a rest and return to explore and bag a new but easier peak. As for Yawash Sar I, the joke was over for this year. The mood in base camp was subdued with lots of chat about going home. We spent the morning chewing the fat, practising knots, and teaching each other different ways of tying them.

Nigel, Wasim, Karim and I dragged ourselves away from 2.15pm next day for high camp and were in bed by 7pm. With the alarm went off at 2am neither of us felt like getting up but an hour later we were marching up the

A consolation first ascent of Peak 5798m.

Ghidims glacier and towards the col marked at 5,644m on Jerzy Wala's map. Nigel and I both felt super-tired. The weather was glorious but incredibly cold and all of us had cold feet. I was tempted to turn back as mine simply would not warm up.

Once at the col we turned left and taking care to stay away from cornices to the east we headed to the summit in shade, swimming through deep snow. Our feet got even colder but we pressed on and reached the summit at about 8am, too tired and cold to feel elated even though the moment felt significant. Karim suggested we name our peak KNN Sar. Views were spectacular, of Yawash Sar II peeping over Peak 6072m and numerous others. There was no question of continuing along the corniced ridge to the next peak. We were simply too cold and energy was lacking.

Back at camp soon after 9.30am, Nigel and I retreated inside the tent, now like a greenhouse, to thaw out and snooze the day away, still exhausted from our earlier attempts. It snowed in the night and we woke at 5am, having been horizontal for nearly 20 hours. We delayed a decision about what to do but then the heavens opened and snow really started coming down. We did all we could to pack from within as the snow built up and a big avalanche rumbled. Then we emerged to cram everything into our sacks and by the time we were read to go the weather had started to brighten.

The weather began to brighten and we were ready to go by 8am. Our descent was beautiful, even warm, and gave us a chance to bid farewell to our home, on and off, for the past week or so. The sun did its best to burn through the clag and with the fresh snow gave us some atmospheric views. We got a final glimpse of Yawash Sar I. Maybe we will be back.

Winter had come to base camp, bringing blustery snow flurries and biting cold. It was the first time snow had settled there. The forecast suggested it would not be radically better in the morning so it made sense to start our return a day early. Thankfully we woke to blue skies to start the journey home. It was no less stunning in reverse: the scale of the landscape was immense and at the Boisum pass we met a herd of yaks we'd seen before from the valley.

On the way we stopped at the base camp of an Austrian couple and their team. Karim knew the guides and were given a warm welcome with tea and biscuits. They were at the beginning of their trip, hoping to climb some established routes nearby but were struggling with altitude. Then we continued. Light snow was falling on our last day but the weather improved and the sun came out. We met a friendly shepherd who made us tea. He was on his way to the shieling at Mandikshlakh (4129m) to tend his 50 sheep. He told us how he had seen a snow leopard here the previous year and also a pack of five wolves. Eagles, he said, were a threat to the sheep.

Almost three weeks after leaving we were back in Shimshal. The village was more autumnal, colours that contrasted beautifully with the snowy peaks above. Back in Hunza, we discovered that disaster had struck the Austrian team close to the Boisum pass; an avalanche had left one dead and another injured. We had been the last to see them and it was hard to process the news. The route they were climbing involved a narrow valley with snow on both sides, which must have been loaded by the recent falls. After dinner Karim produced some Hunza water, made from apricots and mulberries, which we drank with two of his close friends. We raised a glass to our Austrian friends.

JACOB COOK

Time Is a Construct

First Ascents in the Arctic

After four days stuck on portaledges pictured below, Jacob Cook takes advantage of a brief window on Qaersorsuaq, also known as Sanderson's Hope, on the west coast of Greenland, to push for the summit. *(Jaron Pham)*

Over 65 days, our team of six travelled 350km north along the west coast of Greenland via inflatable sea kayaks and established new routes on some of the giant granite cliffs rising straight out of the Arctic Ocean. The team included my wife Bronwyn Hodgins and four of our friends from Squamish, British Columbia: Zack Goldberg-Poch, Kelsey Watts, Angela VanWiemeersch and Jaron Pham.

I don't love using terms like 'fair means', 'self-propelled' or 'self-supported' to describe our trip. Ultimately, all of these expeditions are pretty arbitrary; for me, the reason to go on an expedition like this is not to tick a box in

Jacob Cook paddling the 450km sea-kayak approach starting just north of the abandoned community of Nuugaatsiaq. *(Jaron Pham)*

someone else's style rulebook. Rather, it's to have a smaller, more personal experience. I wanted to go with this particular group because I knew we aligned on the type of experiences we were seeking. For all of us, the goal was to experience the landscape on its own terms. To move slowly. To feel small. A small group of friends in a giant landscape.

Due to a slight delay in the arrival of our shipment of food and gear, we opted to take a short boat ride from Uummannaq on 5 July to set us on schedule. From 6 to 16 July we kayaked north past the former community of Nuugaatsiaq, abandoned due to lasting hazard after a fatal tsunami in 2017, and up to the northern tip of Ukkussisat fjord. On 16 and 17 July we dragged our kayaks upstream through tidal mud flats and from 18 to 24 July we portaged 20km across land connecting a series of small lakes, the larger of which we paddled across. Each leg of the portage required three loads per person, meaning we covered about 100km on foot.

When we reached the ocean on the north side of the portage, we immediately noticed a change in the landscape. The huge and chossy granite walls to the south had been replaced by beautiful red granite domes. We allowed ourselves a well-deserved rest day and then climbed two of these domes across from our camp, in two teams of three. It felt amazing to be finally climbing after over a month's journey with the kayaks. Angela, Zack and Jaron established *Fish Are Friends* (200m, 5.9+), while Bronwyn, Kelsey and I put up *Wears Your Paddle?* (250m, 5.11).

A few days further along the journey, our next objective became clear as we rounded a point and observed a majestic red cliff rising 400m straight out of the ocean. It's no wonder the few teams of climbers who had explored this area by sailboat had already established some lines on this face,

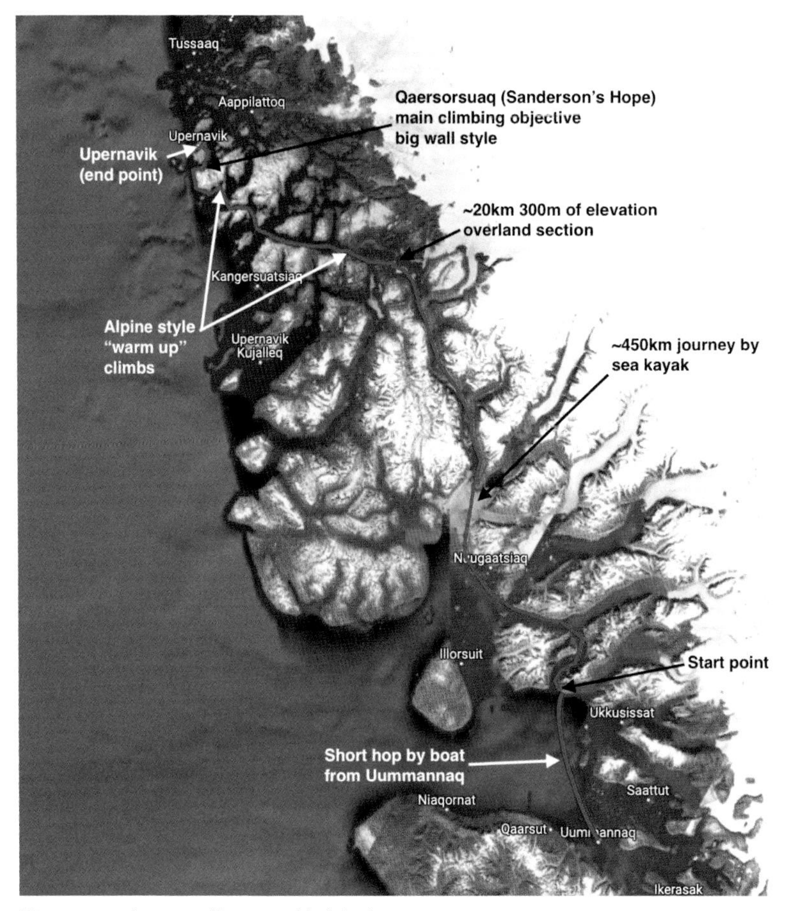

The approach route. *(Bronwyn Hodgins)*

known as Red Wall by climbers, but Agparssuit by the locals, which translates to 'where the gulls stand in a row.'

The rock quality was phenomenal. We scoped some lines and then camped on a beach about two kilometres away to rest and prepare. The boys repeated a stunning continuous crack system up the central prow in 28.5-hour push from camp. This route, *Seagull's Garden* (5.11+) was put up in 2011, the work of Nico Favresse and Ben Ditto who accessed the cliff from Bob Shepton's sailboat. Beginning their route was particularly tricky. I aid climbed about 10m in my dry suit and water shoes and the other two followed on jumars. Then the three of us hauled the kayak to the low anchor, deflated the boat and stashed it there. The rest of the route was climbed free and on sight. From the top, we hiked down to our campsite in the bay west of the wall.

Meanwhile the girls set off on a new line on the unclimbed right part of the wall. In a 50-hour push with an unplanned bivy, they established *Time is*

Angela VanWiemeersch brings her kayak ashore during the approach. *(Jaron Pham)*

a Construct (400m, 5.11, A2). The 24-hour daylight and the seemingly never-ending climb added to the feeling of timelessness as they pressed on for the summit.

Our major climbing objective was to attempt the first free ascent of Qaersorsuaq, also known as Sanderson's Hope, rising 900m straight out of the Arctic Ocean. The cliff lies about 15km from the town of Upernavik (our final destination) and had been successfully aid climbed twice before by an Italian team in 2000 and a Canadian team in 2002.

We set up camp across the 2km-wide channel facing the wall so we could study the formation. Our team chose to climb a new line on the right part of the wall, following nearly continuous cracks from sea to summit. There were two blank crack switches in the middle of the wall, which posed major question marks. We then spent the next 10 days climbing the lower half of the route, leaving fixed ropes in place and stocking a wall camp at about 600m height where there was a small natural ledge.

Several days of rain slowed our progress on the lower half of the wall. With the temperatures dropping, we knew we didn't have long before the cliff could become covered in ice and snow as the short summer season ended. The Italian team had spoken of climbing through rime ice in the upper pitches in late August. The weather continued to look unstable, but we decided to commit to the wall regardless, since we could wait out a storm in our portaledges with their expedition flies.

We jumared a final load to our high camp and, seeing as the sun was still shining, Kelsey, Zack and Angela pushed the ropes three pitches higher before we settled into our ledges for the night. We spent the next four days confined to the portaledges sitting out two storms. At least we were able to

In mid July the team hauled their kayaks for two days across tidal mud flats before portaging 20km through a series of small lakes. They walked 100km covering this section. *(Jaron Pham)*

collect as much water as we needed since our route became a full waterfall. During a small window we attempted a push for the summit but were forced to bail in a blizzard.

On our fifth day on the wall, the rain and snow stopped but the rock was soaked and camp was engulfed in thick cloud. I announced I wanted to climb, and Kelsey and Bronwyn joined me pushing the rope higher with numb fingers on wet rock. At the top of the third pitch, however, we miraculously popped out above the clouds and were greeted with sunshine. We were above the storm. We radioed for the other three to jug the ropes and then all six of us pushed for the summit. The entire route went free at 5.11+, with the crux pitch being the very last, a wildly exposed slab crux followed by a steep hand crack right to the very summit. We went from our wall camp to the summit and back in a continuous 24-hour push on 21 August.

Next day, after 12 hours collapsed in the portaledges, we rappelled the route and cleaned our ropes, leaving only the minimum gear as rap stations on the way down. Bringing all our belongings down the face to our stashed kayaks and then across the channel, we returned to base camp via a 28-hour push and within minutes of the start of the next storm. In total our team hand drilled five bolts, four at belays and one on lead to protect the very last pitch. At other anchors we left behind rappel stations of nuts and cord at roughly 60m intervals to descend the wall.

Our route *Sea Barge Circus* is one of the best moderate adventure climbs of its type I have climbed anywhere in the world, rivalling the *Scott-Hennek* on Mount Asgard and the Lotus Flower Tower in the Cirque of the Unclimbables. It could easily be repeated in a long day by a strong team of two.

Bronwyn Hodgins at the portaledge on Qaersorsuaq during the first ascent of *Sea Barge Circus. (Jacob Cook)*

Belaying in mixed weather from the portaledge. Three pitches were fixed above this point before two storms closed the team down. *(Jacob Cook)*

A last throw of the dice was rewarded as the team climbed three pitches through cloud on wet rock to be rewarded by clear skies above. *(Jaron Pham)*

Angela VanWiemeersch on the first ascent of *Sea Barge Circus*. *(Jaron Pham)*

Kelsey Watts climbing. *(Jaron Pham)*

The impressive wall of Qaersorsuaq with the line of *Sea Barge Circus*. *(Jacob Cook)*

The two routes climbed on Red Wall earlier in the expedition. *(Bronwyn Hodgins)*

Summary

First ascent of *Sea Barge Circus* (900m, 5.11+) on Qaersorsuaq (N 72°42'56.2" W 56°06'07.7") by Bronwyn Hodgins, Jacob Cook, Jaron Pham, Zack Goldberg-Poch, Kelsey Watts and Angela VanWiemeersch over 20 days with seven days camped on the wall for the summit push in August 2022.

First ascent of *Time Is a Construct* (400m, 5.11, A2 with sections followed cleanly up to 5.12d) on Red Wall (N 72°39'23.9" W 55°52'52.7") by Bronwyn Hodgins, Kelsey Watts and Angela VanWiemeersch over a 50-hour push on 1-2 August 2022.

Repeat of *Seagull's Garden* (400m, 5.11+, Favresse-Ditto, 2011) on Red Wall by Jacob Cook, Jaron Pham and Zack Goldberg-Poch over a 28.5-hour push.

First ascent of *Wears Your Paddle?* (250m, 5.11) at N 72°30'00.2" W 54°38'10.7" by Bronwyn Hodgins, Jacob Cook and Kelsey Watts on 26 July 2022.

First ascent of *Fish Are Friends* (200m, 5.9+) at N 72°29'20.9" W 54°35'51.0" by Jaron Pham, Zack Goldberg-Poch and Angela VanWiemeersch on 26 July 2022.

TOM LIVINGSTONE

A Winter in the Alps

Rob Smith on the north-west face of the Aiguille du Blatière, climbed on 27-9 January 2023 at WI4+ and M6+. *(Tom Livingstone)*

As the autumn days became compressed by longer nights and the snow line slunk down the mountains, I found myself re-reading Korra Pesce's description of climbing *Directe de l'Amitié* with Martin Elias. This route forces a straight line up the north face of the Grandes Jorasses, one of the most impressive walls in the Alps and, according to Korra, is 'the most challenging route up the Jorasses and the line that satisfied me the most.' I liked the humour in Korra's writing: 'Martin patiently starts up the pitch and then asks me whether this might possibly be the fearsome expanding flake pitch. I don't need to double check: yes, it's the one. And that's why I sent you up first! Have fun!'

The route was long ago climbed in good style, which I like. When Nick Colton and Roger Baxter-Jones made the second ascent of *Directe de l'Amitié*

The line followed by Smith and Livingstone on the Blatière. Starting up the ice route *Mini Blast* the pair took ground similar to that of Joe Brown and Don Whillans on their first ascent of their famous summer route. *(Tom Livingstone)*

Symon Welfringer on thin mixed ground on *La Croisade. (Tom Livingstone)*

in September 1977, Nick wrote, 'our girlfriends called for a helicopter as we didn't return by the time we had stated we would. The helicopter came and hovered above us on our way down into Italy, just below the summit. Roger and I were not sure what to do but after discussion we decided to send the helicopter away and walk down ourselves on the grounds that if we were trying to do the climb in a better style than those who did the first ascent then we really shouldn't use a helicopter to get down.'

Now that my home mountains are the Alps, I've been playing my pointless-yet-entertaining game of trying to free existing hard routes. It's a challenge to link difficult pitches of ice, rock and snow up a big mountain and it demands a high level of climbing ability. There are routes that had sections of aid where I've managed, through a combination of luck, specific training or sheer bloody-mindedness, to be the first to free them. Two highlights include *Vol du Dragon* on Les Droites in 2021 and *Voie des Guides* on Les Drus in 2022. I thought the famous Jorasses might also provide an opportunity to play this game and the *Directe de l'Amitié* had been burning in my mind since last autumn. My ego also wanted more than just two first free ascents because I always want more in my climbing, so greedily I looked around.

But January has short days and bitter temperatures and I knew from experience I must be patient to avoid jumping the gun. Rob Smith and I discussed objectives and he pointed at the Chamonix Aiguilles.

'There's one idea up there: the couloir above *Mini Blast*, on the Blaitière,' he said. 'I've been looking at it for two years from my kitchen window.'

We'd already trained and climbed together a lot that autumn and winter

The line of *La Croisade* (M7+, A2, V+, 5+, 600m), north face of the Aiguille des Pèlerins. This starts up the hard classic *Beyond Good and Evil* before taking the huge roof at half height. *(Tom Livingstone)*

Tom Livingstone tackling the monster roof on *La Croisade*. Although done with aid, Livingstone said it would go free at M9 or M10. And as Livingstone puts it: 'M7 in the mountains is hard.' *(Symon Welfringer)*

but our first attempt saw us straight back to the climbing wall; we didn't want to cross a sketchy avalanche-prone slope on the approach. Rob and I didn't discuss it much before turning around. At least we were practising our patience. We make a good team and are perseverant.

A few days later conditions had improved so we followed our original track back towards the Blaitière. It was freezing hard. The daytime temperature was -21°C as we soloed the five pitches of ice up *Mini Blast*. Our cheeks were numb and I swung my hands to flush blood into my fingers. Yet I was happy to be moving towards an Alpine goal. The line followed a wide granite couloir, which then narrowed and turned a corner. So with curiosity we began questing, switching from ice to névé and (slightly crumbly) rock. 'This pitch is insane,' Rob and I agreed. It made me think of Alaska, where the couloirs are steep and striking. Popping out of the couloir at the top and enjoying some sunshine, we moved up and right, then found a tent-up bivy. We agreed that was also insane.

Following our noses next day, we started up a giant shield of granite. I pulled through steep ground and then rocked onto a slab with tiny crystal footholds, shouting 'watch me!' as I went. My crampons zipped and I shocked onto my arms but gripped the axes tight. My patience had been tested and now I was climbing, I loved it and wanted to rage. 'Fuck yeah!' A helicopter buzzed us and we later learned someone had told the PGHM to check us out, saying 'surely no-one could climb up there in January.'

Above the shield the line returned to more conventional terrain and the valley was hidden by fluffy white clouds. And just after dark on our second day we straddled the summit of the Blaitière. We rapped down and reached

John McCune picking his placements on *Les Barbares*. Established over five days in February 2003 by Frenchmen Stéphane Benoist and Patrick Pessi, *Les Barbares* follows a logical 500m line up the north-west face of the Pointe Pré de Bar in the Argentière basin. Not repeated until 2010, it's now regarded as a challenging one-day route. The French used aid on the first ascent but the route is now free. *(Tom Livingstone)*

The questionable rock of the expanding flake on the Grandes Jorasses classic *Directe de l'Amitié*. *(Tom Seccombe)*

The north face of the Grandes Jorasses. *(Tom Livingstone)*

our bivy platform later that night. We'd been wondering whether we should've left our tent, sleeping bag, mattresses, extra food, stove and gas at this bivy and climbed light to the summit but were unsure how long it would take. Neither of us wanted to bail if we were still a long way from the summit late at night, so we had carried the whole lot, only to have wished we'd left it there. Oh well, good training I suppose.

Back in the valley, I feasted at the bakery and basked in the comforts of home with Christelle. Although climbing brings pleasure, there is an enormous sweetness to life on the ground. Yet once again I was thinking of the Jorasses: patience, patience, I reminded myself. Instead, I roped up for a new variation on the Pèlerins with Symon Welfringer and *Les Barbares* in the Argentière basin with John McCune. Whilst climbing with Christelle I'd seen the line of the latter route and noticed the good conditions: *placage* was surprisingly abundant this year. Both of these were excellent routes with an equal mixture of high-quality climbing and long, tiring descents.

'Warmer' weather arrived and I knew it was time for the Jorasses. I felt fit, psyched and somewhat accustomed to the unusually cold winter temperatures. Tom Seccombe agreed to attempt to free *Directe de l'Amitié* on the

Tom Seccombe getting comfy on the inflatable portaledge. *(Tom Livingstone)*

Livingstone making a winter ascent of the British route on the north-east face of the Piz Badile. Climbed first in July 1968 by Mike Kosterlitz and Dick Isherwood (who had failed to locate the *Corti route*), the Czechoslovakian team of Zuzana Hofmannová and Alena Stehlíková made the first winter ascent in February 1982, a milestone in female alpinism. In February 2008 Fabio Valsechini made the first winter solo. *(Gašper Pintar)*

north face. Previous teams had freed all except one pitch: the expanding A2 flake that Korra Pesce had mentioned. The clue is in the name, I guess. In hindsight I should've known that a rotten and slightly dangerous aid pitch isn't going to make for a free attempt. But still.

'Big routes demand big packs,' I told myself as I shouldered my bag and staggered out of the Aiguille du Midi station with Tom. The wind cut into our cheeks but I was happy. The Midi really is an incredible feature, one part tourist attraction with a giant rocket sticking out of its head, and one part teleport between Chamonix and the massif. By nightfall, Tom and I were comfortably camped beneath the Jorasses, practically using the 1,000m north face as a headboard. A familiar cocktail swirled around my head: excitement, anticipation and fear. Alpine climbing is such an uncertain game, where events can change everything in an instant. Reaching the top is never guaranteed, especially when trying to climb on sight and free. Persistence is a very useful attribute. I began to doze but in a blink, the alarm went off.

My memories of climbing the *Directe de l'Amitié* are now condensed. I remember the squeak of ice axes and crampons as Tom and I plodded up the initial ice field, taking turns carrying the enormous haul bag. Moderate pitches quickly ramped up and Tom made some brilliant leads. Then I took over and 'fought like a bastard' too. I don't remember where the bivy was, except that we used my inflatable G7 portaledge; without it we'd have been slumped miserably in our harnesses all night. Still, it was very snug to fit two big guys on a single mattress. Everything took ages and it was a miracle we didn't drop anything. We acted as if handling an unexplored bomb. The first M8 pitch felt alright, but the second was tricky. I rocked onto the belay pretty pumped but would still give it M7+.

The second bivy was a happy repeat of the first: make an anchor for the

Livingstone on the summit of Kukova Špica, Slovenia after climbing the south-east ridge. *(Aleš Česen)*

portaledge, crampons off, hang up all the gear in a mess, squeeze onto the ledge, shuffle into the sleeping bag, don't drop the stove, nice hot food, crash out, wake up, do it all in reverse. The expanding-A2-flake pitch was just that. Cams crunched grossly when I weighted them and I told myself to breathe more calmly when I made a few moves aiding off my axes. From the belay at the top I was psyched to be finished with it but not psyched to try for the redpoint. We continued up.

Getting to the top, on the other hand, really was sweet. The last pitches dragged, as did the haul bag, showering rocks. 'It's a chossy crag,' Tom remarked. The Jorasses isn't great rock and we'd occasionally hear a sickening, elongated *whiz* as something bombed past. At the final pitch, I could taste the sunshine on the summit ridge but couldn't find a belay amongst the shit rock. 'Can we move together?' I shouted down. My brains were getting boiled by the choss. 'Er…' came the reply. Tom carried the haul bag as well as the second's pack for about five metres until I could flop onto the south face and thus give him a belay and start pulling up the pig.

Six hours later, my mates Alex and Harry were handing us pizza in the car park. I've forgotten all the bad bits and the hunger and the fatigue and not freeing the pitch and mostly remember that pizza. It was another great adventure with Tom; and he's a total machine and very determined. I was happy to have waited for slightly warmer weather; trying to climb in the Baltic temperatures of January would've been unproductive. I was a bit disappointed not to have done the first free ascent of a route on the Jorasses but at the same time that expanding A2 pitch was not one to attempt free. Another time, another route, hopefully.

For a change of scene, I visited Slovenia with Christelle, where we enjoyed

After the austerities of winter, Livingstone moved on to sport climbing and the overhanging limestone of Saint-Léger du Ventoux, pictured here working his project *Le Nabab* (8b+). *(Aaron Hockey)*

catching up with good friends. Then we returned to Chamonix and I climbed *Ecaille Épique* on Les Droites in a day with Symon and Silvan Schüpbach. Or at least, until we reached the *Tournier Spur*, where at about 150m below the top I was sick everywhere with a bad stomach. After much deliberation, we called for a helicopter. I'd like to go back for this route.

At the very end of the winter, everything worked perfectly when I climbed the *British* route on the north-east face of Piz Badile with Gašper Pintar. We'd arranged to go climbing in the past but never actually tied in together until now. Our 'blind date' showed patience pays off. We'd waited until we had the right objective at the right time with suitable weather. On the route, we got lucky and the high-quality pitches went fast and on sight. It proved a satisfying end to my winter.

Breaking Glass

'Rhone Glacier with Mont de la Fourche', print after Philip James de Loutherbourg, made by Jacques-Henri Juillerat, published by Christian v. Mechel, Basel. c1795-1800, etching with hand-colouring, 50cm × 64.7cm. *(British Museum)*

ELAINE ASTILL

'A Tremendous Exertion for Ladies'

Images from the First Female Crossing of the Col du Géant

Fig 1 'Geant. Upon the Snows', watercolour inscribed with ink, 22.6cm × 12.8cm, 1822. All illustrations by Elizabeth Campbell. Double-sided and backed with *Fig 8* 'Summit of the Col du Geant'. *(All illustrations courtesy of Tony Astill.)*

While every picture tells a story, there was unusual intrigue generated among Alpine collectors recently with the unexpected appearance of a handful of diminutive watercolour drawings. Dated 1822, one of these drawings, in a rather naive hand, depicts a group of five figures, including two ladies in long dresses, ribboned bonnets and nailed shoes, crossing the snows adjacent to the unmistakably crooked magnificence of that great shard of rock perched high on the Mont Blanc massif that is rather ignominiously named the Dent du Géant. This is the story behind that picture.

There has been much written about the early exploits of women in the Alps, although few women to write of who were active before the Golden Age of Alpine exploration in the mid 19th century. Of those few, the identity of two English ladies in particular, a Mrs and a Miss Campbell, had remained an enigma to mountaineering historians until now. However, the year 2022 not only marked the bicentenary of the most celebrated achievement of these two women, but was also the year in which their full identity was established via the extraordinary survival of Mrs Campbell's watercolour record.

On 19 August 1822 Mrs and Miss Campbell, already 'celebrated for their

Fig 2 'Le Jardin, Mont Blanc, Geant', watercolour and ink inscribed with title and date, 21.6cm × 28.5 cm, 1 August 1822.

intensive and courageous excursions among the Alps,'[1] left their footprints in history when they became the first women to cross the Col du Géant, from 'Chamouni' to Courmayeur. Although offering the shortest passage from one valley to the other and therefore avoiding the 'tedious' alternatives, the rigours of the Glacier du Tacul had long deemed the route to the col 'impracticable', and even as 'despairing' by Bourrit.[2] Yet by 1788 de Saussure had made the spot memorable by his extraordinary 16-day residence there. Nevertheless, in 1822 it remained a hard and unfrequented passage rising to over 11,000ft at its crest. Even by 1843 Forbes still determined 'notwithstanding its immense height it would be frequented but for the dangers of the glacier on its northern side.'[3]

What had prompted their ambition can never be known but by coincidence on the very same day the two ladies set out for the col, the Englishman Frederick Clissold left the Hotel Union at Chamonix to commence his own momentous ascent of Mont Blanc. He had, in vain, he later noted, hoped to 'hail them' from above en route. However, news of the ladies' successful passage, and their 'determination to ascend to the summit of Mont Blanc, at the next season of their return to Chamouni'[4] reached Clissold upon his return to the Priory. Indeed he reported 'that the two English ladies had passed

1. F Clissold, *Narrative of an Ascent to the Summit of Mont Blanc, August 18, 1822,* London, 1823, p8.
2. J Forbes, *Travels through the Alps of Savoy*, Edinburgh, 1843, pp216-8.
3. Forbes, ibid.
4. Clissold, ibid, p22.

Fig 3 'A nob of Ice on the same (Tacul) Glacier obliged to be crossed crevaces [sic] on all sides', 22.6cm x 12.8cm 1822. Double-sided backed with 'A passage on the glacier'.

Fig 4 'Bridge of less than a foot wide on the same [Tacul] Glacier. Steep banks of Ice & Crevaces on all sides', 22.5cm x 12cm, 1822. Double-sided backed with *Fig 6* 'The Cachat Impossible'.

the Col du Géant two or three hours before we reached the Petit Mulet, and that while we were near that rock they were descending at Courmayeur.'[5]

Both were extraordinary feats which were, of course, celebrated in print: Clissold communicated his account, including a note of the two ladies' crossing, in a letter to his banker that was initially published in the *Bibliothèque universelle* and was in turn handed to the British press,[6] and privately published the following year; the renowned Dr Paccard sent a note to the *Journal de Savoie* detailing Clissold's summit, and concluding 'On the same day two English ladies, Mrs and Miss Campbell crossed the Col de Giant [sic] having ascended the Buet the preceding day.' Paccard's article found a route to the British press[7] and as far afield as India via the *Government Gazette*[8]; and, another contemporary traveller, Count Theobald Walsh, who 'happened to be in Chamouni on that very same day' confirmed that the two ladies had indeed trained for the feat, by first going to the Jardin and then the Buet.[9]

5. 'Ascent of Mont Blanc', *Bibliothèque Universelle* 30 Sept 1822, pub Perthshire Courier 15 Nov 1822, p4.
6. Ibid, p4.
7. 'Dr Paccard of Chamonix', *The Sun*, London, 24 September 1822, p1.
8. 'Dr Paccard of Chamonix', *Government Gazette*, Madras, 22 May 1823, p6.
9. C Engel, 'Early Lady Climbers', *Alpine Journal*, vol 54, 1943, pp51-9

Fig 5 'The Experiment. Position in which we remained a considerable time while the four Guides were seeking a passage in which they failed – but ourselves discovered an issue [?] which finally saved us', 22.5cm × 13cm, 1822. Double-sided backed with *Fig 9* 'Arrival at Night'.

Reading the report of another 'arduous and perilous' yet successful English ascent of Mont Blanc in 1825, by Capt Markham Sherwill and Dr Edmund Clark on 26 August, it is clear that the ladies' intention to attempt their own ascent of Mont Blanc 'the following year' continued as a subject of discussion amongst the British in Chamonix and in the British newspapers. The *Leeds Mercury* published a lengthy piece under the title 'Letters from the Continent'. This included a detailed report from one of the guides accompanying Clark and Sherwill, and 'subjoined' the note Dr Clark had made in the travellers' book in Chamonix, in which Clark's careful analysis of the pleasures, displeasures and final justification of his experience determined: 'The excursion would, I fear, be too painful for the female constitution; fourteen hours on the snow is more fatiguing than generally conceived.' With a sense of certain bewilderment the editor concluded: 'You will scarcely believe, after this account, that ladies are about to attempt the ascent of Mont Blanc. Yet it is true,' he continued, 'Mrs Campbell and her daughter who have already performed wonders in this way have announced their intention of ascending next year; both Capt. Sherwill and Dr Clark advise them to relinquish their design. … This is a tremendous exertion for ladies.'[10]

Some years later, in 1862, Walsh picked up the theme of the constitution of the two ladies and neatly summarised their commendable achievements.

We still talk today about the courage and muscular strength displayed by two Scottish women, Mrs Campbell and her daughter, about 10 years ago. They, the first of their sex, crossed the Col du Géant to go to Courmayeur, followed

10. 'Letters from the Continent', *Leeds Mercury*, 28 Jan 1826, p4.

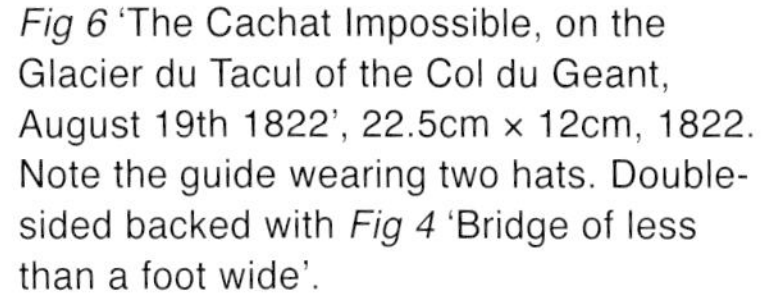

Fig 6 'The Cachat Impossible, on the Glacier du Tacul of the Col du Geant, August 19th 1822', 22.5cm x 12cm, 1822. Note the guide wearing two hats. Double-sided backed with *Fig 4* 'Bridge of less than a foot wide'.

Fig 7 'Passage on the Glacier du Tacul. ascending Col du Geant 19th Aug. 1822, 22.6 x 12.8 cms. Double sided backed with A nob of ice.

the whole length of the Mer de Glace to visit the Jardin, a rock covered with vegetation and flowers, which forms an oasis in the middle of these icy solitudes, they climbed to the top of Buet, the most difficult point to reach in this whole chain. These different routes last ten or twelve hours, and a great part of the way is silent on snow and ice, across crevices and along precipices.[11]

Moving from contemporary commentary to that of a mountaineering historian of the mid 20th century, Claire-Éliane Engel included a precis of the Campbells' crossing of the Col du Géant in a piece she wrote for the *Alpine Journal* entitled 'Early Lady Climbers'. Their identity, and nationality, still a mystery she commenced, 'There are two Scottish ladies about whom I long to know more than I do now.' Quoting both Clissold's *Narrative* and Walsh's earlier 1823 *Notes en Suisse*, and elaborating on both the strategy and the stamina of the 'plucky and sensible' women Engel lamented: 'Nothing more is known about them.'[12]

11. T Walsh, *Voyage En Suisse et en Piedmont*, Paris, 1862, p377-8. Translation by author.
12. C Engel, 'Early Lady Climbers', *Alpine Journal*, vol 54, 1943, pp51-9.

Yet Mrs Campbell had kept a journal and a visual record of around a decade of European travel although the three Grand Tour sketch albums she created were known only to her family until sold at auction in 2020.[13] The title page of one of these albums clarifies the extent of these travels and reveals her full name as the artist: 'Original sketches in the environs of Geneva, Chamouni, Savoy various parts of Switzerland, France and the Isle of Elba made during the years 1818, 19, 20, 21, 22, 23, 24, 25, 26, 27 by Elizabeth Campbell.' Of the nearly 500 sketches Elizabeth Campbell produced, just a handful are under discussion here, and of those it is only one annotated image that allows the only extant link with the artist and her daughter and their historic crossing of the Col du Géant.

Mrs Campbell was born Elizabeth Turner in the county of Yorkshire in 1783, the daughter of Yorkshire politician Sir Charles Turner of Kirkleatham and Mary Shuttleworth. Elizabeth's father died when she was young and following her mother's remarriage and early death she was raised by her stepfather the eminent Sir Thomas Gascoigne, eighth baronet and MP, on his estate at Parlington, near Leeds. There 'Elizabeth witnessed the practical application of Gascoigne's wide ranging enlightenment interests in history, agriculture and horticulture,'[14] and accordingly developed her own extraordinary depth of character heavily influenced by this milieu. In 1801, aged 18, she married Lt Col William H Campbell and their only child Thomasina was born around 1804. Elizabeth was widowed after ten years of marriage.[15] Now, as an intelligent, educated, plucky, artistic and informed wealthy widow, Elizabeth was able to emulate her stepfather's passion for travel and from 1818, as her watercolour sketchbook reveals, Elizabeth and her young daughter Thomasina embarked on a decade of annual European tours.

By 1828 Elizabeth had settled in Scotland, renting Kilravock Castle between Nairn and Inverness, where she became well established in the local community, managed her castle policies and home farm,[16] entertained and indulged her other liberal interests which included a passion for archaeology, her formative years clearly still bearing effect on her achievements here in Britain, as they had in Europe. For it was her explorations here in Britain that have left a more visible trail; in the late 1820s, Elizabeth opened the tombs now known as the Clava Cairns, raising the question of whether she was Scotland's earliest female archaeologist.[17] This allowed an alternative approach to researching Elizabeth's life that had, by strange twist of fate, remained a void for the years of her European travels. Agreeably, each line of research now neatly dovetails together.

In 1818 Elizabeth caught her first glimpse of the Mont Blanc range. She may have stopped en route to paint 'The Mole, Mont Blanc from the road

13. 'A collection of three Grand tour Sketch albums by Elizabeth Campbell circa 1818 to 1830 depicting various parts of Europe, Ireland and Britain', Moore Allen & Innocent, lot 314, sold 18 Jan 2020.
14. M Cross, 'The Campbells: Digging into the history of women in archaeology', Historic Environment Scotland website, 30 Sept 2022.
15. Ibid.
16. Ibid.
17. Ibid

Fig 8 'Summit of the Col du Geant 19th August', 22.6cm × 12.8cm, 1822. Double-sided backed with *Fig 1* 'Géant. Upon the Snows'.

Fig 9 'Arrival at Night 19th August 1822', 22.5cm × 13cms, 1822. Note the addition of a small dog to the party on the descent to Entrèves. Double-sided backed with *Fig 5* 'The Experiment'.

to Coligny, 1818',[18] to outline crisply the topography of a landscape that was yet to be explored. In contrast her sketchy 'L'Aiguille de Dru & end of the Mer de Glace 1818', cleverly stresses her diminutive viewpoint from very close to the glacier wall; Elizabeth allows the moraine, meltwater and seracs to entirely dominate the picture plane. In 1819 the view of the picturesque 'Bridge at St Martin over the Arve' was captured from the roadside. And in 1820 several views of the village of Chamonix were taken with the Arve and the Priory as her focus, with just a few foreground figures to aid perspective. Similarly on 4 August 1822, the year of their crossing, Elizabeth also painted the village from the chapel close by. Views of 'Montanvert', the 'Mer de Glace', and the 'Glacier des Bois' dated 1827 are Elizabeth's latest known drawings of the Chamonix valley which had clearly captivated her. Regrettably there is no known written account of these years of travel although Elizabeth did keep a journal to accompany her watercolours for her 1825 excursion to Sicily.[19]

There is a naivety and honesty to those small, annotated watercolours, painted back to back that depict the Campbell's actual crossing of the Col du Géant. They reveal the real dangers the party was forced to overcome.

18. Annotated on reverse.
19. Mrs Campbell's travel journal and watercolours illustrating her journey through Sicily in 1825 are in the possession of a London gallery.

The ladies prepared well for the arduous traverse. Their excursion to the Jardin took place on 1 August that year. Elizabeth's watercolour 'Le Jardin, Mont Blanc, Geant 1st August 1822' (Fig 2) skilfully summarises the ladies' ambition; it is a record of reconnoitre. Clearly visible to the two women for the first time is the objective and the route and it is possible Elizabeth first forged both her col and summit ambitions from this viewpoint. She depicts her daughter and the guides surveying the vista from the shelter of the Jardin, following their extensive glacier walk. No less taxing was their ascent of the Buet on 17 August, which was considered a most difficult and tedious climb at the time,[20] with steep scree slopes and a glacier walk to the snow-covered summit. Their reward was the stunning view directly across the valley toward the shapely dome and flowing glaciers of Mont Blanc,[21] which may well have further prompted their goals.

The two ladies would have taken the same opportunity of settled weather as Clissold, who had 'remained ten days in expectation of'[22] it. Accordingly, so his narrative reports, 'On Sunday 18 August Mrs and Miss Campbell … started at mid-day with eight guides from the Priory at Chamouni',[23] though Elizabeth's drawings reveal a smaller party. The guides were equipped with standard though scant equipment for glacier excursions at the time: packs, a pikestaff to fix into the ice and ropes. Whilst the whole party wore shoes armed with sharp-headed nails,[24] the cumbersome and inadequate attire of the ladies is clear (Fig 3). Clissold had been made aware of the ignorance of their guides leading him to comment, 'These two ladies have shown how female intrepidity may finally surmount danger even when the experience of guides may fail.'[25] It seems that the guides' inability to handle the ropes had caused the ladies more difficulties than he had faced on the mountain. Indeed, using Forbes' account of his reverse crossing of the col 20 years later[26] it is possible to grasp the ladies situation, and Elizabeth's focus in her sketches on the challenge of forging a route on the Tacul glacier. And, although Engel considered 'the seracs were probably easier to cross … as the glacier was much higher'[27] at that time, the ladies' great difficulty is well conveyed in the drawings (Figs 4-7). Forbes describes the precipitous situation, the 'wilds of ice' encountered in which the most 'terrific chasms and rents are hidden like a ditch in a *ha-ha* fence … a chaos of impassable fissures … a labyrinth,' and most telling of all is his short sentence, 'The spectacle gave us pause,'[28] which aligns so well with Elizabeth's annotation in Fig 5 'The experiment position', bringing to mind Walsh's previously quoted comment.

After successfully navigating the perilous maze of seracs the party would have endured a cold and uncomfortable bivouac 'passing the night at the

20. Walsh, ibid.
21. C Engel, *Mountaineering in The Alps, An Historical Survey*, Allen & Unwin, London, 1971), pp29-30.
22. 'Ascent of Mont Blanc', *Bibliothèque Universelle*, ibid.
23. Clissold, ibid, p8.
24. 'Letters from the Continent', *Leeds Mercury*, 28 Jan 1826, p.4.
25. Clissold, ibid p22.
26. J Forbes, *Travels through the Alps of Savoy*, Edinburgh, 1843, pp216-243.
27. C Engel, 'Early Lady Climbers', *Alpine Journal*, vol 54, 1943, pp51-9.
28. Forbes, ibid. p237.

foot of the rocks of Tacul',[29] 'sleeping on the snow at the elevation of over eight thousand feet above Chamouni',[30] after which 'easier but long slopes of snow'[31] lay ahead to the col at 11,140ft (Fig 1).

This was clearly a place for both celebration and shelter. In her record of their achievement 'The summit of the Col du Géant 19th August' Elizabeth depicts the party sharing wine whilst she and Thomasina use umbrellas against the wind (Fig 8). It must be hoped that Elizabeth and Thomasina took a moment during their rest at the col to absorb the ethereal beauty of this impressive site. Engel writes of it as 'a place of vision ... a world of its own, a large snowy plateau encircled far and near by the most impressive rock pinnacles of the Mont Blanc range.'[32] It had captivated de Saussure, who had felt elated, and written ecstatic descriptions of the place to his wife.[33] Although de Saussure's hut had long been destroyed[34] at the time Forbes passed through he noted 'a board and a considerable quantity of straw ... yet remained there, preserved for half a century. There was also an empty bottle, entire.' This was possibly 'a relic of another illustrious guest M Elie de Beaumont, the last traveller but one who, seven years before, had passed the wild spot.' Forbes also recalled his admiration of the scene, how his 'wide glance' of the southern panorama 'filled my mind with a pleasing confusion of images of grandeur and beauty' and how from there he considered 'the summit of Mont Blanc as perfectly distinct ... close at hand although still 4600 feet above the spectator,'[35] an opinion closely shared by a later observer who reflected that from the col 'Mont Blanc looked so near that one felt as if it would not add much to include him in a day's work.'[36] Perhaps it was also this, the foreshortened proximity of the summit that further inspired the women's ambition to scale the mountain, although that was not to be. Not forsaking the perfection of the view from the col, 'from the gap at the foot of the wild ridge crowned by'[37] what Forbes described as 'the great tooth like form of the Aiguille de Géant', the descent, 'a long uniform slope of nearly 8000 feet',[38] still lay ahead. The ladies arrived at Entrèves in darkness (Fig 9).

There remains much more to tell of these two English ladies. And, whilst the historic significance of their crossing of the Col du Géant has not gone completely unrecognised through the years, Mrs Campbell's watercolour record of it certainly remained unknown, lost in time. Now, in this bicentennial year, via sight of just one small watercolour drawing, Elizabeth and Thomasina Campbell's full identity has been established and these two resolute English ladies can rightfully occupy a slightly wider niche in history.

29. 'Ascent of Mont Blanc', *Bibliothèque Universelle*, ibid.
30. 'Letters from the Continent', *Leeds Mercury*, ibid.
31. C Parker, 'Passages in 1860, Without Guides, of the Strahlegg, Schwarzerg, Weissthor, Col d'Hérens and Col du Géant', *The Alpine Journal*, vol 30, London, 1916), p42.
32. C Engel, *They Came to the Hills*, London, 1952, p60.
33. Engel, *Mountaineering in the Alps*, ibid, p58.
34. Engel, 'Early Lady Climbers', ibid.
35. Forbes, ibid, pp225, 228 and 235.
36. Parker, ibid.
37. Engel, *Mountaineering in the Alps*, ibid.
38. Forbes, ibid, p.225.

SUZANNE STRAWTHER

'I Was Accompanied by My Wife'

The 'Discovery' of Mrs J Curtis Leman

One of Edward Whymper's lantern slides of the Matterhorn, taken in 1893, 16 years after Margaret Curtis Lemon's ascent in 1877.

Written in the *Führerbuch* of the Zermatt guide Franz Biener is a short sentence written by Alpine Club member J Curtis Leman.

Franz 'Weisshorn' Biener accompanied me as guide on the 28th August up the Weisshorn and on the 31st when I was accompanied by my wife up the Matterhorn. [Signed and dated] Zermatt Sept. 1st 1877.

These few words both intrigued and excited me when I first read them; 1877 was only six years after Lucy Walker's first female ascent of the Matterhorn. Who was this 'wife'? My curiosity was further piqued when I crossreferenced other sources and found a second entry about the climb in the *Führerbuch* of Aloys Pollinger, the St Niklaus guide, also written by J Curtis Leman.

> *A Pollinger accompanied me as second guide up the Matterhorn on the 30th, 31st August when I was accompanied by my wife to whom he was more particularly allocated in the ascent. I was entirely satisfied with his care and attention and can recommend him as a careful and attentive guide.*

I felt affronted on the wife's behalf. She had not signed her name to the entry as often happened with climbing parties, certainly as Mrs E P Jackson always did. She would sign: 'Mrs M Jackson CAF'. And Edward Patten Jackson wrote in Aloys Pollinger's *Führerbuch* on 15 September 1878, '... he has accompanied us ...' and 'We have found him an Excellent Guide ...'

Führerbücher are quite small notebooks, to fit into a jacket pocket, and it became customary in the 1840s and 1850s for Alpine guides to carry them and for their clients, who had engaged them for a particular climb or climbs, to write a few words in them about the climb and the conduct of the guide. Their status altered when the various guides' corporations were set up; they became proof of a guide's right to work, bearing the annual stamp of the authorities under which the Alpine guides were organised. Detailed physical descriptions were included so there was no chance of impersonation. Also included was a detailed list of tariffs charged for each climb. (Clients were also responsible for the expenses of a guide: transport, food, lodgings and any porters used.)

Climbing with a guide was the norm until the early post-Second World War years. Practically it made sense, with few written descriptions of routes. The Rev Arthur Gilbert Girdlestone's book *The High Alps Without Guides* (1870) was badly received by his contemporaries; he was seen as foolhardy. Ball's Alpine guidebooks, published in the 1860s and 1870s and written by John Ball, the Club's first president, did little more than point you in the right direction. So engaging an experienced Alpine guide who knew the route made good sense. Though the system was not foolproof: the Misses Pigeon, Anna and Ellen, two sisters from Clapham, complained in their book *Peaks and Passes* (1885) how they were 'out for 17¾ hrs and no summit!', when their guide failed to find it.

So who was 'the wife'? And who was her husband? Never having heard of either of them, it was lucky I was in the AC Library when I discovered the Curtis Lemans so I could start immediately on the trail to find out more. One reference led to another, and I was able to follow a paper trail that revealed further details about their Alpine climbing and more particularly Mrs J Curtis Leman's achievements.

The entry for him in Mumm's *Alpine Club Register* gives the date of his election to the Club as March 1876 and he died a member in 1897. In 1862 he

Lucy Walker, photographed for the Ladies' Alpine Club during her presidency, which began in 1913. Walker made the first female ascent of the Matterhorn in 1871. Margaret Curtis Lemon's ascent was therefore an early female repeat. No extant photograph of her could be found.

had married Margaret, born Jane Margaret Hart in 1834, daughter of Lt Gen Henry George Hart, the originator of *Hart's Army List*, in Calcutta, now Kolkata, in Bengal. The eldest of nine children, her mother was Frances Alicia Okes of Wynberg, South Africa. Three of Margaret's brothers served with distinction in the army. Gen Sir Reginald Clare Hart won the Victoria Cross in the Second Anglo-Afghan War, when aged 30 and a lieutenant, the date of his bravery being 31 January 1879. He received his decoration from Queen Victoria at Windsor Castle, and his son later recalled that the pins from which the medal was suspended were pushed not just into his father's tunic but into his flesh.

Mrs Curtis Lemon's guide, Franz Biner.

James Curtis Leman, a London solicitor, was born in London 1833, the eldest of nine children of James Leman, president of the Incorporated Law Society in 1863-4. Curtis and Margaret married at St Mark's, Surbiton on 14 August 1862. They had seven children. The first in 1863 was stillborn but they went on to have Caroline Margaret, born 1864, Alicia Isabel in 1865, George Curtis in 1867, Downton Curtis in 1868, Reginald Curtis in 1871 and finally Ethel Maud in 1874: seven children in 11 years.

It is interesting to link the ages of the various children with Margaret's Alpine seasons and speculate on the practicalities involved. The 1881 census for their home address at 2, Ravenna Road, Putney Hill, London, lists in addition to family members, three servants: a cook, a housemaid and Caroline B Kage, a 17-year-old nurse born in Switzerland. So presumably nurses were engaged to look after the children whilst Margaret went off climbing: radical in itself for the time.

Her contemporaries tended to be either unmarried, like Lucy Walker or the Misses Pigeon (until Ellen married after their last Alpine season of 1876), Meta Brevoort, aunt of W B Coolidge. The son of Mrs Aubrey Le Blond, Arthur St Vincent Burnaby, was looked after by his grandmother, while Mrs Henry Freshfield's son Douglas (AC president 1893-5) was actively involved in the planning and execution of the family's Alpine excursions from an early age (see *AJ* vol XXX, pp187-9).

Fortunately Mumm does mention Margaret's climbs alongside those of her husband and though not mentioned by name, Curtis mentions his wife, a guide and himself as witnessing a circular rainbow on 7 August 1871, whilst standing on the summit of the Brevent at about four or five in the afternoon, according to his article in the *Alpine Journal* (vol XII).

That same season of 1871 Margaret climbed the Strahlhorn, Breithorn and Monte Rosa. In 1877 she climbed the Matterhorn and Weisshorn, in 1878 Mont Blanc and in 1880 the Grivola, Col de Lauzon, Col de Valpelline, Rimpfischhorn, Rothorn and Furggjoch. For 1881 there is no reference to Margaret in Curtis' list of climbs that season.

Their season in the Dauphiné in 1882 was particularly successful. The Lemans' climbs were recorded in the *Annuaire de la Société des Touristes du Dauphiné* for that year. Curtis was a member, as were a number of AC stalwarts of the day: the Pilkington brothers, Frederick Gardiner, Coolidge.

(The society's name rather belies its intent and purpose.) So: 16 August 1882, Col de la Lauze; 17 August, Col du Clôt des Cavales; 18 August, the Tête de la Maye. *'Première ascension par une dame anglaise'* is recorded for this last but was probably true of the other climbs.

It was on 28 August that she made the first female ascent of Mont Pelvoux. The party induced the Curtis Lemans, the guide Pierre Gaspard *fils* and two porters. They left the Refuge de Provence at 4am and arrived at the summit at 11am, where the party was met by bad weather, snow and squally wind. *'La courageuse ascensioniste,'* i.e. Margaret, sheltered out of the wind on Pointe Durand, whilst the rest of the party made a brief visit to the second summit Pointe Puiseux, 11m higher. They returned to the hut in five hours and then down to the valley and Vallouise for midnight.

In 1883 there are only references for Curtis' climbs in Mumm. Margaret died in 1896 and her husband in 1897. Unfortunately, there is no obituary in the *Alpine Journal* for Curtis, despite still being a member on his death. He is buried in Highgate cemetery with his mother and father and two of his sisters, Caroline and Julia. Again, unfortunately, I could find no record of Margaret's grave. Curtis Leman's brother Robert Edward Leman was also an AC member (elected February 1876), Robert's father-in-law Henry Trower was an original AC member, as was Henry's school friend William Longman (AC president 1872-4) of the publishing house Longman, Green & Co. I mention these familial interconnections to give a flavour of the world in which Margaret lived.

It is frustrating that there is no record of her 'voice', of her reactions to her achievements. A platform for recording exclusively female climbs and accounts only appeared in 1907 with the founding of the Ladies' Alpine Club and in 1921 with the Pinnacle Club.

The Longman connection is interesting in so much as it was the Longmans who published Mrs Henry Warwick Cole's book *A Lady's Tour round Monte Rosa* in 1859. (Henry Warwick Cole was an AC member and a London solicitor.) They also published Mrs Henry Freshfield's *Alpine Byways* (1861) and *A Summer Tour of the Grisons and Italian Valleys of the Bernina* (1862) and similarly Amelia Blandford Edwards' *Untrodden Peaks and Unfrequented Valleys* (1873).

Unlike these women, finding information about Margaret's climbs and who she was had to be done through her father and husband. Mrs Jackson, mentioned earlier, née Margaret Anne Sanderson, was invited to submit an article for the 1889 *Alpine Journal* and to read a paper before the Yorkshire Ramblers' Club in November 1903. Margaret Leman presumably was never invited or encouraged to record her achievements; tantalisingly we shall never know. A recent symposium in January 2023 addressed the question of why so few women go on expeditions. We might equally ask the question of why so few women wrote and indeed write about their exploits. I am not sure what this all says, or means: I shall leave it up to you. But I am very glad that I stumbled across her.

Franz Weisshorn Biener
accompanied me as guide
on the 28th Aug up the Weisshorn
and on the 31st when I was
accompanying my wife up
the Matterhorn –
I have no reason to alter
my estimate formed some
years back of his capabilities
& powers and I strongly
recommend him as a good
& careful guide for any
[illegible] difficult
expedition. J. Curtis Lemon
Zermatt Sept 1st 1877.

On Sept: 3rd Franz Weisshorn
Biener accompanied me and
some friends over the St. Théo-
dule pass. I was so much
pleased with him that I
engaged him for the ascent
of Monte Rosa on the 5th. We
made the ascent by the rocks
on the Col de Lys side. I found
him in every way a first
rate guide, and as pleasant
a companion as he was a
careful helper in the difficult
parts. He is to be much recommended; and I shall certainly
employ him in any more
ascents I may have to make
E. H. C. Wellesley

The entry in Biner's Führerbuch detailing Mrs Curtis Lemon's ascent of the Matterhorn.

RACHEL HEWITT

In Her Nature

Alpinism and Suffragism

Elizabeth Hawkins-Whitshed (1860-1934), better known to posterity as Lizzie Le Blond, first president of the Ladies' Alpine Club, Irish heiress and mountaineering author.

Out of all sports, mountaineering was especially relevant to suffragists' fight for representation; in part because outdoor leisure activities such as hiking were already widely accepted to be fundamentally political pastimes in the context of 'right to roam' campaigns. In a 1908 short story called 'The Suffragette', author Frank Savile made sure that the fictional women's rights activist was a 'lady mountaineer'. Marjorie Milsom thought that early 20th-century female climbers brought to mind 'thoughts of window-breaking suffragettes ... emancipation, in fact – another aspect of the new feminine attack on masculine sanctuaries.' Suffragist mountaineers directly embraced the political symbolism of their sport. In 1909, a group of women ascended Mount Rainier (in the Cascade mountain range of the Pacific Northwest) and placed a 'Votes for Women' pennant at its summit. One of the group's members Cora Smith Eaton, was a founder of the Grand Forks Equal Suffrage Association and treasurer for the Washington Equal Suffrage Association, and when she subsequently climbed Glacier Peak in the same range, she wrote 'Votes for Women' after her name on the register. In 1911, the American mountaineer and suffragist Annie Smith Peck unfurled a yellow 'Votes for Women' banner on the 21,000-foot peak of Nevado Coropuna in Peru, and the following year, Fanny Bullock Workman was photographed holding up a newspaper with a 'Votes for Women' headline on the Siachen glacier in the Himalaya.

Enough members of the Ladies' Alpine Club were ardent suffragists that, in 1909, the British *Votes for Women* newspaper suggested that its membership roster would make a good recruiting ground for militant campaigners. The Club's most prominent mountaineering-suffragists were friends Eva McLaren and Frances Heron-Maxwell. Eva was known to be engaged in 'long and strenuous work for the enfranchisement of women': she served on the central committee of the National Society for Women's Suffrage, was a leading member of the Women's Liberal Federation, active in the Union of Practical Suffragists and the Liberal Women's Suffrage Union and, with Frances Heron-Maxwell, she co-founded the Forward Suffrage Union in 1908. Although a few upper-class women were wary of associating themselves with the militant suffragettes who smashed the windows of gentlemen's clubs, the majority of the Ladies' Alpine Club's members were sympathetic to the cause. Early member Violet Roy-Batty served on the ladies' council of the Conservative and Unionist Women's Franchise Association, which expressed the conviction that women should play a greater part in 'the government of the country'.

Lizzie Le Blond confessed that 'I am not a suffragette, because I lack the courage of my opinions' – but she promised that privately, her views 'entirely coincide with those of the that courageous sisterhood' and that she hoped that, if the suffragists 'make themselves sufficiently unpleasant during a sufficiently long time, they will get [the vote]'. All of the female climbers who comprised the Ladies' Alpine Club had experienced how mountaineering could radicalise women and offer a taste of freedoms that they subsequently wanted to be granted elsewhere. As Mary E Crawford – a member of the

Alpine Club of Canada, president of the Political Equality League in Winnipeg and campaigner for women's rights in the Province of Manitoba – explained in 1909, outdoor leisure helped a woman to 'know herself as never before – physically, mentally, emotionally', to 'gain confidence with every step' and to 'gaze out upon a new world'.

Lizzie spent her middle age with the Ladies' Alpine Club, finding ways to claw back freedoms despite the marginalisation of women in sport and public life that had stolen many of the glorious liberties of her youth. Her final two decades were also seen out in this long-lasting era of male backlash. In those years, Lizzie came to see how her skills in mountaineering were relevant to political issues beyond female suffrage – such as international relations and women's role in global diplomacy.

• Extracted with the permission of the author and publisher from *In Her Nature: How Women Break Boundaries in the Great Outdoors* by Rachel Hewitt, published in 2023 by Chatto & Windus. See p307 for Heather Dawe's review.

ADÈLE LONG

Why Do So Few Women Go on Expeditions?

Katy Parrot, speaker at the Expedition Essentials for Women Explorers, on Broad Peak.

Listening to BBC Radio 4's PM programme some 15 or so years ago, I remember hearing an illustrious mountaineer being interviewed about a recent expedition he and his male partner had made in the Greater Ranges. There must have been some narrow escape involved to make the national news. In addition to the usual questions – 'Why do you do it?' – the interviewer asked him why he thought so few women go on expeditions. My ears pricked up and I listened intently to his reply.

Because I think they can't deal with the hardship; it can be really tough.

Symposium organiser Adèle Long, second from right, at event venue Plas y Brenin.

My reaction was mixed. How dare he say women can't deal with hardship? History shows that women have coped with hardship in every generation, country and culture. Yet, there was a niggling thought. Could he be right? I think he may have been alluding to the physical and mental attrition that wears you down the longer you are away from home, the higher the altitude you reach and the greater the technical challenge of your goal. This is self-inflicted hardship, not imposed due to war, poverty, oppression or the like. Is there a barrier more pertinent to women than men, which makes them reluctant to deal with the voluntary hardship of remote mountain exploration? Or is it something quite different?

It's not that women don't go on expeditions at all. The first recorded all-female expedition[1] was that of Monica Jackson, Elizabeth Stark and Evelyn Camrass who in 1955 reached the summit of Gyalzen (6151m, formerly Gyalgen) in the Jugal region of Nepal. Seven years later Jo Peacock and Barbara Spark made first ascents of two 6,000m peaks during their expedition to Kulu in India and then, with Dorothea Gravina, Denise Evans, Pat Wood and Nancy Smith, climbed Lha Shamma (6412m) in Nepal and six other previously unclimbed peaks. The American Arlene Blum led an all-female expedition to Annapurna I in 1978, the first to an 8,000m peak, while Rhona Lampard and Wanda Rutkiewicz made the first female ascent of Gasherbrum II in 1989. These women paved the way for a more recent generation of female mountaineers, with the likes of Louise Thomas, Glenda Huxter, Julie-Ann Clyma and Cathy O'Dowd making significant expeditionary ascents in the Greater Ranges. Many other women have made expeditionary first ascents and continue to do so.

1. In this context an expedition is a planned journey to reach and attempt to climb previously unclimbed peaks in a remote or unexplored mountainous region.

Fay Manners, leading female alpinist, with her recent haul.

However, the fact remains that while women are in abundance on crags and climbing walls around the world, and an increasing number are enjoying alpine climbing and mountaineering, relatively few go on expeditions. Only a handful of grant applications to expedition funding sources[2] are from women and even fewer are from women as expedition leaders.[3] This has caused concern among those allocating grants and they were keen to understand why this might be. In addition to having the fundamental desire to explore, going on an expedition requires money, skill, knowledge, experience, commitment, freedom from home responsibilities and time. These potential barriers apply to men as well as women, except, arguably, the last two are weighted more strongly against women. Fund holders wanted to know if a dedicated Alpine Club women-specific expedition grant would help overcome real or perceived barriers to level the playing field. As the old adage goes: 'when in doubt, ask. When not in doubt, ask.' So we asked.

This was a bit like asking a chocoholic if they want a bar of chocolate. The reply was an emphatic 'yes please'. But there were some caveats, primarily that more information was needed and that a symposium or workshop would be helpful. We asked what such an event might cover.

Recent research into women involved in mountain training[4] reported women having self-doubts about their ability in the mountains despite having met the requisite skill levels. Family and social constraints caused them to question their belonging in the expedition environment and cultural

2. Mount Everest Foundation, Montane Alpine Club Climbing Fund, British Mountaineering Council.
3. In the last 10 years applications to the Montane Alpine Club Fund have ranged from 0% women to 10% with an average in the region of <5%. Applications to Julie Tullis Award, available to women, all-female expeditions and disabled climber of either gender, are between one and six each year for last 13 years, with an average of between three and four.
4. J Hall & A Doran, 'Researching Women in Mountaineering', Sheffield Hallam University, 2020.

barriers such as 'grade-ism' favoured a more masculine approach. Although by no means universal, misogyny was still in evidence; this was however countered by men who preferred the 'softer' approach of a female trainer. In an equally harsh environment, a 2022 report by the National Science Foundation[5] found female workers in the Antarctic context experienced widespread sexual harassment from their male colleagues, with their complaints often being dismissed. Would the symposium mirror these concerns?

Taking action, the Alpine Club got in touch with the Mount Everest Foundation, the British Mountaineering Council and current AC climbing-fund partner Montane to organise an event specifically for women who want to go on expeditions. Five months later, on 28 and 29 January 2023, Expedition Essentials for Women Explorers was held at Plas y Brenin in north Wales. The purpose was to provide information, share experiences and discover what the real and perceived barriers might be and how they might be addressed.

Over 60 women (and two men) engaged in a series of lectures, workshops and talks for a day and a half. The programme covered all aspects of planning and executing an expedition. In addition to the more conventional subjects, and building on the feedback we had received, topics such as managing personal hygiene were included. In addition, the psychological aspects of success, managing conflict and confidence building were discussed in workshops. After dinner speakers Fay Manners and Katy Parrot gave highly entertaining and genuinely inspirational talks. Fay, a British alpinist based in Chamonix, and her climbing partner Line van den Berg completed the first female ascent of *Phantom Direct* on the south face of the Grandes Jorasses and the *Cassin* on Denali as part of an all-female team. Katy is a Montane endurance athlete; in 2016, aged 24 years, she was a finalist in the BBC programme Ultimate Hell Week: Special Forces. Since then she has participated in numerous challenges including being the second woman in the Montane Lapland Arctic Ultra in 2022 as well as reaching the summit of Broad Peak (8051m) in Pakistan. An unscheduled presentation from Freshta Ibrahami, an asylum seeker from Afghanistan, on her Unstoppable Project[6] reminded everyone that, unlike women in more fortunate countries who are benefiting from the progress that has been made in gender equality, women in Afghanistan and Iran are experiencing a decline in their basic freedoms.

Did Expedition Essentials for Women Explorers meet its objectives? A wealth of information was presented with access to further resources on the Alpine Club website, and delegates were open and enthusiastic to share experiences in what was described as a 'safe' environment. Women-only programmes can provide an atmosphere of care, cooperation, collaboration and informed choice that 'resist the subtle influences to conform to facilitator or programme values, or masculine norms'. Although women-only spaces do not necessarily challenge the dominant masculine discourse that can

5. https://phys.org/news/2022-10-women-antarctica-assault-legacy-exclusion.html
6. https://unstoppableproject.com

lead to social change,[7] a factor that should influence future events. Feedback indicated that the event had surpassed expectations. Delegates were surprised to discover how many expedition funding grants were available and how many specifically targeted women.

Did we learn why women are less likely to go on expeditions than men? Delegates mentioned feeling more confident after the event; they hadn't been sure they were 'up to it', but now realised that they were. Family commitments were raised as an issue and these were at least partially dispelled by suggesting forward planning (12-18 months) and an unwavering commitment to the task. Coping with periods and the menopause were discussed frankly and as a result were seen in a different, more manageable, perspective. Tips on how to cope with stressful situations, be they conflict with other team members, a sense of isolation, concerns about fitness or acclimatisation, were discussed in workshops; the message being that openness is positive and everyone has a right to be heard: expeditions are a team event even if not everyone reaches a summit.

The symposium gave women the chance to share their concerns, their achievements and the excitement of exploration. Now this group of women at least have the information, tools, resources and contacts they need to go on an expedition. Around 30% of delegates said they would be applying for an expedition grant now or in the future. One month after the event, two had already applied. But to ensure a lasting impact, with more women participating in expeditions, we must hope that these women rise to the challenge and become the inspiration for future women. To do that necessitates the full support of the funding bodies, and their partners at home and on the mountain.

Interestingly there was no mention of coping with 'hardship'.

7. K Warren, 'Gender in Outdoor Studies', *Routledge International Handbook of Outdoor Studies*, Abingdon, Routledge, 2016, pp360-8.

JOHN MIDDENDORF

'A Delicate Sense of Balance'

How Miriam O'Brien Inspired America

Miriam O'Brien on a gendarme in the Mittelgruppe of the Engelhörner, taken from her book *Give Me the Hills*. A member of the Ladies' Alpine Club, she was among a significant group who resigned their membership when women were admitted to the Alpine Club. *(Adolph Rubi)*

Before and after the First World War, there were a significant number of women climbing at a high standard in the Dolomites. Dutchwoman Jeanne Immink, for example, whose brief, five-year climbing career included the second ascent of the *Schmitt Chimney* on the Fünffingerspitze, despite its originator Robert Hans Schmitt predicting it would never see a repeat. 'I challenge the male mountaineers to follow in my steps,' she once said.

Gertrude Bell, left, was an early inspiration to Miriam O'Brien. Bell's attempt on the Finsteraarhorn had impressed O'Brien but her own experience on the mountain was harrowing. With Adolf Rubi she made the third ascent in 1930 in a 20-hour round-trip, climbing steep rock in mitts and overcoming phenomenal challenges of route finding and loose rock. In *Give Me the Hills*, she titled her report of this climb, 'the only grim chapter'.

There were the Slovenians Pavla Jesih and Dana Kuraltova, who made the first all-female ascent of the north face of Triglav in 1925. (Jesih's career was ended by a 100ft fall in 1933.) Or the Austrian Irma Glaser who in 1911 shared the first ascent of the spectacular Piaz ridge on Delago Tower, westernmost of the Vajolet Towers, with Giovanni Battista Piaz and the guide and hut guardian Jori Francesco.

In 1903, Vineta Mayer, who was born in Trieste the year Whymper climbed the Matterhorn, made the first female ascent of the Campanile Basso. (She would die by her own hand in 1945 as the Russians approached her home city of Vienna.) Ilona and Rolanda Eötvös were the two surviving daughters of the Hungarian physicist Loránd Eötvös. The fact they were often guided by Antonio Dibona, along with the family's wealth, meant their achievements were often unfairly discounted. Yet the number and quality of their first ascents, including, in 1901, the south face of Tofana di Rozes, one of the classic south facing routes in the Dolomites, speaks for itself, and they were among the first women to climb together guideless. Käthe Bröske was born in 1870 into an ethnically German family in what is now the Russian city of Volgograd but later moved to the Polish Tatras with her husband, a keen alpinist. She climbed in the Dolomites too, making the traverse of the Vajolet Towers with Tito Piaz. I haven't yet needed to mention more familiar names from that era, like Mira Debelak, Paula Weisinger and Mary Varale.

CLUB ALPINO ITALIANO

RIVISTA MENSILE

Luglio-Agosto 1928

DUE NUOVI ITINERARI
SULLA TORRE GRANDE D'AVERAU

I. - VIA MIRIAM.

Dietro il Rifugio Cinque Torri, nei pressi di Cortina d'Ampezzo, sorge la Torre Grande, la

(Fot. E. Y. O' Brien).

TORRE GRANDE D'AVERAU.

.... Via Versante Nuvolau (comune).
------- Variante Angelini Sperti.
— — — Via Miriam.

salita (la prima fatta da turisti). Noi ci trovavamo a Cortina da qualche giorno ed avevamo fatto una sola scalata d'allenamento, preparazione alquanto inadeguata per un'impresa tanto difficile; ciò non pertanto eravamo molto ansiose di accingerci all'impresa al più presto possibile.

Il punto d'attacco si trova in quella parte della base ove le rocce raggiungono il livello più basso, e precisamente dietro ed a circa dieci minuti dal Rifugio Cinque Torri del C. A. I. La prima parte è costituita da una ripida parete che richiede per circa 30 metri uno sforzo continuo ed ininterrotto, sorpresa alquanto brusca per dei muscoli abituati alla vita comoda e molle delle città. A metà strada c'è un passaggio veramente difficile: uno sbalzo di rocce rosse che bisogna superare. Un passo a sinistra rende il problema meno arduo. Sorpassate le rocce rosse c'imbattiamo in un crepaccio di tre o quattro metri, ancora un passo a sinistra e la prima parte dell'ascensione è quasi finita potendoci portare un poco più avanti per una parete liscia che offre alcuni appigli. Sulla sommità c'è un appiglio per legarvi la corda, piccolo ma sufficiente; alcuni passi ancora in su ed eccoci ad una cava: eccellente osservatorio per riposarsi e per osservare le acrobazie degli altri compagni.

Un piccolo crepaccio non molto difficile, che si trova al dissopra della cava, ci guida per circa 8 metri ad un sito ameno e dominante con uno sbalzo di roccia in alto e, per quanto il nostro sguardo potesse abbracciare, con una parete levigata a destra. Quivi giunti, l'unica

G. Ghedina, Cortina d'Ampezzo (By Permission)

TORRE GRANDE OF CINQUE TORRI
South Wall, "Via Miriam"
(See page 165ff.)

Report in the Club Alpino Italiano's *Rivista Mensile* on the first ascent of the *Via Miriam*, on the Cinque Torri's Torre Grande. The route became a European rock climbing test-piece for the East Coast Appalachian Mountain Club (AMC) members. Elizabeth Knowlton climbed it with the Dimai brothers in 1928.

Among English-speaking climbers the better-known leading women were more often from the French and Swiss Alps, like Marie Marvingt[1] before the Great War and after it Micheline Morin and Alice Damesme, who with Nea Morin, Micheline's sister-in-law, made the first all-female traverse of the La Meije in 1933, and Hettie Dyrhenfurth, who went to Kangchenjunga in 1930 with her husband Günter and Frank Smythe.

There wasn't as much written in English alpine journals about female pioneers in the Dolomites and few clubs kept eastern Alpine journals in their libraries. Nevertheless, Miriam O'Brien, in the 1920s one of America's leading female climbers, was inspired by one of those Dolomites pioneers, a pre-Great War alpinist familiar with the potential of the 'special techniques' developed in the Eastern Alps, one of those extraordinary women pushing the boundaries of convention on the most feared rock climbs of the Alps: Gertrude Bell.

Bell's reputation rests on her extraordinary diplomatic career but in her short climbing life (1899-1904) she amassed a phenomenal list of climbing accomplishments, still enviable decades later. Among her visionary projects was an improbable line up the steep, knife-blade north-east rib of the

1. Some of these pioneering women were not just climbers but excelled in other spheres. Pavla Jesih, after her career-ending fall, became a movie-theatre impresario in Yugoslavia. Marie Marvingt became famous as an aviatrix, flying combat missions in the First World War and developing the idea of air ambulances. She tried to enter the Tour de France but was barred for being a woman. She rode anyway, a little behind the official race, and finished, unlike most of the men who competed. In the Second World War she worked in the resistance and was awarded the Croix de Guerre.

Finsteraarhorn, the most prominent peak in Switzerland. Her 1902 attempt on this elegant route ended short of the summit and their descent became the epic tale of that era, as bad weather set in at a particularly perilous section of tenuous route finding. Bell and her guides Ulrich and Heinrich Fuhrer spent two days retreating through avalanches and desperate bivouacs, managing endless rappels with frostbitten hands and feet. Only through incredible teamwork, courage and perseverance did the team survive. When this route was eventually climbed in 1904, it established new levels of commitment on long alpine rock routes. (See 'The Other Gertrude Bell', *AJ* 2020, pp168-78).

Many of Bell's more difficult climbs were made possible with state-of-the-art tools becoming available at the time in the Eastern Alps. In her journals, she writes of some training routes:

> *BERNER OBERLAND August, 1901: Yesterday my guides and I were up at 4 and clambered up on to the Engelhorn range to take a good look round and see what was to be done. It was the greatest fun, very difficult rock work, but all quite short. We hammered in nails and slung ropes and cut rock steps – mountaineering in miniature. Finally we made a small peak that had not been done before, built a cairn on it and solemnly christened it. Then we explored some very difficult rock couloirs, found the way up another peak which we are going to do one of these days. ... I shall probably stay here till Sunday morning which will give the snow time to get right. Then I shall return to my great schemes...*[2]

Miriam became serious about her alpinism in 1926, the year Gertrude Bell died two days short of her 58th birthday, from an overdose of sleeping pills. Bell's line on the Finsteraarhorn, only repeated once since its first ascent, would become a major objective for the American climber Miriam O'Brien. In 1931 she reflected on Gertrude Bell's great schemes in an *American Alpine Journal* essay 'On Some of Gertrude Bell's Routes in the Oberland', a tribute that revealed her own focus on steep and visionary new rock climbs. In previous eras, mountaineers were often modest in their published reports; some were reluctant to make any claim at all, as in the case of the talented Benedikt sisters, Elly and Karin, who roped up with Conrad Kain. Miriam's eight-page article on Bell, on the other hand, dispenses with modesty and explains the raw commitment and severe challenges Gertrude Bell overcame, based on her own experiences and successes on the hardest test-pieces of the day. In the late 1920s and 1930s Miriam became a leading climber among a group of East Coast American rock climbers that included several talented women: Margaret Mason Helburn, Elizabeth Knowlton, Marjorie Hurd, Betty Woolsey, Florence Peabody, Winifred Marples, Julia and Julia

2. There are several other references to Gertrude Bell's use of pitons (then known as 'nails'), notably in 1902 on the Wellhorn, where she succeeded only 'with the aid of an iron nail driven in the worst place and of a double rope.' Miriam O'Brien wrote of this: 'At that time, apparently, pitons were not so much in disfavour with English Climbers as they later became!' (*Give Me the Hills*, 1957). Regarding 'cutting rock steps', note that sculpting hand and foot-holds in rock with a hammer (or ice axe) was a tolerated technique well into the 1930s (see Rudatis, 1931).

Ilona Eötvös (1880-1945) in the Dolomites. She and her sister Rolanda (1878-1953), pictured right, were introduced to alpinism by their father, the Hungarian physicist and politician Loránd Eötvös and were dubbed the 'Hungarian baronesses' for their ability to hire top guides like Angelo Dibona and Antonio Dimai. Despite the criticism, they were dedicated and capable alpinists.

Colt (mother and daughter), and Jesse Whitehead, a Briton who moved to the USA in 1925.

Precisely when and where Miriam O'Brien was born is surprisingly uncertain. Writing Miriam's obituary for the *American Alpine Journal*, her friend Marjorie Hurd claimed Lisbon, New Hampshire as her birthplace in 1899. Hints in her memoir *Give Me the Hills* and other sources suggest the year may have been 1898. Other sources suggest Forest Glen, Maryland as her birthplace. The confusion is understandable. In the late 1890s, her father Robert Lincoln O'Brien was working as Washington correspondent for a Boston newspaper, the *Boston Evening Transcript*[3]. He would later edit that newspaper before moving to the *Boston Herald*. After that, from the early 1930s, he served in Herbert Hoover's administration as chair of the US Tariff Commission, continuing in post when Franklin Roosevelt was elected.

If anything, Miriam's mother Emily Young O'Brien was more notable. (Her father was a merchant in Lisbon, New Hampshire, and she may have chosen to return there to have her first child.) Despite becoming a mother in her early twenties, Emily continued with her ambition to become a doctor, despite the hurdles placed in her path by the male establishment. While living in Washington, she campaigned with other notable suffragists Ellen Spencer Mussey and Alice Stern Gitterman to establish a juvenile court, which was passed into law in 1906. During the Great War she worked with conscripts and was later head of the Disabled Veterans' Hospital Services. She was a dedicated mountaineer and later in life, at the aged of 59, traversed the Grépon and at 63 did the Jungfrau, Mönch and Wetterhorn.

3. T S Eliot wrote a poem titled 'Boston Evening Transcript', *Poetry*, vol VII no 1, October 1915, p21.

Emily made sure to take her two young children on her adventures. In *Give Me the Hills*, published first in Britain in 1956, Miriam begins with memories of a family trip into 'a remote wilderness region of New Hampshire', recollecting how 'I got there my first taste of the wild, uncrowded places of the earth, and even at six years old, I liked it.' In 1914, Emily took Miriam and her younger brother Lincoln to Europe, where Miriam and her mother climbed up to the Brévent while in Chamonix. Soon after, while in a remote mountain town in Switzerland, war broke out and Miriam witnessed the mobilisation of all able-bodied Swiss men heading to the mountains with 'rucksack, climbing rope, ice-axe, and heavy nailed boots'. They had time to look round the Zermatt mountains before a much-interrupted train journey back to Paris, where they witnessed 'refugees pouring out of the city, and we seemed to be alone in wanting to go in.' Eventually the trio made it safely back to America but for all the O'Briens, their first trip to Europe and the taste of being in the mountains would lead to a lifelong pursuit of mountain adventures.

Miriam first roped up in 1920 on the Grand Muveran during one of her annual summer family vacations in Switzerland. She loved this moment and each summer returned to the mountains. In a hut, she met George Finch, who suggested she not waste time on trivial routes. 'You can do the Matterhorn,' he told her. Why not, she agreed. On local Boston crags and later on climbing trips to the American West, she discovered a natural affinity for balance climbing on steep rock. In March 1926, she joined Margaret Helburn on a winter road-trip with the 'Bemis Crew', a group of hard-core alpinists and rock climbers within the Appalachian Mountain Club. The trip cumulated with steep rock climbs on 'the walls of the cirques of Katahdin', the highest mountain in Maine. Inspired by the steep unclimbed rock walls, a few months later, she travelled to the Dolomites, looking to engage the 'right' guides to learn the craft. She wrote in her autobiography:

> *Rock climbing was what I wanted. I would start in the Dolomites and later go on to Chamonix and its granite aiguilles. ... In common with many women, I felt that these Dolomites were made just to suit me with their small but excellent toe- and finger-holds, and pitches where a delicate sense of balance was the key, rather than brute force. While it helps of course to have tough muscles, the prizefighter would not necessarily make a fine Dolomite climber. But the ballet dancer might.*

Miriam proved herself a prima ballerina on rock. In a few prolific Alpine seasons between 1926 and 1928 she graduated to leading top-level climbs, becoming well known on both sides of the pond. In her first year, after a few training routes, she climbed the Punta Fiames by the *Spigolo*, the futuristic 400m line that follows a bold arête, established by Käthe Bröske and Francesco Jori in 1909. Her understated report in *Appalachia* ('Notes on Three Dolomite Climbs', 1926), notes how her guide, Angelo Dimai, led a difficult pitch with only a small fish line attached, as 'the weight of the regular rope

Left: the brilliant Slovenian alpinist and entrepreneur Pavla Jesih (1901-76), who suffered a serious accident in 1933 that ended her climbing career. She went on to own and run cinemas. Right: the famous Italian inter-war alpinist Mary Varale (1895-1963), who climbed with Comici and Cassin but denounced the CAI as 'hypocrites and buffoons' for overlooking the ability of female alpinists, resigning from the club in 1935.

would be enough to upset his balance and pull him over backwards.' Though Miriam was second on the rope, this climb would have been considered harder than any of the long rock climbs in Colorado at the time, such as *Crestone Needle* or *Alexanders Chimney*, and thus harder than anything in America. Miriam would soon be leading routes of this difficulty.

She reported no pitons on the *Spigolo* in 1926 but in the following years many were added, some by none other than Angelo Dimai, who later repeated the route with Albert I of Belgium. Miriam recounted Angelo's explanation of the extra pegs.

> *'I put most of those in myself,' said Angelo, 'when I took King Albert of the Belgians up this climb. It wouldn't do, you know, to have any accident happen to the King … Of course, when it's only you,' he added quickly with the customary twinkle in his eye, 'it wouldn't matter.'*[4]

In 1927, her second Dolomite season, Miriam's first route was 'one of the most difficult in the whole Dolomite region', the south wall of Torre Grande in the Cinque Torri, a guided climb with her partner Margaret Helburn. This was a state-of-the-art route, with piton belays and anchors strategically placed for the V+ free climbing: the top of the free climbing scale. Their guides were the father and son team of Antonio and Angelo Dimai. Antonio's two sons, Angelo and Guiseppe, and the Cortina guide Arturo Gasperi had

4. M Underhill, *Give Me the Hills*, Methuen, London, 1956.

previously climbed and pre-equipped the route with strategically placed pitons in preparation for Miriam's arrival that season and honoured her by naming the climb the *Via Miriam*. A week later, Miriam and the team climbed it in three and a half hours, falling a few times and weighting a piton at one point, and later devoting three gripping pages of detail about the difficulties in her autobiography.

In Italy, the route was news and a feature article by Miriam appeared in the 1928 *Rivista Mensile*, the journal of the Italian Alpine Club. In Britain, the route was controversial. The style of *Via Miriam* was considered in the 1933 edition of the *Alpine Journal* as 'facilitated' by ironmongery, the correspondent claiming that the modern guide's 'mountaineering' skills had been replaced by piton-protected 'acrobatism', considered 'more or less *unjustifiable*'. In contrast with the honoured Antonio Dimai, who reportedly only used pitons for belays in his long career and was described by E L Strutt in 1941 as 'the finest cragsman in the Eastern Alps', the *Alpine Journal's* consideration of Antonio's avant-garde sons was less flattering. They 'inherited their father's skill' but failed to inherit 'all of his methods'.

Miriam had no such qualms about the new methods, at least then, and throughout her life she was proud of the route named in her honour. For Miriam, it was her first direct exposure to the techniques that would soon enable the rise in big-wall standards in America. Her complex relationship with the ethics of pitons, which she frequently shared in her writings, also begins.

Miriam's relationship with tools was complex; in her writings, she frequently made attempts to explain what she termed the 'morality' of pitons: the line of acceptable use as they became adopted during her career as a climber. Of her early days (pre-1928), she writes of a climb that went awry: 'Not one of us in those days would have stooped to carry a piton.' Yet as we've seen, she had already climbed some very difficult piton-protected routes with guides by that time. Climbing without 'artificial aids' was the goal, and big routes like the north wall of Cima Una, an 800m route which she climbed with Antonio Dimai in seven hours in 1928, were climbed piton-free; she laments how subsequent climbers added many 'unnecessary' pitons, and ponders the balance between risk and skill, a central theme in all realms of climbing. In her later years, she wrote:

> *But the piton for security is something else. We have all heard younger climbers tell us, with impatience, that they do not use pitons to help them get up, but merely to make the climb safe, and that it is exactly the same climb it was before, only safer. It most definitely is not the same climb. These modern climbers are getting from their pitons enormous help without admitting or, perhaps, even realizing its extent. And in this, to my mind, lies the more questionable ethics of the piton.*[5]

5. M O'Brien Underhill, *'Ironmongery Then and Now', Yearbook of the Ladies'* Alpine Club, London, 1957.

In the 1950s, when she wrote this, America was undergoing a big shift in technological climbing. Reusable chromoly steel pitons were coming online, allowing a smaller rack for bigger climbs; big walls like El Capitan were being considered. 'I have no quarrel whatever with direct-aid pitons,' she wrote; her concern was for the adventure lost on overly protected free climbs:

> *It is not the same climb [with more pitons], because the piton removes or greatly mitigates the penalty for failure. … For even if the modern climber never needs to use these pitons, they are there, removing from his mind a great weight of responsibility.*[6]

Yet in her early days, Miriam's attitude toward pitons was softer. In 1931, she recognised the standards of difficulty were higher than in the 1920s due to 'recent developments in rock climbing technique and skill' and wrote: 'The raising over the years of standards of difficulty is due in large measure to the use of improved equipment, and particularly of pitons.' This was a period of rapid expansion of piton-protected climbs in Europe, which was followed by a similar wave in America a few years later. She comments on how Armand Charlet, a critic of pitons except for roping down, had no qualms about leaving his jammed ice axe in cracks to protect difficult sections. 'Morally, I see little difference between using a piton and jamming in the ice axe.'

It was not just hardware that Miriam adopted as she became America's leading rock climbing maestro. She learned from the best and developed a holistic understanding of the new climbing systems. Of potentially catching a fall on a climb in France in 1926, she wrote, 'the chief rule is: don't try to stop the fall abruptly but let the rope run a bit and brake it gradually,' perhaps the most succinct explanation of a dynamic belay until Richard Leonard's analysis in 'Values to be Derived from Local Rock Climbing' in the June 1934 *Sierra Club Bulletin*, then to a larger audience in 1946, in his more widely read book, *Belaying the Leader* (1946). Miriam also developed nuanced skills in the use of karabiners and slings, as evidenced by the impeccable team-work with her partners, especially on her efficient all-female alpine ascents. She understood the advantages of longer ropes, sometimes equipping herself with 150ft ropes for certain climbs at a time when 120ft ropes were standard. And she was an expert in rock-climbing footwear, the *scarpa da gatto*: shoes with layers of woollen cloth ('best when old and therefore well-conditioned' but which only lasted a dozen climbs), and the trade-offs with the rubber soles of sneakers also becoming popular around this time.

After each summer season in the Alps, Miriam would bring all this knowledge and information back to the many local crags of the East Coast, where, almost certainly, these new techniques were first practised in the USA. But it was her on-and-off early climbing partner and future husband

6. Ibid.

Alice Damesme (1894-1974) and Nea Morin (1905-86) on the summit of the Aiguille de Blaitière in 1934. Together with Nea's sister-in-law Micheline Morin, the pair were pioneers in 'manless' climbing. *(Micheline Morin)*

Robert Underhill, who would in the early 1930s become the main spokesperson for these new tools and techniques, despite the breadth and depth of his experience on cutting-edge routes in the Alps being much more limited than Miriam's. In this early period, at the height of her rock-climbing career, Miriam was content as a writer to focus on her experiences and avoid the ethical dilemmas that came with exposing the new tools and techniques.

That wasn't true of her husband. As chair of the rock climbing committee of the Appalachian Mountain Club, Robert Underhill published a piece in the *Sierra Club Bulletin* in 1931 entitled 'On the Use and Management of the Rope in Rock Work'. This seminal piece is recognised as the article that created a leap in climbing standards and styles in the USA. It was not that he invented the techniques he described. In fact, his contribution was offering the first explanation in English of the more complex rope techniques that had been developed in the Eastern Alps in the previous three decades. But the timing and information presented in his illustrated 24-page article created a new general awareness of rope-work and exposed new realms of vertical rock that could be climbed with reasonable safeguards, given that Underhill was also an early proponent of the use of pitons as protection for lead climbs. The article and research in the journals provided an advancement in shared climbing knowledge that surpassed G W Young's *Mountain Craft*, then considered the best and most complete instructional book in English. It's worth asking the question: how much of this shared knowledge was gleaned from Miriam?

She continued to develop her skills with Angelo Dimai for many years, often leading crux pitches on routes new to both her and him. A guide letting a client lead was rare: Antonio Dimai would always climb first but, Miriam wrote, 'with Angelo I could lead all I liked, just so long as we were out of sight of his father.' They shared some epic adventures like Miriam's attempt with Angelo on the *Fehrmann* route on Campanile Basso, where they had to sit out a gusting sleet storm on a six-inch ledge. The full range of her climbing experience is still not properly appreciated. In 1931 she published, in the *Canadian Alpine Journal*, one of her best articles, entitled 'European Rock Climbing', the best overview of continental rock-climbing areas to appear in English up to that point. She details objectives in the Dolomites, the Kaisergebirge, the Engelhörner, Bregaglia, Chamonix, Courmayeur, the Dauphiné, Valais and Swiss Oberland, as well as references to bouldering at Fontainebleau, which she visited in the winter of 1928-9. ('The most astonishing feats are performed on the twenty or thirty centers in the Forest.') She hadn't yet visited all these places: the Kaisergebirge for example. But she had plans to and most likely did. It's frustrating that we don't have a full account of her climbing record.

In the Western Alps we know she made all-female first ascents of the Matterhorn, Jungfrau and Mönch, as well as endurance traverses. Yet Miriam got most attention climbing rock test-pieces like the Grépon multiple times and by various routes, including her famous 'manless' ascent in 1929 with Jesse Whitehead and Alice Damesme, who led the Mummery crack on that occasion. Though by no means her hardest climb, this ascent got global attention when her account of manless climbing was published in the August 1934 edition of *National Geographic*.[7]

> *The essence of guideless climbing consists in taking, oneself, the entire responsibility for carrying the climb through to a successful finish. This is a lot of fun, and I saw no reason why this pleasure should be closed to women, although some of my friends among the French men mountaineers tried patiently to explain to me why it was theoretically impossible for a woman to lead a mountain climb taking the entire responsibility herself without at least masculine 'moral support'.*[8]

Her growing ability had fuelled her guideless – and manless – climbing ambitions and she consequently became known for decades afterwards as 'America's foremost woman climber', still noted as such in the March 1961 edition of *Summit* magazine.[9]

In her seasons on the Chamonix Aiguilles, Miriam was no less accomplished than she had been in the Dolomites, climbing many of the hardest alpine and rock routes in the Mont Blanc range. In 1926, she began with moderate guideless climbing with her brother Lincoln, eight years her junior, and others, noting that she 'planned soon to do more and on a bigger scale'. In France, she also found the right guide for her progression, Alfred Couttet, one of the

7. M O'Brien Underhill, 'Manless Alpine Climbing: The First Woman to Scale the Grépon, the Matterhorn, and Other Famous Peaks Without Masculine Support Relates Her Adventures', The National Geographic Magazine, vol LXVI No2, Washington, August 1934.
8. While Miriam was trying to make a serious point, and I love what she wrote, the editors framed the piece in cutesy, sexist terms with captions like this: 'A strong wind bothers a lady, though she has no skirt to worry about.' Such captions must stand for the regular drumbeat of patronising comments that often prevailed in the media about women's climbs in that era.
9. Not all women climbers approved. O'Brien recalled in the Ladies' Alpine Club *Yearbook* how at Zermatt 'one of the officers of the LAC took me aside and said, with some embarrassment, but still doing her duty as she felt she should: "I feel I must tell you that the Ladies' Alpine Club does not approve of manless climbing."'

first French guides to adopt pitons for harder routes. 'Couttet was using pitons, and using them skilfully. But at the time he wished it kept a secret!' she wrote. Couttet also broke guiding convention by seconding Miriam's leads on hard climbs. In their second season together they climbed a long new route on the Aiguille de Roc that involved 12 rappels to descend; it was an auspicious start to Miriam's expansive repertoire of hard climbs in the Alps with and without guides, and many with other top women climbers of the day.

In 1928, Miriam climbed all five pinnacles of the Aiguilles du Diable with Robert Underhill and guides Armand Charlet and Georges Cachet. Reading typical climbing histories, you might conclude that the Aiguilles du Diable traverse was Miriam's most significant climb. I would disagree. It might make her top 10, but while the route has some very technical sections it was not on the same scale as some of her climbs. What we can say, though, is that it was most likely the hardest climb her future husband Robert Underhill[10] achieved in the Alps. Simply put, there's a persuasive argument Miriam was the better climber.

By 1930, Miriam was ready for her hardest climbs yet, long alpine rock routes in the Swiss Bernese Oberland following in the footsteps of her inspiration Gertrude Bell. After a 19-hour ascent of the Dreieckhorn, she wrote, 'Why not repeat some more of her climbs, so engagingly described in *The Letters of Gertrude Bell*?' She found yet another guide, Alfred Rubi, who did not mind being second on the rope, and she often lead every pitch on long climbs of 'great endurance and fortitude'. 'I enjoyed climbing rapidly,' she reflected in her autobiography and indeed, many of her climbs broke records for the shortest time, a big advantage in the wild mountains where sudden weather changes are deadly. In succession, she climbed the Engelhörner and Wellingrat, and made the third ascent of the north-east ridge of the Finsteraarhorn, which the previous ascensionists had noted would always require a bivouac.[11] She and Rubi, with Rubi's younger brother Fritz as porter, climbed the 1,000m route in 13 hours with a seven-hour descent, the first one-day ascent of this spectacular line. Of Miriam's most impressive climbs, many were at a level of commitment that would have been the career best for most climbers of her day, male or female.

Miriam had her first child in 1936 but climbed throughout her whole life, with many productive trips to Europe and the American West, including new routes in Idaho's the Sawtooths and the Beartooths and Mission Ranges

10. In 1983, the American Alpine Club named their most prestigious annual climbing award for Miriam and Robert Underhill, given 'for the highest level of skill in mountaineering through the application of skill, courage, and perseverance'. In 2022, the AAC announced it would rename the award after letters emerged in which Robert Underhill expressed anti-semitic views, even after the Second World War, when the horror of Nazi Germany's crimes against humanity were widely understood. Miriam Underhill's name was also removed from the award, despite the allegation only being made against her husband.

11. The experience was not one Miriam enjoyed. 'Even today,' she wrote in her 1956 memoir, 'the climb remains a very unpleasant memory. It is the only climb I have ever done which I cannot think about with pleasure. Not that this was the only occasion in the mountains when I have ever been frightened, but it was the occasion when I was most badly frightened, and for the longest period. I may as well admit that I haven't the kind of courage it takes to do such climbs as that. Fun, to my mind, is the only reason for climbing mountains, and the North-east face of the Finsteraarhorn was not fun.'

in Montana. She also became an expert skier. In her obituary for Miriam, Marjorie Hurd was at pains to say there was a lot more to her than her mountaineering. Perhaps her greatest achievement, with her manless climbing, was to break the glass ceiling that women weren't leaders. As Janet Adam Smith put it, while reviewing Miriam's memoirs, her 'traverses were a notable landmark in women's progress from being regarded as a special kind of mountaineer, who was to be praised for expeditions that would cause no comment if made by men, to being judged on their own merits as mountaineers pure and simple. As happened also in many other fields of women's rights, it was only through a display of feminism that masculine bias could be counterweighed, and a right balance attained.'

For Miriam, breaking the male hegemony on leading was key because it was in leading that the deepest rewards of alpinism lay. 'Very early, I realized,' she wrote in her famous article about manless climbing, 'that the person who invariably climbs behind a good leader ... may never really learn mountaineering at all and in any case enjoys only part of the varied delights and rewards of climbing.'

Art & Photography

'A Hilly Landscape with a Winding Road', John Robert Cozens, undated, brush drawing in grey wash, 48cm × 61.7 cm. *(British Museum)*

JOHN CLEARE

In the Light of Yosemite

The Climbing Life and Art of Glen Denny

On every foothold and ledge along the way Glen Denny was making photographs that are so much more than action.

John Long

Glen Denny was the foremost chronicler of the Golden Age of Yosemite climbing: the 1960s and 1970s. There were other excellent photographers and many other notable writers, but Denny, one of the leading pioneering climbers himself, was both. His outstanding images place him among the doyens of American climbing photography.

Born in Modesto in California's Central Valley in 1939, he was schooled in the outdoors by his father, a high-school teacher, who would take him on backpack fishing trips in the Sierra that Glen would document with his camera. Later, having absconded from an organised scout hike in the mountains, he set off to attempt Mount Humphreys, a rocky peak of almost 14,000ft in the High Sierra but wisely retreated when faced with exposed, technical scrambling. Intrigued by the challenge of surmounting steep rock, he determined to learn to climb properly.

Reading every climbing book he could find, he soon learned that Yosemite was the place where it actually happened and so, aged just 19, and to his parents' dismay, he dropped out of college and set out in his old car to find and investigate the Valley.

Below El Capitan he found the road blocked by stationary cars and crowds of tourists gazing up at the stupendous cliff. Borrowing binoculars he picked out two tiny figures high on the wall. It was 1958 and Warren Harding and his rope-mates were making the first ascent of the Nose.

It was the most inspiring thing I had ever seen. Instantly I realized I'd come to the right place. I didn't know how they were doing it but I was going to find out.

Supporting himself with a kitchen job at Yosemite Lodge, he mail-ordered some basic climbing equipment and with a workmate, a guidebook and a how-to-do-it manual he started on easy routes, progressing to Class 4 scrambles, 'where a rope is used only because a fall would be fatal.' He'd heard that the real climbers hung out at Camp Four, so one spring day he wandered down to locate the place. Warren Harding was in residence, they got chatting and Harding offered to teach him to climb. And Denny never looked back.

Robbins leads the zebra section on the second day of the first ascent of *Tis-sa-ack* (VI 5.9, A4), a 2,000ft (600m) line on the north-west face of Half Dome in October 1969. The climb, with Don Peterson, took eight days. A powerful, graphic image in a situation where a long focus lens was essential. Long lenses flatten perspective, an effect used creatively here where a wall of blank rock – of vertical texture– is split by a great black feature down which the eye travels to stop at the lonely figure working his way slowly upwards, still with a long way to go. Little man, big mountain indeed: always a good formula. *(All images Glen Denny/courtesy of Peggy Denny)*

Meanwhile he continued to record his doings, supplementing his notebooks with snaps with his camera but he became frustrated in his attempts to capture in words the essence of the climbs, the climbers themselves and the life they led. It was only when confronted by published climbing photographs of Tom Frost and others that he realised his camera might well be a better means of record and self-expression than his pen. It was.

> *Climbing was the most important thing in my life and I didn't want the experience to disappear. It seemed too special … I could show what it was like and not have to explain it.*

He took his camera on every climbing trip: a slim, folding, Kodak Retina 2A with a good, fixed 50mm lens: a fairly simple, robust but decent quality

North America Wall (VI, 5.8, A5). Tom Frost leads the third pitch during an early unsuccessful attempt. The key to this classic image is its symmetry. The rope meanwhile leads down into the camera, a useful ploy that integrates the viewer with the climb, a process accentuated by the leader, who is seen calling down with a comment.

camera but with no built-in light meter. Practice makes perfect, and in the fairly consistent lighting conditions both on climbs and in the shadowed woods of Camp Four, Denny's exposure calculations were obviously pretty successful.

> *... so a camera strap was added to the cluster of slings around my shoulders and under my arm a small folding camera as handy as my hammer: when the image appeared it had to be captured right now before it disappeared.*

He was learning that 'the moment' was important, it could often be anticipated, but should it happen, it would happen fast.

Before long he was aware of the historical importance of the scene of which he was now part: the late 1950s and the ensuing decade encompassed the first generation of American big-wall climbing, what in retrospect we now know as the Golden Age of Yosemite. Conscientiously Glen Denny now set about recording it.

He was soon repeating many of the most challenging routes in the Valley, often climbing with Harding or other leading Yosemite names such as Chuck Pratt, Layton Kor, Gary Colliver, Tom Frost and Royal Robbins, and making first ascents, not only in Yosemite but before long elsewhere in the Sierra and up in the North Cascades of Washington State but always carrying and using his camera. Experimenting with his lenses and his subjects and learning fast, he nevertheless considered that it was a couple of years before his climbing images had any real merit.

Down at ground level he made portraits of the denizens of Camp Four and recorded their doings, their careful preparations for the big climbs, along with the scruffy tent and basha-dotted clearing among the pines where they hung out, often to the chagrin of uptight park rangers. He shot on Kodak Plus-X film, and in poor light on the faster Tri-X film which, if working by firelight or at night, he might push a couple of stops. Until 1965 his film was processed in the local camera shop where 3in × 5in prints were run off from his negatives and larger prints developed as necessary. Some of his pictures were published in the local press and it became obvious he had an eye: a strong sense of composition and the ability to exploit what he saw on film.

Warren Harding on the final 'horrendous' roof pitch of The Rostrum *North Face* (IV, 5.8, A3). Eye-catching in any gallery, this image is purely graphic, a powerful, stark and at first puzzling design, until one realises that gravity doesn't lie. Perspective is non-existent and in this instance irrelevant.

Now captivated by photography, Denny pored over the landscapes of Ansel Adams and the work of such celebrated photographers as Henri Cartier-Bresson and Edward Weston. He was especially stimulated by images, published in art-book form, from the celebrated 1955 'Family of Man' exhibition curated by Edward Steichen at New York's Museum of Modern Art, arguably the most famous photographic exhibition ever hung (and an inspiration for many other young photographers, including the present writer). Many of these images feature action of people in a landscape, which of course is the essence of so many great climbing pictures.

Taking photography really seriously entailed using more versatile equipment. Promoted to barman at the Ahwahnee Hotel where generous tipping was the norm, he was soon able to equip himself with a Nikon F single lens reflex camera and four lenses: a 35mm widish-angle, a 50mm standard lens, a longish 105mm and a 200mm telephoto, as well as, at last, a light meter. The 200mm lens Denny reserved for landscapes and long, tripod shots of 'climbers as small specks on big walls'.

It is no coincidence that I too selected the same combination of lenses for my own work, not just for rock climbing but also for my general business

The agony of the big-wall game. Shadows and shapes form another story-telling image at the final stance on the *Wall of the Early Morning Light* (850m, VI, 5.8, A4). The way that Harding's gnarled, hard-driven hand, complete with tattered finger-tip plasters, rests on his gear after 27 continuous days on the wall says much about the man, while the jumble of karabinres, pegs and tapes suggests that the climb has not been easy going, but it's done: a complex yet sympathetic image.

assignments, but I added, and frequently used, a 28mm true wide-angle lens, a lovely perspective but one Denny eschewed for it slight distortion, an effect I utilised carefully on our so much smaller Welsh crags to good effect. (I was always aware that the coverage of a 50mm standard lens is rather less than the coverage of a human glance and was not what my eye saw.)

Denny eventually decided he must pursue a proper career and in 1965, biting the bullet, he enrolled at San Francisco State University to study photography and film. Yet whenever possible he continued with his alternative climbing career. He was now able to handle all his own darkroom work and his striking images were being widely published, for Yosemite climbing now attracted worldwide interest. That same year he was invited to join editors Allen Steck and Steve Roper as picture editor of the first four issues of the new annual *Ascent*, that beautiful publication, sponsored by the Sierra Club, which was for many years a Californian icon for discerning English-speaking mountaineers and remains a collector's item.

Although colour photography had by now come of age, Denny always preferred to use black and white for his serious work. Like Ansel Adams, the landscape photographer he most admired, he considered the monochrome medium, like painting a translation of the actual, to be the true creative art form of photography. With his fine eye for shape, Denny used the harsh light, the strong shadows, the textured rock and the bizarre geometrics of crack, flake and roof to construct his images. A genius of the moment, his figures reflect the exhilaration, the camaraderie and the ordeals of living in a vertical world, often for days at a time. He emerged from college with a master's degree in photography, cinematography and fine arts.

Back in Yosemite, Denny's peers considered him an excellent rock technician and an innovative aid climber. Indeed, for big-wall climbs he invented a twin jumar-and-leg-pumping technique for easier sack hauling. By 1970 he

Back at Camp Four Yvon Chouinard organises his hardware before a big climb. This arresting composition once again tells a story. Essentially the picture is split into two contrasting images, each dominated by an eye-catching – yet vaguely similar – rounded shape: the lower half with its powerful circle of pitons, the upper half by the crouching figure, an unusual combination of form and texture.

had been involved in no less than 18 first ascents in the Valley itself, most iconic perhaps being *Dihedral Wall* on El Capitan climbed with Ed Cooper and Jim Baldwin in 1962. The following year he made the third ascent of the Nose itself with Layton Kor and Steve Roper. Of that climb he wrote:

How strange it felt after the climb. Walking and not having to hold on to anything. Sleeping on the ground – you couldn't fall off. All the water you could want – just turn on the faucet.

Not one for fame, he eschewed the commercialism and publicity that attended some of the more spectacular Yosemite ascents, falling out with several erstwhile companions who would brief reporters and TV channels before attempting a major new line.

Not surprisingly there were epic moments. The following excerpt, taken, with permission, from Denny's essay 'Quicksilver' in his book *Yosemite in the Sixties*, details an early attempt on North America Wall with Royal Robbins.

My climbing partners got used to annoying new phrases like 'Hold it!' or 'I'm changing film', or even the dreaded 'Could you do that again?' I didn't say that to Royal while he was leading the third pitch of North America Wall. He had placed a long line of marginal pitons, and the situation was tense. But the light on the rock was beautiful. He had been on his last peg for quite a while. It seemed solid so I raised the camera. Suddenly he got bigger in the viewfinder and the belay line started zinging out as if I'd hooked a marlin. I dropped the camera and grabbed the rope with both hands. It hurt like hell, but there was nothing to do but grab harder. After what seemed a long time, things stopped moving.

I looked up. Royal was a lot closer now. He looked down and said 'Nice catch'. The gradual arrest had pulled out only a few pins; I didn't tell him why it had been so dynamic. The rope burns made my palms look like raw salmon fillets.

Camp Four c1968. A casual scene at the very informal camp ground between the foot of Three Bothers and Yosemite Point where climbers hung out in the 1960s and 1970s. The arrangement of the figures in several planes gives an almost three-dimensional feel. To employees of the Curry Company, the franchisee operating the Yosemite Valley, climbers were initially 'parasitic wretches who deserved to live in squalor' until, with the advent of a climbing school concession in the early 1970s, climbers were tolerated as local colour.

Denny's pioneering climbing in the Valley itself continued for another decade, but he was not only a rock aficionado. In the Canadian Rockies with George Whitmore he climbed Mount Robson and other major peaks and in 1964 with Gary Colliver he made the first ascent of Jirishanca Norte (6015m), in Peru's Cordillera Huayhuash. Six years later with Jeff Dozier he made both the first ascent and a film on Koh-i-Marchech in the Hindu Kush.

For some years he worked as a freelance photographer and film maker but admitted, when looking back later that he 'didn't enjoy using his visual skills on commercial assignments photographing junk.' Then for a spell he taught photography while continuing to climb seriously in the Valley and elsewhere, though no longer on the big walls. At one stage Denny enjoyed a spell working in the Napa valley 'producing higher quality wine than the stuff we drank at Camp 4.' And in 1982 he settled down, married Peggy and took a post at the Stanford University library.

Eventually he tried writing again, utilising his notebooks at last, but this time with more success. His first book, *Yosemite in the Sixties*, was published in 2007. It contained many of his favourite pictures, won several awards and was followed in 2016 by *Valley Walls: a Memoir of Climbing and Living in Yosemite*. His major films are *El Capitan*, which took 10 years and was finally completed in 1978, and *Nyala* (1966) featuring a solo ascent of Cathedral Peak in Yosemite's high country.

With the advent of digital photography he had all his negatives professionally scanned and delighted in the quality, tonal range and sharpness of the exhibition prints that digital methods produce. Denny lectured widely in the US, Japan, Europe and here in Britain both at the AC and the Kendal Film Festival, leaving this rather apposite tip for aspiring climbing photographers. 'It's not easy,' he warned, 'to do two full-time jobs at the same time. When you're on a [climb], the more you get involved with a shot, the more you need to check that you're still tied in.' Indeed. Travelling in Britain he especially enjoyed the architecture and tranquillity of English cathedrals and a pint of ale in a local hostelry. He still enjoyed the mountains and continued to make long solo hikes in the Sierra until the last month of his life. Glen Denny died in 2022. John Long, like no one else perhaps, understood what Denny had achieved.

Robbins rests during his descent from Half Dome summit after his eight-day ascent of *Tis-sa-ack*. Shot from an unusual and telling angle, this portrait accentuates the tired limbs, the exhaustion and also the anti-climax of an incredible achievement by an athlete in his prime.

> *Of all those who have recounted the Golden Age of Yosemite climbing, none captured its soul more faithfully and more aesthetically than Glen Denny … While Denny's first ascents are venerated among climbers, his artwork tends to move everyone who's exposed to it.*

• The author and editor thank Peggy Denny for her help in publishing this article.

DAVID SEDDON

In the Shadow of Nanga Parbat

T H Somervell in the Rupal Nallah

The 'rapid sketch' of Nanga Parbat that Somervell made from bear the Tragbal pass on 19 May 1933. *(Courtesy of Tony Astill)*

By early 1933, Howard Somervell (1890-1975) was almost desperate to see the Rupal face of Nanga Parbat[1]. He had seen the Kangshung face of Everest and the north-east face of Chomo Lonzo in 1922 and the north face of Nanda Devi in 1926. He was to write, 'I longed to see the immense southern precipice [of Nanga Parbat]', to 'enjoy Nanga Parbat, not to climb it – to paint it, not to struggle with it.'

With his wife and two young sons in the United Kingdom, an opportunity arose to fulfil this ambition. In early May, Somervell set off alone on the five-day rail journey from Cape Cormorin to Rawalpindi, followed by a two-day bus journey to Srinagar. There he had arranged to stay with Dr Eric Neve (1861-1946), brother of Dr Arthur Neve (1859-1919). For many years the Neve brothers had provided medical care to the people of Srinagar and Kashmir. They were both climbers and between them had achieved many first ascents in Kashmir. Eric Neve introduced Somervell to a local hunter,

1. T H Somervell, *After Everest*, Hodder & Stoughton, 1936, pp156-9.

Abdullah Ganai and his son Aziz. Father and son had been porters variously with the Duke of Aosta and Bullock Workman expeditions and most recently with the 1932 German-American expedition to Nanga Parbat. Over the next few days, Somervell and Aziz Ganai climbed Mahadeva and other peaks either side of the Sind valley.

On 17 May, his party of four travelled by covered boat across Wular Lake to Bandipur. Somervell noted '… the delicate blue beauty of the Pir Panjal to the south east'. Two days later, they reached the summit of the snow-covered Tragbal pass to be rewarded with a distant view of Nanga Parbat. Somervell recorded the next few days in both breathless prose and sketches. He must have been aware that he had not only climbed higher than the summit of Nanga Parbat in 1924 but, at camp six on Everest, had slept higher as well.

> ***Friday 19 May**: 'Up at 5.30 … and trudged up to the [Tragbal] pass. The sky was cloudless in all directions, and as we got higher peak after peak appeared, until at the top we saw one of the finest mountain panoramas I have ever witnessed. There was a long succession of summits to the west and towering over everything else Nanga Parbat rose clear and majestic to the north. A bitterly cold wind was blowing, so we could delay on the top [no] longer than enabled me to take a few photographs and did a rapid sketch of Nanga Parbat'*

A few days later, and in deep snow, his party crossed the Burzil pass, before descending to the village of Das Khirim and the Astore valley.

> ***Wednesday 24 May**: 'A varied march, at first through rather ordinary scenery until the terraces of cultivated land at Das Khirim are reached, and then the Nanga Parbat begins to appear. I went high up on the valley side to get a good view, and was rewarded by a magnificent one. What a mountain it is! Quite unlike any other I have seen, so far above anything else – 26,000 feet in a district where most things are 13,000-16,000.*

> ***Thursday 25 May**: … gorgeous views of Nanga Parbat, sixteen miles away to the northwest. It was cloudless and absolutely clear, and every detail of Nanga's magnificence was plain. Needless say I tarried here for sketching and photography.*

On Friday 26 May, Somervell climbed into the Kamri valley to the east of the Burzil pass. From about 5,000m, and across two pages of his sketch-book, he painted a dramatic panorama of Nanga Parbat and its east ridge as far as the middle Chongra peak. At 23cm × 56cm, this is perhaps Somervell's largest known watercolour.

> *Nanga Parbat burst into full view in all its magnificence. What a mountain it is! The main peak at the western end sends down colossal 15,000 ft precipices to the Rupal Glacier, and the ridge extends to the east for some 10 miles presenting a succession of beautiful subsidiary peaks, with the wonderful ice-architecture only to be seen in the higher Himalaya.*

Nanga Parbat from Das Khirim painted on 24 or 25 May. All pictures are watercolour unless described otherwise.

Nanga Parbat, Rakhiot and Chongra peaks from the Kamri valley, 26 May.

Rupal face of Nanga Parbat, 27 May.

Before returning to Srinagar, Somervell climbed high on the south side of the Rupal Nallah, possibly climbing what is now known as Rupal Peak, and spent an hour or so on the summit.

> ***Saturday 27 May**: Up at 4.15 … to climb a mountain opposite Nanga. Nanga Parbat from here is simply amazing. The actual precipice from the top to the Rupal Glacier, is some 15,000 feet high. In the evening the clouds gathered round and presented, I think, the most beautiful sight I have ever seen anywhere. It was simply indescribable. I tried a sketch, but though it was a fairly successful one, it was impossible to get an inkling of the beauty, as so much depended on the actual luminosity of the clouds.*

On 29 May, Somervell and his companions crossed the Kamri pass in deep snow, before re-tracing their steps to Srinagar.[2] He returned to south India with a folio including nine watercolours (23cm × 28cm) sketched between 19 and 27 May, including the first and third pictures in this article. This folio remained unseen until sold at auction in 2021. In addition, he painted four larger watercolours (26.5cm × 35.5cm), including the second and fourth images seen here. These were exhibited at the Alpine Club in 1936.

Somervell may have seen Nanga Parbat again, albeit from a distance. In 1951, during his last long period of service as a surgeon in south India between 1948 and 1953, he may have visited Gulmarg, a hill station in the Pir Panjal, south of the Kashmir valley. Two pictures seem to show Nanga

2. Ibid. See also: T H Somervell, 'A Pilgrimage to Nanga Parbat', *Fell and Rock Climbing Club Journal*, vol 10, 1934, pp89-100; T H Somervell, 'Some Minor Expeditions in the Himalayas', *Himalayan Journal*, vol 13, 1946, pp28-40.

Nanga Parbat from Gulmarg, 1951. *(Courtesy of Lakeland Arts Trust)*

An oil painting of Nanga Parbat from 1952. *(Alpine Club)*

Parbat from this viewpoint, one dated 1951 and an oil dated 1952. The latter is in the Alpine Club Collection and for many years had been catalogued, incorrectly, as 'Kangchenjunga'. In 2006, this picture was exhibited at the Alpine Club. Mike Westmacott and George Band were able to provide the correct identification as Nanga Parbat. A second oil picture may remain with the family. Somervell exhibited nine watercolours of Kashmir and Nanga Parbat at the Alpine Club in 1936 and a further six oils and four watercolours at the Club in 1954.

• I am grateful to Tony Astill (***www.mountainpaintings.org***) for his help with illustrating this article.

DONALD M ORR

The Light of the North

Peder Balke and the Mountains of Norway

The art of any country can be greatly affected, even directed by its topography and climate. Perhaps none exhibits this more than Norway where soaring verticality and forbidding beauty have shaped an artistic structure, where glacial hardness has rendered sharp, clear landscapes reflecting life on the margins of Europe.

A painting of a mountain can hold an eternal timelessness within its frame 'but in its momentariness reflects also its endless shiftings – it is a moment of time caught in the seeming eternity of the landscape.'[1] So the artist not only records form and topography but also documents the passing of time and the structuring of memory. Mountains especially have that capacity to provoke a tangible landscape of memory. Places that had a profound effect on you, that perhaps made you, may alter you to become more like them. What the youthful mountaineer initially discovers and possesses in the mountains may, in the end, be what possesses them.

That a landscape could imbue a sense of self and of isolation yet at the same moment endorse a feeling of solidity, of belonging, of knowing the land and its history, was a development of Romanticism. Landscape can maintain a purity, mirrored in art, but also a darkness and atmosphere that few mastered better than Peder Balke (1804-87). The main features of his mountain landscapes are dramatic lighting and subject matter. This Norwegian landscape artist quickly became an explorer within his own terrain. This attitude became known as Romantic Nationalism and revealed a pride in his homeland, its history and folk traditions that drew him into the empty places.

Balke was attracted to extreme images where the immensity of the mountains and the vastness of the sea allowed intense and exciting colour structures. The desolation and rawness he found in his homeland was painted delicately and skilfully; there was never an attempt to revel in the harshness of the terrain but to record accurately the colour structures he found and the vivid atmospherics surrounding them. From his interest in national history, he drew from the landscape a form of realism that was never based in nostalgia or folk memory. What he captured was the spirit and essence of the landscape in its emptiness; absence became rendered as presence.

The artist becomes explorer, beginning 'a journey from acute and precise observations of the peculiarities of nature and natural phenomena'[2] to a

1. D Jasper, *The Sacred Desert*, Blackwell, Oxford, 2004, p110.
2. Jasper, p111.

resolution about time and space, colour, and form. This is a journey that mountains can activate and embody in an emblematic stance. We respond to the demands of the mountain environment and in that demand, we are at once the insignificant dot on the massif and an organ of perception extending many miles over the landscape, contacting it, touching it. These are aspects of the world neither beautiful nor hostile in themselves: 'a place pure and simple, on its own terms, absolute'.[3] One of the defining aspects of these unique places over and above the recording of the topography is the interpretation of atmospherics. Whether stormbound or bathed in sunlight the impression of a mountain is radically altered by the mood of the weather. Any sense of character will be greatly enhanced by an accurate analysis and execution of the sky and climatic conditions.

Peder Balke was born on the island of Helgøya in Hedmark in 1804 into a household whose name was Anderson. They were a family of landless farm labourers, and his childhood was stark and impoverished. His father disappeared from Balke's life at an early stage in the boy's life and thereby education was not an option. By the 1820s he was training as a house painter and quickly established himself as a craftsman with a high reputation that secured him many commissions. Around 1825 he spent a long period at Vestre Balke farm where he was very well treated and he adopted the name Balke thereafter. Interested in expanding his abilities he spent several months working alongside Ole Nielsen (1750-1838) at Fåberg who had studied at the academy in Copenhagen. While developing new techniques he still regarded himself as an ambitious artisan who had several apprentices working under him.

He narrowly avoided military conscription and arrived in Christiana (Oslo) in 1826. At this point he had decided to become a master painter in the capital and to that end worked with the painters Heinrich Grosch and Jens Funch, in addition to attending classes at the Royal School of Drawing. Between house decorating contracts and donations from wealthy friends Balke financed his art education so that by 1828-9 he was producing his own work, albeit somewhat imitative of the style popular at that time. In the next few years, he travelled extensively through northern Norway discovering the dramatic unrecorded landscape, and also to Copenhagen and Stockholm visiting artists and collections to increase his knowledge and ability.

In 1830 Balke made an ambitious journey on foot through the Telemark region and over the mountains to western Norway. 'He walked to Rjukan and up the notoriously dangerous path beside the waterfall, crossed the Røldal Mountains and descended to Kinsarvik in Hardanger'[4] and continued on to Christiana. He had travelled further than any other Norwegian artist and returned to Stockholm in 1831 where the king purchased his studies of the mountains and of the new road to Trondheim. He made his first journey to the far north of Norway in 1832, sailing from Trondheim via the Lofoten Islands to Trømso and recording landscapes illuminated by the midnight

3. Jasper, p126.
4. M Lange, *Peder Balke*, National Gallery, London, 2017, p16.

sun. A military convoy took him to Vordø, sailing past the North Cape 'around which swirled the mighty waves of the Arctic Ocean.'[5] In 1836 and again in 1843-4 Balke visited Dresden where he polished his style alongside Johan Dahl and Caspar David Friedrich and advanced his understanding of German *Stimmungsmalerie*, 'mood painting', 'which ultimately would be the decisive influence on his view of nature.'[6]

Several journeys through Germany visiting collections and galleries, friends and fellow artists, seeing diverse forms of architecture and design showered Balke with new impressions. A trip to Paris introduced him to the work of Isabey (1803-86), Huet (1803-69), and Gudin (1802-80) whose striking compositions amazed him. Despite these new fascinations Balke found it difficult to sell his work at home as there were few exhibitions in Norway and relying on private commissions from a small clientele was precarious.

The three examples selected show recurring motifs in his work and developed a distinctly northern iconography that shaped the history of Norwegian painting and informed the art of Europe.

'From North Cape'[7]

This feature is situated on the extreme north coast of the island of Magerøya, on the northernmost part of Europe. In this painting (see p114) Balke presents darkness visible with a light at the end of the tunnel: a quality that recalls aspects of Genesis and a spirit moving over the waters but well within the Norse framework of an ancient land structured by Norse gods. The boat in the central foreground is in darkness about to penetrate the light. That is where Balke takes us to the edge of discovery and exploration.

Darkness frames the canvas curving across the top of the image centring the light, allowing us to see into the primordial blackness. As viewers we are placed in attendance at the discovery of this feature. The two bars of moonlight on either side of the cliffs stand as creational dividers measuring the span and distance of the rocky feature as if newly formed. We travel from the dimness of a dull reddish tone reminiscent of a vast amniotic fluid spreading over a dark, calm sea towards the light and a stark topography of the seemingly emergent North Cape.

This is an image of fear and wonder, an awesome spectacle few would be brave enough to venture towards. Here light delineates form, and form is monumental. What is offered is a bold challenge to approach this feature, to travel north, accept the dangers and explore beyond the North Cape.

'Mountain Range Trolltindene'[8]

Trolltinden (2018m) is in the heart of the Rondane mountains inside the Rondane National Park. Despite the large marine foreground and the receding folds of terrain in the mid ground, and an area of dramatic sky

5. Lange, p20.
6. Lange, p52.
7. P Balke, 'From North Cape', oil on board, 67.5cm × 84cm, National Gallery, Oslo, 1840.
8. P Balke, 'Mountain Range Trolltindene', oil on canvas, 30.8cm × 41.9cm, Nordnorsk Kunstmuseum, Tromsø, 1840.

'From North Cape' by Peder Balke. *(National Gallery, Oslo)*

equalling the foreground in scale, it is a darkly dominant mountain ridge that confronts us. The turbulent clouds fill the lower valleys with mist and violent waves on the sea set the tone of the picture. Balke's deeply serrated skyline overshadows the image, rendering a ferocity to the atmosphere that at once repels and draws us into this strange landscape. The peaks and horns of the Trolltinde demand closer inspection and exploration. This volatile glimpse only whets the appetite and has the capacity to remind us of other extreme mountains at the far ends of the world, as in Patagonia. Cloud spilling down and around the base of the cliffs creates a mystical presence, adding a mythological quality to this feature in northern Norway. Balke's gift is the realisation that such seemingly mythic landscapes exist in reality.

For the Romantics, the life of emotion was at the core of their philosophy and their notion of the sublime. If the concept of the sublime was centred on things that overwhelmed the individual and caused fear and alarm, then the dramatic landscape of northern Norway held it in abundance.

'Mountain Range Trolltindene'. *(Asbjørn Lunde Collection)*

Another interpretation of the Trolltinden; Balke returned to favourite subjects like the North Cape and Stetind several times.

While storms at sea and moonlit landscapes were a common characteristic of the Romantic era, Balke 'translated these motifs into an idiom that could convey the far north's unique atmospheric conditions.'[9]

'Stetind in Fog'[10]

This dramatic rock feature is situated in the Stefjord near the head of the Tysfjorden and was selected in 2002 as Norway's national mountain. Located an hour's drive south-west of Narvik in Nordland, it is about 15km north-east of Kjøpsvik. Smooth sides reaching down to the fjord give the granite mountain of Stetind (1392m) an almost obelisk-like form that dominates this corner of the Scandinavia mountains.

Grey fog envelopes and isolates the peak, creating a dramatic, precipitous and apparently inaccessible rock tower. The diminutive figures in the foreground boat along with those ashore looking out to sea form a human counterpoint indicating humanity's status in mankind's relationship with the forces of nature. This majestic landmark was first climbed in 1910 by Ferdinand Schjelderup, Carl Rubenson, and Alf Bryn. Arne Naess introduced aid climbing to Norway in the late 1930s at Stetind and claimed the first winter ascent of the mountain by the east wall.

Several versions of this scene were produced over the years alongside many drawings and colour studies. Twenty-six sketches of the area were sold to Louis Philippe I of France and are now in the Louvre while other images of the mountain are held in the National Gallery in Oslo and in the Metropolitan Gallery in New York.

In his lifetime, several European monarchs purchased Balke's paintings: Karl Johan of Sweden and Norway, Louis-Philippe of France, and Frederick William IV of Prussia. Yet by the 1850s his work had become unpopular. His pictures may have lacked the intricacy and finesse expected by the Norwegian public and at his death he was known as a respected member of Oslo society but as an artist was totally forgotten. Interests and themes in painting had moved on and he left no successor in the field of dramatic reproduction of the Norwegian north. Yet it is this severity that attracts the viewing public now. The darkness, atmosphere and boldness of his paint handling are recognised as strengths and no longer a lack of academic refinement.

Given the nature of these paintings and the profound impact they had on the Norwegian public of the day one could ask if this was a case of landscape as a reflection of the national psyche? Where 'the fragility of man confronted by brute force'[11], the force projected by this seeming emptiness, was adopted as national characteristic? The north was a fearful, lonely place and sparsely populated. Balke was not trading in anxiety and dread but revealing, through his ability to render atmospherics accurately, the symbolic hardness of life within his country. His ability to create the moods and effects

9. Lange, p52.
10. P Balke, 'Stetind in Fog', oil on canvas, 58cm × 71cm, National Gallery, Oslo, 1864.
11. Lange, p62.

'Stetind in Fog'. The first ascent of this rocky peak was made in 1910 by Ferdinand Schjelderup, the Himalayan pioneer Carl Rubenson and Alf Bryn, author of *Peaks and Bandits*. William Cecil Slingsby described Stetind, which he failed to climb, as being the ugliest mountain he had ever seen. *(National Gallery, Oslo)*

of the weather, uniquely indicating their power and authority in nature, was his gift. If, as Thubron claimed, 'a journey is not a cure. It brings an illusion, only of change, and becomes at best a spartan comfort'[12] then Balke achieved this in his canvases, where a moment in the eternity of time is captured, but also the 'spartan comfort' of natural phenomena within the striking northern climate. Was this what possessed Balke in old age?

12. C Thubron, *To a Mountain in Tibet*, Vintage, London, 2012. p10.

His paintings are held in many major and national collections. Seventeen of his works are housed in the Norwegian National Gallery in Oslo. These are images of endless confrontation yet symbols of resilience also in the face of nature's indifference. He possessed a unique perseverance that over time formulated a visionary landscape for his time and place. A form of this manner of painting was briefly touched on by Bierstadt's symbolic heightened visions of the west, which emerged as a kind of glorification. Balke's work was never concerned with adoration but the profound need to reveal the beauty of the far north. His visual interpretations may have flown in defiance of the conventions of the day, yet it is still the reason we enter the beautiful chaos of the mountain regions and set out on those thrilling adventures.

TERRY GIFFORD

The Way Down

Julian Cooper's 'Lines of Descent' Exhibition

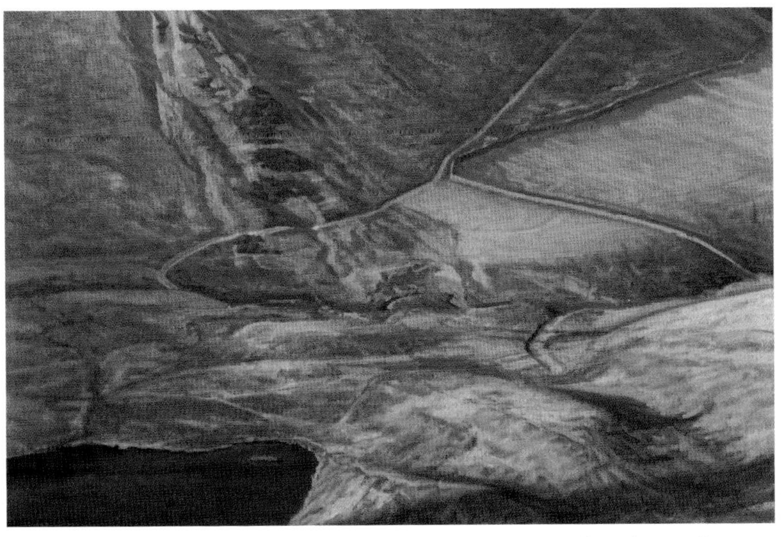

'... a vibrant winter warmth at a cold tarn corner, a crossroads, a descending coffin route, a human battlefield with the conditions, a bloodied beauty beyond the postcards'. Julian Cooper's 'Winter Sun, High Nook'. *(All images courtesy of Julian Cooper)*

Julian Cooper has always sought to be innovative in extending the tradition of Lake District landscape painting that he inherited in a line of descent from his father and grandfather, William and Alfred Heaton Cooper. In doing so he has made original contributions to the British tradition and none more strikingly innovative than his recent 'Lines of Descent' exhibition at his loyal London dealer's Art Space Gallery. As I write, this show is still ongoing, but already it has been almost a complete sell-out. So what is it about 'Lines of Descent' that been so distinctively striking?

At an AC talk in Bristol last February John Porter showed a picture of himself aged 11 years old on his first summit where he was struck by a vision that was new to him. 'Suddenly the earth is beneath you,' he said. This may seem obvious. We all know that revelatory feeling when we turn around on a summit. It's a commonplace experience for all hill-goers. But John invested it with an internalised profundity: 'Climbing takes us to a place we've never been to before, beyond our everyday experience.' That place is looking down.

'Barn Ghyll', revealing 'every sheep-trodden little terrace betrays the imprint of human culture, never mind that pathetic straight-line fence, a kind of residue of attempted colonisation of wild fell …'.

So why have painters not looked down, as well as upwards or outwards? Why has the inwardness of looking down not been explored in paint on canvas, the ancient art of making marks that make us question what we see when we look down, 'drilling down', as it were, in self-discovery?

Cooper's 1998 work 'Brenva Face, Mont Blanc'. Cutting out the summit suddenly 'released all this energy'.

We all know that our lines of descent are often our most dangerous. Accidents can happen on the way down when tired and, relieved, we are often rushing against darkness, not paying sufficient attention. And that's the point that these paintings make. They are not necessarily views from the summit, but moments of pause, of attention, on lines of descent. It's not that they do not need horizons, it's that horizons distract and detract, tempting thoughts of future lines of ascent. It's about the density of landscape to be revealed without horizons – a different kind of grandeur and grace and stark reality without horizon.

What exactly is going on beneath us, down there in those lines of deep-cut ravines, sinuous brackened slopes, raw rolling screes, walled plots of ancient economies, clustered barns of family farms, rocky roads of former commerce, sawing streams to unfathomable tarns? What is flat and what has depth? How do we read what we see? What do these colours really conjure of the changes through the long past? What inherited quality of animal husbandry is still held by that figure on the quadbike? What does a quadbike's shape and colour, its sound and smell, say at the base of this almost overwhelmingly descending landscape? Is it a dramatic mechanical contrast or is it humble human adaption? Is it subsidised sheepwrecking of the land, or georgic continuity with the land? The paintings of 'Lines of Descent' challenge the viewer with question after question. They also offer, perhaps, a new kind of beauty

For his latest exhibition, Julian Cooper made sculptures, following the practice of his mother, Ophelia Gordon Bell.

and celebration in a landscape we thought we knew and with which we have become overfamiliar, not least from the prints of the Heaton Cooper Studio.

There's a map in the catalogue of this exhibition showing the locations of some of these paintings which were all made within a 20-mile radius of Cooper's home in Cockermouth, often, he says, 'when walking at mid-height on the fells'. So these are Anthropocene paintings that radically re-orientate the focus of our attention to our home. Over more than four decades Cooper has carried his canvasses and yard-long brushes through the Alps, Andes, Tasmania and the Himalaya, always examining the intersection of nature and culture, not always explicitly, as in quarrying in Peru and Tasmania, the marble of Carrara in Italy and Little Langdale, but often in the cultural meaning of mountains such as Kailas or the Eigerwand. So, partly a reflection of Covid-19 travel restrictions and a growing reluctance for long-haul flights, these paintings rediscover the same big questions present in Cooper's backyard. And look, those questions, seen from mid height, are asked by lines of descent, lines of colour and form, vegetation and scree, water and walls, tracks and mine-tailings, to be interpreted by the painter, as he puts it, 'stretched by the demands of the subject'.

In his catalogue essay Robert Macfarlane is right to identify as a key to Cooper's being stretched, as a painter, by his subject, the moment when he first reduced and then abandoned a skyline. The painter explained to Macfarlane that in the painting 'Brenva Face, Mont Blanc' (1998) cutting out the summit suddenly 'released all this energy'. It must have been as though all the cultural clutter of what Mont Blanc's summit meant evaporated to offer an insight into the real dynamics at work in the forms and shades of the living mountain. When Ruskin had first looked up at this mountain he found himself 'associating fraternally with some ants'. When Cooper looked inwards he was challenged by the new 'demands of the subject'. He discovered that 'a concentration of dynamics comes from closing the landscape.' It is perhaps misleading to go on, as Macfarlane does, to call the paintings in this exhibition 'closed landscapes', for although the frame encloses a complex of past and present, historical human land-use and current reshaping by water and weather, these paintings rather open up new visions that result from, and answer to, the Anthropocene.

None more so than the miracle that was always there in 'Winter Sun, High Nook', but which it takes this painter to show us. It is a vibrant winter warmth at a cold tarn corner, a crossroads, a descending coffin route, a human battlefield with the conditions, a bloodied beauty beyond the postcards. In many of these paintings the lines of walls delineate the edge of a hard-won battle with bracken and ask the question Robert Macfarlane posed in conversation at the opening, 'What is a field?' Lines in the green indicate hay-cutting in 'Gatesgarth', where the eye is drawn from the thin road just in the bottom of the picture towards the lines of structure at the isolated farm, but also onwards into the sunlit slope beyond. Here an ancient wall cuts across lines of vegetation that are the same on either side of it as though the battle has long been relinquished as it has in the water-holding bog to the right of the farm. Vertical lines of a few trees offer pathetic shelter to the farm. And yet the mowed lines in that singing green, taking up the lower half of the painting, lead the eye past the farm to wild sunlit slopes and the tone of the painting is actually more celebration of nature than desperate farming culture. 'What is a field?': here, indeed. This question is asked more starkly in 'Rannerdale Field' where deep-cut becks, descending between rock outcrops, seem to threaten the thin green horizontal and vulnerable field. The huge scale of this work (275cm × 137cm) suggests what is at stake for both the farmer and the painter. It is priced at £20,000.

There is a moment of tenderness as a farmer, Dave Allen (Cooper got to know all of his subjects), leans from his quadbike to feed milk to a calf in 'Above High Nook'. But this large vertical painting is dominated by the dark fall of rocky, eroded fellside above. The red plastic bowl on the front of his bike, no less than the light on the flanks of the sucking calf, all seem about to be overwhelmed by the conditions in which, as Ted Hughes put it in 'Crow Hill', 'Between the weather and the rock / Farmers make a little heat.' On the other hand, a girl dives in daring descent from a waterfall into a rock-backed pool in 'Deep Pool 1'. She is at home here, open-eyed, spearing deep, past water-worn rock that, by contrast, is seen rough and lit above. We are now familiar with water surface level photography and Cooper is here using the work of Robert Macfarlane's father John work in making this striking image, again on a large scale (214cm × 132cm). Indeed, the lake level painting 'Across the Lake 1' requires the same close attention that the painter is making to see, at its far right end, a wild swimmer with small red buoy, lost in a vast horizontal landscape of falling scree and cold, still lake water. The viewer's discovery is literally breathtaking.

Less successful, perhaps, are the small, close studies of eroding banks in 'High Nook Beck 3' where the thick brushstrokes overwhelm and blur differentiations within the painting. The subject is, of course, an important one and the dynamics at work between water and soil, grasses and rocks, farming and land are what this show is all about. But the technique better suits a larger scale like 'Coledale Beck', or the brilliant 'Barn Ghyll'. This painting looks into the black depths of a golden fellside being cut deeper still by a series of silver waterfalls. Its jagged edges are rock teeth as it makes a savage vertical smile. Along its left side is one of those timeless fences that feign control and up its right flank is the zigzagging echo of a feint path. Here, human primacy is diminished by more ancient forces still in full flow. It repays close attention and distanced reflection. Each brushstroke denotes a distinctive rock or patch of grass or moss. It is still in wild, unstoppable evolution, like the Anthropocene. And, like the Anthropocene, every sheep-trodden little terrace betrays the imprint of human culture, never mind that pathetic straight-line fence, a kind of residue of attempted colonisation of wild fell, which continues now in contested overgrazing.

Finally, there are three painted plaster sculptures: 'High Rigg', 'Langstrath Rock 1' and 'Langstrath Rock 2'. These are both a new departure and an obvious continuity, not least with Cooper's long interest from his sculptor mother, Ophelia Gordon Bell. Certainly these look like replicas, such that Sheffield climbers might make in their cellars of challenges they need to overcome outdoors. But they are not. They are creative responses to the close study of rock textures and formations, the ultimate distillation of gravity's work upon the medium through water, frost and heat that invite human contact with fingers and toes. Their power is immediate – tactile and visual – but hard to explain. As artworks they are staggeringly beautiful, yet hard and resistant: seductively ochre in mineral leakage, yet chillingly silver in thrusting challenge to the viewer. Ever innovative, Julian Cooper says that there is more to come in this mode, once again stretching to the demands of his subject. Printed opposite is a creative response to 'Lines of Descent' in a different mode.

- Julian Cooper's 'Lines of Descent' Exhibition was at the Art Space Gallery, London, 17 March – 29 April, 2023.

Reading the Hills Downwards: 'Winter Sun, High Nook'

I found my eye had not been trained to view [from] so prodigious an height.
Charles P Moritz, 1782.

Do not, any more, lift your eyes to the hills.
Lift your boots to the hills and then turn
to see your ancestors' labours, and your
neighbours' work now, for your food,
in the hayfields below, the sheep trods,
the walls, the tracks, in the buzzing heather,
the bracken, the enclosed woods, water-
powered gullies, the trout tarn sleeping
beyond watercressed fringes, deer-lapped.

Each change of colour and tone tells
a story of three thousand years continuous
human husbandry and fallow – letting go –
for generations of family hill-farming ideas
trying for something slightly different over
the same familiar ground. Father and son

clashed, wives and daughters dared to opine
before the hearth into the candled dark.
Look down. See their debates alive now.

Terry Gifford

ROBIN N CAMPBELL

Robert Wylie Lloyd

Mountaineer, Collector and Public Benefactor

Robert Wylie Lloyd stands between Josef Pollinger and Adolf Pollinger. The photograph was reproduced in the Alpine Journal in 1943 to accompany obituary notices for Josef. 'With the death of Josef Pollinger,' Lloyd wrote, 'I have lost my greatest friend.'

This year's section frontispieces are drawn from the mountain prints and watercolours bequeathed to the British Museum by Robert Wylie Lloyd (1868-1958) from his collection.

Lloyd's life is well described elsewhere,[1] so I will limit myself to a bare sketch here. He was born in Oswaldtwistle, Lancashire into a family engaged in cloth printing. When his parents separated he moved with his Scottish mother Rachel Wylie to Balham, eventually becoming a very successful businessman himself, operating like a one-man private equity concern, acquiring privately-held businesses, mainly in the cloth or paper trades, and managing them into profit. Perhaps his most stunning coup was to become chairman of Christie's auction house and instantly taking it private. As a young man, he collected beetles and butterflies. This took him to the mountains of Norway, which stimulated an interest in mountaineering.

He began his Alpine career in 1896, and joined the Alpine Club in 1901. He seems invariably to have climbed with guides and after engaging Josef Pollinger of St Niklaus in 1904, Lloyd remained with him through 30 seasons until stopped by health difficulties in 1939. Together they made a number of innovations, mostly on the north sides of Valais and Mont Blanc peaks. His business background brought him inevitably into Club posts such as auditor and treasurer, in which post he acquired a reputation for being good at raising money but reluctant to see it spent.

Lloyd never married and after his mother died he occupied rooms in that rich bachelors' lair the Albany, Piccadilly until his death. The Albany was convenient for the Club premises in St Martin's Lane, Savile Row and South Audley Street; one doubts whether he would have favoured Charlotte Road. He also had country residences: at Treago Castle in Herefordshire and latterly a place at Bampton in the Cotswolds. His wealth and absence of family allowed him to give full indulgence to his collecting passions. To the pre-existing insect collections he added old Swiss prints, English watercolours and Alpine books of the rarer sort, as well as Japanese swords and Chinese lacquerware. His print collection ran to five thousand or so. A gift of a Turner watercolour set him on that path and he amassed 60 of Turner's best available works on paper, as well as a considerable collection of watercolours by other English artists.[2] These he preserved most carefully, requiring the art dealer Thomas Agnew's to put each purchase into bespoke frames equipped with blinds to exclude light.

On his death in 1958, Lloyd was buried in his mother's grave at Glasgow Necropolis.[3] His will left his entomological collections and library to Manchester Museum, his print and watercolour collections and Oriental antiques to the British Museum, and his Alpine library (c2,000 items) to the National Library of Scotland. These legacies to public collections invite

1. See *AJ* **63**, pp229-40; A Cain, *Oxford Dictionary of National Biography*; L Cook, *Entomologist's Monthly Magazine*, 155, p3-14. The latter is available at *www.researchgate.net* and offers a most complete and illuminating account; see also footnote 2.
2. K Sloan, *J M W Turner: Watercolours from the R W Lloyd Bequest to the British Museum*, British Museum Press, London, 1998. Sloan's text includes a well-illustrated account of Lloyd as a collector pp9-35 and an appendix listing other British watercolours Lloyd bequeather to the British Museum.
3. Although his burial is recorded in the interment register there is no inscription on his mother's gravestone.

comparison with Paul Mellon's extraordinary generosity to American institutions. Perhaps there is a story explaining why he left nothing to the Alpine Club but I have been unable to discover it. After all, he happily funded Ynys Ettws for the Climbers' Club in 1950, although he was not even a member of that club.

In selecting pictures from the vast Lloyd bequest for presentation here as frontispieces I have of course looked for those with mountaineering interest. I have avoided the 60 Turners. In the main they do not feature mountains – there is one of the modest Ben Venue at Loch Katrine, but it is reduced in detail by strong aerial perspective – and they have already been beautifully presented and described by Kim Sloan. I regret not being able to include some fine Swiss artists such as Jean Antoine Linck (1766-1843) and David Alois Schmid (1791-1861). I have listed and commented on the prints and drawings used in rough chronological order.

'Jungfrau from near Unterseen'

This is a very early depiction of the Jungfrau's north face, and it is remarkable for its very accurate drawing of the mountain. Johann Ludwig Aberli (1723-86) was a well-known Swiss painter and etcher. Born in Winterthur, he moved to Bern in the 1740s. He toured the Bernese Oberland in 1762 but the watercolour on which the present print is based may have been done much earlier. (Biographies in the online *Dictionnaire Historique de la Suisse* and on the British Museum database.)

'Lauterbrunnen Valley and the Staubbach Fall'

James Tobin, a Bristol sugar merchant put together an album of 20 Swiss drawings by Samuel Hieronymus Grimm (1733-94) after he moved to London in 1770, where he settled and where Lloyd eventually bought this album. The drawings were based on Grimm's own sketches made 10 or more years earlier as print studies for Gottlieb Sigmund Gruner's *Die Eisgebirge des Schweizerlands* (Bern, 1760). The Alpine Club Library holds a copy of this three-volume rarity. Grimm had moved from Bergdorf to Bern in the 1750s to work with Johann Ludwig Aberli (see above). Although his high mountain drawings are poor, with unrecognisable peaks and fantastical glaciers, this valley drawing is exemplary and well composed. Biographies as for Aberli.

'Rhone Glacier with Mont de la Fourche'

The sharp peak on the right is better known as the Furkahorn, which is connected by the Galengrat to the Galenstock, and of course the Rhone glacier is now much reduced. Nevertheless, there is no doubt that this beautiful image of Philip James de Loutherbourg's (1740-1812) is faithful to topography. Although the print was not published until late in the century, de Loutherbourg's travels in Switzerland date to 1768-71, whereafter he moved to London and settled there. The British Museum's notes also record a later visit to Switzerland in 1787. French by birth, he was made an academician in Paris in 1767, and RA in London in 1781. Although the print is described as *Peint par* rather than *Dessiné par*, the original was evidently watercolour over pen outlines.

'A Hilly Landscape with a Winding Road'

There is no information about this large accomplished drawing in the database and the sheet bears no inscriptions. We do not know what place is depicted, when it was drawn, who owned it before its acquisition by Lloyd, nor how Lloyd came to acquire it. It is not mentioned in the catalogue raisonné of John Robert Cozens' drawings.[4] The attribution to Cozens is therefore uncertain. It could well depict somewhere in the Alps, where he made many drawings, but it could also be a British subject. The beautifully drawn trees could very well be English trees. I offer the suggestion that there is a very fair match to the Screes Buttresses of Whin Rigg in the Lake District, as viewed from the road to the east of Nether Wasdale, and that this possibility is worth pursuing. Comparison with drawings of these buttresses by Ellis Carr in Haskett-Smith's *Climbing in the British Isles: England* (Longmans Green, 1894) and by Alfred Wainwright in his *The Southern Fells* (Westmorland Press, 1960) is not at all discouraging.

'The Glacier of Montanvert, Chamonix'

Lloyd collected 18 watercolours by John 'Warwick' Smith (1749-1831), so he was his second choice after Turner. This large and attractive composition depicts the source of the Arveyron, a popular venue for Chamonix visitors, often painted, and the terminus of the Mer de Glace, then called the Glacier des Bois. That terminus is nowadays somewhere up near the Dent du Requin. We recognise the Aiguille Verte on the left and the Grandes Jorasses in the distance. Although dated 1802, it is no doubt based on sketches made by Smith during his journeys through the Alps with Francis Towne in 1781, or with the Earl of Warwick in 1786.

'On the Ascent to Snowdon, from Llyn Cywelyn'

Smith produced many attractive Welsh landscapes at this size, although not many are detailed mountain studies. Lloyd secured this picture along with seven others from Lady Gunning in 1927. If the mount inscription is interpreted correctly, then it shows the route from Llyn Cwellyn via the Snowdon Ranger path, which follows the crest of Clogwyn d'ur Arddu. Certainly the light is in the right place, to the right, but the topography seems rather exaggerated. It would be interesting to know what members think.

'View of the Lower Grindelwald Glacier, and of the Eiger' and the Fischerhörner

Like Johann Ludwig Aberli (see p128), Johann Jakob Biedermann (1763-1830) was born in Winterthur and moved in 1778 to Berne, where he worked for Aberli. This is another very attractive and topographically accurate early

4. C Bell & T Girtin, 'The Drawings and Sketches of John Robert Cozens', *The Volume of the Walpole Society*, 23, 1934-35.

Oberland print, with both mountains beautifully rendered and coloured. Biographies as for Aberli.

'Waterfall (at Dawlish, Devon?)'

There is little information about J S Barth (fl1790-1810) beyond what is inscribed on his pictures. This one is inscribed with 'J S Barth N 228 High Holborn London/Dawlish in Devon Agt 1810' on the verso. Despite Barth's low profile the British Museum has acquired eight of his works, including two bequeathed by Lloyd, and this is a large and impressive watercolour. The question mark in the description is well deserved. There are no large waterfalls in Devon and next to nothing near Dawlish. In fact, 'Dawlish' appears in inscriptions on other works of Barth's which have nothing to do with Devon, and again accompanied by '288 High Holborn', the business address of Cribb, Barth's print-seller. So Dawlish is surely Barth's address. The figures in the picture make clear that what is depicted is a very large waterfall, and the two servants with dog positioned on the right wear Welsh hats, so it is probably a waterfall in Wales, possibly Pistyll Rhaeadr in the Berwyns. Again, perhaps members familiar with Wales may be able to provide better information.

'Gormire Lake, Yorkshire?'

Lloyd acquired three drawings by John Sell Cotman (1782-1842), the foremost artist of the Norwich School. This one was exhibited by Cotman at the Royal Academy in 1804, then at the Tate Cotman Exhibition in 1922 and several times at the British Museum following Lloyd's bequest. Although Cotman exhibited a drawing with title Gormire at the RA in 1804 (cat 928), he exhibited several other drawings, including one titled 'Near Barmouth, North Wales' (cat 375), now in the Eton College Collection. Kim Sloan's notes about the drawing (op cit p140) suggested that the present drawing is 'probably a view of Cader Idris from Barmouth', but this opinion has now disappeared from her notes in the museum database. However, it is a very good fit for Cader Idris from the sands east of Barmouth and it definitely looks like a high mountain, rather than the Whitestone Cliff which rises only 500 feet over a forested hillside above Gormire Lake. I have discussed the matter with Cotman authority Prof David Hill of Leeds University,[5] and he has agreed, following discussions with Jeremy Yates, an artist and another Cotman expert, that there has been a transposition of titles at some stage in the drawing's history and that it should be re-titled as a 'View of Cader Idris from near Barmouth'.

'La Montant sur la Pitz Val Rhein et Glacier du Rheinwald?'

As the curator notes on the museum database, this beguiling painting by Johann Ludwig Bleuler (1792-1850) 'emphasizes the danger of alpine expeditions.'

5. David Hill helped me greatly when presenting the Club's Ruskins in AJ 2019 and I record my gratitude again. Members with an interest in old watercolour might care to visit his blog site *sublimesites.co* which reports his journeys 'following the footsteps' of Turner and Ruskin in the Alps.

'Gorner Glacier with the Zermatt Breithorn and Klein Matterhorn', Elijah Walton, undated, watercolour touched with white, 35cm × 24.7cm. *(British Museum)*

Indeed, and one might add 'the expense needed for guides and equipment.' The two *Herren* appear to require the support of at least 12 guides and porters. Sorbonne art historian Danijela Bucher has discovered that the mount description was added later and believes that the depicted scene is on the Glacier des Bossons, flowing down from Mont Blanc. Certainly if an ascent of the Rheinwald glacier in 18th century garb is depicted, the painting could only be a recollection of the famous ascent of the Rheinwaldhorn (3407m) by Fr Placidus à Spescha in 1789, an ascent not repeated until the mid 19th century. However, Coolidge, discussing the monk's considerable achievements, declares that he had a horror of glaciers and would not set foot on them.[6] It is much more likely that Bleuler has painted an early ascent of Mont Blanc via the Bossons Glacier, as Dr Bucher has suggested. It could also be that Bleuler's drawing is merely comedic and fanciful. Biographies as for Aberli.

'East Side of Monte Rosa, and Jägerhorn' and 'Moonlit Mountain Landscape'

These three fine watercolours (the third illustrates this article) by Elijah Walton (1833-80) were not purchased from dealers, and may have been got by Lloyd from other Club members, or bought at Club exhibitions. This is certainly true of the Monte Rosa drawing, which belonged to C E Mathews. I identified the subject of the Breithorn-Klein Matterhorn drawing to the British Museum and Tony Astill suggested the location of the moonlit landscape to it: looking south over the Lauterbrunnen valley from the Mürren Alp. This small drawing has the spooky and romantic quality found in so many of Walton's Alpine pictures, which is absent from the other two. If Tony Astill's identification is correct (and I do not doubt it) then we see a portion of the Jungfrau on the left, and the distant peaks are perhaps the Gletscherhorn and Ebnefluh.

6. W Coolidge, *The Alps in Nature and History*, Edinburgh, 1908, p212.

Environment & Nature

'The Glacier of Montanvert, Chamonix', John 'Warwick' Smith, 1802, watercolour touched with body-colour, 53.5cm × 82.3cm. *(British Museum)*

ANNIE DARE

Cold Comfort on Chomolungma

Going, going, gone? Seventy years on from the first ascent of Everest, the Khumbu glacier is disappearing at an accelerating rate. *(Alex Treadway)*

Seventy years after the first ascent of Everest, some of the world's most famous climbers are backing a new campaign to save the ice and snow of Earth's tallest mountain, and the entire Hindu Kush-Himalayan region. Scientists say there's no time to waste.

This spring, Catalan athlete Kilian Jornet was training around Everest, in Nepal. This was his 10th visit to the Khumbu region, but it was the first time he and his partner Swedish athlete Emilie Forsberg were accompanied by their two youngest children. Jornet, the son of a mountain guide who reached the summit of his first 3,000m peak at the tender age of three, was hoping to plant the seed for his daughters to develop a love for the people and nature of the Himalaya to equal his own. He delighted in seeing the girls playing with people and in places he felt so connected to.

All change in the Icefall. Always dangerous, climate change is impacting on this key section on the ascent of Everest.

Kanchha Sherpa, last surviving member of the 1953 expedition that put Hillary and Tenzing on the summit. *(Tenzing Chogyal Sherpa)*

Yet the trip was bittersweet. A climate advocate who consciously limits how often he flies in order to try to drive down his personal carbon footprint, it had been 10 years since Jornet had first seen Everest, or Chomolungma, 'goddess mother of the world' in one translation of the Tibetan. 'The changes that have taken place in the snow and glaciers here, just in the space of that decade, are so immediately obvious, and so dramatic,' Kilian told me. 'It's happening so, so fast.'

The family's visit came just before dignitaries from the climbing world gathered at the base of the mountain, in Namche Bazaar, to mark the 70th anniversary of Sir Edmund Hillary and Tenzing Norgay's first ascent. The glaciologists and researchers I work with at the International Centre for Integrated Mountain Development (ICIMOD), which for 40 years has monitored the cryosphere across the entire 3,500km long expanse of the Hindu Kush Himalaya (HKH), used the moment to zero in on the specific impacts of climate change on Everest. Their data provides incontrovertible scientific evidence to corroborate climbers' increasingly alarming eyewitness accounts, such as Jornet's, or that of Lukas Furtenbach, who saw puddles on the South Col in 2022, or another climber who, when climbing Gasherbrum IV in 2021, was shocked to find water cascading down a rock at 7,000m. Worryingly, ICIMOD scientists found that the 79 glaciers around Everest had thinned by over 100m in just six decades and that the rate of thinning had almost doubled since 2009. The iconic Khumbu glacier itself is disappearing up the mountain. And the further east you go, the worse this thinning becomes.

Tenzing Chogyal Sherpa, an early-career glaciologist at ICIMOD, travelled to Namche to join his grandfather, the last survivor of the first ascent, Kanchha Sherpa, and Helen Clark, the former prime minister of New Zealand,

and Hillary and Norgay's descendants for the anniversary events. Together, this group launched a campaign asking climbers to raise their voices to press for faster action to avert catastrophic, irreversible changes to Everest and other mountains under the banner of *#SaveOurSnow*. The campaign asks members of the public, but particularly climbers, scientists and mountain communities, to share stories of the climate impacts they're seeing on social media and to add their name to a declaration that asks for governments to honour their commitments to limit warming as set out in the 2015 Paris Agreement.

'The sporting community needs to step up,' Jornet, one of the signatories of the declaration, says. 'Alongside scientists studying these mountains, and the communities that live here, it is those of us who return year after year to these mountains, to work and to train, who can see with our own eyes the extraordinary pace of changes to mountain glaciers, snow and permafrost. These changes are not only aesthetic, of course. They also pose new dangers to climbers in terms of unstable terrain. But the much more profound impacts are the dangers these changes pose to the people and nature that rely on these mountains, for water, for livelihoods, for habitat.'

Climate impacts across the world's cryosphere are fast outpacing scientists' previous projections, with the fight to save summer ice in the Arctic declared essentially lost earlier this year, and revised forecasts suggesting Antarctica is vulnerable to devastating and permanent impacts at just 1.5°C of temperature rise. At 2°C of warming, glaciers in the Alps, the Andes, Patagonia, Iceland, Scandinavia, the North American Rockies and New Zealand are all set to disappear completely, while according to ICIMOD's latest report *Water, Ice Society, and Ecosystems in the Hindu Kush Himalaya* around half of glaciers in the Hindu Kush Himalaya would be gone. That even just half might remain is unlikely: our current emissions trajectory sets us on course to smash through the 'safe' 1.5°C ceiling. At the currently plausible 4°C of warming, 80% of glaciers in the HKH will vanish by the end of the century. While glacier loss worldwide will devastate local communities and result in sea-level rise, the consensus is that the consequences of glacier loss, more erratic snowfall and permafrost thawing for people and nature in the hugely populated and bio-diverse HKH region, where 12 of the world's major rivers originate, will be nothing short of catastrophic.

'Nowhere is safe from climate impacts,' says ICIMOD's deputy director general Izabella Koziell. 'But the Hindu Kush Himalaya holds the third largest frozen body of water on the planet, which provides freshwater services to a quarter of humanity. A staggering half of that population already suffer malnutrition. In the past two years alone we've already seen devastating climate-driven humanitarian disasters unfold in this region – in Afghanistan's droughts, and Pakistan's floods: a chilling illustration of what our scientists say will be one of the key climate impacts in our region – the issue of 'too much water, too little water.' The magnitude of the humanitarian catastrophe that will unfold should the reliable water supply that flows from these mountains be lost – undermining the food and water

Himalaya

~ Changing Landscapes

Imja Glacier in the 1950s

An impressive layer of ice covered the Imja glacier in the 1950s. Thick ice falls down from the mountain and the glacier merges with the Lhotse Shar glacier further down. However, even in the 1950s, small meltwater ponds could be seen in and around the glacier. Over the next fifty years, these ponds continued to grow and merge, and by the mid 1970s had formed the Imja lake.

Photo: Fritz Muller, Khumbu, Nepal, 1956 – 1961
Courtesy of Jack D Ives
Archives of Alton Byers, The Mountain Institute

The Imja glacier in the 1950s and 2007, illustrating the formation of the glacial lake near Ama Dablam. The rate of glacial thinning has doubled since then. *(ICIMOD)*

ICIMOD

Imja Glacier in 2007

By 2006, the Imja lake had grown to around 1 km long with an average depth of 42 metres, and contained more than 35 million m³ of water. The Imja glacier is retreating at an average rate of 74 metres per year, and is thought to be the fastest retreating glacier in the Himalayas.

The thin cover of debris on this glacier may actually have accelerated surface melting, as heat is transferred to the ice below. Because of the unconsolidated nature of the lake's terminal moraine dam, the risk of a glacial lake outburst flood (GLOF) may be high.

Photo: Alton Byers, Khumbu, Nepal, 2007, The Mountain Institute

Above: Visible changes seen in the terminus of glacier AX010 from 1978 to 2008. Situated in the Shorong Himal, this glacier has lost almost half its surface area in just the last three decades. Opposite: The terminus of the Rikha Samba glacier between 1974 and 2010. The rate of loss has only accelerated since then. *(Alton Byers)*

security of two billion people in Asia – is almost beyond imagining. Yet this is what the science tells us will happen unless world leaders act decisively now.'

The case for action is compelling. With very low emissions, most glaciers and snowpack can be preserved for water resources, with scientists saying losses would begin to slow slightly around 2040, with glaciers stabilising sometime in the next century. And the support alpinists have given the campaign has been unequivocal with over 2,000 signatories in the first 48 hours, including Kenton Cool, Rebecca Stephens, Peter Hillary, Wolfgang Nairz, Reinhold Messner, the glaciologist and alpinist Patrick Wagnon, Jamling Tenzing, Gerlinde Kaltenbrunner, Lakpa Dendi Sherpa, documentary-filmmaker Craig Leeson, and Pemba Sherpa. Other backers include the Nepal Mountaineering Association, the Mountain Research Initiative, the UN Mountain Partnership, and the UIAA.

'It's amazing to have had this strong early support from the climbing community,' says Izabella Koziell. 'But it feels like we're barely scratching the surface with what might be possible, in terms of the leadership role alpinists might be able to play at this crucial moment,' says Koziell. 'Not just because of their tenacity and influence, but most of all because of their unrivalled intimacy with mountains and mountain people. Many climbers' lives have often been if not profoundly transformed then at least hugely enriched by encounters with the landscapes and cultures of the Hindu Kush Himalaya.

These experiences give them an intrinsic awareness of how much we stand to lose unless we check emissions that are threatening lives, livelihoods and cultures.

'It's hard to have spent any time among such communities too and not be struck by the sheer injustice of what we're seeing unfold across this region: of the lives of peoples who have trodden so lightly on the Earth for generations being destroyed as a consequence of political and business choices being taken millions of miles away.'

ICIMOD, for its part, is reinventing itself to rise to the challenge of supporting communities and governments in the region that will confront the impacts of the changing climate. The organisation has completely reconfigured its portfolio in order to reduce the region's vulnerability to disaster risks: biodiversity loss; and water, energy and food insecurity. This work runs from installing early-warning systems to forewarn communities of floods and encouraging governments to share data across national boundaries, to advancing the rights and recognition of nomadic communities and the role of rangelands, to identifying incentives for communities to protect biodiversity and forests.

Critically, the organisation is setting out to build an advocacy voice that is commensurate with the region's importance and peril. Because, despite how much hangs in the balance in terms of human population alone, knowledge of the consequences of continued climate inaction on the Hindu Kush Himalaya globally remains low. There was no mention of mountain impacts *at all* within the draft text of this year's critical Global Stocktake process, an integral of the Paris Agreement under the framework of the United Nations Framework Convention on Climate Change.

In collaboration with and on behalf of its eight regional member countries – Afghanistan, Bangladesh, Bhutan, China, India, Myanmar, Nepal and Pakistan – the organisation is setting out to change that lobbying at global fora:

Left: ICIMOD glaciologist Tenzing Chogyal Sherpa in the lap of Ed Hillary in 1992. Right: With his grandfather Kanchha Sherpa. *(Tenzing Chogyal Sherpa)*

for faster action on mitigation globally; for the urgent scaling up of adaptation and ecosystem restoration funds; and programmes and for the mobilisation of loss and damage finance.

In seeking to strengthen its impact, ICIMOD is also looking outwards, exploring the creation of a new regional political mechanism, akin to the models used by the Alpine or Carpathian Convention, with the aim of accelerating political change through closer collaboration among countries to build greater resilience to these issues, many of which are trans-boundary, such as floods, and in securing greater prominence and negotiating power for the region.

'For 40 years, ICIMOD has acted as a knowledge centre for the region, generating and sharing evidence to our member countries to support their policy processes, and this remains our primary work,' says Koziell. 'However, with humanity standing at such a crossroads, and our cryosphere being so central to that, our board, donors, regional member countries and stakeholders were all unanimous that ICIMOD should start to take a much more assertive role.

'I believe that at this moment all of us are being called to go beyond 'business-as-usual' – and that it's for all of use whatever platform we have to urge governments and businesses to transform how we power our lives, feed ourselves, move around so that Earth can sustain life. The science is clear – there really is no time left. Perhaps this transformation will be humanity's greatest summit yet.'

- To sign the declaration go to ***www.icimod.org/SaveOurSnow*** and share your story of impacts using the hashtag *#SaveOurSnow*.

HIMALAYA IN CRISIS

- Glaciers in the region disappeared 65% faster in 2011–20 compared with the previous decade.

- The glaciers could lose up to 80% of their current volume by end of this century.

- Availability of water in the Hindu Kush Himalaya is expected to peak in mid-century, driven by accelerated glacier melt, after which it is expected to decline.

- Snow cover is expected to fall by up to a quarter under high emissions scenarios – drastically reducing freshwater for major rivers such as Amu Darya and Helmand where it contributes up to 74% and 77% of river flow respectively. Floods and landslides are projected to increase over the coming decades

- Two hundred glacier lakes across the HKH are deemed dangerous, and the region could see a significant spike in glacial lake outburst flood risk by the end of the century

- Effects of the changing cryosphere on fragile mountain habitats are particularly acute. The HKH holds four global biodiversity hotspots but cascading impacts of a changing cryosphere are already being reported in most ecosystems and most inhabitant species, with species decline and extinction already reported, along with range shift of species to higher elevations, ecosystem degradation and decrease in habitat suitability.

- Ice and snow in the Hindu Kush Himalaya are important sources of water for 12 rivers that flow through 16 countries in Asia, providing freshwater and other vital ecosystem services to 240 million people in the mountains and a further 1.65 billion people downstream.

Data drawn from ICIMOD's new report: Water, Ice, Society, and Ecosystems in the Hindu Kush Himalaya. You can download the full 'HI-WISE' report at: ***www.icimod.org/hi-wise***

JIM LANGLEY

Meltdown

Climate Change and the Greening of the Alps

Left: The Mont Blanc massif photographed by Walter Mittelholzer in 1919. The Swiss pilot and entrepreneur was the first man to fly over the snows of Kilimanjaro. Right: The Mont Blanc massif photographed by researchers from Dundee University in 2019.

With another summer of record temperatures and heat waves across Europe the signs of a warming planet are all too evident. The effects of climate change have significant consequences for plants and animals, their habitats and their ultimate survival. This article takes a look at the changing climate in the European Alps where it is having a pronounced and visible impact on both the physical environment and the living world.

Last year was exceptional in many ways in terms of climate. It followed a trend in which 16 of the past 17 years have been the warmest on record. The winter before saw little snowfall in the Alps and very mild conditions too. A hot, dry summer followed across Europe and the Alps experienced rapidly deteriorating conditions. These conditions have been widely reported with major Alpine events including the tragic news of a serac collapse on the Marmolada glacier in the Dolomites that killed 10 mountaineers in its worst recorded incident. Rock collapse, widening crevasses and generally

A large moraine abandoned by the retreating Glacier du Râteau.

poor glacier conditions have also led to the closure of some normal routes up major Alpine peaks including the Matterhorn, Mont Blanc and Jungfrau.

Impacts of Climate Change

At the scale of the European Alps, over the course of the 20th century, temperatures have risen by 2°C which is double the increase recorded in the northern hemisphere. This rate of warming, observed since the industrial revolution, has accelerated in the past 40 years (see fig 1 overleaf). Data recorded by MeteoSwiss in 2022 reported a record-high freezing point of 5,184 metres – an altitude higher than Mont Blanc – compared with the normal summer level of 3,000m to 3,500m. This temperature change impacts all living things and represents an upward movement of about 100m. As a consequence, in order for species to be able to stay in the same temperature conditions they will need to move 100m upslope. This forms a major challenge for biodiversity as species try to keep pace with such rapid changes.

Snow Cover

The rate of warming is amplified in the mountain environment as many different habitats occur over a small area. Snow beds are reduced in size and length of time, ice melts from screes and rocky ridges earlier and meadows are exposed for longer periods. These habitats are all experiencing reduced snow and ice cover, which presents several problems. Snow and ice reflect the sun's rays keeping the ground cold but when they melt they are replaced by rock and vegetation. These both absorb the sun's heat increasing ground temperature, which contributes to more melting. These effects have been

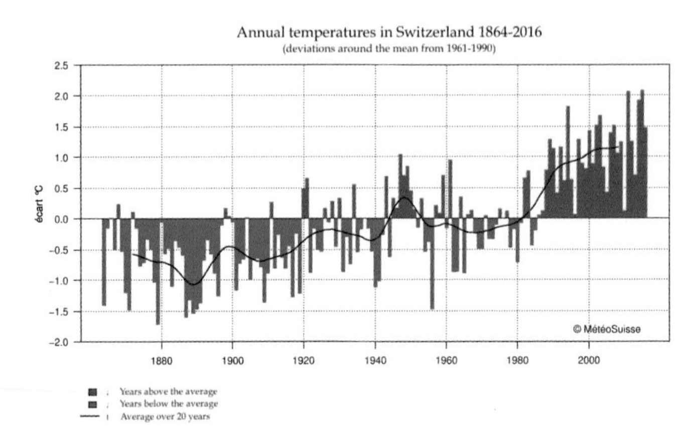

Fig 1. Annual temperatures in Switzerland based on the 1961-1990 average.

recorded on the Mont Blanc massif, which has lost one month of snow cover, at mid elevation, in the past 40 years. This trend is predicted to continue and an equivalent reduction is likely by 2050.

Drought

Europe had its hottest summer and hottest August on record in 2022. Associated with these heat waves is drought due to a lack of rain, warmer soils and enhanced evaporation due to the high temperatures. Yet as southern and central Europe baked, Scandinavia soaked this summer. According to scientists global rainfall patterns have changed little over the past century, however, regional and seasonal changes have been observed and we are witness to this in Europe. A noticeable consequence I observed last summer was with Switzerland's drinking water fountains. These are normally a constant flow of fresh spring water but many were turned off to conserve water supplies. Thanks to the risk of wildfires, no fires were permitted which included during the Swiss day celebrations when fireworks displays are traditionally seen across the evening sky on 1 August.

Glacial Volume

Global heating is supercharging extreme weather at an astonishing speed. High temperatures have a dramatic effect on glacial ice volume causing retreat to occur at an alarming rate. Since 1850 glaciers in the Alps have lost between 30% and 40% of their surface area and half of their volume. The speed of loss has accelerated and since the turn of the millennium the Alps have lost about 17% of their ice volume. Iconic glaciers such as the Mer de Glace in the Mont Blanc massif and the Aletsch glacier in the Swiss Valais have experienced huge reductions in ice volume. The Mer de Glace experienced a seven metre loss of thickness this summer alone and the Aletsch glacier, the largest in the Alps, is contracting by five metres or more each year.

Pioneer plants colonising rock debris following the retreat of a glacier.

In 1919, the Swiss pilot and photographer Walter Mittelholzer flew over Mont Blanc in a biplane to photograph the Alpine landscape. Exactly 100 years later, researchers from the University of Dundee in Scotland recreated his photographs to show the impact that the changing climate has had on the mountain's glaciers (see p146).

Permafrost

Permafrost is the permanently frozen ground and consists of soil, rocks and sediments usually bound by ice. Permafrost generally occurs in the Alps from around 2,300m altitude. Investigations into the link between permafrost thawing and rock collapses were started around the time a large part of the Bonatti pillar on Les Drus collapsed in 2005 but have been the subject of speculation about since the 1970s. Long-term monitoring has revealed progressive warming and degradation of permafrost, which has a profound influence on the evolution of the mountain landscape and the stability of the mountains. The potential for natural hazards such as rock falls, landslides and debris flows, will become more frequent and will impact not just mountaineers but settlements, infrastructure and all living things in the Alps.

Impacts on the Natural World

Such rapid changes in the physical environment have significant effects on all living things. The effects of climate change on alpine flora and fauna are noticeable and are already contributing to changes in species distribution and abundance. They have to keep pace with the evolution in order to survive but the gradual greening of the Alps illustrates the changing distribution of species.

Glacier crowfoot a high alpine specialist.

Growing Season

Alpine plants are specialists at survival. They are at home in the harsh alpine environment with its extreme climate and short growing season. As snow cover melts earlier the growing season lengthens and this will begin to favour the less well adapted and more competitive species usually confined to lower elevations. Gradually the high-altitude, alpine specialists will become restricted to newly exposed areas uninhabitable to the invading plants. The rise in spring temperatures, combined with earlier melting of the snow cover allows the majority of species to develop earlier in the season and to produce more biomass over the course of the growing season. This is generally a positive effect but some species are sensitive to frost, especially in early season, so this can increase the risk of damage to species such as bilberry.

Vertical Migration

Over the past decades, with the warming climate, a rise in elevation of both plant and animal species has been observed. Plants are rising vertically at a rate of about 30m per decade with animals rising about 100m per decade. Forest trees have migrated around 30m over the 20th century. This vertical migration increases the competition for space and resources and combined studies across the Alps indicate an increase in plant species found on summits over the past few decades.

Phenology

This is the timing of events in nature. It is when plants come into flower, when eggs are laid and when you see the first swallow of summer. It also focuses on

Ibex.

how plants and animals respond to the climate. In order to survive changes in climate species can either migrate to preferable conditions or they can adapt to the new environmental conditions. Examples of this are: the arrival of migrating birds advancing by about 15 days over the past 30 years; common toad eggs being laid about a month earlier than 25 years ago; and plants flowering between two and five days earlier per decade.

Grazing Animals

The changing in the times of spring is also having a great effect on grazing animals such as ibex and chamois. They are becoming desynchronised with peak vegetation production in the spring with dire consequences for their young. Their mating season is in the autumn and young are born in the springtime. During relatively warm winters peak plant production is out of synch with weaning their young. As a result higher mortality of young ibex and chamois has been observed due to a lack of suitable food.

Summary

It is without doubt that the Alps are entering a period of unprecedented change. Climate change continues to alter the alpine ecosystem and there will be winners and losers. While alpine species will lose significant areas of habitat, colonising plants and forest trees will expand their territories. As individuals, we have our role to play in mitigating climate change. The decisions we make regarding how we travel, what we eat and what we buy all have an important impact.

VICTOR SAUNDERS

On the Future of Mountain Guiding

Mountain business: Edward Whymper's image of the Compagnie des Guides in Chamonix. *(Alpine Club Photo Library)*

I qualified as a mountain guide in 1996 after a 20-year career as an architect. As an architect I had spent every holiday and quite a bit of flexi-time in the hills, from the Cairngorms to the Karakoram. I looked forward to turning my hobby into my job and vice versa. And so I brought the exuberant enthusiasm of an amateur climber to my work, which would be increasingly based in Europe. The sky was blue with promise and I can say now that promise was fulfilled, for me at least.

Even though I was by then in my mid forties, like everyone else starting out in a new job I was quite naïve. So my feeling that the guiding world in the late 1990s was more freewheeling may just be subjectivity born of my newness in the role. But I do think that the British Mountain Guides are a tighter and more professional body now than they were in the mid 1990s when I started. It seemed that all I had to do was show up in the Alps, show my carnet and I was good to go.

Of course, it didn't stay like that. Even before I moved permanently to France at the turn of the millennium I had thought it a good idea to apply for my *carte professionnelle*, my 'carte pro', a form of identification required by many occupations in France. While I didn't have to take any new exams, this did require me to get my original guiding certificate translated into French by an officially recognised translator. I had to do the same with my birth certificate, except that in France a birth certificate is more like a life certificate, since it is updated with marriages and children.

In early 2016 the European Union introduced the European Professional Card (EPC), the 'Carte professionelle éuropéenne', allowing some nurses, pharmacists, physiotherapists, estate agents and mountain guides to move around the European Union using their existing qualifications. But its arrival has made the authorities pay more attention to where and how mountain guides are working.

Brexit has further complicated this situation and I am now going through the process of becoming a French citizen. This one issue alone has cast a long shadow over the future of British guiding. On top of that is the more existential crisis of climate change. It's hard to avoid the conclusion that the challenges I faced in my first 25 years as a guide will be less significant than those facing young guides in the next quarter of a century. Will guiding even exist? To try to answer these questions I need to go back to some basic definitions.

The Meaning of Profession

To practise a profession, to be a professional is to be a member of an association that guarantees its client public two things: competence and integrity. These guarantees are backed by tests and examinations (competence) and sanctions (integrity). A body that claims to be professional but does not control its members in this way is little more than a trade association or a political lobby.

Professions have differing levels of recognition by the government depending on the country. For example, in the UK the highest level of recognition protects both the name and the work. A good example is medicine. A lower level in the UK recognises the name but not the work. For example, it is illegal to call yourself an architect if you are not registered with the Architects Registration Board but it is not illegal to perform architectural services without being registered.

The lowest level of recognition is none at all and in the UK this is the case for mountain guides. While it would be illegal to misrepresent yourself as a guide certified by the International Federation of Mountain Guide Associations (IFMGA) or a member of the British Mountain Guides (BMG), there's nothing to stop you calling yourself a guide and working as one in the UK. This is not the case in France, where the level of recognition for guides as a profession is at the highest level, like doctors in the UK. The name and work are both recognised and protected. And this level of recognition is more or less the standard throughout the Alpine regions.

IFMGA

The mountain guide community is overseen by the IFMGA, which is essentially a federation of the national associations. In short, while it is the federation that certifies us, we are members of our national associations such as the BMG, which are, in turn, members of the federation. Each nation is entitled to one member association (more or less). The federation sets a common technical standard, which the member organisations have to meet before their guides can be IFMGA-certified. It is an extremely good system, with high standards of safety and technical competence. IFMGA certification is accepted throughout Europe and much of the world where mountains are prominent.

Each national association sets its own syllabus but needs to meet the overall IFMGA standard. The BMG achieves this using four key areas of examination: rock climbing, winter (ice) climbing, alpine climbing and ski touring. This was more or less the same for all member associations until 1990 when Peru was admitted to the federation without the skiing element. Three more non-skiing nations were added: Bolivia in 2004, Nepal in 2012 and Ecuador in 2017. In 2019, the first multinational association, the Eastern European Mountain Guide Association (EEMGA) was admitted as a skiing association. The IFMGA now comprises 25 member associations, although there are in fact 27 members listed since Italy has three IFMGA members associations (Aosta, South Tirol and the rest of Italy) but only one Italian voting representative. And no, please don't ask how that works.

A somewhat controversial element was the approval of the four non-skiing associations. Their members are not recognised for guiding in Europe. Allowing non-skiers to join the federation was justified on the basis that the respective countries have large glaciated mountains but no skiing facilities. The arrangement seemed a little asymmetric to some guides who wondered if the IFMGA had considered swapping the skiing element for a high-altitude guiding exam.

There was, however, an alternative, possibly more compelling, motive: the political one, since it ensured that visiting IFMGA guides would be allowed to operate in those countries. In other words, it could be described as a transactional arrangement. This was perhaps in response to Tanzania, where all climbers on Kilimanjaro are required to use a local (i.e. non-IFMGA) guide. This year, 2023, the Nepali government has ruled that all trekkers in national parks (with the current exception of the Sagarmatha National Park) will have to hire a local guide. This is a ruling that will certainly affect lone trekkers and western trek leaders. It remains to be seen if that ruling impacts expeditions and foreign IFMGA guides.

EU and Regulation

When in January 2016 the EU created the EPC to help professionals travel and work throughout the EU, those who thought it would replace the complex documentation required for working in the various Alpine countries discovered the small print included the stipulation that 'the EPC does not replace the "traditional" recognition procedures foreseen by the Professional Qualifications Directive.'

As I said, when I began my guiding career mountain guides simply needed to show the IFMGA carnet in guest countries, possibly because guides were fewer in number and the existing work permit regulations were lax or largely ignored. From 2016, national authorities began to be more interested in enforcing the regulations for temporary work authorisation. This may have been a result of the increasing number of non-EU guides working in Europe but was also an unforeseen consequence of the EPC initiative. Be careful what you ask for.

In combination with Brexit, the EPC has been no friend to the British guide. It is now time-consuming and difficult for British guides to get an Italian work permit and almost impossible for British guides to obtain an Italian EPC. On the other hand, guides are rarely, if ever, asked for the permits in Italy. Obtaining permission is somewhat more efficient in Switzerland but the corollary of that is the Swiss penchant for delivering swift and hefty fines to those carrying incorrect paperwork. The situation for foreign mountain guides in Spain appears to be unresolved in terms of bureaucracy. In all cases, it is not recommended to have an accident without holding the correct paperwork in any of these places.

Meanwhile the demand for mountain guiding work appears to be growing, especially for the popular iconic mountains. This might be a consequence of the mountaineering industry's growing profile, hot-housed by social media: the 'Insta effect'. We will have to wait and see if it's a passing fashion. What does seem clear is that with increasing guiding work, including cross-border guiding, there will be calls for enforcement of local regulations. Guides can confidently look forward to a more tedious regulatory environment.

Climate Change

Another huge question for mountain guides is the changing climate. While the daily and annual temperature data look somewhat spiky, even random, the changing shape of glaciers shows a clear reversion to the mean. Glaciers across the world are mostly in retreat, notwithstanding the so-called Karakoram Anomaly (the Hunza basin glaciers did not decline between 1975 and 2017).

The most obvious example is right here in Chamonix. In 1988 the Montenvers train and téléphérique led to the edge of the Mer de Glace. By the early 1990s that part of the glacier was thinning at about one metre per year, which, for tourists and returning Vallée Blanche skiers, added about three steps a year from the ice to their ride home. By 2019, just before the pandemic, the rate of thinning had increased to 18 steps a year. Post-Covid-19, the rate

A modern mountain guide at work on the Aiguilles d'Entrèves. *(Maxime Gilbert)*

has accelerated to 35 new steps. That is approximately 10m of ice lost each year. To the increasingly tired skiers (and their old guides) hauling their heavy Vallée Blanche skis back to the téléphérique, those 580 steps seem endless.

There is a similar story at Concordia, that icon of Swiss glaciers. When the first hut was established it was possible to walk off the glacier to the hut. Year by year, in an evolutionary adaptation like the giraffe's neck, or the elephant's trunk, it was easier to add a few more ladders than move the hut. Now there is a magnificent mountain refuge 200m above the glacier, in a location where no one of sound mind would choose to place one.

By the end of the 21st century most of Europe's minor and several of the major glaciers will have disappeared. By halfway through the century the valley ice-climbing season will barely exist. It has already been reduced from four months when I began in 1996 to a little more than six weeks in 2023. Nearly all Gaston Rébuffat's 100 classic climbs have had major glacier or bergschrund changes. The rising permafrost altitude has destabilised many mountain refuges and several routes.

None of the above is very surprising and the guide community has long understood that it will have to adapt. What the future holds for guides may be best understood in relation to the topic at the beginning of this article:

professional recognition and regulation. Guides in Europe have a unique level of training and competence in high mountains and glaciated territory that contributes to their recognition. With climate change literally stripping away ice climbing, will guides have to overlap more with rock-climbing instructors and ski instructors?

This may affect the Austrian and German IFMGA guides less as their nations' guides associations govern skiing and rock-climbing instructors as well. In the remaining Alpine countries – France, Switzerland and Italy – the mountain professions are fractured and less qualified instructors have their own separate organisations, as is the case in Britain. In the non-Alpine European countries I can only say I don't understand the Spanish organisation and I am told the Polish one is even more complicated. But one has to ask if a long-term challenge to alpine guides from climate change will appear in the form of competition from less qualified organisations.

The Future Predicted

It is possible that a much advocated-for decrease in short-haul air travel will impact the guiding world's European client base, though alternative means of travel may offset that. It is probable that carbon-intensive activities such as heli-skiing will become increasingly controversial. This could also affect ski lifts and if the net result is an increase in ski touring (as has been seen since Covid-19) that would be no bad thing. It is more than probable that the regulatory environment both in the Greater Ranges and at home in Europe will be more challenging for mountain guides. It is near certain that many areas with glaciers will see their glaciers disappear and the winter guiding season will, on the whole, shorten.

What is absolutely certain is that the next generation of enthusiastic mountain guides will adapt their routes to the changing climate, find excellent outings which did not previously exist and continue to delight in the real challenges of life, which are not to be found buried in layers of bureaucracy but up there in the air and light. This I can say with confidence looking through my window at the Chamonix Aiguilles.

History

'On the Ascent to Snowdon, from Llyn Cywelyn', John 'Warwick' Smith, 1790, watercolour over pencil, 13.8cm x 20.8cm. *(British Museum)*

J G R HARDING

The Mountain Life of Robin Fedden

The multi-faceted Robin Fedden, sketched by the artist and illustrator John Stanton Ward.

Robin Fedden's name will be unfamiliar to most modern mountaineers for he came to mountaineering late in life and died young. His contribution rests on his accomplishments as a ski mountaineer and the expeditions he led to unusual, little-known ranges. His attainments as a writer, Middle East traveller and mainstay of the National Trust marked him as exceptional: an aesthete with a steel inner core who did everything with style, humour and charm.

Henry Robin Romilly Fedden was born in 1908. His father was the English landscape painter Arthur Romilly Fedden (1875-1939) who studied art in London, Paris and Spain and exhibited at the Royal Academy. His mother was

Fedden spent much of the Second World War in Egypt, where in the autumn of 1942 he married the Alexandrian Renée Catzfelis. They are pictured below the Khafre pyramid at Giza, which they were invited to climb the following year. *(Courtesy of Frances Fedden)*

Fedden on the summit of the pyramid in 1943. While a dedicated walker and skier from youth, he only began serious climbing in his late 30s. *(Courtesy of Frances Fedden)*

the American writer Katharine Waldo Douglas (1870-1939) from whom he imbibed a love for the Basque country. Robin's autobiographical *Chantemesle*[1] records his early upbringing at the parental home in this remote Seine-et-Oise village as a dreamlike evocation of rural France that influenced his attitudes and outlook to become as much European as English.

Romilly Fedden's choice of Clifton College for Robin's secondary education was influenced by the family's Gloucestershire roots. The school's reverence for manly vigour was personified in such alumni as the explorer and Great Game warrior Francis Younghusband and Younghusband's bosom friend Henry Newbolt, poet laureate of high imperialism. Robin was later to play his own game both as an adventurer and prose poet. After graduating from Magdalene College, Cambridge he travelled extensively in the Middle East and was temporarily an attaché at the British legation in Athens before taking up a lectureship at Cairo's Fuad al Awal University: times crisply recalled in *The Land of Egypt* (1939), *Syria* (1946) and *Crusader Castles* (1950).

Robin was lecturing at the university in the spring of 1941 when Rommel's Afrika Corps threatened to overrun Egypt. As an ardent pacifist he refused to enlist for military service in reaction to the severe shellshock his father had suffered after frontline service in the Great War. His stance was misinterpreted by the British embassy as defeatism but he spent that summer as

1. *Chantemesle: A Normandy Childhood*, first published in 1964, is still in print, courtesy of travel specialists Eland.

an ambulance driver with the Free French and British forces fighting the Vichy French in the short-lived Syrian-Lebanon campaign.

Wartime Cairo gave Robin's life a new dimension. As Artemis Cooper evokes in her *Cairo in the War 1939-1945* these were halcyon years for the brilliant set of literati that included the writers Lawrence Durrell and Olivia Manning, the poet Bernard Spencer and the soldier-scholar Patrick Leigh Fermor. Although Robin's natural eloquence was handicapped by a disconcerting stammer, he quickly established himself as a leading member both of this set and an influential group of cosmopolitan Greek friends whose parties King Farouk occasionally looked in on with Prince Peter of Greece acting as the gramophone's DJ. Here, too, Robin met Renée Catzeflis, an Alexandrian Greek who in the autumn of 1942 became his wife and lifelong climbing companion.

As their contribution to the war effort, Fedden, Durrell and Spencer founded *Personal Landscape* 'the most influential literary magazine to come out of the war years' (Turret Books, 1966), intended 'to preserve personal life and values ... in the channel of war' and encourage frontline servicemen to submit their own literary contributions. Another theme that preoccupied Robin during these years of self-imposed exile from German-occupied Greece was the loss of a culture he cherished and the landscape he loved. He never forgot climbing the Thessalian Mount Olympus in June 1939 and the pioneer ski ascent he made of that mountain the following Easter. In 1944, as his Middle East envoi, he made a 10-day traverse along the spine of the Lebanese mountains with Renée and the noted diplomat Bernard Burrows, later number two at the Foreign Office, ending with an ascent of Qurnat as Sawdā (3088m), the highest mountain in Lebanon and the Levant.

After the war, Robin returned to England and joined the staff of the National Trust, first as curator of Polesden Lacey in Surrey, in 1951 as secretary of the Historic Buildings Committee and in 1968 as the National Trust's deputy director general until his retirement in 1973 when he was awarded the CBE and appointed consultant, a post specially created for him in recognition of his long service and the numerous books and articles he had written about the National Trust's history, objectives and the properties it curated.

Robin's love of mountains had long predated his ascent of Mount Olympus. He had skied in the Alps since early youth and on his admission to the Alpine Ski Club in 1958 had already done no less than 33 skiing seasons. His book *Skiing in the Alps* (Hulton, 1956) was both an instructional manual and a guide to 70 different Alpine ski resorts. In 1952 he branched out from piste skiing to embark on his first serious ski-mountaineering tour in the Ötztal where, with Hans Lois as guide, they climbed the Wildspitze's south summit (3769m). In 1954 he completed a 10-day guided traverse of the Silvretta, bagging three peaks including Piz Buin en route.

The turning point in Robin's ski-mountaineering career came in 1955 when he embarked on the Chamonix to Zermatt *Haute Route*. Originally an invention of Alpine Club members who walked the course during the summers

Renée and Robin in the Pyrenees, a range that suited their mountaineering philosophy. Robin Fedden's book *The Enchanted Mountains* captures this period of their lives and was widely praised. *(Courtesy of Frances Fedden)*

Renée in the Alps in the late 1950s. *(Courtesy of Frances Fedden)*

of 1860 and 1861, it was first completed on ski by F F Roget and Marcel Kurz with three guides in January 1911. For many years thereafter this 'most dramatic and sustained of the great ski tours in the Alps' was regarded as something of an achievement and seldom attempted by British parties. Though it has since become wildly popular, when Fedden did it with a French Resistance survivor and a Greek photographer and their guide Marcel Burnet, they met no other parties. Robin's account of their 10-day traverse, *Alpine Ski Tour* (Putnam, 1956), combines history and practical advice in a narrative that reaches literary heights. Their attempt on the Chardonnet by the Forbes ridge in dangerous snow conditions was frustrated 50m short of the summit due to Robin losing a crampon and fast-deteriorating weather. *Alpine Ski Tour* became the inspiration for ski tourers determined to revive post-war British ski mountaineering's near-moribund state and it was Robin who proposed the toast to the Alpine Ski Club's founder Arnold Lunn at the club's jubilee dinner in 1968.

By now, Robin's passion for mountains had gone way beyond skiing and he embraced serious mountaineering with the zeal of the converted. His choice of the Pyrenees, a range to which 'the smiles of the artist and heart of the poet will always turn', reflected his penchant for wild, little-frequented country. After climbing Aneto (3404m) with Renée and John Varney in 1953,

The Feddens traversing the Aiguille de la Grande Sassière in the Graian Alps. *(Courtesy of Frances Fedden)*

he returned the following year with Renée and Peter McColl to make guideless ascents of the Pic du Midi d'Ossau, Pallas, Ariel, Vignemale and Balaitous. In 1955 he and Renée reverted to the Alps to climb the Freiwandspitz (3035m), Kitzteinhorn (3207m), Gross Glockner (3796m) and several rock routes in the Kaisegebirge.

In 1957 the Feddens shared their most memorable Pyrenean year with Basil Goodfellow, a former Alpine Club honorary secretary and fine amateur photographer who added weight to the party. Their tally of 10 of the range's best peaks, culminating in a triumphal ascent of the Encantados that consummated Robin's quest, as he recorded in his magical *The Enchanted Mountains:*

Renée and Robin, left, with Peter Lloyd and Alan Pullinger on the false summit of Castor, having climbed the north face. *(Basil Goodfellow)*

A Quest in the Pyrenees (Murray, 1962), a book whose gem-cut prose transports the reader to share the author's exhilaration, joy and wonder. Later that year Robin was elected to the Alpine Club with his proposer Jack Longland lauding Robin's 'originality in the choice of the mountain districts he has visited.'

Originality remained Robin's mountaineering hallmark, exemplified in his first mountaineering expedition to Turkey's Kaçkar mountains, the culminating massif of the 500km mountain chain that runs parallel with the Black Sea to the Russian border. Known to the Romans as the Pontic Alps after the kingdom of Pontus whose first century ruler Mithridates the Great thrice fought their armies to a draw, the range's lower reaches are smothered in dense deciduous forest surmounted by spikey granite peaks and a scattering of small glaciers. Homeland of the Laz people, a half-forgotten remnant of Caucasian stock whose language is unwritten, it was once part of Christian Armenia whose decaying Georgian churches slumber in the folds of vertiginous wooded valleys. Here too, folk memory distantly recalls Xenophon's epic winter crossing of the range with the remnants of his ten thousand Greek mercenaries in 401 BCE.

Most often swathed in the Black Sea mists that make its heights invisible from the coast, this mysterious range had seized Robin's imagination. During the late 19th century British consuls and merchants based in Trebizond, modern Trabzon, would have taken more than a passing interest in these 'Little Caucasus' that bordered the frontiers of Russia's ever-expanding empire. However, when HMG wound up its Turkish consulates after the Great War, they passed out of British consciousness. A solitary German Karl Koch crossed the range in 1843 but it was Willi Rickmer Rickmers (1873-1965) who undertook the first serious mountaineering exploration in 1894. (Awarded an RGS gold medal for his pioneer mountaineering expeditions to Central Asia and the Caucasus, Rickmers was elected to the Alpine Club in 1899, twice de-elected as an alien during the two world wars, and re-instated as an honorary member in 1958.)

During the inter-war years, Atatürk encouraged German scientific and mountaineering expeditions to Turkey as its former wartime ally. The Austrian explorer-scientist Dr Hans Bobek led one to the Kaçkar but left no traceable climbing records. After the Second World War, military and political constraints made travel in eastern Turkey extremely difficult though Denis Cecil Hills (1913-2004) was an exception to every rule.[2] From 1955 to 1962 he lived in Turkey as a peripatetic lecturer exploring its sites of antiquity and climbing its high mountains, mostly with Muzaffer, a Turkish Army sergeant who he converted to mountaineering. Hills invariably lived rough with shepherds and nomads. His last three years in Turkey were spent living near Trebizond allowed him to explore the Kaçkars: 'a botanist and climber's paradise'. In 1959 he and Muzaffer traversed the range from Ilica to Barhal, climbing the six summits of Altıparmak (3605m) en route. On his last visit in 1962, with the Byzantine scholar David Winfield, their attempt on the highest peak Kaçkar Dağı (3937m), was rebuffed by torrential rain. His book *My Travels in Turkey* (Allen & Unwin, 1964) is a classic.

Fedden and Hills had much in common save for their wartime experiences. Robin also preferred the company of like-minded friends. His Kaçkar expedition included Basil Goodfellow, Patrick Brunner and David Winfield as local expert and interpreter. Robin's two articles in *The Times* (30 and 31 August 1963) lyrically describe the range's Swiss-style chalets, its Lazi women dressed like peacocks, luxuriant forests of gigantic chestnuts, beech and alder, tracts of the native *Rhodendron ponticum* and the swathes of yellow azalea whose honey, harvested from barrel-shaped hives perched high in the treetops to frustrate marauding bears, once maddened both Xenophon's and Pompey's troops.

His nuanced assessment of the mountains as 'good second class peaks' might have been influenced by the 'curious and inconvenient' weather with incessant rain and snow and the insidious Black Sea mist that enveloped their campsites in 'a steady Scotch drizzle' to leave their tents dank and dripping and their sleeping bags perpetually sodden. Despite a misleading military map and magnetic rock that threw accurate compass bearings, they made first British ascents of Kaçkar Dağı and a spectacular neighbouring aiguille (3,450m).

In 1965, Robin set his sights on the Cilo and Sat massifs in Kurdish Hakkari. Tucked away in Turkey's south-east corner, Hakkari's mountains

2. Hills, a scholar at Lincoln College, Oxford, spoke six languages, served as a liaison officer with the Poles in World War Two, fought in North Africa, Iraq, Palestine and Italy and took part in the assault on Monte Cassino. In 1945, when Britain shamefully surrendered Ukrainians, Georgians and Cossacks to Stalin Hills saved many thousands from the cattle trucks and certain death. Hills was acclaimed by *The Spectator* as 'a hero of our times' for defying the Ugandan 'village tyrant' Idi Amin, having been sentenced to death. His daughter, Gillian Hills, had a hit aged 16 with the 'yé-yé' song 'Zou Bisou Bisou' and appeared in the films *Blowup* (1966) and *A Clockwork Orange* (1971).

Renée on the Meije. In her obituary of her friend Janet Adam Smith wrote: 'Many of my best days on the mountains were with the Feddens – weekends in North Wales, a summer in the Dauphiné when we shared a chalet at Villeneuve-la-Salle and took it in turns to stay with the children while the other two climbed.' *(Courtesy of Frances Fedden)*

are the most dramatic in the Middle East with fine alpine peaks and two sizeable glaciers. But the dark shadows of its violent history still lingered. Once a homeland of the Nestorian Christians, condemned as heretics at the Council of Ephesus in AD 431, Tamerlane had scattered them to the winds. They fled to the fastnesses of Hakkari only to find themselves in fractious proximity to Muslim Kurds who massacred most of them at the turn of the 20th century.

Unlike the Pontic Alps, Hakkari's mountains were known to 19th century British travellers. Their exploration had been exclusively British affair thanks to the government's consular posts maintained in eastern Turkey until 1914.[3] During the 1930s German-Austrian expeditions monopolised Turkish exploratory mountaineering, including one to Hakkari in 1937 led by the irrepressible Dr Hans Bobek in 1937. In 1956 and 1958 Austrian expeditions climbed all its major peaks with eight first ascents. In 1957 two Scots, Tom Weir and Douglas Scott, evaded officialdom to become the first Britons for 55 years to climb in the Cilo Dağı described by Weir as 'a paradise with superb mountaineering … the most rewarding in which I have

3. In 1897, Lt Col Maunsell climbed Galianu (3685m) in the Cilo group and narrowly failed on Resko (4170m). In 1899, Earl Percy, on his second Kurdistan mission to assess the strategic threats posed by Russia and Germany and investigate the plight of the Nestorians, traversed the Cilo Dag: *The Highlands of Asiatic Turkey*, Arnold, 1901. In 1909 British consul B Dickson explored the neighbouring Sat group.

Two views of Robin Fedden: photographed in the Alps and painted by Robert Buhler.

travelled' (*SMCJ*, 1958). In 1959 Denis Hills and Muzaffer undertook a month-long trek through Hakkari's mountains, just failing to summit Resko after several brushes with bears. Yet another German party gained access in 1962 and made the first ascent of Resko's formidable north face.

Hakkari was certainly not *terra incognita* yet remained a magnet for small-scale expeditions. Despite vicious guerrilla fighting on the Turkish-Iraqi border waged by Kurdish hero Mullah Mustafa Barzani against Iraqi armed forces, the opening of a major new road through eastern Turkey induced the government to relax travel restrictions to Hakkari: Robin resolved to go in 1965. He was invariably selective in choosing his companions and there was one Englishman long resident in Turkey who exactly fitted the bill: Sidney Nowill. A scion of the Levant's 19th century British mercantile dynasty, Sidney was born in Istanbul and educated at Rugby. At the outset of the Second World War he was working for British intelligence under the traitor Kim Philby, a man he 'cordially loathed'. Scholar, linguist, author, painter, photographer, economist, adviser to British envoys and Turkish politicians, gourmet, wine buff and compulsive traveller, Sidney was also a passionate mountaineer and long-established AC member with wide experience of Turkish ranges. He was also a fluent Turkish speaker.

Having previously climbed with Sidney in Turkey in 1961, I had suggested to him in early 1965 that we might visit Hakkari together. However, when he replied that he and his wife Hilary were already committed to join Robin Fedden's party of Renée, the Everest veteran Peter Lloyd and Robin McCall, I put aside Hakkari as another pipe dream. A Fedden-Nowill *équipe* should have been made in heaven but in late March Sidney wrote to say that it was a non-starter owing to start-date disagreements and because Peter Lloyd 'hates women on a party.' In fact, Renée was always going to come and Peter Lloyd was a happily married man. A more intractable issue was breakfast. Lloyd insisted on porridge, Nowill on grape nuts. A compromise should have been possible, particularly as Renée was acknowledged to be the best amateur cook in London. More likely, it was a clash of two idiosyncratic personalities.

Hakkari Resko (4133m), part of the Cilo Dağı massif in south-east Turkey. The Feddens' expedition there was Renée's favourite: 'the camps on the high pastures, the hospitable Kurdish nomads, the superb flowers, the splendid climbing in wild country.' *(John Harding)*

Having enlisted me as an eleventh-hour substitute, Sidney was determined to steal a march by starting out on 16 June, two weeks before Robin, to give us the advantages of better snow conditions and less oppressively hot weather in the valleys. In the event, Robin made the neighbouring Sat massif his first priority to do a new route on Hendevade (3800m) and two other respectable climbs. Moving on to the Cilo group, they climbed Resko, did an 'exhilarating' 700m rock route on its eastern spur and got to within 100m of Suppa-Durak's 4,060m summit. The Feddens' six routes (including three new ones) over a fortnight was more impressive than our one-week tally of a virgin aiguille on Resko's north-east glacier, Maunsell Peak (3870m) and Resko itself. At least that gave Sidney the satisfaction of Hilary just pipping Renée to a first female ascent by a few days.

In what proved to be the last decade of his life, Robin embarked on a flurry of expeditions. In 1970 he canoed down Turkey's longest river the Kızılırmak, in antiquity the Halys, which runs for over thirteen hundred kilometres from eastern Anatolia to the Black Sea. In 1971, he led an expedition to Peru's Cordillera Vilcabamba with Renée and an eclectic bunch of friends: André Choremi a Greek-Egyptian lawyer and anthropologist, Carl Nater a Swiss mountaineer, champion skier and manager of Cartier, Andrew Cavendish, 11th Duke of Devonshire and a passionate botanist, and Patrick Leigh Fermor, writer, scholar and Cretan resistance hero. Fedden wrote a brief factual report of the expedition in *AJ* 78 (1973) but its flavour is better captured in Leigh Fermor's *Three Letters from the Andes* (Murray, 1991).

Fedden and friends in the Andes in 1971. Renée to his left, the Duke of Devonshire behind and slightly to the right and Patrick Leigh Fermor on the right.
(Courtesy of Frances Fedden)

Robin's main object was to explore a little-known group of mountains in the Nevado Cara Cruz relying on inaccurate sketch maps and Prescott's *Conquest of Peru*. Sustenance for the unfamiliar and uncomfortable experiences the three unfledged mountaineers – Choremi, Cavendish and Leigh Fermor – were to encounter included 14 bottles of airport whisky decanted into transparent jerry cans for a morale-boosting evening tipple. Their 14-day trek through virtually uninhabited country with eight ponies and a couple of indigenous pack-drivers involved a succession of laborious ascents and perilous descents through near-impenetrable jungle, across fast-flowing rivers, camps above the snow line at 14,500ft and the use of ropes and crampons. The mountaineers traversed the three summits of Cara Cruz, including the highest at over 5,100m but their brave attempt on Huayanay IV (5484m) was rebuffed 30m from the summit by waist-deep, avalanche-prone powder snow. Renée cooked 'miraculous' meals while Robin's 'quiet, imperturbable competence in the management of the whole undertaking with comedy and charm' made their trip 'nothing but concord and enjoyment … enhanced by a snowballing mythology of private jokes.'

In the following year of 1972, Robin's long attachment to Greece made it an obvious objective both for him and Renée and also Patrick Leigh Fermor, now resident in the Peleponnese. Grecian mountains may not vie with the Alps but four-fifths of this 'gift of the sun and sea' is mountainous, sparsely populated and altogether wilder. British Victorian mountaineers scoffed at their pretensions but Edward Lear who well knew both the Alps and Corsica and had once painted Kangchenjunga from Darjeeling held the beauty of

Greece's mountains above all others. And although Greece had been overlooked by British mountaineers, in spring 1963 John Hunt, a long-time devotee, made the first recorded south to north 160-mile traverse of the Pindus range with an international party that included Tony Streather, George Lowe and John Disley.

Below the dramatic wall of Huayanay in Peru's Cordillera Vilcabamba. *(Courtesy of Frances Fedden)*

The northern Pindus fall within Epirus, Greece's most atypical and scenic province, rich in classical sites and historical interest. The setting of Byron's *Childe Harold's Pilgrimage* and the subject of Leigh Fermor's travelogue *Roumeli*, it offered Robin serious rock climbing comparable to classic Dolomite routes on the sheer, castellated limestone wall of the Tymfi massif whose northern scarp presents the grandest mountain panorama in all Greece. That June, Robin, Renée, Peter McCall and three members of the Andean expedition, Carl Nater, Andrew Cavendish and Paddy Leigh Fermor, plus a guide, foregathered at Konitza before trekking up the Aoos gorge to attain the recently-built Greek Alpine Club refuge on the Astraka Col. From here, the Feddens and Nater climbed a virgin line up the impeccable limestone of Astraka's (2436m) north-west face. It was Robin's last serious rock climb and with honour satisfied, the whole party reversed much of John Hunt's 1963 Pindus trek. Their journey through largely untrammelled country with its deserted villages, vertiginous gorges, rushing waterfalls, sites of antiquity and monasteries is extravagantly described by Leigh Fermor in his letters to Deborah Devonshire, published *In Tearing Haste*, Murray, 2008: a mountain venture of 20 days, spiced with fun, humour and camaraderie and one of Robin's happiest.

Robin was not yet done. In March 1974 he returned to his beloved Pyrenees with the object of traversing on ski the ground occupied by virtually all the 3,000m peaks from Andorra to the Col de Somport. The first complete ski traverse of the Pyrenees from Canigou to Arette Pierre St. Martin had only been achieved six years earlier in 1968 by the Frenchman Charles Laporte in 34 stages. Robin's was still an ambitious undertaking on account of the range's often foul weather and the fact that few Britons had ever ski toured there. Fifteen separate stages were originally planned involving two separate parties with a support team providing motorised transport to take the skiers

Patrick Leigh Fermor, pictured smoking in his tent, praised Fedden's 'quiet, imperturbable competence', pictured here with Renée at base camp. Their attempt on Huayanay IV ended just short of the summit. *(Courtesy of Frances Fedden)*

to and from the snowline and provision the huts. Typically bad Pyrenean weather frustrated the first, Spanish section and only four of the eight stages were completed. The traverse was recommenced at Espot and after finishing at Gavarnie they were transported to the Pont d'Espagne above Cauterets to complete the next seven stages to the Col du Somport in perfect weather. Now aged 65, Robin's Pyrenean traverse was a remarkable achievement for a man already suffering from deteriorating health. Save for a visit to

Fedden on his final expedition in 1976 at the head of the Kulu valley.
(Courtesy of Frances Fedden)

Kulu and Lahul with Peter Lloyd in 1976, it was to be his mountaineering valediction. He died a year later on 30 March 1977.

Robin Fedden will best be remembered for his 30 years' service with the National Trust preserving a score of historic houses for public enlightenment and enjoyment: a task well suited to his love of tradition and impeccable taste. His powers of evocation and finely tuned ear for language produced writing that elevated him to first rank of English prose-poets. He was an expert and exemplary ski mountaineer and a mountaineer whose originality, enthusiasm and determination, combined with empathy and humanity, won him the admiration and loyalty of all who knew him: a brilliant light extinguished before its time.

• The editor thanks Robin Fedden's daughter Frances Fedden for her help in illustrating this article.

DENNIS GRAY

The Villain

Memories of Don Whillans

Pajama people. Don Whillans ready for bed in the Everest icefall in 1972. *(Doug Scott)*

Better be a piece of broken jade than unbroken tile.

Chinese proverb

A filmmaker contacted me recently with news that a production company were planning to make a film about the life of Don Whillans. What did I think about this? I told him I thought that if it was to be honest and truthful, it would probably need to be what we used to call X-rated. His soubriquet 'The Villain' was not inaccurate. On occasion his aggression was frightening to behold. There were happenings that from my understanding of psychology

A young Don Whillans with Harry Smith. *(Dennis Gray)*

would have labelled him a sociopath. But let us be clear. He was without doubt one of the outstanding mountaineers and rock climbers of any era. When the editor of a continental magazine got in touch, asking me who I thought were the three most memorable British climbers in the history of our sport, I had to admit that Whillans was one of them. It is, with hindsight, a surprising fact that Don and Joe Brown began climbing within a few years of one another and were active together.

I first met him in 1951 when I was 15 years old and he was 17. I was going slowly down the Llanberis track, having just made my first climb on Clogwyn Du'r Arddu with Jack Bloor. I was carrying all our equipment and spare clothes because Jack had gone off on a training spin. He was an outstanding runner, having won the Festival of Britain road race, and a few years later the Three Peaks challenge in Yorkshire, which he established with Arthur Dolphin[1].

As I drew level with Whillans he spat out an 'Ah doo'. He was only as big as I was then, 5ft 3in, but he was twice as broad in the shoulders and he had the angular face and quiff that became his hallmark in early press photographs. I hadn't understood his greeting so he spat out another 'Ah doo'. He looked so aggressive that I stammered 'Hullo' and scuttled off down the track, chased by a shout of 'Bloody stuck up!' from Whillans.

I next met him the following Easter on a Rock and Ice bus trip to Glencoe. I found myself sitting next to him and he didn't let me forget how I had reacted on our first meeting; I was subjected to a flow of acerbic comment the like of which I had not then experienced. Don had a language that was all his own, finessed over the years. If you were easily put off you were 'a drink of water', if you confessed to finding a route hard you were 'a ta-ta',

1. After Bloor's death in 1984, a memorial fund and races were established in his honour in support of young Yorkshire outdoor athletes. See: *jackbloor.co.uk*

The Rock and Ice in Chamonix, 1954. Sitting: Joe Brown, Fred Ashton, Nat Allen, Ron Moseley. Back row: Unknown, Ray Greenall, Don Whillans.

if you advised him a climb was not in good condition you were 'a ninnie', but the biggest put down was if you were 'a little hill man', applied to an individual or generally meant for all and sundry in the climbing world he might be annoyed at.

The climbing partnership he enjoyed with Brown famously began in the spring of 1951. Don was paying his first visit to the Roaches in Staffordshire and wandered by chance into a first ascent on the Lower Tier. Joe had led a crack that was repelling his second. Whillans volunteered to try. He tied on and without too much difficulty reached the ledge where the leader was belayed. He then expressed a wish to try the next pitch and Joe agreed. With a struggle Don managed it. The route was called *Matinee* because a crowd gathered to watch the action.

Brown was impressed that this youngster who had only been climbing a matter of months could lead what was near the top standard of that period, a pitch that was then badly protected. It was in those days generally believed that one had to work up through the grades, build one's experience before attempting extreme climbs. Whillans, like Brown, was a contradiction to that belief. They both climbed difficult routes soon after starting.

Matinee was the beginning of a partnership that lasted for several years, one of the strongest in the history of British climbing. The media loved

Whillans in Chamonix in 1959 with Les Brown, Robin Smith, Gunn Clark and John Streetly. Smith and Clark had just beaten the others and photographer Hamish MacInnes to the first British ascent of the Walker Spur. *(Hamish MacInnes)*

these two working-class heroes; they fitted the belief that society was changing and becoming more egalitarian. Brown became known as the Human Fly while a Stockport newspaper wrote how 'Whillans moved up hold-less slabs balancing like a fairy.' He let it be known that if the journalist referred to him as such again 'he would deal with him.' In later years he was more content to be referred to as the Andy Capp of the climbing world.

I kept in touch with the Rock and Ice after that bus trip to Glencoe, particularly Ron Moseley. He sent me details of routes Whillans had pioneered on limestone at Stoney Middleton and Pickering Tors in Dovedale, both in the Peak District. In the spring of 1953, John Ramsden and I travelled by train, bus and foot to Stoney, where I led *Frisco Bay* and repeated some other routes Don had put up but we had no other names and even pioneered a route of our own, *Little Capucin*. How we then travelled to Dovedale I don't know but despite many attempts both Ram and I failed on the route across the roof of the cave at Pickering Tors.[2]

When I was posted to Manchester for national service in February 1954, I climbed mainly with Joe, Ron Moseley, Ray Greenall, Joe Smith and other members of the Rock and Ice but Whillans not so often. He worked Saturday mornings and so much of his activity was confined to outcrops he could reach after his work finished that day. He was a plumber and proud of that fact. I remember how he reacted when Joe was also referred to as a plumber

2. Pickering's Overhang (E1 5b) appears in many guidebooks as a Joe Brown route. The author recalls it as one of Don's.

Chris Bonington and Don Whillans Eiger-bound in 1962. Bonington's ascent with Ian Clough later that year caused tension between them.

in a media profile. 'Nat Allen and I are plumbers,' he spat. 'Joe is a bleedin' property repairer.' It was obvious that he thought this inferior.

I did visit Cratcliffe and Froggatt with Don. After a route on Froggatt Pinnacle he simply jumped off the top, across the gap and onto the hillside opposite. Until a motorcycle accident in 1961, when he badly injured a kneecap, he was impressive at this sort of leaping. I was once at Curbar with him leading Eric Beard up Joe's route *Short Slab*, quite a bold HVS, and he soloed up behind wearing boots. Beardie found the route hard and was telling Don so as they arrived together.

'You can easily jump down this route,' Don replied and without hesitating he turned round and ran back down the slab.

On another day's climbing I asked him why he hadn't done national service. 'Because I failed the medical,' was all he would say. At the time I found that unbelievable. At that time I thought him physically an outstanding figure and at the time I was mixing with some of the best athletes in the country. One of our Manchester athletics team had just managed a four-minute mile. It might surprise some that in these early years Don neither smoked nor drank much alcohol, preferring to stay in the barn or his tent and listen to a small radio whilst other members of the club visited the pub. So I assumed his answer was a joke. But I found out eventually that Whillans suffered from a rare kind of vertigo that had hospitalised him previously and that was why he had failed his medical.

Don was fortunate there were climbers in the Rock and Ice who had Alpine experience. In 1952 he visited Chamonix with Don Cowan and Nat Allen. Under their tuition he learnt the basics of alpinism. On a visit limited in time by work commitments they managed three classic routes on the Aiguilles, including the Mer de Glace face of the Grépon, and from these beginnings his motivation grew. When the Alpine Climbing Group (ACG) was formed in the spring of 1953 Whillans, Cowan and Allen were invited to be founding members. At a later date I was its secretary and Don was one of its keenest supporters but when it formed Joe had not even visited the Alps.

This changed in the summer of 1953, when Cowan, Allen, Don and Joe visited the Alps together. They had an epic on the Crocodile. The climb went well but on descent a sequence of accidents led to a cut rope and Joe falling in his crampons onto Whillans. Don suffered a punctured backside

Cigarettes, alcohol and motorcycles all took their toll on Whillans. Here he is enjoying all three on the summit of Ben Nevis, a publicity stunt for Triumph.

while Don Cowan burnt his hands holding the fall. They retreated back to the Biolay campsite to lick their wounds.

Flicking through the guidebook, Joe discovered that the *Fissure Fix* on the west face of the Blatière was the hardest pitch in the range. But then they met up with Geoff Sutton and Bob Downes from the Cambridge University Mountaineering Club. At that date Sutton probably had the best knowledge of the Aiguilles of any British climber. He told them that a huge rock fall had erased the route on the Blatière, which was ripe as a new route. They set off at the first opportunity, Brown climbing with Cowan and Whillans with Sutton. It was on this first attempt that Joe led the Fissure Brown, a crack that came to be acknowledged as the hardest pitch in the Western Alps. Joe reported it as being no harder than some of the gritstone cracks he had already climbed but I am not so certain of that.

This first attempt was stopped by bad weather after a bivouac on ledges higher up but they were back in Chamonix the following year, and after an abortive attempt on the east face of the Capucin, held up by the weather and a slow party ahead of them, Brown and Whillans wrote their name large in the history of alpinism with a repeat of the west face of the Petit Dru, the third ascent in the fastest time, and by completing their first ascent of the west face of the Blatière. Higher on the route, Whillans led a crack which became the second crux, overcome by a fierce layback.

Whillans saw these successes as the way forward for him becoming a fulltime climbing bum. There was no doubt that with longer periods in the Alps many routes would be within his compass and over the following decade the number of ascents he made mark him out as the leading British alpinist. He was still pioneering in Britain and though at times he was difficult to be with socially, once on a climb or an outcrop one could not wish for a more concerned companion.

I climbed a lot with him in the latter years of the 1950s. I was with him when he made the first ascent of *Cave Wall* on Froggatt Edge and I made the second ascent of *Goliath*, his infamous crack climb on Burbage. He wanted me to tell him if I thought it was hard and worth recording. Currently graded E4, it was obviously one of the hardest routes of that era and among the first of that grade in the world. Don coached me up *Left Eliminate* on Curbar, when I had a blank on the route, although I had already led *Peapod* and the harder *Right Eliminate*, although I had to be rescued on the former when my right boot became immovably stuck in the narrowing crack. He soloed it to show me how it was done and talked me up it after him.

I also climbed with him in the Mont Blanc range and the Dolomites. The hardest route we did together was the east face of the Grand Capucin and although we had no difficulty on the ascent, during the descent a forced bivouac in a storm tested us utterly.

After that summer's Alpine season, we had a Rock and Ice meet at my parents' home in Woodhouse, Leeds. We climbed at Ilkley, Crookrise and Almscliff. My father and Whillans began a surprising friendship that lasted until my father's death. He was in the entertainment industry almost all his life and Don accompanied him on some of his club and theatre dates around the north of the country. It was noticeable, from this time on, that Don became more polished with the one-liners for which he became famous in the climbing world.

In 1957 Don made his first visit to the Himalaya as a member of the Masherbrum expedition led by Joe Walmsley. In retrospect this had a real effect on his future physical wellbeing: travelling to Pakistan by sea took several weeks and during the voyage he started drinking and smoking. Beer was a shilling a pint and he won a raffle prize of a thousand cigarettes and by the time he had smoked them he was hooked. I know from personal experience how hedonistic such sailings to the subcontinent could be, having done so two occasions. There is little to do on such journeys except eat, drink and make merry.

The attempt on Masherbrum was tragically derailed when Bob Downes was taken ill with altitude sickness and died. This had a great affect on Don. He had become close friends with Bob: together they had pioneered the route *Centurion* on Ben Nevis. After Downes' death, Don made a last attempt with Joe Walmsley backing him up, but he had to admit defeat despite being close to the summit.

From then on the Himalaya held him in thrall. Don took part in the Trivor expedition of 1960 and drove back to Lancashire on his motorbike at

Don in the Karakoram in 1983, an éminence grise on Doug Scott's freewheeling team that included, from left to right, Steve Sustad, Alan Rouse, Greg Child and Beth Acres.

its conclusion. Then there was the Gauri Sankar attempt in 1964, which I organised. This expedition was full of incident as we drove from Leeds to Kathmandu. We almost succeeded but I have already written about this elsewhere.[3] I think Whillans' outstanding ascents in the 1960s were his two climbs in Patagonia: the Aiguille de Poincenot in 1961 on an Irish expedition and in 1963 the Central Tower of Paine with Chris Bonington.

Don and Joe were as different as chalk and cheese. Brown is best described as calm and sanguine; Whillans in a temper was frightening. He never threatened me but I saw enough of him when riled and out of control to know not to get involved. On one occasion Morty Smith challenged Joe Brown to a wrestle-cum-fight but included me in his plans. Initially I refused but Joe agreed believing he could handle us both, having grown up on the mean streets of Manchester where he was used to dealing with heavies. Morty and I had a plan: he would take the Baron head-on whilst I crept up behind him and put a stranglehold on his neck. This worked a treat and we nearly killed him and I was so sorry to have taken part, but when he recovered Joe was full of admiration.

'You clever little bleeders,' he observed. Then I realised Whillans was making ready to join in and he came at us! I turned round and started to run but he was after me. Fortunately I was still in training and he couldn't catch me but as I went off up the road towards the Llanberis Pass he shouted after me: 'You're a bloody slippery Jim!' And that's what he called me from thereon.

I saw Don in several confrontations over the years but none as frightening as the night he picked a fight with some members of Sheffield Hell's Angels.

3. D Gray, *Rope Boy*, Victor Gollancz, London, 1970. See also I Clough, 'Gauri Sankar, 1964', *Alpine Journal* 1965, pp96-105.

Whillans in puckish form on Everest in 1971. *(John Cleare)*

This was one winter's night in the Little John pub in Hathersage; they were annoying him as he was sat near the door and every time one of them came through having been to the bar he felt a cold draft. Even so, I was amazed when Whillans stood up and hit one of them with the swinging door as he came through carrying a tray of drinks. The angel went down. Whillans swung round and grabbed a bar stool before fending off the rest of them while his wife Audrey, Morty and I ran outside to my van. I revved the engine and as we pulled away Don came running out and dived in the back.

Unlike Brown, Whillans was a sports player; at school he took part in gymnastics, boxing and rugby, and he was keen to participate in the games sessions of the Rock and Ice. When we played barn rugby he played no holds barred. There was a particularly bloody session in the Wasdale barn in 1960, when the young Doug Scott and Dez Hadlum, both playing for rugby clubs back in Nottingham, also took part. I used to make sure I was on Don's team, even though he was not the strongest physically amongst club members. Morty could do one-arm pull-ups on either hand.

Whillans' other big interest was darts but despite cheating (he used to fiddle his score) he could never beat Eric Beard, who was once in a competition for the best players in the country. A youth spent in the back-to-backs of Leeds 6 had its compensations. When I lived in Derby, Nat Allen, his wife Tinsel and I visited Audrey and Don at their cottage in Crawshaw Booth, Lancashire. Whillans had been sent there during the war as an evacuee and had happy memories of the area. Though the accommodation was Spartan, Audrey was almost saint-like. How she put up with Don and his tempestuous character I never understood but her welcome could not have been warmer. She had married him in 1958 after a long courtship, so she must have well known what their life together would be like.

Crawshaw Booth is near Bridestones, the grit outcrop known to locals as the Kebs; Whillans had pioneered many problems there. I managed *Duck*, which made me quack, and the *Whillans' Jam*, but I failed hopelessly on *The Villain*. Don was offering to buy anyone who could repeat it a pint, which was impressive because he was a notorious tightwad but it was a few years before he had to pay up.

My keenest memory of this visit to Crawshaw Booth was waking up with the Whillans cat licking my face as I lay in my sleeping bag on the floor of the cottage. He was trying to make a living around this time as a freelance lecturer and later as an equipment designer. I suppose in both cases he was eventually successful, for his lectures were hard-core and humorous, and appealed to the climbing fraternity. Some of his designs, including a rucksack, the world's first sit harness and his 'Whillans Box' to replace a tent on expeditions were successes. Others, such as the 'Whammer', were not.

We had one of the first designs of the Whillans Box on Gauri Sankar in 1964. It weighed over 70lb. Carrying it up the 'Little Eiger' and traversing across the north face to put it into an ice cave we had dug completely banjaxed me. Later, Don was to act as consultant to a specialist clothing firm who were trying to develop a range of outdoor clothing. This was aimed at a general market, particularly the golfing and motoring community. For a while Whillans was to be found at the Open or Silverstone but I'm afraid the jackets, while looking attractive, enjoyed limited success.

When I arrived back in Liverpool by sea in January 1965, Whillans and Terry Burnell were onshore to greet me; they had come for their personal gear from the Gauri Sankar expedition.

'You picked a good one there,' Don told me. 'What's next?'

'The south face of Annapurna I,' I laughed and showed him a picture of the face Jimmy Roberts had given me before I left Kathmandu. I discussed the objective with Nepal's foreign minister and he promised they would give us permission to attempt it. We started to plan for the face but the film *Raid into Tibet* was released, causing Nepal to be closed to expeditions for the next few years.

In early 1969 Chris Bonington contacted me as Nepal had opened again and Nick Estcourt, Martin Boysen and he were keen to try Menlungste. Did I think they would get permission for this? I thought not at the time but that the south face of Annapurna I was a possibility. I sent him the photograph of the face Jimmy had given me. I had just married and there was no way I could participate, especially with the organisation. I was more than pleased when Don and Dougal Haston were successful in 1970 but so sad at the death of Ian Clough, one of our Gauri Sankar party and one of my oldest friends.

Don was a member of the 1971 international Everest expedition to the south-west face organised by Norman Dyhrenfurth and the 1972 European expedition led by Karl Herrligkoffer to the same objective. On both Whillans performed well and reached some of the highest altitudes then reached on this objective, but both attempts were rife with dissension and argument. Though replete with stars of the climbing world those stars did not gel. These three expeditions were the apogee of Whillans' Himalayan career and it led to his appearance on the prime-time show *This Is Your Life*. As is wont with these things, the fame was short-lived.

In 1973 I persuaded Whillans to join me at the Leeds University climbing wall, then the most famous such facility in the country. By today's standards it was basic but it was probably the first wall that illustrated what could be achieved with an improved level of fitness specific to rock climbing. Don was unimpressed, however, and couldn't be persuaded to try any of the problems I showed him so we retreated to the Fenton, a nearby pub.

'There is no bloody adventure on climbing walls,' he pronounced over a succession of pints. I wonder what he would say now that there are over 400 walls in the UK and that most newcomers coming into the sport begin their climbing lives in such centres.

When I was at the British Mountaineering Council, I involved Don several times in national events to which the BMC was invited. One was a reception at Manor House in London. The guest of honour was the Duke of Edinburgh. He worked the crowd with an entourage of hangers-on, weaving his way around and eventually arrived at Don and me. He knew vaguely who I was; I was a member of a committee he chaired occasionally. Don, not so much.

'May I introduce Don Whillans, sir, one of our council's most famed members.'

The Duke looked at Don but was a bit taken aback when Whillans, in full Andy Capp rig, came out with his usual 'Ah doo,' and then held out his hand. The Duke's entourage looked on in obvious disapproval but were surprised when their charge grasped the Villain's hand in return.

Even more memorable was our meeting with Margaret Thatcher, when she was leader of the opposition. She wished to meet representatives of national bodies of sport. I won't repeat what happened; it's well known and involves birds and nests. The American climber Jim Donini was puzzled to learn that Whillans, an icon of the working class, was a keen supporter of Mrs Thatcher. I observe from this that as soon as somebody like Don breaks the boundaries of their origin, they often behave thus. As Shakespeare noted, 'He then unto the ladder turns his back.'

Towards the end of 1974, with the approval of the executive of the BMC, I put the names of both Joe and Don to the honours committee for recognition, in view of the great contribution they had made to British mountaineering. This seemed to be proceeding well until Whillans was involved in an outrageous incident that made the national news. ('The day Tiger Whillans took on the law', was the headline in the *Daily Mail*.) In the early hours at the end of March 1975, after a drinking session in the Woolpack, the police stopped Don for speeding and driving erratically. This led to a physical confrontation and Don assaulted the policemen who promptly called for back up. Five police were eventually required to subdue and handcuff Whillans and push him into the back seat of a panda car. Even then Don didn't give up until two of the coppers sat on him.

When the case came to court in Rawtenstall, the only excuse the defence could offer for Don's behaviour was that Audrey had been ill at the time and was in hospital. He was fined a considerable sum and banned from driving for two years. In retrospect he was lucky. If this happened today he might have received a period in custody. In the aftermath, a lady from the honours committee phoned.

'Is this Mr Whillans appearing in the press for his misbehaviour the person your council has put forward for an honour?'

'I'm sorry, yes he is.'

'Oh goodness, we can't have such a person receiving an honour.'

When the birthday list was announced later that year, Joe received the MBE but Don was omitted.

In 1976 Audrey and Don left Rossendale for Penmaenmawr in north Wales and opened a guesthouse. I visited them there and was surprised to find Whillans had become keen on tropical fish with a large tank in one of the rooms. Over the next few years he went on many trips: to Yosemite, to Tirich Mir in the Hindu Kush, on a Doug Scott expedition to Shivling, to Patagonia again, and the jungles of Venezuela with a face climb on Roraima, to Huandoy Sur in Peru with a Scottish party, and sailing down the Amazon with Dave Bathgate at the expedition's conclusion. He was on Broad Peak, again with Doug Scott, when tragedy struck and Pete Thexton died of pulmonary oedema, but his days as the lead climber on prestigious expeditions were clearly at an end. Not everyone was willing to include him, for not everyone was willing to put up with his self-serving attitude.

He found solace in other activities. He and Audrey visited the Red Sea to try scuba diving, and he made a parachute jump, declaring he fell like a meat safe. He spent much of his time visiting old friends: John Streetly in the West Indies, Ronnie Wathen in Spain. But the nonstop heavy drinking and smoking was catching up with him. In girth he looked more like a Sumo wrestler than a mountaineer. One of his last climbs was with Joe Brown, an anniversary ascent for television of their outstanding route on Dinas Cromlech, *Cemetery Gates*. It was sad to see how unfit he was and how he struggled compared to Joe, who was still climbing well.

In 1984, Don was the guest of honour at the National Mountaineering Conference. These events dated from my early days at the BMC. Faced with financial constraints and the competing need to make the BMC more relevant to the mainstream climbing community, these gatherings, held at the Buxton Conference Centre, were a success from the start. The main event was the lecture on Saturday evening, given by someone universally acknowledged in the climbing world: Diemberger, Heckmair, Bonatti and so on.

Don certainly lived up to the occasion. His lecture got off to a good start when a streaker ran across the stage, allowing Don to make one of his most famous one-liners.

'Well I'll be buggered.' (Pause.) 'And so will he if I can catch him!' A full house roared its appreciation.

Earlier on the Saturday we organised a cabaret. That year half a dozen of us dressed up in drag to satirise the Miss World competition, with a jury of women climbers chaired by Rosie Smith of *Mountain* magazine. This was won by Donna Whillans, who, when asked, declared her ambition was 'to

Street fighting man. John Cleare's portrait of Don Whillans at Heptonstall. *(John Cleare)*

become a fat, hairy climber!' All this done to raise funds for the purchase of the Alex MacIntyre hut at Onich.

In his last years Don was back working as an emergency plumber in the Manchester area. So when we had a water leak in our toilets at the BMC I phoned him. He arrived on his motorbike and I could see at once he had been in some kind of confrontation. His leather coat was torn and his face bloody. 'What on earth has happened to you?'

'I was knocked off my bike by a car.'

'Crikey, are you okay?'

'I got up off the road and chased after them, overtook the car and stopped in front of it. They had either to stop or run me down!'

'Bloody hell Don, it sounds like the Dukes of Hazard.'

'The driver got out of the car and I flattened him but none of the others. There were three of them in there but they wound the windows tight and I couldn't get at them. But I had my boots on, so I kicked hell out of their car. Then I drove off.' Don was over 50 and you would have thought past such escapades.

'Nothing has changed, has it Don?'

'You're bloody right Slippery Jim,' he replied.

That summer of 1985 he rode to the Dolomites on his motorbike. At Alleghe he ran into old friends Derek Walker and Roger Salisbury, but the latter noted how unfit and slow he was. Most of the time Dan sat around sun bathing and drinking. With nothing to do but talk about the old days, it wasn't a long trip. His drive home was plagued by heavy rain and he stopped off in Oxford, wet and dispirited, at the house of old friend Derek Bromhall. After a welcoming meal and a few beers he went to bed and simply didn't wake up, having suffered a major heart attack. He was 52. Don's funeral at Bangor crematorium drew hundreds of climbers from all over the country. I gave the oration and concluded that his was a unique character, difficult to assay but unforgettable.

His friends felt there should be some kind of memorial and the original proposal was a campsite in Chamonix. Derek Walker and I met with local officials there but the only offer was a site with avalanche warnings for winter and spring use. Talking with Audrey, we settled on a hut at one of the main climbing areas in Britain. Fundraising began, under the leadership of Derek. My contribution was to organise a Don Whillans memorial evening at the Free Trade Hall in Manchester. Doug Scott, Nat Allen, Joe Brown and Chris Bonington spoke of their climbs and memories of Don. Printer friends of mine wanted to help, producing leaflets for us, free of charge: 'Buy a Pint for Don!'

Derek and the other members of the committee raised a total of £50,000. Rock Hall Cottage at the Roaches came up for sale, and with extra funding from the Sports Council and other bodies, and a volunteer management scheme run by the BMC, the Don Whillans hut was secured. The Roaches seemed more than appropriate: the crag where he met Joe and where he did *The Sloth*, one of his finest new routes. The Roaches was also where Don met Audrey. She opened the hut at a ceremony in 1993.

JOHN C WILKINSON

The Aiguilles du Diable in Winter

A Complementary Account

The Aiguilles du Diable, the Devil's Needles: the traumatic first winter ascent left a trail of cruel injury and bitter recrimination. *(John Wilkinson)*

My interest in the drama surrounding the first winter ascent of the Diable ridge (see Eric Vola's 'The Devil's Needles', *AJ* 2022, pp176-93) stemmed in part from the fact that while still a beginner I had an intensive month's climbing with Christian Mollier in 1965 during leave from the oil company I worked for in Oman. One of the great routes we did, with his friend Marc Martinetti and client, was the Diable. Marc was tragically killed with Lionel Terray in the Vercors the following September. But my main interest arose while translating my wife Anne Sauvy's book *Secours en Montagne* (Arthaud 1998). In chapter XV, she discussed rescue cases that led to litigation and referred to the Diable winter ascent. Typically, Ken Wilson immediately wanted to know all about it, as he'd found no references in English sources. So I dug around and my account was published as appendix III of the English translation, *Mountain Rescue Chamonix-Mont Blanc* (Bâton Wicks 2005).

By now I was intrigued by anomalies and inconsistencies in the various accounts and these I continued to pursue (see sources in next section, 'The Climb'). The story is, inevitably, a great deal more complicated than Eric Vola's account. Written, appropriately perhaps, in the dramatic present, Vola's version is based on three cited sources, for Raymond Lambert the *Bulletin du Club Alpin Suisse* 1939 and the section in Lambert *À l'assaut des 'quatre mille'* (1953). (Note that this latter source is the version augmented with Lambert's account of Everest. The original *À l'assaut des Quatre Mille*, published in 1946 by Editions de la Frégate, was a collection of 10 accounts recorded by Claude Varennes from Lambert. Of itself it adds nothing new, but it did give a wider circulation of Lambert's account at a time when controversy with Marcel Gallay was once again flaring up.)

For Gallay, Vola's account is solely that of 1940, *Une tragique aventure au Mont-Blanc*, a work that was supplemented in a second publication the same year with his *Étude médicale sur mes congélations*. He does not reference subsequent Gallay publications; not surprisingly as some were published during the war when Swiss affairs were not to the fore in most people's minds. However, Vola also overlooks some pre-war accounts of relevance, notably that submitted to the *Annales* of the GHM (June 1938, pp221-2) by Robert Gréloz, one of the Genevans equally involved in the rescue. That shows that one way and another some 50 people were concerned in the rescue operations during the horrendous conditions that prevailed.

In Vola's 'Aftermath' there is nothing recorded of the bitter recriminations about responsibility between the three main protagonists, let alone mention of two court cases, ending with a libel settlement in 1964. Lambert, who nearly summits Everest on the stubs of his frostbitten feet is, perhaps understandably, his hero, while poor Gallay's bitterness is satisfactorily directed at Mme Amstutz, Erica's mother, a sort of Queen of the Night figure, the only baddie of the scenario. Even so, in the accounts that are cited, there are inconsistencies that might raise questions for the inquiring mind: sleeping bags, for example, a vital element that played an essential part in determining the degree of frostbite affecting our three protagonists.

More surprising is the question he poses at the end of his 'Aftermath': 'Considering the extreme weather conditions, why did Chamonix guides agree to a rescue party?' He goes on with a veiled hint at their failure to respond to the winter tragedy that befell Vincendon and Henry. True, attempts to answer his own question may have valid elements, yet the blindingly obvious he does not see. The extreme costs paid in terms of financial loss, amputations, including some guides losing the ability to pursue their professional livelihood, meant that they had learnt a bitter lesson. They were not prepared to get involved again in further foolhardy ventures in winter conditions

Christian Mollier climbing L'Isolée in 1965. *(John Wilkinson)*

18 years later. That refusal in turn played a major part in reorganising the system for rescue in Chamonix, ultimately the responsibility of the PGHM, as my late wife describes in her 1998 book.

So it is, that for some 20 years I have sat on the results of my research, hesitating whether to publish or not. My prevailing sentiment was that of the editor of GHM *Annales* concerning Gréloz's 1938 report: 'This terrible ascent makes any comment inappropriate, except to pay tribute to the unfailing courage displayed by all in this drama.' So I let sleeping dogs lie. But now Vola's publication has made it imperative that this should not be the final record in a publication so influential as the *AJ*. This 'Complementary Account' is necessary to fill in some gaps and context in his account, but above all to explain the subsequent history of bitter relations that developed between the three main protagonists, however unpleasant. None comes out clean. That is the real tragedy of the first winter ascent of the Diable arête.

The Climb

First, it may be useful to remind the reader in a brief summary from my own notes of the climb described more fully by Eric Vola. The rescue is dealt with in a separate section based essentially on Gréloz (1938) and information from Christian Mollier of the report as recorded by the Compagnie des Guides de Chamonix. On the first day, 7 February, the three climbers reach the Requin hut. On day two they reach the Borgna hut, the original at the Col de la Fourche. Next day, day three, they start the route, missing out the Corne du Diable and aiming straight for the Chaubert. The climbing goes well, the Chaubert followed by the Médiane, the only mishap being snowshoes torn off a sack. Their first bivy is a good site 10m below the summit of Médiane. At midnight the weather suddenly changes and the real trouble starts.

On day four, the problem lies in the abseil descent from Carmen to the brèche and up the other side. Gallay belays from the bivy site and protects Stagni who can help belay Lambert during these complicated manoeuvres. Sacks are hauled across a Tyrolean and one smashes into the wall: they lose all their provisions. Bypassing the Isolée they follow the ridge of the Tacul.

There, on the Chamonix side, they are hit by the full blast of the storm. They endure a terrible second bivy on the lee side, just below the east summit of Tacul (4247m). The following day, they find it impossible to descend from Tacul to Col du Midi so instead turn towards Col Maudit in a blizzard and total whiteout. Stumbling across a hole, which opens into a sort of horizontal crevasse, they improve the site and settle there. Having not eaten for two days, all they have is a bit of chocolate, three dried fruits and a Maggi powder soup plus some aspirin tablets. They bivy again, licking ice, cut up leather of a shoe to chew etc. On day six, after their third bivy, they endure more suffering, try and burn shavings off an ice axe, drink urine and endure a fourth bivouac. Lambert dubs the crevasse 'the hotel of slow death'.

On day seven there's a ray of sun and an exit. Here a degree of detail is necessary to understand subsequent accounts. In Vola's reconstruction it runs as follows. In the morning Gallay punches a large hole in the door they had blocked off with snow and ice when they first arrived and sees the sun. After digging themselves out with considerable effort they realise they are on a precipitous spot near Col Maudit, but the wind conditions are such they retire back inside. Their eventual stumbling attempt to reach the col is a failure. Back in the crevasse their attempt to enlarge it results in part of the ceiling collapsing, letting in the intense cold. They are sure that by now their Genevan friends must be looking for them. Lambert realises the only hope is for him to go down on his own. For the subsequent period until the rescue, the accounts of the wait in the crevasse by Gallay and Stagni are to be treated with reserve (see 'Discrepancies' below). What we do know is that when Charlet's team rescued Stagni, she was found wrapped in a sleeping bag, alone and naked. The horrors of that third terrible day and night in the crevasse – the fifth bivy – with everything sodden and soaked through, freezing in the bitter cold and Gallay unable to get his boots back on speak for themselves, whatever the accuracy of the accounts.

Nor is it necessary to detail Lambert's adventures on the descent, which clearly demonstrate all his best qualities. Starting off on the wrong side in bad visibility (the north side, i.e. towards the Grands Mulets) he finds himself in a maze of crevasses and has to climb back up 300m, re-passing their snow hole (but not telling them). Eventually Lambert staggers down and is spotted by one of the Genevan groups; he insists on going down with them under his own steam to the Requin, where Stagni's family physician, Dr Ody, has been sent by Mme Amstutz. On day eight the three Chamonix guides reach them and straightaway whisk off Stagni, leaving Gallay, but telling him there are others coming. Conditions are still incredibly harsh and some of the Genevans and guides renounce. But a party of Chamonix guides, Armand Charlet, Luc Couttet and Jerôme Bozon and Genevans, Francis Marullaz and Walter Macquart, reach Gallay and drag him off down). At the Col du Midi, they meet Dr Ody who has come up to join the others and gives him some basic treatment, saying he will see them at the Requin hut. But when they arrive Ody and most others have left for the valley accompanying Stagni.

An earlier image from the Aiguille du Diable, the work of guide and photographer Francis Marullaz, who was seen as the philosophical heart of the influential Androsace group. The photograph illustrated Marcel Gallay's book on the 1938 tragedy. *(Francis Marullaz)*

On the ninth day Gallay is brought down to the valley still tied to skis. He is first treated by a local doctor before carrying on to the private Clinique de la Colline at Geneva to join the other two, plus frostbitten rescuers of Stagni. The first thing Mme Amstutz says to him is: 'Ah, there you are. Are you insured?' Gallay is sent to the public hospital where he is equally well treated but separated from his companions and rescuers. The trauma of that separation gives him plenty of time to brood and build up the rancour that was later to develop with his climbing companions and more immediately Mme Amstutz.

The Climbers

The first winter ascent of the Aiguilles du Diable on Mont Blanc du Tacul in February 1938, the resulting rescue and the aftermath was, in a prominent 1947 review of Raymond Lambert's *À l'assaut des Quatre Mille*, described thus: 'In all the history of Alpinism, I know nothing which reaches the tragic horror of the chapter which complements the painful account formerly [in 1940] given by Marcel Gallay.' Yet, as already shown, it is a story that is unfamiliar to the British climbing public and the aftermath is virtually unknown, even though the history ran on and on, much as did the story of the first ascent of K2. So although the actual climb and the rescue with its resulting polemics were certainly well known in the tight world of the leading French and Swiss alpinists, the outbreak of war, the fact that Mlle Stagni fully recovered and restarted serious climbing, and Lambert was able to reach 8,600m on Everest on the stumps of his feet in 1952, meant that few knew the ins and outs of Gallay's bitterness. It was certainly not a matter for public discussion. Yet 12 years after being the highest man in the world, Lambert was having to sue Gallay, whose leg had finally been amputated 25 years after the Diable ascent, over a circular letter he had sent round the Club Alpin Suisse (CAS) saying that for him Lambert was the lowest of the low, whatever heights he may have reached on Everest.

My early interest in the case revived when out climbing with François Damilano who was helping Lambert's son Yves Lambert tick off the 4,000ers and who recounted how Yves had recently done Everest wearing the scarf Tenzing had given to his father in gratitude. Yves proved most helpful and provided me with a photocopy of Lambert's *Carnet de courses* kept by guides, along with a copy of the judgement given in the September 1964 libel case. But the Diable ascent took place a quarter of a century before he was even born and his own knowledge of the affair was limited. So he put me in touch with two people who might help: Raymond Darbellay, whom Anne and I already knew, and Ernest Hofstetter, a good friend of Lambert who was with him on the Swiss expedition. But although very much alive, at 94 his memories of people and events nearly seven decades on may not have been of the clearest, particularly since he was not directly involveded. Nevertheless, in a long discussion over the winter ascent, he clearly hinted that the young Lambert of those days was not yet the respectable figure of his later years. To put it tactfully, his involvement with Erika Stagni was not confined to his professional activities. The importance of that observation will become apparent in due course.

Raymond Lambert and Erika Stagni in happier days outside the Tour Rouge hut under the Grépon, with the Aiguille Verte behind.

The extremely important help given me by my old friend Christian Mollier of the Chamonix guides included obtaining for me the official records of the guides company concerning the rescue, as too was a discussion with Jeannot, son of Arthur Franchino, who was one of those badly frostbitten. To all these people I would like to extend my thanks for the help given. There is one other source worth mentioning, a compilation (archeo-gallay.ch) containing some useful nuggets of 58 pages, *La Tragédie des Aiguilles du Diable*, put together by Alain Gallay to illustrate a reconstruction of events. If this is the same person (1938-2021) who was professor of archaeology at Geneva University, he was a nephew.

Yet the fact remains that at the end of the day there remain hidden aspects of the story, of guilt, of responsibility, of self-justification or pity, that we can never know. The real tragedy of the ascent lay not so much in the events, horrific as they were, but that a story of much courage and suffering shared between three friends should have finished with the bitter mutual recriminations it did.

Raymond Lambert (1914-98) was an extremely tough and pushy mountaineer. In 1934 he had done a summer ascent of the Diable with Loulou Boulaz and in the following year they were involved in the competition for the first ascent of the north face of the Jorasses. In the end they found themselves climbing the Croz spur alongside Gervasutti and Chabot, 48 hours behind Peters and Meier who had just done the first ascent. The same year he was in a party of four attempting the north face of the Dru and on return to Montenvers found Allain and Leininger who'd just made the first successful ascent, which he and Loulou repeated the following year. He had early on been attracted by full winter ascents and twice did the traverse of the Grépon (1932, 1934) and ascents of the Triolet (not the north face) and Chardonnet.

From his *Carnet de courses* one suspects he was also doing a bit of unofficial guiding. In 1936 he climbed a series of big Swiss mountains with the Japanese Kimchi by the ordinary routes. True, the regulations in those days were somewhat less strict and in that same year he was formally granted the diploma of assistant guide by the Club Alpin Français. But as a Genevan it was under the aegis of the CAS and the État de Valais that he did his guides' course, the sole lowlander amongst the traditional mountain families of the high Swiss Alps. After a gruelling 17 days under the direction of Alexander Graven and L Thétaz he passed out top.

However, it was not through occasional guiding in the high mountains supplemented by a bit of gardening that he would earn a decent living. That came when the Ecole d'Alpinisme de Genève started up in 1936 and gave him the chance to develop his clientele. Courses were based on the Salève with a final session in the nearby French Alps along with ski courses in winter. Salève, although technically in France, was the great rendez-vous for the remarkable galaxy of Genevan climbers of that epoch and it was there that he got to know Marcel Gallay, who was particularly powerful on rock. Together they did the first winter ascent of the Caiman on 12-13 January 1937, a major undertaking of what was then a remote peak. Since November, they had been planning to make the attempt in February but one day when out training on ski Lambert decided that the conditions were right and they left there and then, without telling anyone. They arrived at Tines at 1pm and flogged up for five hours via the Chapeau, then the standard route to the Requin hut, the base for all climbing in the great cirque of the Vallée Blanche. The major problem next day was the deep powder on the Glacier des Plans, both on the approach and descent and they arrived at the Col Supérieur du Plan totally knackered at 9.30am (See Gallay's account in *La Montagne*, June 1937, pp223-300). On the traverse of the Crocodile, Gallay lost a glove and his hand started freezing until Lambert finally remembered he had a spare pair. They reached the summit of the Caiman at 3.45pm, Gallay having led the main rock pitch in espadrille, and finally in the dark, after something like 25 hours on the go, got back to the hut, (Lambert gives the time as 21h 10m for the ascent). Given the conditions and the primitive equipment – they stuffed the inside of their boots with paper, greasing the inside of their boots and feet and sprinkling them with mustard powder – the shortness of the winter days, the sudden decision to go, the ascent shows not only Lambert's determination to push the limits, but also a certain insouciance which is not totally to be attributed to his youth. It was after this successful Caiman outing that they decided on a winter ascent of the Diable. And it was round December Lambert announced that Erika Stagni would be coming too.

Mlle Erika Stagni must have been a godsend to Lambert. He probably met her on a course at Salève but the first record of climbing with her in his carnet is the 27 May 1937 when they did the traverse of the Grépon. Up to then Kimchi had been his main client and with the Japanese he had already done the Grand Combin and Mont Blanc that year, but now he totally disappears from the scene. Stagni was a good athlete and a particularly fine horsewoman, but she had recently caught the climbing bug, to the disapproval of mama (Mme Amstutz) who did not appreciate the kind of people who indulged. However, she was very rich in her own right, young and fit. Before his guides' course in June he managed to fit in the Clochetons of Planpraz and the Dru and Mlle Stagni was now Erika.

As soon as he got back they were out regularly training at the Salève and that summer they did the Verte, the *Mayer-Dibona* on the Requin, the *Mummery-Ravanel* traverse, the *Ryan-Lochmatter* on the Plan, the Frontier ridge on Mont Maudit, and then an eight-day campaign on the Aiguilles, with the first descent of the *Allain* on the Caiman, a new route on the Pointe des Nantillons, the traverse of the Grépon, Aiguille de Roc, Mer de Glace face of the Grépon with a final flourish of traversing the Fou, Ciseaux and Blaitière summits, 20 hours roundtrip from Montenvers. And in this campaign they were accompanied by Fernand Gros and André Roch: no mean company. No wonder Lambert considered her capable of accompanying them on the Diable, particularly as it would mean all necessary supplies provided and a big fat fee of a thousand Swiss francs. And to give her proper due, there is no evidence in any account that Erika Stagni was a burden. That she was the only one that came out of the adventure without surgery is not entirely due to the fact that especial care was taken of her.

So the winter saw Erika training hard with Raymond on ski tours during a prolonged period of fine weather but various illnesses and indispositions meant the projected departure date had to be postponed. Indeed, when they did set off Lambert was still suffering from a bad attack of flu which made the ascent to the Requin a misery, although next day he suddenly felt over it. The weather was still brilliant and there was no reason it should not remain so. And even if it did change Lambert was confident he could deal with the situation.

Marcel Gallay.

The Objective

Two people used the word *gonflé* (foolhardy, hair-brained) to me in describing Lambert's goal. It was reflected in Lambert's overconfidence and culpable irresponsibility in failing to leave any information in Chamonix about where they were going. The result was that neither Stagni's mother nor the Chamonix guides knew where to look and it was only a week later that the Genevans who alone knew where to search arrived on the scene.

The remoteness of the climbers' objective cannot be overstated, particularly in the conditions of -30°C to -40°C in which they were caught. But outside the Chamonix valley there was no communications system and any coordination was through personal contacts. Nor were there weather forecasts. Indeed, the breakthrough in understanding the formation of depressions that caught them unawares was not made until 1940. There was a railway to Montenvers but that was seasonally closed and the standard way in any case to the Requin hut, the sole proper refuge but unguarded in winter, passed (and still did after the war) by Tines and Le Chapeau. Neither the Midi nor Torino lifts had been built. The Diable was certainly in French territory, but it was close to Mussolini's Italy, one of three fascist regimes now surrounding France, which since 1936 had moved to the Left. Any rescue would have to come from the French side.

The Rescue[1]

The failure of Erika Stagni to give any details concerning what she was up to meant that Mme Amstutz, with no news of her daughter, made no attempt to contact Genevan climbers, even if she knew how to, and instead rang the Hotel des Alpes on the evening of Friday 11 February. The hotel put her on

1. Sources: primarily the R Gréloz account given to the GHM as published in *Alpinisme* June 1938, supplemented by Mollier's information from the guides' records.

to the guides' office. Next morning, they sent Michel Démarchi and Anatole Bozon to the Requin hut. They returned that evening because of the appalling weather, reporting they had found some of the climbers' effects there. On the same day a party of 20 climbers from Geneva, including R Dittert, R Gréloz and F Marullaz left Geneva and spent the night at the Chapeau, where they met the two French guides on their way back down. On the Sunday the Swiss reached the Requin and Loulou Boulaz, Aubert and Dittert immediately carried on and searched the bergschrund of the Col de la Fourche while Gréloz, Marullaz and Marquart explored the rimaye of the Col du Diable on the other side.[2]

In the meantime, M and Mme Amstutz instruct the guides to save Stagni at all costs and so at 3pm a first caravan consisting of Michel Payot, Paul Démarchi and Arthur Franchino leave Chamonix, while a second is being organised. But with nothing specific to go on, Mme Amstutz consulted a *radiesthésiste* (diviner, or douser) who advised to look in the Rochefort Mont Mallet area (in fact a not entirely unreasonable suggestion). At about 2pm, the Swiss searchers were forced to give up because of conditions but as they turned the foot of the Capucin in a clearing saw Lambert descending as though he were an *automate* (automaton). He insisted on carrying on down with them, reaching the hut at 6pm. Gréloz and Boulaz continued to the valley to get help and on the way crossed the three Chamonix guides coming to look in the direction Mme Amstutz had instructed, diverting them to the Requin. There, the guides questioned him several times to ensure he was not hallucinating, but he insisted they carry straight on, afraid that having not seeing any rescue the two in the crevasse would make a last desperate attempt to descend. At 11pm, despite a temperature of -31°C at the hut and probably -40°C on the Tacul the three set off, climbing in soft powder where all trace of Lambert's passage had disappeared but managing nevertheless to find the crevasse without too much casting around at first light: 6am. They began taking Stagni down attached to skis and told Gallay that another party was on its way up and should arrive at the latest in another two or three hours.

This second caravan, made up of Armand Charlet, Luc Couttet and André Bozon, had left Chamonix about 7pm the previous evening. Joined by some of the Genevans, they immediately carried on from the Requin to the Col du Midi where they met up with the three guides bringing Stagni down. The Chamonix guides with Francis Marullaz and Walter Marquart, friends of Gallay, then set off, although the three others reported he was a gonner according to Gallay'a account. With the tracks of the previous party to follow, the official guides' report says they reached him about 9am. According to Gallay they did not arrive until midday and had lost time searching too high and only found him through his yelling. They reached the Col du Midi three hours later where other Genevan friends took over and carried on to the hut. It is only there that the frostbite suffered by the rescuers became clear.

2. Lambert's account differs somewhat, saying it was Loulou Boulaz, Dittert, Aubert, Muller, Gréloz, Bader and Bonnant who see him.

Gréloz's account continues with the frostbite damage. Of the climbers, Stagni lost nothing but Lambert had major amputations while the toes of Gallay, though not yet operated on, were falling off of their own accord. Demarchi had one foot amputated, well behind the toes, while the 'porters' spent four weeks in hospital but finally lost nothing. The Swiss Marullaz lost the end of his toes of one foot.

Discrepancies

Two intertwined sets of discrepancies in first-hand accounts concerning the days in the crevasse explain how the split between Gallay, Lambert and Stagni finally developed into the bitterness which ended in two court cases. None therefore should be taken at face value, and all versions examined as far as possible with a degree of scepticism.

First, the sleeping bag mystery. According to Gallay (1944), written after he had broken with both Lambert and Stagni (see below), Stagni claimed that on Friday 11 February, their second night in the crevasse, he abandoned his bag against her advice. Gallay rebuts this, stating that Lambert and Stagni had moved with their bags (plural) to the back of the crevasse to be warmer but he had to abandon his own. The lie to that is given by Gallay himself in his original account when he describes how, with the wind blowing in at the entrance and the snow covering their feet and creeping up their legs, he got out of his sleeping bag to push it back and block the entrance with a pair of snowshoes. This more or less concurs with that of 1952 (*La tragédie des Aiguilles du Diable*, Editions Franck Luthi). In both versions he still has a sleeping bag to himself when they arrive in the crevasse.

A further complication to the story comes from Stagni who claims that she tore her sleeping bag in two so as to share it and various pieces of clothing with Gallay. This statement he rightly totally rejects, continuing that when she was rescued she was in a complete sleeping bag of her own and that was how she was taken down. That version was correct (see 'Rescue'). He on the contrary was found sitting on the ice with his legs bare and holding his ungloved hands between his thighs for warmth when finally rescued. So it seems Stagni herself had something to hide. What?

Both Gallay (1940) and Lambert (1946) concur that all three had a sleeping bag at the summit of the Tacul (second bivy). Stagni was installed in a relatively sheltered place and the two men shared a bag in a more exposed location. Gallay (1952) states they were each in their own sleeping bag but next morning his was so frozen it was abandoned: a subtle difference. Although saying nothing specific about sleeping bags, Lambert does note that one of the problems about the bivy at the Tacul was that the sacks were going to get soaked. So the pair of them huddled together in one sack, and in the morning the other was too frozen to move and consequently abandoned. So there were only two sleeping bags when they arrived in the crevasse, one of which was Gallay's, the other shared by Lambert and Stagni. For some reason Gallay does not want to let on that Lambert's bag is big enough for two, albeit uncomfortably and impossible to do up fully when occupied by two men. But with a man and a young woman? Lambert says nothing about sleeping arrangements in the crevasse.

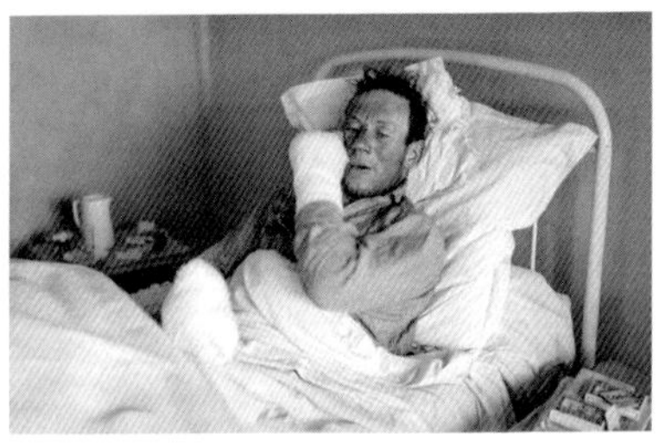

Lambert with his hands heavily bandaged recovering from his ordeal in a Geneva hospital.

The next mention of sleeping bags comes from Gallay after Lambert goes for help leaving them on their own. Gallay states Stagni was tucked up in her sleeping bag with gloves on. And in both his versions, he mentions that an unusable sleeping bag was laid out on the bottom of their crevasse (so why was he not at least sitting on that rather than bare ice?). Stagni's claim that she had torn her sack in two to help Gallay might provide an explanation but makes no sense if she and Lambert were in fact sharing a bag, which they were. It does however provide another explanation for why one of the bags was unusable after Lambert set off, leaving his behind for Stagni. Altogether three explanations are possible. Either Gallay shared a bag with Stagni but does not want to admit it, or else Stagni would not let him, or else it was Lambert's bag that had become unusable and abandoned, so Stagni got her own smaller bag, which could not accommodate two, back from Gallay who was forced to spend the night in a frozen anorak. None stands up to examination.

Gallay's Motives

In his 1940 account Galley states that after their abortive outing from the crevasse, it would have been too long and complicated for all to try and descend and neither he nor Lambert wanted to leave Stagni on her own. In reality Gallay was trying to disguise the fact that he was already in a bad physical state when Lambert decided to go for help. His condition belied the story that it was thanks to him that Stagni was safe and sound, and that his serious deterioration was due essentially to the day and a half waiting before the rescue came. In Gallay's 1952 account, he insinuated he was the equal of Lambert by posing it as a dilemma with Lambert deciding it must be him, for he is the guide. Lambert (1946) on the contrary made it clear that after their attempted sortie to Col Maudit, the other two were in no fit state do descend. So after talking things over he decided the only answer is for him to go alone. It must also be recognised (and Stagni admitted this) that at one stage she implored the two others not to abandon her.

Behind all these discrepancies in fact lie their respective depositions for a court case in 1941 (see below). Lambert and Stagni called as evidence the state Gallay was found in. Gallay riposted that it was invalid to judge his condition when Lambert left by the lamentable state that resulted from a further day and a half of waiting in which he, unlike Stagni, had no sleeping bag. To back up his claim he reported a conversation Lambert had with friends on 1 November 1939 in which he acknowledged that Gallay was

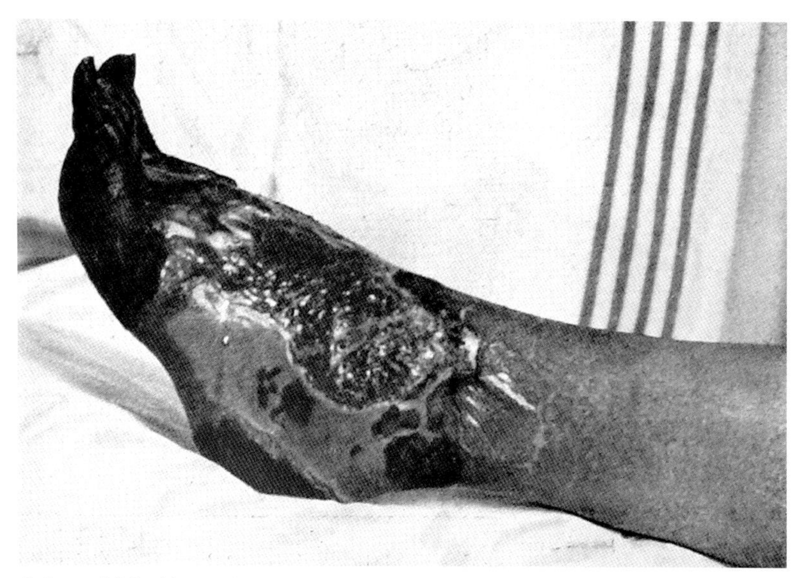

Gallay published harrowing pictures of his injuries to garner support for what he saw as the injustice of his situation.

capable of descending and had there just been the two of them they would have gone together. With three it would have been too long and difficult and Stagni could not be left alone. Not too much should be read into this. Even assuming the conversation was reported correctly, it does little more than indicate that Gallay was not totally *hors de combat* on 13 February and as a pair naturally Lambert would have tried going down with him.

In brief, we may conclude that Gallay was playing his role as best he could. The poor man had to try and make a case for why he should have received equal treatment with Lambert and the guides who rescued him, and morally he was arguably right. But legally to do so he needed to exaggerate and make it appear that Mlle Stagni owed her life, or at least her complete recovery, in part to him. His real anger and bitterness are against Lambert and derive from the fact that he did not back up his story, while Stagni had forgotten her promises that her mother would look after them all, stating it was Lambert alone who saved her. It's interesting to note her comment that women were more resilient than men and that anyhow they all took their chances and some came out of it better than others. It is also relevant that when the three of them arrived in the crevasse, Lambert observed that Stagni had no signs of frostbite, whilst the pair of them had serious concerns about their own state.

Betrayed: Le Guide Acheté[3]

Lambert's first visit to Gallay on 1 July 1938 followed Lambert's second

3. Based on Gallay 27 Oct 1944.

The three publications Gallay produced to argue his case, two in 1940 alone.

round of amputations. He wanted a *déposition*, essentially an affadavit, since Stagni was refusing to pay. This Gallay supplied. A month or so later, Lambert arrived with the Chamonix guides who were in good spirits despite their injuries and only getting 20 French francs per diem for three months from their own insurance system. They were all determined to take a case out against Stagni and wanted him to join them. Gallay declined but did not say why, possibly because he was preparing his own account (1940). In any case it was not obvious what Lambert could sue Stagni for except the thousand Swiss francs for his guiding fee, which he sent to her lawyer.

Mme Amstutz profited from this potential divergence of views, stage one of which was to get Stagni to settle with the Chamonix guides on condition they drop their communal case with Lambert. That, Gallay claimed, was when Lambert changed tactics and finally reached a settlement amounting to 7,000 Swiss francs all told, provided Lambert supported Stagni's account. When Gallay found that she had completely recovered and was back riding and driving fast cars with no care for her rescuer he swore to fight this injustice and threatened a press campaign.

It was carrying out this threat that finally determined Mme Amstutz would do nothing for Gallay, although she did eventually offer a settlement of a thousand Swiss francs provided she heard nothing more from him. Gallay refused this in September 1938 and decided to publish his 1940 account to clarify the situation with a view to starting legal action. In the preface he thanks all the guides and friends who risked their lives, at least those who had not *'marchandé'* (traded) their devotion. He finishes:

> *What I have never been able to understand is the bad luck whereby from the time of the first rescue I was separated from my companions of the route, and always kept away, with no help, nor comfort even from [Mlle Stagni] who came out of this adventure intact.*

As a result of the potential court case Lambert and Stagni gave *dépositions* in 1941 which more or less scuppered Gallay. So he took on the lawyer who originally acted on behalf of Lambert and the guides. Yet the lawyer warns him that what he was going to argue then was quite different from what he would say now.

However, Gallay's plight seems to have stirred a certain amount of sympathy and various people try to get influential institutions to intervene, including the Valais guides association who asked CAS to act, since the whole matter was reflecting badly on the spirit of solidarity amongst mountaineers. The result was, according to Gallay, that Lambert wrote him a menacing letter, which he said he couldn't find, but which ended to the effect that he had made his own ball and chain and that he should make sure that he didn't get crushed by it.

Nevertheless, the fact that Lambert may have given a different slant to his account when trying to get compensation does not mean that he perjured himself. It can suffice to change the emphasis of events to put matters in a different light.The key to Gallay's case was, first, that he was capable of going down with Lambert but that Stagni could not be left on her own and, second, that it was thanks to his devotion, keeping the snow hole blocked and the physical rubbing he provided that Stagni survived with no long-term injuries. Indeed, he argued that it was his legal duty for one of them to stay, citing an interesting case of 1933 in which a young man left his female companion when they got lost in order to get rescue and she died, her body only being found when the snows started melting. The judges considered his behaviour was responsible for her death and condemned him to two years' imprisonment. One would need to look more carefully at that particular case to see whether it really was relevant but in any event, it was an *ex post facto* discovery by his lawyer to justify why Gallay stayed.

The essence of the argument Gallay had to make, if he were to stand a legal chance of getting compensation and damages, was essentially the first issue: the succour he gave is largely secondary since there was not much else either could do but try and mutually boost morale and give such physical aid as was possible. Leaving aside that it was the guide who was the strongest member of the party and that it was his duty to do everything possibie to get rescue for his client, however slim the chances, the question that needs to be answered is: was Gallay in a fit enough state to have gone down when he left? That is where Lambert's testimony would be vital. Clearly, his failure to support Gallay against Stagni's assertions was what kyboshed Gallay's case and caused the rift between the two men.

Mme Amstutz

At this point, we need to examine rather more closely the role of Mme Amstutz. It is easy to dismiss her as an unsympathetic rich bitch, as I originally did, but rich or not, the fact is that the rescue of her daughter, her only concern, was costing her a fortune, and liability becoming open ended. In addition to the Chamonix guides already mentioned, Christian Mollier sent me the names of eight further guides who went up to the Col du Midi to help evacuate the injured and another five who left at 7am on 15 February and brought the last injured back to the Requin, plus two others who helped in the final stages of the evacuation down to the valley: a total of 23, all at Mme Amstutz's expense. Then there was Dr Ody, who was clearly an able skier, at least to judge by his displacements, and certainly not cheap, and of course the *sorcière*. Now she was having to pick up the bill for treatment of the injured guides she'd hired at the private Clinique de la Colline.

Not surprisingly, she determined to rein back. Why should she pay for Gallay or even Lambert, and indeed guides who were rescuing them as well as her daughter? Well, part of the answer is that without Lambert she would not have been saved. And then there is the admitted fact her daughter pleaded not to be left alone and promised her companions that her mother would look after them.

The Court Case

So the case swung on whether Gallay contributed to saving Stagni. That is why her mother Mme Amstutz, despite still holding the purse strings for her daughter, allowed Stagni, who was not yet in her majority, to take over negotiations. She and Lambert came to the conclusion that Gallay was in no fit state to descend. That essentially was why Gallay lost his case. As reported in *La Suisse* on 3 April 1947:

> *La Cour correctionelle de Genève has just condemned Marcel Gallay, one of the members of the terrible adventure of the Aiguilles du Diable (February 1938), from which he came out seriously mutilated. Mlle Stagni, having been accused in the course of the trial, considers it necessary to make clear the following: She rejects having been saved by M Gallay. The credit for the rescue, according to her, was entirely due to the guide R Lambert.*

Having done her mother's bidding, Stagni was now free to cut the apron as well as the purse strings and shack up with her new partner Robert Wohlschlag, nicknamed 'Pellebrosse', or dustpan and brush, on account of his thick red hair. It was hardly the improvement socially that mama would have liked, even though she did end up marrying him. Together, they opened some remarkable new routes, notably on the limestone cliffs of the Arve valley between Geneva and Le Fayet. From then on it was pure rock climbing and she did not again venture into the icy wastes of the Mont Blanc massif.

The Libel Case

The case for libel brought against Gallay in 1963 seems to have had its origins in something Lambert did or said in 1958. As we have seen, Gallay lost his initial case in 1947 when Erika Stagni made it clear that it was Lambert who had rescued her. That was literally true but it was harsh on Gallay. Thereafter, Gallay's attitude, as he told the court in 1963, was to ignore Lambert and that perhaps explains why in his 1952 book he gave no details of the aftermath. Gallay had been condemned over Stagni and her mother and he was not intending to start a war with Lambert. Lambert in turn had not responded to various things Gallay had been saying and writing, notably his 1944 pamphlet and so matters appeared to have settled. The only explanation we have of why they flared up again is the circular Gallay wrote in 1963 stating that his aim was to seek public acknowledgement for 'the moral wrongs' Lambert had caused him 'since 1958'. What was the significance of the year 1958? Was it Lambert's recovery and fame on Everest, his assured job as a mountain pilot thanks to the help given him by his rich new wife? Was it the contrast with Gallay's own sufferings, broken marriage and indebtedness that made him turn his resentment against the man whom he considered had not sufficiently supported him?

Whatever the motive, Gallay started writing again about their dispute. And what led to the dam bursting was the fact that at the end of 1962 Gallay's leg had finally to be amputated.

> *After twenty-five years of fighting and hardships, I have just been amputated for Christmas and this new drama obliges me to reconsider the deplorable attitude you have taken towards me ... For once recognize your cowardice ... I have enough material available to enlighten public opinion concerning the man who was once said to be the highest in the world but who will remain for me the lowest.*

This letter of itself clearly indicates Gallay's intentions of dragging Lambert's name through the mud. Yet once more Lambert had not allowed himself to be provoked. Finally, Gallay decided the only relief he could find for the anguish caused by his amputation was to blacken Lambert's name publicly by circulating a letter to some 500 people, mostly CAS members, in which he stated:

> *... this approach will be the culminating point for the injustice imposed on me by my former climbing partners. The aim is not to acquire financial reparation, but solely to obtain from the principal person responsible, the guide Raymond Lambert, public recognition of the moral wrongs he has caused me since 1958.*

That, Lambert could not ignore and in May 1963 he opened proceedings, suing for 4,000 Swiss francs in damages and a thousand for expenses to meet the cost of contacting the recipients of the letters. The court finally adjudged on 24 September 1964 opining that Gallay had indeed libelled him out of a spirit of resentment and vengeance and that his intention had indeed been to harm his reputation. Lambert was not responsible for the amputation and in no way did it justify changing Gallay's earlier decision to ignore him. In pleading before the court, Gallay had made no attempt to withdraw what he had said or express regret, while recognising he had made errors.

However, there were mitigating circumstances. It was understandable that in his depressed state Gallay might consider that his former fellow climber should have given him greater support even if Gallay had produced no evidence to show in what ways Lambert had fallen short. In any case, they would not justify his explicit intention to damage Lambert's reputation. But the stress permitted a considerable reduction in the damages asked for, since the harm done Lambert was essentially one to his honour and reputation and not financial. The court awarded damages of a thousand francs and another 500 for costs in circulating the judgement to the recipients of the 500 letters whose names Gallay was ordered to produce. He was also ordered to pay court costs, amounting to almost another thousand.

John Wilkinson on the summit of L'Isolée in 1965. *(John Wilkinson)*

Envoi

Thus ended the tragedy of the first winter ascent of the Aiguilles du Diable. They were well named, those needles of granite, and so too the Combe Maudit, the accursed valley, above which they rose. None of the three that had set off so confidently that February of 1938 came out of their adventure with their reputation unscathed. For a quarter of a century the bitterness engendered was to pursue them. Both Stagni and Lambert were cleared through legal proceedings paid for ironically by Gallay whose life had been permanently ruined. Did that absolve them? Did their remarkable subsequent climbing careers dispense them from moral responsibility for their companion's misfortunes? Ironic that Stagni's remarkable ascent of the *Brandler-Hasse* occurred a few weeks after Gallay lost his libel case and is heard of no more. Did she and Lambert brush Gallay's misfortunes aside?

The reader will have their own opinions. All I have tried to do is present the facts concerning the aftermath, in so far I have been able to establish them to supplement Eric Vola's account of those bitter winter days.

PETER FOSTER

One Hundred Years Ago

'Dent d'Hérens at Dawn' by Victor Ellwood. Shown at the Club's photographic exhibition in December 1923 and reproduced in the *Alpine Journal.*

On the evening of Tuesday 4 December 1923, 226 members of the Alpine Club and guests, wearing formal evening dress, illuminated by chandeliers and reflected in gilded mirrors, took their seats for the annual dinner in the plush surroundings of the Edward VII Rooms at the Hotel Victoria on Northumberland Avenue.[a] That afternoon the Club had been 'at home' to about 400 members and friends at an exhibition of photographs in the hall at 23 Savile Row. The subject matter of the photographs was

a. Members had paid £1 2s for their ticket; a proposal to raise the cost to £1 11s so that champagne might be served had been rejected by an abstemious majority at a previous general meeting of the Club.

overwhelmingly Alpine, reflecting the activities of members who, five years after the Armistice, had returned in increasing numbers to their playground to enjoy classic climbs of the pre-war years.

During the summer season the weather in the Alps had been generally good and by August Chamonix was heaving with visitors: 'all the huts were crammed, and the Couvercle had as many as a dozen or more people sleeping outside. What the inside must have been like is easily imagined.'[1] On 17 August George Bower and Fred Pigott set out from Montenvers to make the first guideless ascent of the Mer de Glace face of the Aiguille du Grépon. Eleven and a half hours later they reached the final tower and were faced with the notorious final crack which on the first ascent Joseph Knubel had overcome by jamming his ice axe and using it as a horizontal bar. It was snowing gently. Bower tried hard but failed to climb the crack; he invited Pigott, who earlier in the year had made the third ascent of the *Flake Crack* on Central Buttress on Scafell, to have a go but Pigott stuck at the final chockstone, where from the summit block, six feet above, he heard a voice: 'voulez-vous la corde, monsieur?' and a rope end brushed his nose. 'Er, s'il vous plaît,' Pigott answered in his best French. In a few seconds he was on top of the Grépon.[2]

Swiss huts were busy, too.[b] One evening at the Mountet hut, 40 schoolgirls arrived. 'Their harassed mistress could not keep them quiet. They effervesced. And all through the night spluttering giggles went off like fireworks,'[3] complained a sleep-deprived Dorothy Pilley. Bivouacking offered a more tranquil alternative and for their ascent of the Weisshorn's *Schaligrat*, Raymond Bicknell and Harold Porter adopted a minimalist approach, simply donning a woollen waistcoat and extra pair of socks and lying down on the dry rocks of the Schalijoch. A cold and sleepless night followed making the next day's climbing up the pinnacled ridge arduous: 'long before we got to the top' Bicknell recalled vividly, 'I was beginning to feel like a microbe crawling around the unending edge of a circular saw.'[4]

In the Oberland, Pilley and her husband, Ivor Richards, with their guide Joseph Georges, escaped the crowds thronging the Jungfraujoch by making the second ascent of the north-east ridge of the Jungfrau, a long route involving some difficult climbing on sometimes rotten rock. Approaching the summit the party was caught in an electrical storm, a particular feature of the weather in the region.

> *To the peculiar feeling in the muscles which tells of a big electrical disturbance was now added music from the axes. The party was slightly reassured by discovering that one was rendering 'God Save the King' and the other 'Rule Britannia'; what J.G.'s axe was doing we had no means of ascertaining.*[5]

Ninety-five years later in 2018, a party comprising Ben Tibbetts and two recent past presidents of the Club, Mick Fowler and Victor Saunders, en-

b. In 1923 the total number of visitors to all the SAC huts was 41,186, a 25% increase on the previous year.

A similar view by Ben Tibbetts, illustrating the growing impact of climate change on the mountain's snow and ice cover.

countered similar alarming conditions on the route, as Tibbetts recounts: 'Every time I raised my hand to pull in rope, it fizzed and vibrated. Soon my head was buzzing; even the rocks were humming.'[6]

During a fortnight in August, a 28-year-old Austrian, Alfred Horeschowsky, who had already caused a stir with his solo ascent of the Pallavicini couloir[c] on the Grossglockner, made a meteoric appearance in the Western Alps. He traversed the Grandes Jorasses, climbed the Aiguille Blanche from the Brenva glacier, continuing via the Peuterey ridge to Mont Blanc and made the first attempt on the north face of the Matterhorn, reaching the base of the couloir that slants rightwards up the middle of the face and is the key to the route, but 'continuous stonefall made it impossible to gain a single inch of height' and they were forced to escape by difficult rocks to reach the Hörnli ridge, 'a few steps from the Solvay hut'.[7] Horeschowsky's technical competence and endurance drew admiration from Percy Farrar, recent past president of the Club, but he worried about the willingness to take 'outrageous risks': 'If Mr Horeschowsky continues like this he will not go on long, which would be regrettable.'[8] Horeschowsky died in 1987, aged 92.

Another prodigious talent, Willo Welzenbach, a 22-year-old engineering

c. The first ascent in 1876 had been a remarkable feat. The guide, J Tribusser, cut 2,500 steps in seven hours. Forty-five years elapsed before the second ascent.

Alfred Horeschowsky

student from Munich, was on his first visit to the Valais where he made the first continuous traverse of the Matterhorn and Dent d'Hérens, spending a night at the Italian hut on the Matterhorn where 40 climbers competed for space in the hut designed to accommodate 12. From a point high on the east ridge of the Dent d'Hérens, Welzenbach observed a 'mysterious trail of cut steps curving like a string of pearls'[9] that rose from the glacier terrace extending across the north face at mid-height, the track made 10 days earlier by George Finch and his companions on their attempt to climb the north face. Their route had avoided the obvious challenges of the ice wall to gain the terrace and the steep snow and ice slope above. Two years later Welzenbach would return to make a direct route, ushering in a new age of technical ice climbing.

To the east in the Bregaglia, Walter Risch made the first ascent of the north ridge of the Piz Badile with his client Alfred Zürcher who declared that Risch's ascent of the crux slab 'without exaggeration, reaches the extremest limits of human possibility.'[10] One hundred years later it is not unusual to find a dozen parties on the now classic route.

References

1 *Alpine Journal* **36**, p44.
2 P Brockbank & E Byrom, *A Short History of The Rucksack Club* 1902-1939, privately published from a 1977 MS, 2011, p76.
3 D Pilley, *Climbing Days*, London, 1935, p224.
4 *Alpine Journal* **36**, p56.
5 *Alpine Journal* **35**, p171.
6 B Tibbets, *Alpenglow*, privately published, 2019, p64.
7 *Alpine Journal* **36**, p156.
8 *Alpine Journal* **36**, p409.
9 E Roberts, *Welzenbach's Climbs*, The Mountaineers, 1981 p57.
10 *Alpine Journal* **37**, p147.

Area Notes

'View of the Lower Grindelwald Glacier, and of the Eiger and the Fischerhörner', Johann Jakob Biedermann, c1800, etching with hand-colouring, 35cm x 51.8cm. *(British Museum)*

LINDSAY GRIFFIN

The Alps 2022

The north-west face of the Roda Val della Neve with (1) *Jack Canali*, (2) *Niedermann* and (3) *Tierra del Fuego*. *See p218 (Romano Salis)*

With an odds-on prediction that before 2027 our overheated world is likely to surpass a key 1.5°C global warming threshold, three publicised incidents in 2022 produced sober reminders that climate change remains ever present in the Alps.

On the first Sunday in July, a large section of the diminishing Marmolada glacier below Punta Roccia collapsed. Sadly, it did so at the wrong time, sweeping down smooth rock on the face below and across the normal route, where it killed 11 people.

In late August, the area of blocky granite ridge around the Col de la Fourche bivouac hut collapsed, precipitating the small building onto the glacier below.

Two views of Roger Schäli rope soloing on the north-west face of the Roda Val della Neve, high above the Val Bregaglia. *(Romano Salis)*

The hut was located on the Brenva side of the Frontier ridge, which that summer was completely denuded of snow. The original shelter, constructed in 1935, was replaced by a newer model in 1985 and gave access to routes on the Brenva face of Mont Blanc.

A few days later a large section of the south flank of the ultra-popular *Cosmiques Arête* also collapsed. Fortunately, a party on the glacier below was to one side of the fall line and no one was injured, though climbers on the adjacent *Rébuffat* route got a fright.

The Solo Ascents

One of the most notable winter ascents of the year was the first solo of *Rolling Stones* on the north-east face of the Walker spur, **Grandes Jorasses**, by Charles Dubouloz. This somewhat enigmatic route, which has seen few repeats, was first climbed by a four-man Czech team in 1979. The second overall and first winter ascent was made in 1984 by Benoît Grison and Eric Grammond. It was climbed free for the first time in the winter of 2014 by Slovenians Luka Lindič and Luka Krajnc at M8. Conditions for Dubouloz's back-roped ascent in January were unusually hard, with temperatures down to -30°C and a north-easterly blowing directly onto the face. He carried a small hammock and made five bivouacs, sustaining a little frostbite. The route is known for its loose rock (the clue's in the name) and due to dry conditions during the ascent, this was one of the biggest problems faced by Dubouloz, though apart from two crux (aid) pitches, he managed the route free.

Raphaël Georges, a 31-year-old guide, made the first solo ascent of the 900m *Lesueur Route* on the north face of the **Grand Dru**, free at M7. Beginning from the valley on 21 March, he finished up the top section of the Dru couloir on 23 March, finding conditions very dry. The route, which was ahead of its time when first climbed in the summer of 1952, did not see a second ascent until 1975 courtesy of Rab Carrington and Al Rouse. Andy Parkin and Thierry Renault made the first winter ascent in 1983. It was eventually climbed free (at M8+) in 2012 by Ueli Steck and Jon Griffith, using several variants.

The three summits of the Zermatt Breithorn seen from the north-west. From left to right: Breithorn East (4141m), Central (4160m) and West (4165m). Marked is the new mixed route *Essere o non Essere* on the Breithorn Central. *See p223.* *(Lindsay Griffin)*

One of the most accomplished speed soloists currently operating in the Alps is the Italian resident Filip Babicz from Poland. On 23 September Babicz made an un-roped solo of the *Swiss Route* on the **Grand Capucin**, taking the *O Solo Mio* finish. He scorched up this popular combination, which at 6a/6a+ is the easiest line on the Capucin, in a remarkable time of 49 minutes. Babicz started at the bottom of the face, rather than near the top of the gully on the left where the original route begins, giving him 570m of climbing. Preparing for this ascent, he climbed the route seven times, three of these alone. While he did not carry a rope for the speed ascent, he did use aid in a few places. However, the difficulties would have been well within his comfort zone: one of his notable ascents from 2022 was a roped solo of *Appointment with Death* (E9 6c) on Wimberry: his first ever gritstone route.

A notable winter achievement in the Écrins took place on 9 February when Arthur Sordoillet made the first solo winter ascent of the 1975 *Cambon-Francou* (1,000m, ED1 6a/b A1 WI4 M4) on the north face of the **Pic Sans Nom** (3913m). After fixing the first pitch the day previously, Sordoillet climbed the route in 14h 30m, alternately free and aid climbing. Conditions were favourable, with dry rock in the lower section and the freezing level at around 3,500m. The first winter ascent of this steep and superb line was not made until 2012.

On 25 March, statistically just a few days after the end of the official winter season, the Austrian Laura Tiefenthaler made what is likely to be only the second female solo ascent of the *1938 Route* on the north face of the **Eiger**. On 8 March, with the German woman Jana Moher, she had made a winter ascent of the route in one day. Starting at 1.30am from Eigergletscher the two reached the summit at 6pm. On 24 March she tried it solo. However,

Line van den Berg climbing the 1,600m *Phantom Direct* on the north face of the Grandes Jorasses, completed with Fay Manners in a 31-hour push during the winter season of 2022. See p226 Tragically, van den Berg died aged 30 in an apparent avalanche while on her way to climb the Grosshorn in May 2023. Her two companions died with her. *(Fay Manners)*

despite previous knowledge, she made a route-finding error, lost two hours and decided to retreat. Next day, starting at 1am and back roping all the hard pitches, she was on the summit at 4pm. Such is the popularity of the face when in good winter conditions that she shared the climb with three other parties. The first female solo in a 17-hour day and in winter was famously made in March 1992 by Catherine Destivelle.

The **Roda Val della Neve** (2626m) in Bregaglia is a mountain of two halves. From the Albignia valley to the east it is no more than a low, broad, grassy ridge, but the north-west face, high above the Val Bregaglia overlooking Vicosoprano, is a 600m compact granite wall. It feels remote yet is easily reached from the Albignia dam via the Passo Val della Neve. Classic routes include the *Jack Canali* (600m, D, V A0, Bozzi-Canali-Merendi, 1959) on the far left and the Niedermann (600m, TD VII, Frei-Hurlimann-Naf-Neidermann, 1975). On the far right the steepest rock, a 350m pear-shaped buttress, rises to the west-north-west ridge and holds the *Nigg Route* (Blattler-Neeracher-Nigg, 1968, VIII- but generally climbed with additional aid). Over five days during the summer, Roger Schäli rope soloed a new route up the centre and steepest part of this buttress at 6c A2+. *Tierra del Fuego* was climbed ground-up, with traditional protection throughout (though the belays were bolted). Once above the buttress, 250m of III/IV led up the west-north-west ridge to the summit.

In September 2002, Christoph Hainz made a redpoint ascent of his own route *Moulin Rouge* on the **Roda di Vael** in the Catenaccio group, climbed a few months previously with Oswald Celva at IX- or 7b/7b+. The 11-pitch route, which has sections of friable rock, lies to the right of the classic *Buhl Route* (Brandler-Hasse, 1958, VI A2, or VIII) and is considered one of Celva and Hainz's best ascents. Twenty years later, on 20 June 2022, the route was audaciously free soloed by Jonas Heinz, son of Christoph. Widely considered the most outstanding free solo in recent years, it took Hainz just an hour and five minutes to complete his ascent.

Sadly, this one climb will remain his greatest legacy, as just a few months later the 25-year-old died trying to solo a peak in the Reiserferner Group, Hohe Tauern.

Tom Livingstone climbing the Quartz Vein pitch on the free ascent of the *Guides Route*, on the Petit Dru. *See p226.* *(Tom Seccombe)*

The Traverses

In early May, two rapid crossings of the Mont Blanc range were made on ski. Bastien Fleury and Bastien Lardet began in the Swiss village of Champex, crossed various cols, including the difficult Col des Cristaux, to reach the Vallée Blanche, then continued over Mont Blanc. Crossing the Col de Miage they arrived in Les Contamines after 21h 47min (65km, 6,450m of ascent). A week later, starting in Les Contamines and progressing eastward over the Dome de Miages, Aiguille de Bionnassey and Mont Blanc, Mathéo Jacquemoud and Benjamin Védrines crossed the Cols des Cristaux, du Passon, and Supérieur du Tour to arrive at Trient in a little over 20 hours (70km, 7,300m of ascent).

Traversing the Mer de Glace skyline has been in the minds of alpinists for many decades. Martin Moran and Simon Jenkins tried it several times in the late 1980s starting up the Aiguille Verte, their best attempt reaching the Aiguille de l'Eboulement. Subsequently, François Damilano would cover much of the ground during his solo traverse of the Mont Blanc range. Frédéric Degoulet and Benjamin Ribeyre attempted the skyline traverse in 2021 but poor weather and conditions stopped them less than halfway. On 8 July 2022, they left the church in central Chamonix and during the following nine days crossed the Aiguille Verte, Droites, Courtes, Triolet, Aiguille de l'Eboulement, Petites and Grandes Jorasses, Rochefort, the Frontier Ridge over the Tour Ronde and Mont Maudit, and finally a complete crossing on the Chamonix Aiguilles before returning to the church on 16 July. The heatwave meant they could travel lighter and faster but also meant negotiating more loose rock. At that time of year, during the voyage from the Verte to the Torino hut, they met only two other parties.

Tom Seccombe climbing the big corner above the niche on the *Guides Route*. *(Tom Livingstone)*

Another most impressive traverse, this time in the Eastern Alps, was Simon Gietl's three-day crossing of the entire **Catinaccio range**, solo and in winter. This south to north ridge traverse is eight kilometres in length and involves 5,000m of ascent. It includes such famous summits as the Roda di Vael, Vajolet Towers, Punta Emma, and the Cima Catinaccio itself. A complete crossing of the main ridge had never been achieved in any season but a colleague of Gietl's, Egon Resch, had climbed many sections in summer with a friend, Daniel Habock. The three decided to give it a try in late February. They were going well until the second day when Resch was hit by stone fall that fractured his hand, forcing a retreat. Undeterred, Gietl returned on 1 March to try it solo, an audacious undertaking as he had very little previous knowledge of the massif. Setting off with an 18kg rucksack and climbing in high mountain boots throughout, he back-roped and sack-hauled the difficult pitches, thought to be VI, and negotiated sections of very airy ridge work and rappels. He saw no one during the journey, which as the South Tyrol guide stated was 'exactly what I wanted.'

The Valtournenche Effect

The guides of the upper Valtournenche are increasingly active opening hard new routes and making significant repeats in their back garden, taking opportunities as they arrive. In recent years the most prolific have been François Cazzanelli and Francesco Ratti. Apart from the selection reported below, Cazzanelli notably fitted his personal Alpine climbing around his guiding profession and an expedition to Nanga Parbat, where he first climbed a new start to the standard *Kinshofer*, then later made a record speed ascent of the *Kinshofer* to the summit.

Tom Seccombe climbing one of the final tricky pitches on the third day of their climb. *(Tom Livingstone)*

On 9 February, Cazzanelli, Ratti and Jerome Perruquet created a new mixed route on the north-east face of the **Becca di Salé** (3,107m), a locally well-known peak with a mix of older traditional routes and facets that have been developed more recently for sport climbing. It overlooks the Cignana dam, south of the Grandes Murailles and is approached directly from the Valtournenche. The three took advantage of the lack of snow on the 1,200m approach to reach the base of the new line, climb it to give *Su per Cignana* (600m, M6 75°) and negotiate the tricky descent of the south-east ridge in the same day.

If that wasn't enough, by next morning Cazzanelli and Perruquet were in the Vallée Blanche, Mont Blanc range, where they climbed a new mixed route towards the right side of the north face of **Pic Adolphe Rey**. The Italian pair was after the second ascent of *Changing Corners*, a line put up on 25 January by Christophe Dumarest and Tom Livingstone. This takes a series of corners up the wall immediately left of the obvious crack and chimney line in the centre of the face climbed in 1962 by Bernezat, Revillod, Riboud and Robbe (250m, VI obl and A2, first winter ascent over three days in 1990). *Changing Corners* (250m, seven pitches, M7) gives thin dry tooling.

Arriving at the bottom of the face, Cazzanelli and Perruquet found a Swiss party already engaged on the second ascent, so moved to the far right side of the face where they climbed *Impulso Geniale* (250m, seven pitches, M8), starting up the broken corner system leading towards the Brèche du Pic Adolphe before moving left onto the face. Near the top they came across a couple of ancient pegs and although details of previous lines on this part of the face are lacking, it is known to have been climbed in 1961 by Cesare Gex and Franco Salluard. From 27-29 February, Cazzanelli, Ratti and Emrik Favre made the first winter and second integral ascent of *Padre Pio, Echelle vers le Ciel* on the south face of the **Matterhorn**.

In 2002, after three previous attempts with different partners, Patrick Gabarrou, France's most prolific Alpine new router, teamed with Cesare Ravaschietto to climb the crest of the Pilastro dei Fiori, completing a 650m climb on generally sound and compact rock at 6c+/7a, 6c obl. Their exit point was close to the Furggen ridge, on which they finished. Reflecting Gabarrou's religious nature, the line was named *Padre Pio Pregga per Noi*.

Over the next 13 years, with seven different partners, Gabarrou returned

Two views of Les Drus: (1) *Lesueur* to the Grand Dru and (2) *Guides Route* to the Petit Dru. *(Lindsay Griffin)*

to force a direct finish up the steep rock above, left of the crest of the Furggen Nose. The result, in 2015, was *Echelle vers le Ciel* (650m, 7b). It was finished with his old friend Pierre Gourdin but the line had been pieced together either by traversing in from the Furggen Ridge or rappelling from above. Gabarrou returned the following year with Pierre Gourdin and Nicolas Magnin to make the first integral ascent of *Padre Pio, Echelle vers le Ciel* (1,300m, 41 pitches, 7b, 6c obl), one of the longest and most demanding rock routes at altitude in the Alps.

The lower *Padre Pio* has been repeated on several occasions, including a first winter ascent in 2004 by Hervé Barmasse and Massimo Farina, but the

entire 1,300m line had not seen a second ascent until Cazzanelli, Favre and Ratti were able to profit from the dry winter to make their three-day climb in daytime temperatures of around -10°C.

Guiding and expeditions now intervened but on 13 October Cazzanelli, Perruquet and Stefano Stradelli climbed a new route on the north-north-east face of **Breithorn Central** (4159m). The sustained *Essere o non Essere* (550m, AI5 M7 85°), lies between *Settro Glauco* (TD, Grassi-Ravaschietto-Siri, July 1985) and the *Gabarrou-Steiner Direct* (TD, September 1979). A demanding climb with steep runnels, thin smears and a crux in the final exit corner on very steep rock, the new route takes similar but independent ground to the 1980 Italian rock route *Via della Torre Maggiore* (TD/TD+, V+ A1, Castiglia-Crivellaro-Manera-Persico-Pezzica).

Full winter conditions on the north-east face of Piz Badile. Marked is the *Isherwood-Kosterlitz*, rising out of the north couloir of the Col della Cengalo. See p226. *(David Hefti)*

On 27 November, Cazzanelli, Perruquet and Stradelli made the 900m approach from Cervinia to the east side of **Punta Sella** (3878m) in the Grandes Murailles, then climbed the 900m *Hyper Couloir della Grandes Murailles* at AI4+ M4. The new line lies to the right of *Banana Sprint* (850m, V/4 M4, Cazzanelli-Ferraris, March 2014) and arrives on the ridge immediately north of the col between Punta Sella and Becca di Guin (3805m). Descent was made by rappelling the route.

On 1 December, Cazzanelli, Perruquet and Ratti climbed a new line on the east face of **Cresta Albertini**, the ridge that runs south from the large snow shoulder at c4,040m on the east ridge of the Dents d'Hérens. *Triplo Zero* rises around 600m from the Mont Tabel-Chérillon glacier, directly above Cervinia, to finish on the Albertini ridge not far south of the Col des Grandes Murailles – technically the north ridge of **Punta Margherita** (3903m) in the Grandes Murailles. The line lies right of two established routes: *Petit Lumignon* (600m, IV/4 M4), climbed in 2003 by Hervé Barmasse, Massimo Farina and Ezio Marlier; and *Bonne Année*, climbed in 2017 by Barmasse and Stefano Perrone. The new line has 13 pitches with difficulties up to AI4+ M7 and was descended via 60m rappels. It was first attempted in 2017 by Cazzanelli, Ratti and the late Roberto Ferraris and at that time given the proposed name *Triplo Zero*. The zeros are the final digits of the three climbers' birth years: Cazzanelli was born in 1990, Ratti in 1980 and Ferraris in 1970.

The Repeats

Over five days in January, Léo Billon, Sébastien Ratel and Benjamin Védrines made the first alpine-style winter ascent of the entire 1966 *Harlin Route* on the north face of the **Eiger**. This demanding route has rarely been repeated, and most of those repeats have exited via the classic 1938 Route, rather than take the original and harder finish up the Fly.

Ten days later the same three were standing on top of the **Grandes Jorasses**, having made a three-day ascent of *Directe de l'Amitié*. They had climbed the 1,100m route free at M8, except for one pitch of A3 on the second day. This is another rarely repeated route on the north face of Pointe Whymper, noted for sections of difficult climbing on rotten rock. It was completed over most of January 1974 by Louis Audoubert, Michel Feuillarade, Marc Gally and Yannick Seigneur; the final ascent lasted nine days. The second ascent was in September 1977, carried out in just five days, alpine style, by Roger Baxter-Jones and Nick Colton.

To complete their trilogy on the three great north faces, on 9 February the three Frenchmen made the first known one-day ascent of the original 1969 *Cerruti-Gogna Route* on the Zmutt Nose of the Matterhorn. To date the route has received no more than a dozen ascents, around four of these in winter when successful parties have quoted grades of VI+ M7 A3.

Since January 2020, when Yann Borgnet and Charles Dobouloz made the much acclaimed and long-awaited second ascent of Giancarlo Grassi's *Phantom Wall* on the south face of the **Grandes Jorasses**, there have been three more ascents, all taking place in January 2022. A Spanish team climbed it on 19 January, and on 26 January a Belgian-Italian pair and the Chamonix-based British climber Fay Manners with Line van den Berg from the Netherlands, the latter pair making the first female ascent. Remarkably, these two teams completed the route in a single push from the car park in the Val Ferret, the first in a round trip of 21 hours. After a difficult bergschrund, which cost them time, the two women made consistent progress, reaching the crucial traverse at 1.45pm. As always with the upper section of this route, it was a race for the top. Moving together, they climbed the upper funnel with increasing tiredness and blustery cold wind, taking a variant out right to the upper Hirondelles ridge, and eventually reaching the summit at midnight. Seven hours later, and 30 hours after first setting out, they collapsed into the Boccalatte hut.

In the middle of March, Tom Livingstone with Tom Seccombe made what is likely to be the first free ascent of the *Guides Route* on the north face of the **Petit Dru**. The original ascent of this 850m line was something of a tour de force when it was climbed over a week in February 1967 by Michel Feuillarade, Claude Jager, Jean-Paul Paris and Yannick Seigneur. The French quartet used around 220 pegs and climbed at a grade of V+ A2. A German team repeated it over five days the following summer and then over three days in August 1975 by Bob Milward and Steve Parr. Livingstone either led or seconded every pitch free during his three-day ascent and felt the crux pitches somewhere between M7+ and M8+. From the summit the two descended the Dru couloir in 14 rappels.

On 17 March, Silvan Schupbach and Peter Von Kanel made a winter ascent of the 1968 *Isherwood-Kosterlitz* on the north-east face of the **Piz Badile**. While there have been previous winter ascents of this 600m line, which has difficulties of VI A1/A2 or VIII if climbed free, this recent ascent may be the first to free climb the route in modern mixed dry-tooling fashion. The two carried bivouac gear but finding no suitable ledges kept going to arrive on the summit 22 hours after leaving the Sciora hut. They found the rock to be solid, the climbing continuously steep, hooks and torques excellent, pitches easy to protect and difficulties up to M8.

Dick Isherwood and Mike Kosterlitz, both accomplished British rock climbers of their era, climbed the route by mistake, hoping at first to repeat the original 1953 *Battaglia-Corti* line on this part of the face. The first winter ascent of the British route was a landmark in female alpinism and still ranks up there with the most significant ascents in women's mountaineering. From 11-15 February 1982, Zuzana Hofmannová and Alena Stehlíková from Czechoslovakia battled full winter conditions to become the first unaided women's team to make a first winter ascent on a big alpine wall.

The on-form Federica Mingolla repeated *Bellevista*, Alex Huber's spectacular route on the north face of the **Cima Ovest di Lavaredo**. She tried the route over two days in August 2021 but was unable to free the crux (originally 8c but now thought to be 8b+). An accident that broke both heels then put her out for the season but she returned in mid June having not long before on-sighted 8a. Having just passed the crux, she fell and then retreated when rain set in. Next day she made a flawless ascent, leading every pitch. Her celebratory scream on reaching the belay at the end of the 8b+ pitch was so loud it roused applause from occupants at the nearby Lavaredo hut. However, on joining the upper section of the *Cassin* route, around half-height on the wall, she found it streaming with water and made a difficult descent from this point. This is the third female ascent, after Sasha Digiulian in 2013 and Barbara Zangerl in 2015.

The Messner Routes

Simon Messner, largely with regular climbing partner Martin Sieberer, continues to explore the Eastern Alps and a few of his 2022 new routes are described. A line on the west face of **Lagazuoi North** (2,510m) in the Fanes group had attracted Messner for years but he had been put off by apparently compact and often yellow rock. He finally attempted it over two days in July with Barbara Vigl, the pair climbing to two-thirds height before being stopped by an overhang. Messner returned on 3 August with Martin Sieberer, straightened the line and free climbed all eight pitches to the ring band, giving a relatively sustained climb with an VIII- crux. A degree of boldness and endurance are needed to repeat this route, which the authors named *La Vita e Bella*.

Jonas Hainz's solo was not the only event of interest on the **Roda di Vael**. In July, Messner, Philipp Prunster and Sieberer climbed a new line on the right side of the face, which they spotted while repeating the *Casarotto* a few days previously. Described as a little gem, the rock on *Manner di auf Wande Starren* is good for most of the seven-pitch climb, and the crux (VIII obl) is where it should be, right at the top.

The **Sagwand** (3227m) in the Austrian Zillertal has made several appearances in these pages over the last few years, not least for the first ascent and subsequent free ascent of *Sagzahn Verscheidung*, climbed in 2018 after four previous attempts by the late David Lama with Peter Mühlburger (800m, M6, A2). Two years later, and in much better conditions, it was climbed free by David Bruder and Martin Feistl at M6, WI4. The route arrives on the col between the Sagwand and, to the left, the **Schrammacher** (3410m). On the north-west face of the latter, close to *Sagzahn Verscheidung*, Messner and Sieberer opened *Goodbye Innsbrooklyn*, having made four attempts spread over the previous five years. The pair originally envisioned it as a mixed winter route (there are numerous loose blocks that need to be frozen in place) but felt unable to climb the smooth granite slabs with axes and crampons. March 2022 was the driest on record for this area, so on 24 March the two skied to the base of the wall, used axes and crampons for the lower easier section, then climbed the upper 485m in rock shoes at VIII-, with the crux moves past a rounded roof some distance above protection. The route terminates just left of the Schrammacher-Sagwand col, and the name reflects Messner's move from Innsbruck to live with his girlfriend in the South Tyrol.

Other New Routes

Two new routes were climbed from Combe Maudit in the Mont Blanc range. On 28 March Niccolo Bruni and Gianluca Marra climbed the north face of the **Col Occidentale de la Tour Ronde** in six pitches to give *Goulotte Desparados* (IV/4+ M7), where the last pitch crux on fragile rock was protected with two bolts. Then, over two days, 17-18 April, Gosia Jurewicz and Jozek Soszynsk put up *Resurrection* (nine pitches, M7+ A2), a dry-tooling route up the steep slabby wall to the right of the Androsace Pillar on **Mont Maudit**. The climbers descended by rappel from the shoulder at the top of the pillar where all its rock routes join. They found solid granite with good cracks and protection.

On the east-northeast face of the east ridge of **Aiguille Noire de Peuterey**, Jon Bracey and Matt Helliker climbed a deep couloir leading to a notch in the ridge. The 350m *Mad Vlad* gave steep mixed climbing, with sections of suspect rock and little protection. Bold climbing is reflected in the grade of M7 R, or Scottish IX, 8. Accessed via the lower Brenva glacier the new route was completed on 28 February.

The **Douves Blanche** (3664m) lie south of the well-known Aiguille de la Tsa on the east side of the Arolla valley in the Valais. The name is derived from large white rock scars on the north-west flanks. It is best known for the classic *Douves Blanche Arête*, the south-west ridge to the South Summit (3641m): a magnificent rock excursion on excellent gneiss (D, V). The north-west face of the South Summit is an austere wall and has been climbed on the right side by a hard rock route involving dangerously loose blocks and flakes. On 11 November Silvan Schupbach and Peter Von Kanel decided to try a right-slanting, central line of weakness in this wall, approaching from the left. The lower section was slabby, though not entirely straightforward, leading right to the line of weakness, which was steep and sustained. There were excellent pitches of dry tooling but as the pair approached the top, the rock worsened and the last two pitches comprised large loose blocks poorly wedged together. It was here they found old pegs. The two reached the top, Pointe 3582m on the south-west ridge, at dusk, then rappelled the route, arriving back in the valley 17 hours after leaving. The name of the line, *Frigo Combo* (450m, M7, 6a) refers to the fridge-size blocks in the upper section and the climb being a combination of new ground and an existing route.

From 6 August to 6 September Philipp Hans, Josef Pfnür and the now 57-year-old former competition climber and co-founder of the Red Chili brand, Stefan Glowacz, created a big new route on the north-west face of the 3,360m **Scheideggwetterhorn** in the Bernese Oberland. The new route takes a steep part of the wall between *Baston La Baffe* (1,100m, 34 pitches, 7c, Burdet-Zambetti-Zambetti, 1996-1998 and then 2004) and the classic *West Pillar Direct* (ca.1,000m, 5c/6a, Trachel-Von Kanel, 1970), still considered one of the best long rock routes in Switzerland. *Wirklich oben Bist du Nie* (1,100m, 33 bolt-protected pitches, 8a+ but not yet redpointed), which roughly translates as 'You're never really up there,' is a quote attributed to the late Reinhard Karl on reaching the summit of Everest.

In the Arolla: (A) Aiguille de la Tsa, (B) Douves Blanche North (3664m) and (C) South (3641m) from the west. The sombre wall below the south summit is climbed by the new mixed route *Frigo Combo. (Lindsay Griffin)*

In the Civetta group of the Dolomites, on the big south face of the **Torre Trieste** (2458m), home to the ultra-classic pre-war routes of 1934's *Carlesso-Sandri* (750m, VIII- VI+obl) and 1935's *Cassin-Ratti* (700m. VII+ VI+obl), two strong Italian teams independently created parallel lines. Alessandro Baù, Alessandro Beber and Nicola Tondini completed the 28-pitch *Enigma*, while Simon Gietl, Vittorio Messini and Matthias Wurzer climbed an adjacent 20-pitch line. It has been many years since new routes were added to the Torre, so it came as a surprise to both parties to find each other simultaneously attempting first ascents on this historic wall. Both routes were completed to the summit from September to November but the arrival of bitterly cold temperatures meant that free ascents will need to wait until 2023. Given the talent of respective parties, both lines will undoubtedly be hard and most likely climbed entirely with traditional gear.

In the Brenta, the south face of **Campanile Alto** (2937m), Fabio Bertoni, Andrea and Antonio Zanetti put up *Via delle Mamma* (c500m, VII) with bolted belays and rappel points but only pitons and threads left in the individual pitches. The Alto lies opposite the famous Campanile Basso and the new route lies to the left of the historic but classic *Via Graffer* put up in 1927 by Giorgio Graffer and Renzo Videsott, a 500m V that was considered hard for the day.

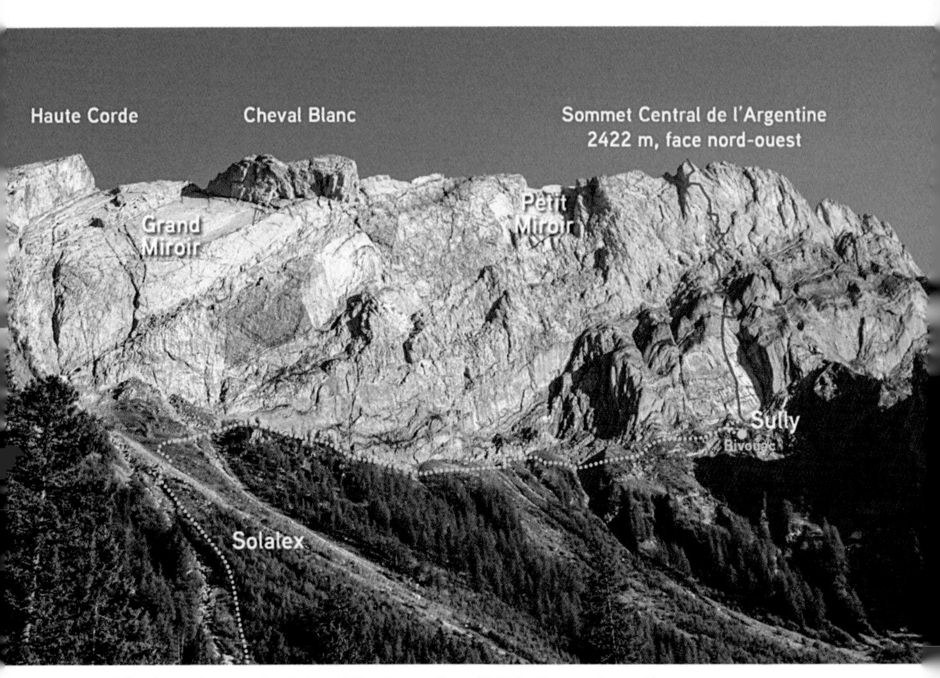

The broad summit vista of the Argentine (2421m), see from the north-west with the line of *Sully* marked. *(Claude Remy)*

Not all quality winter new routing in the Dolomites has to be desperate. In mid March, Marco Longo and Pietro Simon noticed a wonderful rectilinear couloir splitting the middle of the west face of **Cima Immink** (2850m), immediately south of the Pale di San Martino. It was such an obvious line in a region steeped in climbing history that they were amazed to find it unclimbed. The two resolved this by creating what they felt to be a classic mountaineering route with no serious difficulties. Conditions were dry, meaning that a few of the rock sections encountered would be covered with snow and ice in a normal season. *Scivolo del Riky* (45°-75°) was climbed without placing a single peg. The summit is named after Jeanne Immink (1853-1929) from the Netherlands, who towards the end of the 19th century was consistently climbing grades III and IV with her guides, perhaps the first woman to do so. She shot to fame through her partnership with Theodor Wundt, a pioneer of mountain photography, who published images of her climbing steep, exposed Dolomite rock, which was more or less unheard of for a woman at that time.

The Pre-Alps

The centenary of the first ascent of the famous Miroir, on the **Argentine** above Solalex in Switzerland, was celebrated in May. A couple of months later Marcel Remy passed away aged 99. He had climbed on the 450m west face of the Miroir countless times and was noted for his last ascent aged 94

Claude Remy leading on the upper section of *Sully*. Jean-Michel Pauchard is on belay. *(Gilles Damay/David Haefeli Coloria.ch)*

Jean-Michel Pauchard climbing the upper section of *Sully* on Argentine Central, while Nicolas Bossard makes a wing-suit BASE jump. *(Claude Remy)*

Fred Moeesner leading the diedre on the upper section of *Sully*. Jean-Michel Pauchard belays. *(Claude Remy)*

via a combination of routes up to 5b. Shortly before his death he was still leading 4c on a local climbing wall. Remy was the father of Claude and Yves, who themselves climbed many new routes on the Argentine and are credited for shaping modern climbing in the country, dubbed 'the heavy metal brothers who bolted Switzerland,' for their love of good protection and the powerful genre of rock music. During the summer there were second, third and fourth ascents of Claude Remy's latest addition *Sully* on the northwest face of the Central Summit (2422m) right of the Miroir.

There has been little climbing on this 500m wall: the lower section contains much bad rock, while the upper is vertical and compact. Remy and Jean-Michel Pauchard quickly decided that a ground-up ascent would, even with much aid climbing, prohibit satisfactory cleaning, particularly of large loose blocks. Instead, they opted to work the route from above using fixed ropes. It took 40 days, starting in 2019, until their first clean ascent on 20 August 2021 at 7a. More than 600 bolts were placed on the 27 pitches and statements from the parties repeating the ascent in 2022 include 'an incredible route – you must do it immediately.' During the ascent, 10 harder variation pitches were created to the right of *Sully*, and these have become *Sabaton* (6c obl, 7b/7c not yet freed).

In 2011 Stéphanie Bodet and Arnaud Petit began a new alpine sport climb to the right of the 600m east pillar of the **Pic de Bure** (2709m) in the Massif du Dévoluy. Since then almost a dozen climbers have nibbled away at the line, adding pitches and equipping. One of these, the French guide Aymeric Clouet returned in July 2022 with the young Italian Federica Mingolla. Over two days the pair made the first free ascent at 8a. The route is sustained, generally at 6c and above with two pitches of 7c+, two of 7c and the crux high on the route. *Voyage au Buristan* lies to the right of the *Desmaison Route* (Bertrand-Desmaison-Pollet-Villard, 1961, 20 pitches, VI with many pitches of aid, now 7a.) The second ascent of this classic line on the east pillar took place in June two years later, when it was completed over a couple of days by two talented rock climbers, the Scot Stewart Fulton and American Gary Hemming, whilst 'training' for their successful first ascent of the south face of the Fou just one month later. It is believed Desmaison discovered this area of the Dévoluy while attending the funeral of his great friend and climbing partner Jean Couzy, who was killed by stone fall on the peak next door to the Bure. Couzy put up many significant Alpine routes (often with Desmaison), took part in the 1950 French Annapurna expedition and later made the first ascent of Makalu.

• Thanks to Rodolphe Popier and several route authors for their help in compiling this report.

Fred Moessner in the lead with Jean-Michel Pauchard in the diedre on the upper section of *Sully*. *(Claude Remy)*

The east side of the Pic de Bure in the Massif du Dévoluy. The new route *Voyage au Buristan* climbs the steep walls to the right of the east pillar seen in profile.

SIMON RICHARDSON

Scottish Winter 2022-23

Chris Huntley on the first ascent of *International Groove* (IV,4) climbed during the International Winter Meet. *(Simon Richardson)*

In 2016, Greg Boswell and Guy Robertson raised the Scottish winter climbing bar by climbing three new Grade Xs in the same season. Since then, standards have remained largely static, but they moved forward again during the 2023 winter despite often limited snow and patchy conditions. In December, Boswell and Robertson made headlines with the first winter ascent of *Nihilist* (IX,9), an oft tried problem on Lochnagar, followed by *Vortex* (X,10): a bold and technical route breaching the main wall on Cùl Mòr. But it was Tim Miller and Jamie Skelton who turned heads with the first winter ascent of

Stone Bastion (X,10) on the Shelter Stone in early January. This seven-pitch route up a sustained summer E4 deep in the Cairngorms is one of the longest Grade Xs climbed to date and caught everyone's imagination. A little gloss was taken off when they explained that they had pre-inspected the crux pitch from above.

A week later Greg Boswell revisited Lochnagar with Jamie Skelton and Hamish Frost. The weather was poor with spontaneous avalanches cascading down the gullies but Shadow Buttress A was free from danger. Boswell set his sights on the three-metre horizontal roof guarding the blank looking wall on the right side of the buttress and after two false starts he rounded the lip to do battle with the technical headwall above. *Bring da Ruckus* (XII,13) is the highest graded route in Scotland to date. The two existing Grade XIIs (*Anubis* on Ben Nevis and *Banana Wall* on Cairn Gorm) had taken numerous separate attempts but *Bring da Ruckus* was climbed on the first visit and sits fully within the ground-up ethic.

Boswell and Robertson continued their new-route campaign with first ascent of *Delusion Direct* (X,9) in Coire an Fhamhair on Beinn Bhan. This six-pitch line is the direct version of *The God Delusion* and takes the obvious continuous crack-line cutting straight through the wandering lower wall in two long, hard and sustained pitches (both IX in their own right). In March they visited An Teallach's Hayfork Wall to climb the *Headmaster* (X,10), the most difficult of their routes on the wall to date. Also of note were the second and third ascents of *Banana Wall* (XII,12) in Coire an Lochain in the Cairngorms by Calum Muskett and Dave MacLeod.

Away from the cutting edge it was a relatively quiet season but several good mid-grade routes were found. In early December, Jack Morris and Neil Kerr climbed *Last Resort* (VI,6) on Church Door Buttress in Glen Coe which takes the left side of the rock needle that rises from the centre of Central Gully. Later in the month Joe Barlow, Rosie Rothwell and Bruno Cullinan visited Druim Shionnach in Glen Shiel where they climbed the excellent looking *Aubergine Pickle* (V,6) that takes the exposed right side of Boxer's Buttress.

Nathan Adam added two good new routes to Skye in January. Together with Dominic Mackenzie and Ben Smith-Price he climbed *Slaying the Badger* (V,6) on Am Basteir. This striking, left-facing chimney corner high on the left side of the north face starts from the traverse line of *The Deadline*. Fortunately, it was much easier than it looked and was very accommodating for placements and runners. Four days later, Adam visited the west face of Sgùrr a' Mhadaidh with Ali Rose, where they climbed *Sunshine Rib* (V,7) to the right of Thuilm Ridge. On Ben Nevis, S Pigden and O Miller climbed *Icarus* (VII,7), a bold route starting up the short left-trending corner left of *North-West Face*.

The Scottish Mountaineering Club organised the 2023 Scottish International Meet that ran from 25 February to 4 March. The meet was based at the CIC Hut on Ben Nevis and comprised eight guests from Korea, Poland, Italy, Germany and Singapore hosted by 12 British climbers. Ice conditions were excellent high on the mountain and the weather was superb.

Greg Boswell on the first ascent of *Bring da Ruckus* (XII,13) on Lochnagar. *(Hamish Frost)*

Over 120 ascents were made ranging from the great classics of *Tower Ridge* and *Point Five Gully* through to modern offerings such as *Big Wednesday* and *Flight of the Condor*. Eight new routes were climbed including *Hot Barszcz* (V,6), the icy wall left of *North-West Face* on Observatory Buttress by Willis Morris and Jan Gurba from Poland. The same pair also climbed *Red Aurora* (V,6) the ice line that cuts through *The Blue Horizon* on Raeburn's Wall. On The Comb, Scott Grosdanoff and Italian climber Dario Eynard had a good find with *Solar Wind* (VI,6) which takes a series of direct variations to *Naïve Euphoria*, and on the Carn Dearg Summit Buttresses, Chris Huntley and Simon Richardson found *International Groove* (IV,4), which is set in a magnificent position at the head of Castle Corrie.

There were several good additions in the northern Highlands. On Stac Pollaidh, Iain Young and John Higham climbed the spectacular *No2 Buttress* (IV,6), which approximates to the summer line first climbed in 1956. In the Glen Carron area, Mark Robson, Roger Webb and Neil Wilson found the excellent *Still Life* (V,5) on Glas Bheinn, and on Sgòrr Ruadh, Will Rowland and Garry Campbell ascended *Wide Buttress* (IV,5), a natural line left of *Narrow Gully* on Raeburn's Buttress.

In early March, Hamish Frost, Guy Robertson and Greg Boswell visited An Teallach and climbed *Grand Old Master* (VI,6), a magnificent 300m route taking the right crest of Major Rib. Most appropriately, the route was named in memory of the great pioneering Scottish winter climber Jimmy Marshall, who had passed away a few days before.

IAN WALL

Nepal 2022-23

Himlung remains a popular 7,000m challenge but changing glacier conditions are making the approach more difficult. Climbing a fixed line up a steep moraine bank.

Towards the end of every season, guides, agents and expedition owners start to return from their offices and the mountains to their favourite cafes in Kathmandu. Conversations always turn to what kind of a season they have had. The usual response is, 'Well, not so good but not so bad. Fingers crossed for next season.' And so everyone had high hopes for the autumn season of 2022. Expeditions to the 8,000m peaks showed a high booking rate but as the monsoon lingered on optimism began to wane.

In the western Karnali region, late monsoon rains in the second week of October killed dozens of people, made thousands homeless and washed away chunks of the Karnali highway, a new road already in a state of disrepair. The World Food Program (WFP) has, in recent years, taken a more proactive approach, using predictive analytics and weather forecast data to respond more quickly to avert disasters. That approach allowed a fast response to flooded communities in the Karnali river basin. The WFP sent early warnings and emergency cash to 3,000 households in areas the data deemed to be high risk. Climate change is undoubtedly changing monsoon patterns and the need for such schemes will only increase.

Autumn 2022

The world's eighth-highest mountain **Manaslu** (8163m) was more popular than ever, with many people trying to reach the 'true' summit having previously claimed the 'fore-summit' as the summit until Jackson Grove's video exposed so many false (or ignorant) claims in his video. Early in the season Kristin Harila, Pasdawa Sherpa and Dawa Ongchu Sherpa reached the summit followed a little later by Sanu Sherpa and Hu Tao. However, there had been days of rain on the higher slopes of the mountain making the snow very unstable and the inevitable avalanches happened, creating havoc on 23 September. The Department of Tourism had issued 404 permits to foreign clients for Manaslu, double the number in an average year. This number increased to over 700 people on the mountain when including Nepali guides and staff.

On 28-9 September, while guides and clients were spread out between camps three, four and the summit, two heavy snow avalanches broke away, seriously injuring four Sherpas and sweeping away more than 13 clients and Sherpas. Bad weather hampered rescue operations keeping several helicopters grounded in Samogaon, while one was forced to land above camp one with an injured client and a Sherpa, as well as the pilot. Crowded camps also created problems for pilots trying to evacuate ill or injured clients and staff, problems only compounded by politics and delays in obtaining national park clearance permits, even in the case of extreme medical emergencies. Higher up the mountain, above camp four, a large number of people were trapped as an avalanche had swept away the fixed ropes and clients lacked the skills to descend without them. This created more safety concerns as many people were on supplementary oxygen, which, in all the chaos, was inevitably running low.

On 2 October another avalanche hit Manaslu base camp, destroying more than 30 tents. After that, and several other avalanches, the agencies finally admitted that trying to get everyone up and down the mountain safely was suicidal and withdrew their teams in the face of increasing criticism on social media. There were avalanche fatalities including two Nepali expedition staff. The well-known American skier Hilaree Nelson, a former National Geographic Adventurer of the Year, fell to her death while attempting to ski down from the summit on the same day Anup Rai died in an avalanche.

Dawa Chhiring also died in an avalanche days later. Nelson's body was retrieved by her husband Jim Morrison, who had been skiing ahead of her and saw her fall, and a Sherpa team from around 6,000m on the south side of the peak.

Two statements stood out from media reports. Himalayan veteran Ralf Dujmovits, a high-altitude expert trying to reach the true summit, said that when he reached the top of the fixed ropes on a previous climb he hadn't realised it wasn't the true summit. 'A strong wind blew that day,' he said of his first climb in 2007. 'I wasn't able to look behind the supposed summit cornice. The sky was full of spindrift. I climbed another three metres further, but I didn't see a higher point.' He also stated that Manaslu is no longer the 'easiest' 8,000m peak since those who have little or no real mountain experience found the steep sections difficult, both technically and physically, despite the fixed ropes. Slow climbers caused much of the crowding and traffic jams on the lower half of the route. Adriana Brownlee, a newbie to the 8,000m speed game, said: 'this has taught me how dangerous this mountaineering world really is.'

Just as the Manaslu season was winding down, Grace Tseng of Taiwan and three Nepali guides set off from base camp at 6.30pm local time reaching the summit at 7.30am, 13 hours later. Tseng used no supplementary oxygen, although the three Sherpas supporting her did. Tseng's claim to have reached the summit of Kangchenjunga in October 2021 came under scrutiny with the conclusion being reached that she had not. Tseng has since told the media that she intended to revisit Kangchenjunga but on the next occasion it would be without supplementary oxygen. French mountaineers, Helias Millerioux, Charles Dubouloz and Symon Welfringer canceled their attempt on Manaslu's west face due to unstable snow conditions.

Expeditions to **Dhaulagiri** (8167m) also closed down early in the season due to bad weather and avalanches which forced all climbers to descend from no higher than camp three including Mike Arnold, Mathieu Maynadier, Vivian Bruchez, Matheo Jacquemond and photographer Bertrand Delapierre who had aspirations to make the first complete ski descent. David Goettler and Hervé Barmasse also called off their winter attempt. On **Everest**, extremely bad weather forced Andrzej Bargiel to cancel his attempted oxygen-free ascent and ski descent.

The world's sixth-highest mountain **Cho Oyu** (8188m) remains the focus for Sherpas intent on finding a new route to the summit from the south side but last year's winter expedition called off their attempt at 7,300m. The cost of the enterprise was supplemented by paying clients including Kristin Harila and Adriana Brownlee, both chasing the 8,000m speed record. Harila and Brownlee's lack of experience on non-fixed routes and the magnitude of the challenge in winter, on a highly technical route, without oxygen, attracted some criticism. (Harila is, if nothing else, a strong athlete: at the time of writing she has just climbed K2, the last of her 14 8,000ers achieved in 92 days, smashing Nims Purja's record, along with Tenjen Sherpa.) On Cho Oyu, strong winds destroyed high camps and other essential equipment and the expedition was ultimately cancelled. Commercial expeditions don't often include the cost of staying on the mountain for several weeks if the initial summit bid fails. This often results in a short expedition and the use of helicopters for the return leg to Kathmandu.

It was an extremely busy autumn season on **Ama Dablam** (6812m) with over 500 clients attempting to summit. Fixed base camps are now established at the foot of the mountain pre-season and they remain there, along with Sherpa staff, until December with the staff repeating the ascent as each new party of pre-booked clients arrive. With this approach, the surrounding environment is being impacted, particularly by human waste.

The Grey Couloir is a 100m long, 70° section of mixed terrain just above camp two that leads to the so-called Mushroom Ridge and camp three. Towards the end of the autumn season the couloir was unusually swept by rock fall that not only cut but also flushed out some of the fixed ropes. This is a critical part of the route, often taking several hours for clients to climb. Climate change is undoubtedly having an effect on the stability of this couloir. While the surface is refreezing, deeper internal dampness within the cracks and fissures is not and this gives climbers a false sense of security.

Robert Mads Anderson led an expedition to **Himlung** (7126m) that reached the summit on 17 November. While the expedition was 'trouble free', changing glacier conditions, once again caused by climate change, have created an objectively dangerous approach.

An expedition comprising Topo Mena, Roberto Morales and Joshua Jarrin of Ecuador left base camp on 14 October for **Langtang Lirung** (7234m). The team got caught on the crux section of thin and delicate ground at 5,800m in the heat of the day and decided to abseil back to base camp. With conditions not improving they wrapped up their attempt early.

A large Russian 14-member team led by Oleg Afanasiev, Sasha Eliseev and Andrey Dergachev reached the summit of **Annapurna IV** (7525m) on 13 November but Afanasiev was evacuated with frostbitten fingers and toes. The German solo climber Jost Kobusch succeeded on **Chulu West** (6419m). That was not his original goal but as on many other mountains, conditions were not good with his potential routes overloaded with snow and a high avalanche risk. To complicate his plans, Kobusch contracted dengue fever and his season came to an early end.

An American team had the north face of **Jannu** (7710m) in its crosshairs but due to appalling conditions curtailed their expedition. Still in the Jannu region, a Spanish team attempted **Jannu East** but one member was evacuated early on also due to contracting dengue fever. Previously unclimbed **Chumbu** (6859m) lies near the Tibetan border to the north-west of Gorak Shep got its first ascent from a Czech team comprising Zdeněk Hák, Juraj Koren, Radoslav Groh, Jaroslav Bansky and Petr Kejklicek. Juraj Koren had to withdraw, another victim of dengue fever, but Hak, who recovered from his dengue, and the remaining four set off from the Gaunara glacier, climbed the west face and descended south toward Changri Nup glacier. 'Because of snow conditions and unknown terrain, it was a very difficult climb. We assessed

Radoslav Groh on the first ascent of *The Last Flight of the Falcon* on the west face of Chumbu. *(Zdeněk Hák)*

the overall classification as TD+,' Hák said. They called their route *The Last Flight of the Falcon* as a tribute to fellow mountain guide Andrzej Sokołowski, who died in September 2022 in the Tatras. Sokolowski was a Polish climber, instructor and rescue worker. They camped twice at 6,350m and 80m below the summit which they then reached on 27 October.

Kisuke Goto and two other members of Japan's Himalayan Camp team attempted **Pungi** (6523m) but because of altitude sickness and bad conditions on the mountain they abandoned their expedition at 6,150m. **Pomlaca** (6187m), also known as Phamlahaka and Ngole East, is situated in Khumbu near Thyangbo village. Slovenian climbers, Bor Levičnik, Žiga Oražem, and Matija Volontar made a first ascent via the west face but it was not, as they believed, the first ascent of the mountain, which

Topo of the new Czech route on the west face of Chumbu. *(Zdeněk Hák)*

The line of the Canadian new route *Tiny Changes* on the north-east face of Khang Karpo.

was possibly climbed first in 2002. Already well acclimatised, the team climbed in a single and extremely fast sub-nine-hour push. The route was continually steep, between 70° and 90°, with some multi-pitch sections at 90°. They descended the east ridge. The trio, who met as part of the Slovenian Youth Alpine Climbing Team, named their route *Screaming Barfies* (1,100m, AI5, 70°-90°, IV-V), referring to the pain of 'hot-aches' that they endured during their ascent.

The closest 6,000m peak to Kathmandu is **Ganchempo** (6387m), which is situated in the Langtang region and was climbed via a new route up the south-south-east side of the mountain, also known as the Sindhupalchok side (after the closest village) by an all-Nepali team comprising of Rabindra Aryal, Ram Kaji-Prayas and Ashok Sharma Battha led by Sanu Sherpa and Lal Bahadur Waiba. Maarten van Haeren and Ethan Berman from Canada completed a new route on **Khang Karpo** (6646m) in Rolwaling: *Tiny Changes* is 1,200m and graded TD+, M5, AI4. This was the first ascent of the north-east face from the rarely visited Chulle glacier basin. The descent took two days down the line of ascent. The alternative descent on the south side seemed objectively hazardous and descent to the north would put them in Tibet. **Chekigo** (6257m), Rolwaling, was attempted by an experienced Japanese party, Hiroyoshi Manome, Yukio Ueda, and Makoto Kuroda alpine-style, they did not summit but made it up the south face to the main ridge before descending in poor and dangerous conditions. **Khembalung** was climbed in November 2022 by American climbers Ted Hesser, Garrett Madison, and one unnamed other. This is believed to be the first ascent of a nearly 7,000-metre peak that is relatively close to Everest. The name comes

Matija Volontar climbing the initial ground on the first ascent of the west face of Pomlaca. See p242. *(Bor Levičnik)*

Higher on the west face of Pomlaca.
(Matija Volontar)

Good conditions on the middle part of the Slovenian route which they called *Screaming Barfies*. *(Matija Volontar)*

A topo of the Slovenian route. Despite the Slovenians believing otherwise, this was not the first of the mountain, which was likely first climbed in 2002.

The Japanese line on Chekigo Peak. *(Hiryoshi Manome)*

from the village all their Sherpa team call home. The route is 1,400m with difficulties up to 5.6 to 5.8 with significant mixed terrain.

On 22 October the *Nepali Times* published an article indicating that the tourism-dependent municipality below **Machapuchare** (6993m) wanted the decades-old ban on mountaineering expeditions on the iconic Himalayan peak lifted. Wilfrid Noyce and David Cox, members of the 1957 expedition led by British Gurkha Lt Col Jimmy Roberts, had to turn back from 50m below the summit due to poor weather and technical climbing on the last stretch. Roberts later became defence attaché at the British embassy in Kathmandu and is said to have convinced the Nepali government at the time to keep the mountain out of bounds. Mountaineers had been forbidden from climbing it ever since, although that didn't stop New Zealand climber Bill Denz from claiming an ascent in 1982. At the moment the jury is still out.

The term 'trekking peak' is often misinterpreted. Mountains thus classified are still a challenge. British mountaineer Andrew James Clayton died at 5,000m in a high camp on **Lobuche** on 6 November, his deteriorating condition forcing him to return to base camp on advice from expedition guide Nims Purja. Clayton said he was okay and planned to go to Everest Base Camp next day with his guide. He went for a short sleep but never woke up. This was the third fatality on lower Khumbu peaks last autumn. Previously, Mingma Wangdi Sherpa and Jean-Marc Morschel of France died on **Ama Dablam** in separate incidents. Meanwhile in Manang, two Thai women, Rataya Philaisengsuri, 49, and Penny Aranlum, 37, died at 4,200m at the foot of Mesokanto La (5330m) as they were descending towards Tilicho lake. They were part of a large party of 22 and accompanied by eight porters and two guides.

Other ascents, apart from those on commercial expeditions, from the autumn 2022 season include Baruntse, Bhrikuti Shail, Dolma Khang, Khatung Khang, Metalung, Nagoru Far East and Tengi Ragi Tau South. According to the tourism ministry many permits were issued for lesser-known peaks around 6,500m in the autumn of 2022, including Sat Peak, Chandi Himal, Dogari Himal, Lachama North, Mansail South, Sharphu V, Sherson Peak 3, and Jobo Rinjang.

Expeditions to the far west of Nepal suffered particularly in the unseasonably late monsoon. Julian Freeman-Attwood, Nick Colton and Ed Douglas made the eight-day trek from Simikot to a base camp in the **Chandi Himal** just shy of 5,000m and then established advance base just below the Ganglung glacier. Douglas was another climber struck down with dengue. Having recovered, he and Colton put a cache high on the glacier with the intention of climbing Chandi next day. That was the last good weather of the expedition and after three days of snow they were forced to make a difficult descent to base camp. Four days after that, and with snow still falling, a sat-phone call confirmed mules could not reach within four to five days of base camp and the team called for an air evacuation that picked them up on 11 October.

From an optimistic start to the season, albeit with a long-lasting monsoon, the autumn ended with appalling conditions and weather bringing all big mountain expeditions to an early end. The style of modern commercial expeditions, their overuse of helicopter support, over-crowding, the excessive use of oxygen and staff along with the huge amount of fixed ropes resulted in many specialist media running negative reports of events and questioning the state of modern commercial expeditions.

Winter 2022-23

Simone Moro, the Italian mountaineer and helicopter pilot, returned to **Manaslu**. The Basque Alex Txikon was also on the mountain and reached the top on 6 January but not without controversy. Mountaineering is now a closely scrutinized activity with questions being asked of Txikon's, mask-free ascent while his team working with him were all using bottled oxygen.

During January 2023 the issue as to when winter in the Himalaya is not winter again surfaced. Adam Bielecki suggested that the astronomical (calendar) winter is the best way to define the climbing seasons, for a logical reason: you can apply the same definition all around the world. 'If we used the meteorological winter definition based on the coldest days, we should have to set different dates for every mountain in the world,' he explained. 'Better to stick to the simple calendar: four seasons, three months each, based on astronomy.'

Bielecki also spoke about the current evolution of Himalayan winter climbing, including using helicopters for the approach or acclimatising in different areas with more comfortable resources: 'it's part of a natural process,' he said, 'just as it was in the Alps. There was a time when the Alps were isolated, without roads, no lifts and nearly no huts. Climbing there was tough.

Now we can start from the valley, climb a 4,000er and be back at a restaurant at the end of the day.' He also aired his views on the use of oxygen: 'the biggest obstacle to climbing 8,000m peaks is the lack of oxygen. When you remove that, it is not the same. If you climb without O_2 but the people around you are using it, the style falls somewhere between an O_2 and a no-O_2 climb. If there are people with O_2 around you, there is always a chance that if things go really wrong, they'll share their masks,' he said. 'Only with no gas available can you prove that you are physically and mentally capable of reaching the summit without oxygen.'

Spring 2023

A total of 1,009 mountaineers received climbing permits to scale 23 mountains in the 2023 spring season, accumulating $5.5m in royalties for the Department of Tourism (DoT). Once again the weather played an all-important card. Adam Bielecki, Felix Berg and Mariusz Hatala were aiming to establish a new route on **Annapurna** while expedition outfitter Mingma G was planning to use **Thorong Peak** for his team to acclimatise on, with possibly two ascents and a summit camp before being airlifted to Annapurna base camp. Then it snowed and everything that could go wrong did go wrong. Again, a large number of climbers got stuck in high camps in very bad weather, eventually running out of food, fuel to melt snow and supplementary oxygen. Some of the exhausted climbers and Sherpa sustained frostbite. Sadly, Noel Hanna passed away in his tent at camp four. The usual mixed communications coming from the agencies, or no information at all, led to more confusion. One remarkable rescue on Annapurna was that of Anurag Maloo who, while descending from 5,800m fell into a deep crevasse, where she was later spotted by rescuers from a helicopter and eventually winched to safety and transferred to Kathmandu for extensive medical care.

Bartek Ziemski and cameraman Oswald Rodrigo Pereria of Poland planned ski descents on Annapurna and Dhaulagiri. After a swift ascent without oxygen or personal Sherpa support, the climbers reached the top. Ziemski then descended all the way on skis. He rappelled down several sections amid the seracs between camp three and camp two but kept his skis until the snow ended while Pereira made it back down to base camp on foot. Their physical strength, experience and self-sufficiency saved them from getting stuck in a difficult situation.

A new technological issue arose this season with the use of tracking devises on Annapurna. Some climbers who reached the summit used their InReach devices to share their locations live. All the trackers had two theoretical points in common. First, they all went to the same point, which was, logically enough, the end of the fixed ropes. The second point was not so obvious. All the climbers seemed to stop at a secondary summit on Annapurna, far from the spot marked on the map with a red summit triangle and Annapurna's name in Devanagari. The trackers put the altitude somewhere between 7,800m and 7,900m. It has transpired that the trackers were correct but the maps were not. Expert commentator Rodolphe Popier also observed that the contours on the InReach map were amazingly 'inaccurate'. His colleague Eberhard Jurgalski agreed. 'I think the trackers are correct but the contours are quite wrong,' said Jurgalski. 'They have marked the highest point at the central summit, not the main one.'

Climbers on **Manaslu** were also experiencing unfavourable conditions. However, the dangers were increased as a result of those seeking speed ascents pushing Nepali staff into going up to fix ropes in less than ideal conditions.

Peter Hamor along with Nives Meroi and Romano Benet succeeded on climbing a new route on the unclimbed west face of **Kabru South** (7394m) while climbers heading to **Kangchenjunga** in the spring of 2023 included Domi Trastoy and Gonzalo Fernandez Garcia of Andorra. Trastoy had already climbed Everest, Cho Oyu, Manaslu and Lhotse. Also headed to Kangchenjunga was the German guide Luis Stitzinger, whose experience on 8,000m peaks stretched back a quarter of a century and who was noted for his ski descents. He planned on skiing down Kangchenjunga but was found dead at 8,400m. His body was recovered and the cause of death given as pulmonary oedema.

Nepal issued a record 478 permits for **Everest**. Factor in that for every two climbers there are three staff and the number actually at Everest was more like 1,200. There were fears of overcrowding but a cold spring and persistent illness at base camp sent a lot of climbers home early. The cold weather also caused more frostbite injuries than usual. As a consequence there were even more flights on Everest, with approximately 200 flights to camp two during the season. These flights were also used to ferry equipment over the Icefall and by climbers not wishing to descend the Icefall to return to base camp. Helicopters are also being used increasingly to bring supplies to base camp without the need for traditional transport.

Despite the helicopters and huge support, the 2023 season developed into the deadliest on record with 17 fatalities. Within the first few days of the season three Nepali porters working for outfitter Imagine Nepal were caught in an avalanche in the Icefall: Tenjing Sherpa, Lakpa Sherpa and Badure Sherpa did not survive. Despite this, the Sherpa team fixing the route reached the summit in mid May.

There were a few interesting records. Kami Rita Sherpa, now 53, and Pasang Dawa both climbed the mountain twice in the season, taking their respective tallies to 28 and 27 respectively. Kenton Cool set a non-Sherpa record at 17. Some of the most impressive ascents were from disabled climbers, most notable the former Gurkha Hari Budha Magar who became the world's first double amputee to reach the summit. A number of climbers attempted the peak without bottled oxygen but the cold conditions worked against that. Among them was Kilian Jornet who made an impressive solo attempt on the west ridge of Everest. That attempt ended after a small avalanche several hundred metres up the Hornbein couloir swept him 50m down, prompting the Spaniard to abandon his attempt.

'I'm a big believer in the how is way bigger and more important than the what,' he wrote on his Instagram account, 'and in that sense the climb was just perfect. Like a big puzzle with all the pieces but one, the summit one.' A fine sentiment.

Just two climbers reached the top without gas on the regular route: Colombian Mateo Isaza and the Pakistani Sajidali Sadpara. Another of those who tried was the Hungarian Szilárd Suhajada who went missing and was seen next day in distress near the bottom of the Hillary Step. They radioed his position but when a rescue team arrived he had disappeared and has still not been found. In fact, four of the 17 fatalities remain missing, which begs questions of the companies responsible. Commercial practice on Everest continues to cause concern with multiple thefts reported as high as the South Col, including oxygen bottles, and inexperienced clients saving money with cheap local operators who don't follow best practice. These dodgy dealers can declare bankruptcy if there are any problems and reopen for business next year. The authorities continue to show little or no appetite for challenging any of this.

On a more positive note, great credit must be given to Gelje Sherpa working for Seven Summit Treks. Spotting a Malaysian climber, Ravichandran Tharumalingam, in distress and abandoned high on the mountain, he persuaded his Chinese clients to let him rescue the man, giving up his own summit attempt to do so. (Gelje had climbed the peak six times previously.) Working with Nima Tashi Sherpa, the pair carried the stricken climber on their backs from the Balcony to the South Col where others were able to help. Tharumalingam was eventually evacuated in a long-line helicopter rescue from camp three and proved surprisingly reluctant to acknowledge the part the Sherpas played in surviving his ascent.

Sixteen Chinese climbers reached the summit from the north side of the peak, part of a group maintaining the weather station installed last year. China did say it would issue permits but did in this in March when it was too late for anyone to do anything about it.

Another sad loss, someone many readers who have trekked in the region will have known, was the death of Pasang Lama, the Everest trail builder who worked tirelessly to ensure that paths were safe and accessible for trekkers and who could usually be found sat on his chair beside the trail collecting donations.

While all the expected dramas played out on the commercial expeditions Czech climbers Marek Holeček and Matěj Bernát headed to the north-west face of **Sura Peak** (6764m). They completed their route in five days and called it *Simply Beautiful*. 'It was pure alpinism, a beautiful and untouched face. One battle tent, a backpack with gear, a rope like an umbilical cord [between us], our plan and determination. Nothing useless.' They estimated difficulties to be M6, the average slope 70° with 90° and the length of the route at 1,500m. See Holeček's article 'The Gods Are Kind on Sura Peak' in this issue of the *Alpine Journal* for a full account.

Finally, on **Chandi Himal** (6142m) came news of a likely first ascent.

Nima Tashi Sherpa carries Malaysian climber Ravichandran Tharumalingam on his back down to the South Col, photographed by Gelje Sherpa who instigated the rescue and took turns in rescuing him. *(Gelje Sherpa)*

The late Pasang Lama, right, who for almost 40 years worked and then coordinated trail repairs in Khumbu, starting near his home in Dingboche and then expanding his efforts across the region. His efforts were recognised in Nepal, if not by the authorities then by the 'everyday hero' award from a Nepali newspaper. His age was uncertain, but Pasang was likely in his mid 80s.

Setting off before dawn up the north-west face of Sura Peak. *(Marek Holeček)*

Spaniard Jaime Iranzo and Pemba Sherpa succeeded in climbing this peak in Humla after a nine-day approach. The expedition was the brainchild of Matt Powell who recruited team members through the Potomac Appalachian Trail Club in the Washington region where Iranzo was studying. The ministry has not always been a reliable source of information on peaks in this area and peaks have been confused with each other. It's likely that some of these peaks have had 'unofficial' ascents but Powell thought this was a first ascent, a view shared by the British team who visited in the pre-monsoon.

Since 1950 nearly all expeditions have employed Sherpa staff. When asked, why do you risk your life for foreign mountaineers, they often reply, 'So that I can pay for my children to have a better education so as not to have to work in a dangerous occupation.' Previous generations have grown up in high-altitude villages, doing hard manual labour to sustain the family. If they did go to school that would often entail walking up to several hours to school and back home again, often carrying heavy bags of books and of course playing and running around along the way. This hard life at altitude developed resilience and a tough physical character.

These days it is rare to see youngsters in the high Himalayan villages; they are all studying at lower altitude in Kathmandu or abroad. Does this mean the present generation of high-altitude Sherpa workers will be one of the last to work on 8,000m expeditions? Being a guide is far more physically demanding in the Himalaya than in the Alps. Many 8,000m guides physically assist clients, carrying their rucksacks or oxygen, in ways not often seen in the lower ranges. If Sherpas withdraw from the industry, what will the impact on the Everest industry be? What will be the impact on the casualty rate? The issue is not an immediate concern but surely one that will arise in a few years' time.

Starting up the rock band at two-thirds height on Sura Peak during the first ascent of *Simply Beautiful*. *(Marek Holeček)*

Trekking Permits

An issue that has rumbled on for years is the threat to make guides compulsory for all trekkers. On 11 June 2023, the Nepal Tourist Board finally made it reality, issuing new guidelines for foreign trekkers banning them from visiting Nepal's national parks and conservation areas without a registered guide or porter. (These changes were described as 'guidelines' in the NTB's statement but look more like mandatory rules given the sanctions for breaking them.) The new rules say that a government-registered trekking company must arrange the guides or porters. Foreign visitors also have to obtain a trekkers' information management systems (TIMS) card before going trekking. These cost NR2,000.

A trekker found travelling on designated trekking trails without a guide or TIMS card faces a NR12,000: around $100. Officials at check posts have been promised 20% of the fine for stopping illegal trekkers as a special encouragement allowance, according to the authorities. A TIMS card is not required for those holding permits for climbing mountains. Tourists visiting restricted areas with permission from the Department of Immigration do not require the card either. Children under 10 do not require a TIMS card. Diplomats and aid workers don't require a TIMS card if they are working. The rules came with a list of 44 trekking trails across Nepal including Kangchenjunga, Makalu Barun, Everest, Rolwaling, Panchpokharai Bhairavkunda, Helambu, Langtang, Ganesh Himal, Manaslu, Annapurna, Mustang, Dhaulagiri, Dolpa and Humla.

Local authorities in the Everest region have strongly opposed the new rules, saying that they limit the right to free movement of foreigners. Independent trekkers have enjoyed taking advantage of the extensive network of trekking lodges in Khumbu.

By law all foreigners involved in trekking should insure their Nepali staff against illness, injury and death while employed as a guide or a porter. Foreign tourists also need insurance in case of helicopter rescue. Although this is not a legal requirement by law many helicopter agents will not collect casualties unless an insurance document is shown. All agencies expect clients to be appropriately insured.

Prior to these new rules trekkers could hire a guide or trek independently, requiring the trekker to take responsibility for the insurance of staff. At that time the purchase of the appropriate TIMS card covered that issue. Now guides are required to be hired through a registered trekking agency and by law the agency should insure their staff.

Many independent trekkers will be disappointed by these changes but so are many local lodge owners, homestay operators, freelance guides and porters who operate from trailhead centres and will now be required to work through agencies. It has also focussed attention on the quality of certified guides, whose training is often out-of-date or inadequate. A few have false documents.

Scrutinised closely, this seems more about trekking agencies extracting more money from tourists than any genuine attempt to improve safety as claimed. The rules don't apply to domestic trekkers who are no less vulnerable to mishap. Whether these rules will be implemented and monitored is another story. This season many TIMS counters and park check-posts remained unmanned.

TIMOTHY ELSON & ED DOUGLAS

India and Pakistan 2022

Dan Joll leading towards the barrier roof of the west face of Changabang on day three. *(Dan Joll)*

The standout ascent of 2022 in the Indian Himalaya, briefly reported in last year's *Alpine Journal*, was the first repeat of the 1976 British route on the west face of Changabang from an Australian-New Zealand team in excellent style in late April and early May. In the post-monsoon season, poor weather hindered many teams and led to one of the worst tragedies in recent Indian climbing when 29 climbers died in a single avalanche. Three teams from the Alpine Club were active in Zanskar and the east Karakoram, with a party from the Young Alpinist Group making an impressive first ascent on Barnaj II East.

West face of Changabang in profile. *(Dan Joll)*

The repeat of the Shining Wall on **Changabang** (6864m) was finally made 46 years after Pete Boardman and Joe Tasker made the first ascent over 25 days in 1976 in a tour de force of lightweight capsule-style climbing. At the time, it was one of the hardest routes in the Himalaya and certainly the hardest climbed by a team of two. Boardman and Tasker's accounts of the ascent in *The Shining Mountain* and *Savage Arena* added to the mystique of the face and over the intervening decades drew in several strong teams, though few got much further than the Bagini col.

The Australian-New Zealand team made up of Dan Joll, Kim Ladiges and Matt Scholes travelled to India in April 2022 when it was still technically closed to tourists by utilising an invite from the New Zealand High Commission. Prior to the expedition, the team pre-acclimatised in the Mont Blanc massif for six weeks and so arrived in India partially acclimatised for their route. The team's high level of preparation, forethought and planning resulted in a smooth ascent, which nevertheless still sounded incredibly cold and hard work.

They arrived at base camp on 11 April and started up the route just eight days later, fixing all the ropes they had up the initial section of the line. The trio took a slightly harder line that led more directly to the start of the climbing on the west face rather than going straight up to the Bagini col. This turned out to be one of their masterstrokes as it allowed for much easier hauling, a benefit that significantly outweighed the slightly more difficult climbing.

The weather seemed to have a steady pattern for the whole expedition, with a fine start each morning before things gradually deteriorated and developed into storms in the afternoon. This made climbing on the west face

Climbing the summit ice gullies on the west face of Changbang. *(Dan Joll)*

tough and cold, often with only a very short period where the team got any sun.

After a rest at base camp, they set off up the face again on 25 April. From their advanced base camp the route took a nine-day round trip. Each day, one of the team led and one belayed, alternating positions each day for most of the climb and moving their camp up every other day. Although they were a small team, they had around 100kg of equipment with them, including a full big-wall rack, tent and two portaledges.

From 25 to 30 April they made progress up the wall, enduring a terrible bivy in a storm just below the central icefield on the night of 28 April during which one of the portaledges broke. On 1 May they set off from their high camp with only their bivy tent and spent an uncomfortable night sliding off a ledge before summiting safely on 2 May. From the top it took two days to abseil back down before a mega-load-carry got them back to base camp.

The post-monsoon season in India was characterised by unsettled weather and more snow than usual. This led to one of the worst mountaineering tragedies in mountaineering history when a group of 41 from the Nehru Institute of Mountaineering, made up of seven instructors and 34 trainees, were hit by an avalanche on 4 October while attempting **Draupadi Ka Danda II** (5670m) in the Garhwal Himalaya. Tragically 29 of the group, including two female instructors, died after being buried by the avalanche. As one survivor of the avalanche put it: 'Everything happened in the blink of an eye and everything happened in silence.' A large rescue attempt was made and 27 of the bodies were recovered but the tragedy plunged Indian mountaineering into a period of introspection. The worst mountaineering disaster remains the 1990 Peak Lenin avalanche that killed 43.

Mick Fowler and Victor Saunders (UK) returned to the unclimbed **Chombu** (6310m) in Sikkim for the third time. The expedition lasted from late April to mid May and they found consistently poor weather for the whole trip, with persistent avalanche conditions. Their initial aim was to attempt the attractive mixed ramps on the mountain's west face but the good weather that preceded their trip left these bare of snow and ice. The pair therefore turned their attention back to the north-east spur where they had reached 6,017m in 2019. While acclimatising, Saunders suffered a bad cut to his hand, which delayed their attempt until 4 May. From 4 to 10 May the

A glorious view of Hagshu from Chomochior. *(Hugo Béguin)*

pair undertook a push on the north-east spur, but bad weather severely hampered their attempt. They climbed the Fowler couloir, which leads to the glacier shelf below the north face but retreated in the face of high avalanche conditions.

In September, Alpine Club members Derek Buckle, Jamie Goodhart, Steve Humphries, Steve Kempley and Howard Pollitt travelled to the Rassa glacier region of the Nubra valley in the east Karakoram where they made the first ascent of **Dagarpheth Kangri** (6365m). Initially they spent four days in Leh, before crossing the 5,370m Khardung La to the Nubra valley. Setting off from the village of Tirit they trekked for three days up the Tirit Phu where they established a base camp at 4,750m, a little beyond the summer pasture of Arganglas and close to the confluence of the Rassa and Phunangma glacial outflows. From here they scouted the best access to the lower Rassa glacier and set up a camp in a sandy depression on the moraine at 5,100m before setting up a further high camp at 5,500m. From this high camp an extensive reconnaissance was carried out before Pollitt and Kempley made the first ascent of Dagarpheth Kangri on 20 September via the east-south-east ridge (AD). After this, bad weather set in and the expedition returned home.

The west wall of Changabang was not the only significant repeat this year, with a young team from the Swiss Alpine Club making an ascent of the 1988 Everett-Richardson route on **Chomochior** (6278m). The original aim of the expedition had been to try a route on Cerro Kishtwar but the unstable autumn weather meant that this was not feasible. The whole Swiss

An excellent view of Cerro Kishtwar illustrating the thin gully taken by Mick Fowler and Steve Sustad on their first ascent of the mountain in 1993: 30 years ago. *(Hugo Béguin)*

team, comprising Matthias Gribi, Gaetan Simian, Hugo Béguin, Kaspar Grossniklaus, Julian Cavigelli, Niklas Konrad and Thomas Senf, repeated the south-west ridge of Chomochior. They climbed in two groups, separated by a day, from 2 to 5 October. Four of the team went on to try a route on **Kishtwar Shivling** (5780m) while two others made an ascent of a rock climb on Point 5066m which they dubbed *Petit Clocher du Kishtwar* (6b) as it reminded them of the climbing on the Petit Clocher du Portalet.

An American team made up of Tess Smith and Alan Goldbetter returned to the Shimling Tokpo in Zanskar in July 2022, having been there previously in 2019 to attempt **Starikatchan** (5904m). This peak was once again their objective in 2022. They initially tried a route on the east face, which they had previously attempted in 2019. They climbed for two days, encountering difficulties of 5.8 and A2, but retreated high on the face when they came upon a band of shale that was too loose for their liking. Subsequently they moved base camp and approached the peak from the west in order to access the mountain's south ridge. They spent another two days on an attempt, but turned around at c5,800m after running out of time on the second day having left their bivy kit low down.

During August, the Spanish team of Tasio Martin and Marc Toralles climbed a new route on **Punta Guillem Aparicio** (5700m) in the Shafat valley. The valley is known for its high-quality granite and is home of the famous Shafat Fortress. The pair climbed their new route, which they named *Txoria Txori* (740m, 7a+), in a single push from base camp on 23 August. The route was free climbed in its entirety without the use of bolts.

Chiling I and II from the Chiling col. The upper section of the north face of Chiling II is in the shade on the right of the picture. *(Innes Dean)*

A British Team made up of Alex Mathie, Innes Dean and Timothy Elson went to attempt the unclimbed north face of **Chiling II** (6253m) in September and October 2022. Alex Mathie attempted this face in 2018 and succeeded in reaching the top of the initial ice runnel before warm temperatures forced him down. The team acclimatised by heading up to the Chiling Col (c5200m) between the Lalung and Chiling glaciers, which is also the approach to the north face of Chiling II. On reaching the col they found the way to the bottom of the face blocked by a large, fresh landslide. The team spent two days attempting to find a route through this before giving up. They subsequently made attempts on **Lalung I** (6243m) and **Peak 6048m**, but bad weather and avalanche conditions forced retreat on both peaks.

A British-Irish expedition made up of Young Alpinist Group members Dave Sharpe, Will Harris, Callum Johnson, Matt Glenn and Tom Seccombe travelled to the Hagshu Nalla to attempt **Barnaj II** (c6500m) and **Chiring** (6300m). Johnson, Glenn and Seccombe succeeded in making the first ascent of the north face of **Barnaj II East** (6303m), a subsidiary summit of Barnaj II. The ascent was made over three days from 7 to 9 October. The team called the route *Seracnaphobia* (1,600m ED, M5, AI4).

On the first day, the team of three simul-climbed the lower ice-snow face before bivying below a serac. The second day involved climbing harder mixed pitches on the headwall before reaching the ridge at 6,000m where they again bivied. Reaching the summit at noon on the third day, they then descended their line of ascent on abalakov threads. Despite several expeditions to Barnaj II in the late 1970s and early 1980s, as well as attempts by an American team in 2014, the main summit of Barnaj II appears to remain unclimbed. For more details, see the full report on page 14 of this year's *Alpine Journal*.

The north side of Lalung I that had incredibly poor rock. *(Innes Dean)*

The north face of Peak 6048m. The line attempted was the line between sun and shade. *(Innes Dean)*

In October 2022 Ondrej Huserka (Slovakia) and Wadim Jabłoński (Poland) made the first ascent of **Phaalkan Meenaar Tower** (5602m), via a route they called *Gangotri Gambling* (6c+, A0, M6). They were part of a larger expedition whose focus was **Thalay Sagar** (6904m) and climbed Phaalkan Meenaar Tower as a consolation prize after poor weather prevented an ascent of their primary objective. From 14 to 16 October the pair climbed Phaalkan Meenaar Tower, which sits above Kedar Tal valley in the Garhwal Himalaya,

Technical climbing on Phaalkan Meenaar. *(Wadim Jabłoński)*

The line of Gangotri Gambling on Phaalkan Meenaar Tower. *(Wadim Jabłoński)*

by an 18-pitch route comprised primarily of rock climbing with some mixed sections. Phaalkan Meenaar in Hindi means 'falcon tower' and the ascent was dedicated to Andrzej 'Falcon' Sokołowski: a Polish climber and guide who died tragically in the Tatras in September. (See also Nepal notes for another memorial route to Sokołowski.)

Elsewhere in October, Jonas Schild, Andy Schnarf and Stephan Siegrist made the first ascent of a big-wall style climb they named *Between two Parties* (7b, A3, 350m) on Kirti Nose (4950m) below the south face of Shivling. The route, like that above on Phaalkan Meenaar was really a consolation prize, snatched in the poor post-monsoon conditions which thwarted so many of this year's expeditions to the Indian Himalaya.

Tim Elson

Meanwhile in **Pakistan**, the more numerous technical challenges and cheaper, less bureaucratic operating costs of the Karakoram continue to attract many strong teams from around the world. The Trango massif is more usually associated with the summer months but a Polish expedition comprising Marcin Tomaszewski and Damian Bielecki made a first ascent in winter on **Uli Biaho Gallery**, the huge buttress guarding access to Uli Biaho Tower. The original plan was to attempt Shipton Spire with a third teammate who withdrew at the last moment. The two Poles started on 5 December and spent 11 days climbing through extreme conditions. The face has a northern aspect and temperatures dropped as low as -32°C but Tomaszewski and

The line of the new Italian-Austrian route on Shaue Sar (6653m).

The new Italian route on Chikkorin Sar (5810m), which Tomas Franchini dubbed Gypsy Sar.

Bielecki persevered to create *Frozen Fight Club* (780m, A3, M7). Their line goes to the left of the 2014 route *FreeTanga Ecuatoriana*, sharing the top pitch.

Meanwhile on **Nanga Parbat** (8126m), David Göttler and Hervé Barmasse called off their winter attempt of the Schell route on the immense Rupal face. Apart from the intense cold, heavy snowfall shut them down at 6,200m. A forecast of jet stream winds at 8,000m for several weeks made lingering for better weather pointless. 'I never regret any experience,' Barmasse said in announcing their withdrawal. 'Believing (and still believe) that we can climb the biggest wall in the world in winter and in a clean, light, alpine style. A style that respects the mountains and consequently mankind.'

Moving to the summer, Italian Tomas Franchini, Austrians Philipp Brugger and Lukas Waldner travelled in mid May to the Momhil valley. The original plan was to try **Dut Sar** (6,858m), first climbed 30 years ago by an Italian team, but mixed weather prompted the trio to switch objective to an unclimbed and unnamed peak they dubbed **Shaue Sar** (6653m). Starting from an advance base at 4,600m at 3am on 27 May, the three reached the summit in 11 hours via the north face to the north-east ridge at 6,200m, largely climbing unroped except for a steepening near the top. Descent required numerous abseils from abalakovs and they were back at advance base at 7pm after a 16-hour round trip. Before this, on 23 May, Franchini acclimatised with a solo ascent of a peak he dubbed Gypsy Sar but was in fact **Chikkorin Sar** (5810m), first climbed in 1993 by the same Italian team that did Dut Sar. His was a new line though, which he called *Azam* (600m, TD, 80°). On the way out via the Shimshal valley, Franchini climbed solo a rocky summit in the Zartgurben valley he dubbed **Croz von Zartgurben** (4650m) via the west face at VII.

On **Nanga Parbat**, Italian climbers François Cazzanelli and Pietro Picco added a new variation start to the Diamir face's *Kinshofer*. Dubbed *Valle d'Aosta Express*, the line overcame the huge serac at the base of the Mummery spur and then a series of steep snowfields and mixed ground to join the Kinshofer at camp two at around 6,000m.

French alpinists Christophe Ogier, Victor Saucede and Jérôme Sullivan made the first ascent of **Pumari Chhish East** (6850m) via a substantial line they called *The Crystal Ship* (1,600m, M7, 6b, A2). The mountain is located off the Hispar glacier and surrounded by 7,000m peaks. Its south face has three granite prows but despite regular attention from strong teams, its complex terrain and objective threat had until last summer thwarted all-comers.

The French may have benefitted from a long wait at base camp for good weather. This left them plenty of time to study the face, threatened as it is by substantial snow mushrooms on the summit ridge. Their patience paid off, as they found a line up a steep section on the left-hand buttress that was relatively free of this danger. Starting at 2am on 25 June, the trio had cleared an initial snow slope and were established on the wall by the end of the day. The upper steep section took three days on a system of cracks requiring 20 pitches of sustained mixed and aid climbing. For the last few the team switched into rock shoes for 6b free climbing on vertical and at times overhanging rock to arrive at a final fourth bivy on a shoulder beneath the summit. The snow mushrooms proved unnerving but they were on the top early on 29 June and back in base camp that evening.

Low down on the substantial, 2,200m new route *Waa Shakil* climbed by a Basque-British team on Trango II this spring. *(Hermanos Pou)*

On **Trango Tower** (6239m), often called Nameless Tower, Spaniard Edu Marín made the second free ascent of the classic German route *Eternal Flame*, 13 years after Thomas and Alex Huber made the first. Marín had come close in the summer of 2021. Starting at above 5,000m, it's hardly surprising that the hugely attractive free ascent of such a beautiful line involved a protracted effort but several parties. The Hubers finally succeeded in removing the final aid at 7c+, describing it as 'the best and most beautiful free climb on the globe' with its crux above 6,000m. Marín, climbing with brother Álex and father Francisco, thought the crux more like 8a, but by the time he overcame it he had sat out a period of bad weather at 6,000m to ensure a one-push ascent. He spent 28 days altogether on the wall, reaching the summit on 20 July. Perhaps just as impressive was Francisco's summit, achieved at the age of 70.

A few days later, *Eternal Flame* got its third and first female free ascent from Austrian Barbara Zangerl climbing with Italian Jacopo Larcher. Like Edu Marín, the pair had tried in 2021 but last year things went much better. Starting on 18 July, they climbed the route in one push, swinging leads but both leading the hardest four pitches. Reduced to a crawl on days two, three and four by hot temperatures melting snow, on the fifth day they made rapid progress and topped out quickly on the sixth day. The ascent confirms Zangerl

The route was completed in snowy, windy conditions that were more like winter. *(Hermanos Pou)*

Eneko and Iker Pou either side of British alpinist Fay Manners. *(Hermanos Pou)*

status as one of the strongest all-round climbers in the world. With sport ascents up to 8c+/9a, the first woman to boulder at 8b, a free ascent of the *Nose* and the first repeat of the Eiger classic *Odyssee*, she's also a National Geographic adventurer of the year.

On **Uli Biaho Spire** (5620m), Italians Leonard Gheza, Alessandro Baù and Francesco Batti established a significant new route called *Refrigerator Off-Width* (510m, 7a, A2, M5). The line takes an obvious corner in the middle of the east face. Having arrived on the Baltoro in mid June, the team made a strong attempt on *Eternal Flame* before settling in on their main objective. Uli Biaho Spire sits next to its bigger neighbour Uli Biaho Tower (6109m). On 17 July they didn't even make it to the bottom of the cliff, while on 18 July they climbed two pitches before realising they were underequipped and returned to camp for more gear. After making progress the next day, they rested on 20 July and then committed to the wall, climbing six more pitches to a freezing bivouac at two-thirds height. Another six pitches put on the summit on 23 July. 'Viewed from below,' Ratti said, 'the corner is very obvious and, in general, it leads to the top in an elegant way. We saw another obvious corner to the left, which we took. Of course, it would have been more beautiful to stay in the original corner. But we noticed during the bivouac that the straight-up section formed by a chimney was much more difficult and we did not have enough gear to properly protect this section. On the other hand, the system on the left side was more approachable and safer.' Theirs was only the second route on this face.

Moving into the early season in 2023, well-known Basque brothers Iker and Eneko Pou and the British alpinist Fay Manners climbed six new routes in the Trango group. The pick of these was a colossal new mixed route on

Topo of *Waa Shakil* on Trango II. *(Hermanos Pou)*

Trango II (6327m), the first on that peak for some years. Manners described *Waa Shakil* (2,200m, 6b, 70°, M5), climbed in three days, as a 'long alpine-style climb which involved some interesting mixed at the top.' It might have been a different story given how badly the expedition started. Manners and Eneko Pou both had flu and were struggling to breathe properly at altitude. Others in the team had stomach issues. Then they faced heavy snowfall, which shut down access to many objectives. To cap this difficult start, Manners then got word that her close friend and climbing partner Line van den Berg had died in Switzerland. She credited the support from the Pou brothers in getting through what must have been an agonising few days.

After that, and despite a strong desire to return home, Manners and the rest of the team kicked into gear. To acclimatise they climbed *Domage pas de Fromage* (250m, 6c) on **Little Trango** (5700m) with Colombian Andrés Marín, dedicating the route to van den Berg. As the weather became more unstable, the team kept active by adding more rock routes of around 200m on previously unclimbed spires between 4,500m and 5,000m, before pushing back their flights and committing to Trango II. Starting from a base camp at 4,080m and with the weather more like winter, with high winds and low temperatures, the three had their work cut out. They reached the west summit in a storm and descended in a blizzard with slopes avalanching around them. 'We couldn't do anything,' the Pou brothers said. 'Just cross our fingers so that the next one wouldn't come down on us.'

There was still time, however, to climb one more rock route on another unclimbed needle the brothers dubbed **Lady Fay** (5100m) to give *Always Elurra* (260m, 7a+). 'Manners is the living example of a new generation of mountaineering women that has been going very strong,' the brothers said. 'She has been leading on most of our ascents, demonstrating a spectacular physical and technical level.'

Fay Manners, who followed up recent success in the Alps with a major new route in the Karakoram. *(Hermanos Pou)*

Perhaps the most imaginative first ascent in the Karakoram last year came from British guide Will Sim and his German partner Fabi Buhl. They chose as their objective **Gulmit Tower** (5810m), which has resisted all-comers since the first attempt by a French team in 1988. Half a dozen attempts were made from the north-east via the Bulkish Yaz glacier, with problems on the approach from avalanches, seracs and blank rock. The approach from the south is via the Gurpi glacier is simply too dangerous and convoluted for porters. That's when Buhl and Sim had what they described as 'a light-bulb moment' during a skiing-paragliding-climbing trip to the Hunza valley. They could take off from Karimabad at around 3,000m and ride thermals up to 6,000m and simply fly over the Gurpi glacier to land at the foot of the south-west face. Despite being laden with bivouac and climbing gear, and despite the vagaries of the thermals, this they achieved together with fellow pilot Jake Holland who followed their progress next day from the col at the top of the glacier before skiing back to camp and flying out.

Sim and Buhl started at 2am, climbing a 400m couloir in the dark that was usefully frozen to a col. Above that was a steep sequence of cracks and chimneys that led in 10 pitches to the summit. They abseiled the route anticipating another night at camp but when they reached their stash they decided to take advantage of the warm evening air and less than an hour later were back on the Karakoram Highway having saved themselves a three-day walk. 'Our adventure on Gulmit Tower,' Sim said, 'answers a question that Fabi and I have had in our minds for some time: can cross country paragliding and technical climbing in the Greater Ranges work together?'

Tom Livingstone and Aleš Česen planned to attempt the south-west ridge of **Gasherbrum III** (7952m) but were forced to abort due to strong south-westerly winds. Believing they might find more success and shelter from the wind on the mountain's north face and ridge, they relocated and made an attempt from this side of the peak. At 7,800m they came upon a large tower that couldn't be bypassed and which required more difficult climbing than they were willing to contemplate given the altitude and weather. Livingstone notes that the south-west ridge of Gasherbrum III is still a viable prospect due to its fairly solid granite composition which contrasts markedly with the rest of the group.

On the first ascent of *The Pretty, the Bad and the Ugly* (230m, 7a). *(Hermanos Pou)*

American couple Priti and Jeff Wright came within 100m of the summit of **K7 Central** (6858m) having already made important first ascents on the north and east faces of the group in previous years. They reached base camp in the Charakusa valley on 20 June. Dominating the Charakusa valley, in the west of the Karakoram, K7 is divided into three distinct peaks: the western K7 (6615 m), the central and the main (6934m). All three peaks have seen attention in the last couple of decades from some big names but the central summit remained and remains unclimbed. Details remain sparse, but the pair claimed to have climbed 2,000m with difficulties up to M5, AI4 and 5.9 but were shut down when the crack they were climb disappeared into blank rock just shy of the summit. Jeff Wright took two falls trying to makingfurther progress. They descended the mountain's previously untouched central couloir, despite its high objective danger, in just one day back to base camp.

A Hungarian team visited the Hushe and Nangma valleys, reaching the base camp for K6 on 28 June, just three days after arriving in Pakistan. Having assessed the weather and conditions, three of the team, Laszlo Szasz, Bence Kerekes and Viktor Agoston, climbed an unnamed peak near Green Tower via a 600m route they dubbed *Hungarian Dances* with three pitches of 5c rock climbing. They then climbed 12 pitches on an unnamed peak on the north side of the valley, with difficulties up to 6b, before retreating in a rainstorm. They then had to wait 12 days for the weather to improve before setting out on unclimbed **Bondit Peak** (5980m) from Khande village (2900m), camping first at 4,100m and then again on the Bondit glacier at 5,100m. The following day they reached a camp at 5,500m and went to the summit the following day via the north-east ridge with snow and ice up to 80°. They reported significant objective danger from seracs and avalanche. There had been at least three previous attempts on the peak but its altitude had previously only been guessed at 5,780m. The Hungarians GPS reading is quoted above.

The well-known Czech pairing of Marek Holeček and Radoslav Groh attempted a new route alpine style on **Masherbrum** (7821m), reaching 7,300m on a futuristic line on the compelling north side of a mountain that has only been climbed four times by any route. In his inimitable style, Holcček described poor snow conditions as being partly responsible for turning round: 'As we climbed from the north side to the east side, the snow turned into non-sticky powdered sugar. Loose, dried white stuff that sticks in the groove and on the rock for some mysterious reason. As soon as you touch it, it falls over 2,000m to the glacier in big cakes.'

Cornered on the first ascent of *The Prime Minister* (205m, 6c). *(Fay Manners)*

The Japanese climber Kazuya Hiraide had a long love affair with **Shispare** (7611m), in the western Karakoram, first seeing the mountain in 2002 and then making four attempts to climb it, ultimately succeeding in 2017 via the first ascent of the peak's north-west face and the first of the peak in alpine style, a climb that won a Piolet d'Or. (Hiraide has three of them.) During that decade

The first ascent of *Always Elurra* (260m, 7a+) on a previously unclimbed spire dubbed Lady Fay. *(Hermanos Pou)*

and a half, he couldn't help but notice the neighbouring peak of **Karun Koh** (6977m), attempted by Chris Bonington and Al Rouse shortly before an Austrian team made the first ascent in 1984. So Hiraide returned in late 2021 to climb it but suffered dreadful frostbite on his acclimatisation peak. It seemed his climbing life might be over.

By spring, however, his feet had healed sufficiently for him to contemplate returning, which he did last September with his Shispare climbing partner Kenro Nakajima. Finding a line they could trace with certainty up the peak's north-west face proved elusive but they went for it anyway, finding 'a wonderful route that miraculously connects a line of ice through rocky walls, all the way to the summit.' They reached the summit on 21 September after one bivouac and made another on descent, grading the route WI5. Hiraide and Nakajima were back in Pakistan this year climbing Tirich Mir: more details in the next edition of the *Alpine Journal*.

Two views of the first ascent of Gulmit Tower, finally achieved despite a dangerous, time-consuming approach via the imaginative solution of flying in on a paraglider. *(Jake Holland)*

A French-Pakistani team comprising Sebastién Carniato, Sussex-born James Price, Adnan Khan and Hassan Aljabbal made probable second ascents of two peaks in the Batura Muztagh region of the western Karakoram. On 1 September, they reached a col below **Mirshikar** (5464m) and the following day Price soloed a likely new route through seracs to the top of **Pheker Peak** (5462m), west of the col. The day after that, the whole team climbed the east ridge of Mirshikar before descending the south-west ridge to complete the traverse of the mountain. The recorded first ascent of both these mountains was made by Lindsay Griffin in 1984. On 11 September Price set off on an attempt on the Batura Wall traverse, carrying a sack of 30kg and prepared for a three-week outing. Facing bitterly cold temperatures, he came close to the summit of **Muchu Chhish** (7453m), the highest unclimbed peak that's currently accessible.

The K7 group, including K7 Central, almost climbed by Priti and Jeff Wright.

The line of the new Japanese route on Karun Koh.

He tried to wait out 30 hours of strong winds but with a bleak forecast chose to use a short window of good weather to escape the ridge. During the descent he realised that his cold feet were in fact frozen with serious frostbite injuries that cost him several toes.

Ed Douglas

MARCELO SCANU

South America 2022-23

Alvaro Rojas Rivera with his group climbing Cerro del Gallo (5615m) in the Atacama. (Alvaro Rojas Rivera)

Chile

In the Atacama region, Alvaro Rojas Rivera and his group ascended various interesting virgin volcanoes in a remote zone 57km north of Ojos del Salado and near the Paso de San Francisco and the Argentine border. Starting in 2019, three important volcanoes were explored including Volcán del Toro, surely the previously highest untrodden summit in Chile. They were looking out for Inca remains but nothing was found on the summits.

On 24-27 October 2019, Chileans Juan Avalos, Cristóbal Diaz, Danilo Layana and Alvaro Rojas Rivera climbed **Cerro Negro Grande** (5570m). They had seen the mountain from Juncalito (5675m), first climbed 25 years earlier. Thinking Negro Grande was also rarely visited, they erected a base camp at 4,425m and reached what was in fact an unclimbed summit from the north-west after some false tops.

Volcán del Toro (5935m) was marked as Cerro del Mortero on the old 1898 map. After investigating the peak, the group concluded it could be the highest summit in all Chile. From 7-11 December 2021, Claudia Arratia, Inés Carrasco, Ariel González, Antonio Neira, Jaime Paineo, Fernando Toro, Oscar Torres, Mauricio Urrea and Alvaro Rojas Rivera reached the top after leaving their base camp at 4,750m and climbing the west face.

A view from the descent illustrating the vast and desolate landscape in this region. *(Alvaro Rojas Rivera)*

On the slopes of Cerro Negro Grande (5570m) and the spectacular geology of the Atacama. *(Alvaro Rojas Rivera)*

The last volcano, **Cerro del Gallo** (5615m), with its nice pointed summit, was spotted by the group descending Toro. The summit is a small but perfectly formed stone tower. From 1-5 February 2023, a group established base camp at 4,550m. From there Carlos Etchegaray, Fabián Fadic, Ariel González, Danilo Layana, Jaime Paineo, Juan Soto, Oscar Torres and Alvaro Rojas Rivera reached the summit via the north face.

Argentina

In northern Argentina's Catamarca province, on the border with Chile in the northern Andes, Lisandro Arielovich and Glauco Muratti climbed **Cerro El Segundo** (5350m) from the east. They camped in an ancient place called Tres Quebradas (4300m) that has been used since pre-Columbian times to the present, including by the well-known Polish expedition of the 1930s. On top they found an ancient topographic marking and a curious one-metre asymmetric cairn that could be pre-Columbian. It appears it pointed towards an important place for their ancient cosmography. The expedition took place in April.

Located in the Cordón de La Ramada of San Juan province, **Alma Negra** (6120m) is a beautiful 6120 mountain that lies nearby mighty Mercedario. Both mountains were first climbed during the 1933-4 Polish scientific expedition led by cosmic-ray physicist Konstanty Jodko-Narkiewicz. Austrian Christian Stangl reached the summit on 4 December approaching from Paso del Espinacito (4476m), a historic pass used by San Martín to liberate Chile from the Spanish. Stangl made base camp there because his horses couldn't continue due to snow. He made another camp at 4,400m below the south-east ridge. He climbed to a bottleneck between vertical cliffs and camped at a flat zone at 5,200m. On summit day he took the south-east ridge, reaching what he claims as the south summit with little more information. He had to turn a glassy rock band 100m below the south summit by descending a little and traversing towards the east and then went to the highest summit and descended by the same route.

During November, Martin Suso, Lisandro Arielovich, Federico Barberis and Glauco Muratti made the first ascent of **Cuchilla Negra** (5130m), a remote mountain in the Cordón del Potrero Escondido in Mendoza province. Two previous attempts were made in 2016 but both aborted 200m short of the summit, one because of avalanche risk and the other because of tricky penitentes. The group departed from Punta de Vacas and trekked for two days through the valleys of Río Blanco and Potrero Escondido before reaching the first crux, a 300m cliff. As on previous expeditions they climbed this via a narrow and steep ravine on this occasion with waterfalls. This had section of V with the risk of rock fall. Above the cliff they made two camps. The way to the summit had many penitentes and they had to use crampons because of the frost. Some 100m from the summit they deviated from the direct line because of threatening cornices, taking instead unstable rock of no more than II or III but with no possibility of belays. They found better rock higher up and the last 50m was II and III. The double summit was previously unclimbed.

The line of the first ascent of Cuchilla Negra in the Cordón del Potrero Escondido. The deviation at the top was to avoid cornices. *(Glauco Muratti)*

Frederico Barberis leading up the penitentes in the main gully of Cuchilla Negra. The cornices that later collapsed are above his head. *(Glauco Muratti)*

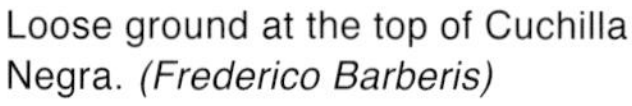

Loose ground at the top of Cuchilla Negra. *(Frederico Barberis)*

The line of the first ascent on the Argentinian side of Cerro Tres Hermanos. *(Glauco Muratti)*

To descend they made two rappels and during the second the team heard an explosion as part of the cornices fell on the route. They hurried to extract themselves from that risky section. They rated the route AD but said that it only describes the technical difficulties and not the distance, or the ascent and descent of technical terrain with heavy packs, the isolation and no possibility of rescue, the lack of information and the terrible penitentes. Muratti says, with truth, there must be an Andean grade system scale to describe this kind of ascent.

With this climb the Grupo Rosarino de Actividades de Montaña and in particular Glauco Muratti finished the exploration of the entire Cordón del Potrero Escondido with eight remote summits at a range of 4,600m to 5,300m. This task took 19 years.

Located in Central Andes of Mendoza province, **Cerro Piloto** (5056m), known also as Cerro Amarillo, lies in the headwaters of Quebrada Benjamín Matienzo near the border with Chile. On 16 December Argentine Gabriel Fava and Frenchman Henry Bizot opened the first line on the south face. They placed three camps, the last one at 4,490m on the morraine just below the face that was in dry condition. They climbed right of a poor snow and ice couloir with penitentes and a 20m rock step. The route was named *Patrick and Elisabeth* (500m, D).

Also in Mendoza, **Cerro Tres Hermanos** (4764m), the 'three brothers' is an interesting and attractive mountain that lies on the Argentine-Chilean border. It's most usually been climbed from Chile since the 1960s. The highest summit,

On the northern summit of Cerro Tres Hermanos in Mendoza province.

the north one, hadn't been climbed from Argentina before 2022. Fernando Martínez and Luciano Barale reached 100m short of the summit by some steep snow gullies on the south-east face. And there was also previous activity in the steep Quebrada Sin Nombre that ends at the Portezuelo de Lomas Colorados (4458m) border pass that was also used by Argentines Glauco Muratti and Federico Barberis. These two made the first ascent of the higher north summit in a four-day expedition that departed Las Cuevas on 11 August in the winter season. The first three days the weather was good, the last one they had snow and whiteout conditions. Facing calf-deep snow, they wished they'd brought skies or snowshoes. Muratti and Barberis climbed the north face, rating it as PD/PD+. Before their last camp at 3,900m they traversed loose and tricky 40° snow, ice and rock. The last 350m were mixed 40°-60° slopes and a II-III rock chimney. The pair climbed unroped and then down-climbed the route.

Peru

In the Laguna Paron region of the Cordillera Blanca, a difficult route was opened in August on the south-west Face of **Caraz II** (6020m) by the Spaniard Ibai Rico and Peruvian Aritza Monasterio. *Fango, Mushrooms and Cornice* (400m, MD+, 70°-80°) finished 20m short of the summit because of an unstable ridge. The east face of this peak is better known with several lines including the serious *Australian* route (720m, ED1, W3, V+, A2), established by Matt Scholes and Ant Morgan in July 2004 and still unrepeated.

During July, Peruvian Juan Benavides and Chilean Ignacio Vázquez Palominos climbed *Juanito and La Luna* (350m, MD+, M4, 6a) on the north face of **Shaqsha** (5703m). The pair rounded the peak's rocky foot and climbed the glacier directly to reach the face where they found a line of rock and ice on its centre-left. The summit was reached on 9 July. On 24 July Chileans Ignacio Vázquez Palominos and Martín Contreras Ried summited

The line taken by Marcelo Delvaux on his first ascent in the remote Chumpe group in the Cordillera de Vilcanota and a more distant view identifying the group's peaks. *(Marcel Delvaux)*

Nevado Huascarán Sur (6768m) via what is certainly a new route: *Agua en Marte*, (MD+, WI4, 80°). On 22 July they bivouacked at 4,980m and next day climbed the bulk of the route, with a hard section (WI4, M4) gaining the 80° ice and snow face and the south-east sub-summit, then the upper south-east ridge with a bivouac at 6,500m On the final day they summited and descended the north side. Huascarán is known in Quechua as Mataraju. Also in July, Slovenians Anja Petek and Andrej Jez with Spaniard Aritza Monasterio climbed the first line on the east face of **Hualcán** (6122m) calling it *Fango Fiesta* (1150m, ED, M5, 60°-85°).

The well-known guide Nathan Heald and Peruvian Leo Rasalio climbed **Lasunayoc** (5936m) in the Vilcabamba range. Their new route, climbed in November, was via the south and then the east faces and was rated 1,000m, TD, WI4. On 9 May, in the Vilcanota range, Heald and Bill Thibeault made the first ascent of **Huilayoc** (5974m), also called Huila Aje, via the west face at AD.

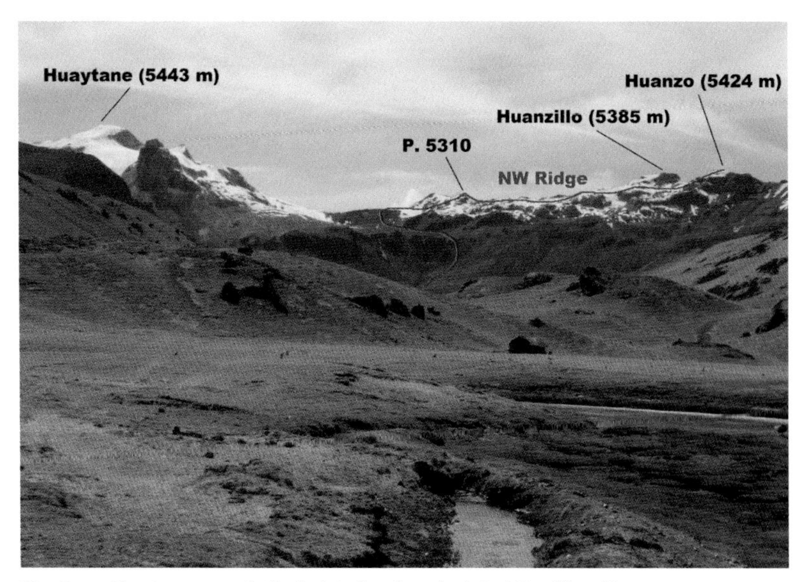

The Cerro Huaytane group in the isolated and rarely visited Cordillera Huanzo.
(Marcel Delvaux)

Still in the Cordillera de Vilcanota, Brazilian Marcelo Delvaux made a nine-day unsupported traverse in May between the villages of Pacchanta and Mallma. His traverse including an unclimbed summit of 5,780m. His itinerary went from Pacchanta to **Abra Jampa** (5068m), Laguna Ticllacocha, Quebrada Jampamayo, Suyrucochapampa, **Abra Huayruro Punco** (5360m), Murmurani, Laguna Sibinacocha, Quebrada Puja Orco, **Abra Chumpe** (5400m), Laguna Chuyanecocha, Laguna Huarurumicocha, Laguna Mullucocha, Laguna Pucacocha, Laguna Singrenacocha and finally Mallma.

Peak 5780m lies on the south-east ridge of Nevado Chumpe (Jatunriti), an enormous massif in one of Vilcanota's most remote zones. He arrived at a base camp on the sixth day to climb the south glacier of Nevado Chumpe, approaching from a glacier tongue just before Abra Chumpe. Once on the glacier he followed the labyrinth of crevasses towards the north-east arriving to the base of Peak 5780m at a zone with falling seracs. He then went to a col between the peak and a secondary summit, finally climbing the south-east ridge to the summit. In the last part he found the crux of 55° ice.

The Cordillera Huanzo is one of the forgotten ridges in the Andes. Because of its isolation, only two expeditions have been recorded, one in 1970 and the other in 2015. In 1970 Sue Tatum and John Ricker made a long traverse between Santo Tomás and Antabamba ascending **Nevado Jatun Huaychahui** (5452m) and the ridge's highest summit **Chancoaña** (5494m): see *AAJ* 1971. Many years later, in 2015, well-known Scottish climber John Biggar and party made the second ascent of Chancoaña by the same 1970 route of north ridge and face. They then achieved the first ascents of **Condorillo** (5213m), called Toro Rumi by Biggar, and **Huaytane** (5443m).

The line of the new route on Cerro Huaytane. (Marcel Delvaux)

During the first days of May, Argentine Julieta Ferreri and Brazilian Marcelo Delvaux headed towards Huanzo and its north-east sector where the bigger glaciers lie. After a complex approach of five days from Arequipa they arrived at Laguna de Huanzo. They then had eight days of activity trekking 50km and climbing three mountains and crossing two passes over 5,200m. They went first to Quebrada Huanzo, then a 5,221m pass between **Cerro Huaytane** and **Cerro Calasaya**, which they called Paso Huaytane, to Quebrada Huacullo and a 5,197m pass north of **Cerro Chancoaña** that they christened Paso Chacoaña, Quebrada Tirane and finishing in the villages of Quiriquiri and Paterio. The first summit climbed was **Cerro Huaytane** climbed by Biggar in 2015 by its north ridge. The pair opened a new route via the south-west face and north-west ridge. Biggar reported the summit as 5,430m, while Ferreri and Delvaux recorded 5,443m.

Next day Ferreri rested and Delvaux went to a mountain that the Instituto Geográfico Nacional del Perú calls **Cerro Huanzillo** and the locals Nevado de Huanzo. He took the Quebrada de Huanzo up to a 5,214m col between Huaytane and Huanzillo. From there he continued to the north-west ridge with rock and snow terrain and some secondary peaks on route. He didn't find any trace of activity along the route or at the summit, which his GPS measured at 5,424m. He decided to call it Huanzo as the locals do, giving the name of Huanzillo (little Huanzo) to a secondary 5,385m summit to the north-west.

After three days of trekking and crossing Hauytane and Chancoaña passes, the pair reached an unknown mountain south of Cerro Huaña calling it **Huaña Sur**. It has two summits with GPS readings of 5,372m and 5,387m. They found cairns on them but don't know who were their precursors. They left the district by lorry towards the city of Santo Tomás.

The first pitch of *Camino del Supay* on the Gran Murallo.

In 2019 Patrick Mikelsons and Ben White, both Australian, made the first ascent of a route in the middle of the north-west face of the mighty **Gran Muralla** (c5100m), the 'great wall' in Cordillera de Quimsa Cruz, La Paz. This wall is good granite and the pair climbed ground up, with aid on three-quarters of the route, which took four days of climbing and a fifth day cleaning and drilling rap stations. The crags were dirty with vegetation so progress was slow. The Australians didn't have time to free it but in August,

Line and topo of *Camino del Supay*.

Mikelsons and Chilean Juan José Catón freed every pitch, finding difficulties up to 5.11c. After the descent and a clean-up it may be more like 5.11-. The route was named *Camino del Supay* (250m, 5.11c). Supay is the Andean subterranean god and nowadays the devil is also known as supay.

The splitter pitch high on *Camino del Supay*.

Patrick Mikelsons and Juan José Catón on the summit.

Expedition Reports

'Waterfall (at Dawlish, Devon?)', J S Barth, undated, watercolour touched with body-colour, 57.1cm × 44.7cm. *(British Museum)*

SUMMARISED BY ADAM BUTTERWORTH

Mount Everest Foundation Expedition Reports

The Mount Everest Foundation (***www.mef.org.uk***) was established as a registered charity following the successful ascent of Everest in 1953. It was initially financed using the surplus funds and subsequent royalties from that expedition. It provides financial support for expeditions of an exploratory nature in mountain areas, and is administered by trustees appointed by the Alpine Club and the Royal Geographical Society.

The exploration is mainly of a geographical nature but may also cover disciplines such as geology, botany, zoology, glaciology and medical research. In return for funding the MEF requires only a comprehensive report, and copies of these reports are lodged with the AC and the RGS. The reports can be consulted at these establishments or online via the MEF website.

The MEF has made total grants of well over £1m to more than 1,600 expeditions with members from the UK and New Zealand. Donations to allow us to continue this work are always welcome. We particularly encourage donations from former beneficiaries of MEF grants. In 2022, 24 MEF-supported expeditions made it into the field with a number achieving notable first ascents or bringing back valuable scientific data. The following notes summarise the reports from these expeditions.

NORTH AMERICA

British Kichatna Expedition 2022 – Mike 'Twid' Turner and Mark Thomas

Taking advantage of a season that saw remarkably good weather in the region, Turner and Thomas established a new route on the east face of Kichatna Spire, the highest of the granite peaks comprising Cathedral Spires. Their line *Thunderstruck* (VI, A3+/A4, 6c) takes a slender pillar on the right-hand side of the face, following a crack-line for much of its length before mixed rock and ice terrain leads to the summit. The pair referred to the route as "the best climb of our lives" and note that the large east face has significant potential for continued route development.

MEF Ref 22-05

Meltwater Drainage through the Mackenzie Mountains –
Benjamin J Stoker, Sophie L Norris and Helen E Dulfer

All three members of this expedition are researchers with a focus on the ice sheets of North America – their extent, their deglaciation and the associated effects on the landscape. The central aim of this fieldwork was to better understand the drainage network created as glacial meltwater passed through the Mackenzie Mountains during the last deglaciation and how this freshwater flux to the Arctic Ocean may have impacted ocean circulation. On 22 June, following a short delay caused by bad weather, the team flew into the Mackenzie Mountains from Norman Wells, setting up base camp next to their landing site. Over the following days, they conducted short forays into the field of 3-5km, observing the landscape and taking a sample from a boulder deposited by an historic outflow. With their research completed in good time, they flew out on 27 June. It is hoped that their observations, combined with the dating provided by the rock sample, will allow them to reconstruct the region's drainage network.

MEF Ref 22-17

Baffin Island 2022 – Maria Parkes, Neil Chelton and Owen Lee

The team flew into Pangnirtung from where they travelled up Pangnirtung Fjord into Auyuittuq National Park. Their primary objective, Mount Turnweather, is located just east of the park boundary. Based on pre-expedition research, they had planned to climb the mountain via its north face but on inspection they decided that the rock was too loose to be viable. They turned instead to the north-east face, where a series of continuous crack systems allowed them to forge a path to the summit. Their new route *Rainy Day Dream Away* (VI, 5.9, A4, 70°) was climbed capsule style, with some use of fixed ropes on the initial section. The team encountered poor weather, with rain almost every day. At the summit tower, they found evidence of previous expeditions in the form of bolts but believe that earlier parties climbed both the summit tower and the mountain by different routes.

MEF Ref 22-20

'Alder in the Arctic' – Millicent Harding, Calvin Heslop, Lauren Church and Nicholas Daley

When two members of the expedition tested positive for Covid-19 on arrival in Alaska, this team were forced to alter their plans, relocating the planned site of their research from Umiat to the Yukon-Koyukuk area in the sub-Arctic. Here the team sampled four tundra sites at varying altitudes, gathering data that will allow them to better understand the plant life of this rapidly changing environment.

MEF Ref 22-22

Sex Differences in Cardiovascular Acclimatisation to High Altitude – Dr Lydia Simpson, Dr Jonathan Moore, Dr Mike Stembridge and Dr Alex Williams

Based at the Barcroft Research Station in California, US, the aims of this research expedition changed to focus on examining the effect of high altitude on vascular function in men and women rather than its effect on cardiac function. Over two weeks, the team examined intra-arterial blood pressure as well as vascular and blood flow responses to high altitude at rest and during exercise in male and female participants. Additionally, the team were able to assess several aspects of blood pressure control at rest. They characterised sympathetic nervous system activation at high altitude and investigated the role of both elevated pulmonary pressure and the input from the body's main oxygen sensor (peripheral chemoreceptors) in eliciting these responses in males and females. Due to the large quantity of useful data collected, the team expect the expedition to result in several peer-reviewed publications.

MEF Ref 22-33

SOUTH AMERICA

Altitude Physiology Expedition (APEX) 6 – Dr Oliver Vick, Dr Alastair Woodhead, Dr Suzanne Green, Dr Isla Petrie, Dr Katie Flower, Dr Ben Warrick and 32 undergraduate students

This scientific expedition from the University of Edinburgh travelled to La Paz in Bolivia and onward to a high-altitude laboratory at Huayna Potosí. The aim of the expedition was to collect physiological and genetic data from individuals exposed to moderate (3640m at La Paz) and high-altitude (4775m at Huayna Potosí) environments in order to improve understanding of the body's response to hypoxia (low oxygen levels). Over three days in la Paz and eight at Huayna Potosí, the expedition team gathered data from a series of experiments investigating the effect of hypoxia on dark adaptation and retinal function, menstrual bleeding, the predictive validity of different measures of lung oxygenation function, white blood cell gene expression and neutrophil survival. Analysis of these results is expected in due course.

MEF Ref. 22-32

GREENLAND & ICELAND

Medusa Climbing Expedition – Tim Luke, Ed Luke and Sasha Doyle

Setting sail from Glasson Dock (UK) on *Medusa*, a Vancouver 34C yacht, the expedition party arrived in Nanortalik, south Greenland after an arduous three-week crossing. After repeating some of the established routes in Tasermuit Fjord, they moved to Tininnertup valley where they made an attempt on Tininnertup 4 (T4) Spire but were unable to reach the summit. Windy conditions led them to relocate to Semersoq Island where they established a new direct line on Punta Alboran (1060m). Following this, the expedition undertook the long journey to Greenland's east coast where they hoped to find more unclimbed objectives. Sea ice prevented them from accessing the Mythics Cirque so they headed instead to the Fox Jaw Cirque where they repeated two existing climbs, made the first ascents of two new routes and made an unsuccessful attempt on an unnamed peak.

MEF 22-18

Greenland Sea to Summit 2022 – Bronwyn Hodgins, Jacob Cook, Kelsey Watts, Zack Goldberg-Poch, Angela VanWiemeersch and Jaron Pham

This team of six set out from Uummannaq on 5 July, paddling north through fjords and tidal mud flats before portaging a 20km section of land which connected a series of small lakes. Once past the portage, the party were able to make two first ascents on the impressive red granite domes on this section of coast: *Fish are Friends* (5.9+, 200m) and *Wears Your Paddle?* (5.11-, 250m). Further north, they arrived at the cliff known locally as Agparssuit. Here the three men repeated *Seagull's Garden* while the women established a new route *Time is a Construct* (5.11/A2, 400m) in a 50-hour push. However, the expedition's main objective was the first free ascent of Qaersorsuaq (also known as Sanderson's Hope), a 900m wall which rises directly out of the Arctic Ocean. In this they were successful, overcoming challenging weather across 20 days on the wall to establish *Sea Barge Circus* (5.11+, 900m).

MEF Ref. 22-27

Angmagssalik Expedition 2022 – Will Rowland, Mike Bauermeister, Noel Williams and Simon Tietjen

This expedition's initial objective was to complete a 25km traverse of several peaks on the west side of Ikasagtivaq fjord. Once underway the team quickly realised that, due to the poor quality of the rock, the full traverse would take four days rather than the three they had planned. After the weather deteriorated on the second day, they abandoned the attempt and relocated to a cirque of peaks on the opposite side of the fjord. Here, along with repeating a number of existing routes, Rowland and Tietjen also succeeded in the first ascent of a 700m rock route on the west face of Niniartivaraq.

MEF Ref 22-35

INDIA

British Chombu Expedition 2022 – Mick Fowler and Victor Saunders

Having attempted this unclimbed peak twice in 2019, first in April and then in October, this pair returned in the hope of finding better conditions in May. Despite promising signs upon their arrival, the weather quickly deteriorated with a degree of snowfall every day. This left the mountain's north face heavily loaded. They turned their attention to the west face, but here the risk of rockfall was too high and so they returned to the north-east Spur which they had climbed to 6,107m in 2019. After waiting for an injury suffered by Saunders to heal, the team began their attempt on 4 May. They made it to the base of the north-east spur on 07 May where foggy conditions forced a bivouac. Additional snowfall followed and the team retreated, considering the risk of continuing to be too great.

MEF Ref 22-04

2022 East Karakoram Expedition – Derek Buckle, Jamie Goodhart, Steve Humphries, Steve Kempley and Howard Pollitt

In September 2022 five members of the Alpine Club travelled to India intent on exploring the Rassa glacier and attempting the first ascent of one or more of the many 6000m peaks which rise from it. Flying via Delhi to Leh (3500m) in Ladakh, they first spent four days acclimatising to the altitude before crossing the 5370m Khardung La to the Nubra valley. After spending a night near the village of Tirit, the team then began a three-day trek up the Tirit Phu to establish a base camp at 4750m. Having identified and optimised access to the lower Rassa glacier, an advanced base camp was subsequently established on a sandy depression in the moraine at 5100m. Further forays identified a suitable high camp on the glacier proper, at the foot of the unexplored second glacial spur. From this camp team members extensively reconnoitred this glacial spur and two members successfully made the first ascent of Peak 6365m (Dagarpheth Kangri) via its east-south-east ridge at alpine AD. Further exploration was precluded by the onset of bad weather, forcing a retreat to base camp and an early return to Leh.

MEF Ref 22-07

Chiling II North Face Expedition 2022 – Alex Mathie, Tim Elson and Innes Dean

Travelling from Leh, the expedition arrived at base camp on 8 September. After establishing ABC at 4500m, they reconnoitred their primary objective, Chiling II (6253m), discovering that a recent landslide had made accessing their intended line on the north face impossible. They turned their attention to the north rib of Lalung I (6243m), but found this to be an unattractive proposition, consisting of little more than frozen earth. Searching for new objectives, the team entered an unexplored side valley of the Lalung glacier where they found a number of attractive unclimbed peaks. They decided to make an attempt on an unnamed peak with a Google Earth spot height of 6048m but abandoned their attempt after triggering a small slab avalanche, which narrowly missed one of the team. Concluding that the conditions were unlikely to improve given the forecast, they packed up early and returned to Leh.

MEF Ref 22-14

British/Irish Barnaj II Expedition – Dave Sharpe, Will Harris, Callum Johnson, Tom Seccombe and Matt Glenn

Upon arrival at their base camp in the Zanskar valley this team found very dry conditions, the monsoon seemingly having failed to arrive. However, the very next day, 1ft-2ft of snow fell at base camp, with possibly more higher up. The fresh snowfall made acclimatisation heavy going, but over a few days, the whole team rotated up to 5,700m and back to base camp. Abortive attempts on the east face of Chiring and Barnaj II's north face followed on 30 September but, after a couple of days' rest, Glenn, Seccombe and Johnson set out for what would prove to be a successful attempt on the north face of Barnaj II. The trio climbed to a subsidiary peak, Barnaj II East (6303m), over three days via a 1400m route which they dubbed *Seracnaphobia* (ED M5 AI4). Upon reaching this subsidiary summit, they elected not to continue along the ridge to the mountain's north summit, reasoning that it would likely take at least three days to complete the traverse and descend. They rappelled their new route on abalakov threads, leaving no in-situ gear behind.

MEF Ref 22-31

NEPAL

British Ganglung Kangri Expedition 2022 – Nick Colton, Ed Douglas, Julian Freeman-Attwood

After obtaining their permits in Kathmandu, the expedition team flew to Simikot from where they began the long trek to base camp. The journey took eight days, during which the weather was consistently unsettled and the expedition party faced difficulties navigating boulder fields with mules. Once base camp was established at just shy of 5000m, an ABC was sited below the access to the Ganglung glacier at 5333m. On 4 October, two of the team scouted their objectives, ascertaining that while Ganglung Kangri was too distant for an attempt, Chandi was definitely a viable proposition. Unfortunately, this clear day of scouting was to be the last good weather of the trip. Late, persistent monsoon weather arrived in earnest, forcing a difficult retreat from ABC by Colton and Douglas. With snow covering the boulder-strewn approach, the team found themselves trapped at base camp with no obvious route back down. A sat-phone call confirmed that mules could not reach within four to five days of base camp and, out of concern for both themselves and their base camp staff, they called for an air evacuation which picked them up on 11 October.

MEF Ref 22-06

British Jugal Expedition 2022 – Paul Ramsden and Tim Miller

The idea for this expedition was born when Ramsden, who was browsing satellite imagery during a Covid-19 lockdown, spotted an impressive north face in the Jugal Himal. Further research revealed that, despite being one of the closest 6000m peaks to Kathmandu, the mountain (Peak 6563m) remained unattempted. He and Miller travelled to Nepal in April 2022 and, after setting up base camp next to the Lingshing glacier, they combined acclimatisation on the west ridge of Dorje Lhakpa, with reconnaissance of their intended face. A break in the weather afforded them a view of a potential route, a thin ice line that seemed to extend almost the full length of the face but with short, blank sections that cast doubt on its viability. Nevertheless, the pair set out to investigate. Climbing alpine style over five days, they succeeded in making the first ascent of the mountain by their intended route, discovering that the blank sections they had observed could be surmounted by three pitches of awkward chimney climbing. They named their route *The Phantom Line* and offered a grade of ED+. Following the ascent, they dubbed the mountain 'Jugal Spire', but subsequently learned that it has also been referred to as 'Dorje Lhakpa II'.

MEF Ref 22-11

PAKISTAN

Virjerab Sar 2022 – Peter Thompson, Philip De-Berger and Murilo Lessa

Having struggled to recruit porters for their approach to base camp, the team was forced to split at Carpogoro with Thompson concluding that he would be unable to make the 26km carry to Virjerab Sar's ABC. De-Berger and Lessa reached their ABC two days later. They made two attempts to access the mountain, first via the north col and then by the west. Despite climbing through the night in the hopes of finding colder conditions, they were forced to turn back by poor snow and the added challenge of navigating significant crevasses in the dark. On 1 July, having relocated 6km down the glacier, the pair were able to make what they believe to be the first complete ascent of Peak 5880m, simul-climbing the entire way. Lessa's GPS measured a height of 5905m on the summit.

MEF Ref 22-08

British Slovenian Gasherbrum Expedition 2022 – Tom Livingstone and Aleš Česen

This pair planned to attempt the south-west ridge of Gasherbrum III but were forced to abort due to strong south-westerly winds. Believing that they might find more success (and shelter from the wind) on the mountain's north face/ridge, they relocated and made an attempt from this side of the peak. At 7,800m, they came upon a large tower which could not be bypassed and which required more difficult climbing than they were willing to commit to given the altitude and weather. They were therefore forced to retreat.

MEF Ref 22-16

Yawash Sar I-IV 2022 Expedition – Nicholas Hurndall Smith, Nigel Bassam, Tom Bell, Paul Winder, Ross Bell and Karim Hayat

This expedition hoped to make the first ascent of Yawash Sar I, a 6258m peak which they accessed via the West Ghiddims valley. Despite making three attempts on the peak; once by the south face, which was turned back by rock and ice fall, and once each by the south-east and south-west ridges, which were abandoned due to loose rock, they were ultimately unsuccessful. However they did not end the expedition empty-handed. Expedition member Karim Hayat and assistant chef Waseem Shah made the first ascent of Peak 5742m in alpine style at a grade of PD. Subsequently, Bassam, Smith and Hayat also made the ascent of Peak 5798m, again climbing alpine style via a route they considered to warrant PD+.

MEF Ref 22-24

Muchu Chhish 2022 – Murilo Gimenes Lessa and Stephen Ashworth

The world's second highest unclimbed peak has had several suitors over recent decades, to which this pair now add their names. Travelling to Pakistan in August 2022, they encountered appalling conditions as the country experienced its highest level of rainfall in 30 years, with widespread flooding.

The poor conditions hampered their approach to base camp but by the start of September, they had succeeded in establishing camp one at 4,900m, just below the mountain's south ridge. At this point, they received a poor weather forecast for the days ahead and decided to abandon their attempt, concluding that they would not have enough time for a serious push. They returned to Aliabad before relocating to their secondary objective: Pregar II (c6000m). Finding their intended route on the mountain's south face to be in poor condition, with scoured, dry rock and loose scree, they called it a day, ending the expedition without success. The team concluded that future attempts on Muchu Chhish would be advised to plan for a longer, six or seven week expedition, with acclimatisation carried out on an alternative, safer peak.

MEF Ref 22-29

Shimshal Expedition 2022 – John Burgess and Rob Reynolds

Taking place two years later than originally planned, this expedition faced difficulties arriving in Hunza, but once there experienced little in the way of bureaucracy and had a more pleasant onward journey to their base camp in the Gunj-e Dur valley (c4400m). High spring temperatures had left the valley very bare, with icy faces where one would expect to find snow slopes. Even so, the team were able to identify two potential summits which could be accessed from the same col. They made their attempt on 29 August, electing to climb to the col and choose between the peaks once there. Upon reaching the col, they noted that the higher of the two summits, Peak 5775m, could only be accessed via a complex rocky ridge. With Reynolds suffering from acute mountain sickness they felt that they could not commit to this approach and chose instead to attempt the lower summit via its more amenable snow slope. However, after only a short distance, the snow conditions worsened and they retreated in the face of significant avalanche risk.

MEF Ref. 22-30

CENTRAL ASIA

Alpine Club Tajikistan Expedition 2022 – Tom Davis-Merry, Alex Hale, Chris Lewis, Alex Metcalfe and Sarah Wysling

This expedition planned to visit the Zaroshkul glacier in the Rushan range of the Pamirs and to attempt a number of the surrounding unclimbed peaks. Despite erratic weather conditions, (this was the hottest Tajik summer on record but also saw the arrival of snow in August), they were successful. The whole in-country team achieved the first ascent of Peak 5357m in alpine style via a route 1km in length with 200m of height gain and an approximate difficulty of PD. Subsequently, Hale and Lewis made an attempt on the west ridge of Peak 5357m but were forced to turn back 300m from the summit due to a combination of fatigue and objective danger. It should be noted that the expedition's original leader, Tom Davis-Merry, was unable to fly out due to illness.

MEF Ref 22-23

EUROPE

Izvor Licanke Expedition 2022 – Christine Grosart, Richard Walker, Mark Burkey, Louise McMahon, Osama Gobara, Mauro Bordignon, Luke Brock, Mitchell Parry and Velimir Vrzic

The Izvor Licanke cave system in Fužine, Croatia has been visited by cave diving expeditions for the last seven years with many of these teams receiving support from the MEF. This year's expedition discovered 938m of new cave passage, both above and below water, bringing the total cave length to some 2819m. This included the diving and mapping of sump five and the discovery of sumps six, seven and eight. Beyond sump 8, the cave continued with a high canyon leading into a huge dry chamber at the end of which was a ninth sump. This sump was not dived during the expedition, but was explored via video and looked promising.

MEF Ref 22-36

ANTARCTIC

Interdisciplinary South Pole Innovation & Research Expedition (INSPIRE 22) – Prof. Chris Imray and team

The aim of this scientific expedition was to build on the work that has already come out of the MEF-supported metabolic research registry, GPAMRR, by assessing the metabolic tariff imposed on both male and female participants by prolonged polar travel. In the process, the researchers also planned to test wearable technologies designed to measure physiological activities and to assess the psychological impact of prolonged polar travel. Following a preliminary expedition to Norway in March 2022 and training exercises in the UK, baseline measurements were taken at University Hospitals Coventry and Warwickshire NHS Trust in October 2022. The team left the UK on 7 November and, following testing in Punta Arenas, Chile, arrived in Antarctica on 21 November before being flown to the starting point of the Messner route on 24 November. Over the next 47 days, the team of nine (three women and six men) skied to the south pole, averaging 23km a day with two rest days. Diet was monitored throughout, with on-ice testing taking place every five days with all participants remaining on freeze-dried food for two days after reaching the Pole in order to obtain additional measurements. The researchers note that all of the participants lost weight. This weight loss was generally concentrated in the fat compartments and was accompanied by the addition of muscle mass. Men appeared to lose more absolute weight and had a greater percentage weight loss. Analysis of the data is ongoing.

MEF Ref 22-03

EAST ASIA

Mulu Caves 2022 – Andrew Eavis, William Yu Pearson, Anthony Radmall, Christopher Blakeley, Colin Boothroyd, David Nixon, Gareth Davies,

Rostam Namaghi, Richard Walters, Rida Rambli, Judith Calford, Martin Holroyd, Christopher Howes, Kevin Munn, Zarris Kem, Andrew Farrant, Ashley Gregg, Peter Hall, Timothy Kent, Andrew McLeod, Joanne White, Andrew Smith, Robert Eavis, Stein-Erik Lauritzen, Christos, Pennos, Hazel Barton, James Koether, Derek Bristol, Jonathan Beavan and Maya Williams

This large expedition party worked in several teams; exploring surveying and photographing 6.5km of new cave passage, as well as resurveying 5km of previously discovered passages. They also made a diving connection between Clearwater Cave and Racer Cave, increasing the length of the Clearwater Cave system by 10km, making it the eigth longest cave in the world. Additionally, laser scanning of 4.5km of cave passage yielded an impressive 3D image of the cave. This scan is likely to confirm Clearwater as the largest cave in the world by volume. Finally, scientific research was conducted into the corrosive quality of the cave air and, in particular, its deleterious effect on artificial fibres. Analysis of the results of this research is ongoing. The expedition team note that there is significant scope for further exploration of the cave system but caution that most of the more easily travelled passages have likely already been discovered.

MEF Ref 22-10

Reviews

'Gormire Lake, Yorkshire', John Sell Cotman, c1804, watercolour and brown wash, 37.2cm × 54.6cm. *(British Museum)*

Reviews

Tom Patey
One Man's Legacy
Mike Dixon
Scottish Mountaineering Press, 2022, 464pp, £30

This monumental work is a fitting tribute to a legendary figure of mountaineering. Mike Dixon, the author, began his research 10 years ago and has been assiduous in tracking down Tom Patey's friends and climbing partners from across the years, including a goodly number who have since died. The result is a book rich in detail and reminiscence, scrupulous in its attributions, with persuasive narrative accounts of many of Patey's key ascents. It portrays a whole man, faults and all, that will be recognisable to those who were privileged to know him. It also portrays an ethos and an era that are receding in memory but that deserve to be memorialised. For those who were there, even on the margins, it is evocative and nostalgic as it explores the myths that have developed around its subject.

Thomas Walton Patey, named for his father Thomas and his mother, née Walton, was born on 20 February 1932 at Ellon, near Aberdeen. His father was a minister of the Scottish Episcopal Church, his mother a keen musician who played the organ. In September 1942, when Patey was 10, his father took him to the summit of Ben Macdui. By the age of 17, shortly before he started studying medicine at Aberdeen University, he was undertaking full winter hill-walking outings in the Cairngorms. Within two years he had graduated to climbing proper, both summer and winter. In 1950 he made his mark with the first winter ascent of *Douglas-Gibson Gully* in Lochnagar.

That signalled the start of two decades during which Patey made a series of key first ascents, at the same time expanding the scope of what was possible in Scottish climbing, above all in winter. Based at first in Aberdeen, his key routes included *Scorpion*, the first winter route on Carn Etchachan with Graeme Nicol in 1952; *Eagle Ridge* at Lochnagar with Bill Brooker and Mike Taylor in 1953, considered the hardest Scottish mixed route of the time; the first winter ascent of *Mitre Ridge* on Beinn a'Bhuird with Bill Brooker in 1953; and the epic first winter ascent of *Zero Gully* on Ben Nevis with Hamish MacInnes and Graeme Nicol in 1957. As Dixon notes, this was still the era of long-handled ice axes, clunky hardware, pre-breathable clothing and frozen hawser-laid ropes. It was also a time of poor public transport,

Tom Patey on the rocky terraces and icy gangways of the route he put up with Joe Brown on the west face of the Aiguille du Plan. *(John Cleare)*

Betty Davidson with her future husband. *(Adam Watson)*

when few climbers had cars: the bothy culture thrived, providing places where climbers would relax, discuss their climbs and misses 'and embellish them for posterity.'

Patey spent 1957-61 undertaking national service with the Royal Marines, adding 12 months to the basic two-year period by signing up as a doctor and eventually serving for four. He was based in Devon but had the bonus of attending winter warfare training in the Cairngorms and Norway, where he made the first winter ascent of the celebrated *Fiva* route on Store Trolltind.

In 1962, he and his wife Betty (they married in 1957) moved to Ullapool with their three children: Rona, Ian and Michael. Patey took over Ullapool's GP practice, at first single-handed, then with a partner. The fabled northern peaks, from Beinn Dearg to Quinag, became his playground. He climbed numerous new routes, heading out of Ullapool in his battered Skoda as soon as his morning surgery was finished.

Many of his first ascents were, of necessity, achieved solo, a practice he justified by saying that there was little difference in risk between climbing alone and leading on a rope. In 1965 came the route which Dixon hails as his greatest achievement during his time at Ullapool and arguably his best route anywhere: the first winter traverse of the Cuillin Ridge, made, at Patey's third attempt, with MacInnes, Davie Crabb and Brian Robertson.

Patey wrote an enchanting account of the traverse for the *Scottish Mountaineering Club Journal*, subsequently published in the collection of his writings *One Man's Mountains*, published in 1971. That deserves to be read alongside the new biography as testament to his supreme gift as a writer and mountaineering chronicler. There is however one important caveat. Dixon adopts Patey's account of the Cuillin Traverse for his book but there is a telling detail that should be examined.

In Patey's own account, he was called late at night by MacInnes with the instruction to set off at once for Skye. In fact, as MacInnes told me, Patey was reversing the roles. As in this instance, it was always Patey who called MacInnes with peremptory instructions, not the other way round. It is clear Patey sometimes observed the dictum, known also among journalists, that you should never let the facts get in the way of a good story.

Between times Patey climbed in the Alps and the Greater Ranges. In 1956 he, together with Joe Brown, Ian McNaught-Davis and John Hartog, made the first ascents of the Muztagh Tower in the Karakoram. His medical knowledge proved vital when Hartog suffered badly frostbitten feet. In 1958, as members of a British-Pakistan services expedition, he and Mike Banks made the first ascent of Rakaposhi, also in the Karakoram. Patey displayed almost mystical mountain sense in leading an immensely hazardous descent to safety, treating himself as well as Banks for frostbite en route. Patey also made regular forays to the Alps, but never succeeded in his long-held ambition of climbing the north face of the Eiger, turning back in 1963 on his most serious attempt, made with Don Whillans, and leaving regrets which he often voiced (including to me) in the remaining seven years of his life.

One of Dixon's final chapters – 'Lights, Cameras, Sea Stacks' – is devoted to the golden age of British climbing outside broadcasts, where the photographer and camera operator John Cleare was a key player in suggesting locations to the BBC and taking a leading role in the filming. (Patey described Cleare as 'the Supremo who pulls the strings … the silent man with the Midas touch.') The most spectacular of those events was on the Old Man of Hoy in 1967, with a stellar cast including, as well as Patey, Joe Brown, Dougal Haston, Chris Bonington and Ian McNaught-Davis. Patey had previously made the first ascent of the sea stack with Bonington and Rusty Baillie in a hard-fought three-day campaign. Some parts of the three routes televised by the BBC were prepared ahead of the broadcast, creating the absurdity that two camera assistants had to hide beneath sacking on a ledge in order for it to appear that the climbers ascending the pitch below them were pushing up new ground. In his article 'The Professionals', Patey made much fun of the event, with his most telling remarks directed at the rasping sensationalising of commentator Chris Brasher.

In 1969 Patey scored another triumphant Scottish first with his Creag Meaghaidh *Crab Crawl*, his solo high-level winter traverse of Coire Ardair. I was there that day, writing an article on Scottish winter climbing for the *Sunday Times Magazine*, with photographs by Cleare. Tom had fun at my expense, depicting me as little better than the Fleet Street hacks so despised in the mountaineering world: remembering the complaints of MacInnes, I bore my wounds with due stoicism. (He did however tell me he enjoyed my article.)

I saw other aspects of Patey's rich life during that assignment, among them above all the lock-in sessions at the Rowanlee, Jimmy Carr's hostelry in Carrbridge, when he sang his sardonic verses about mountaineering and mountaineers, accompanying himself on the accordion and sometimes with Carr on his fiddle. It was approaching dawn when we set off back to Ullapool in time for his morning surgery.

It all adds up to a picture of a supreme figure of British mountaineering. Yet our hero had feet of clay. Scattered through the book's 450 pages are references to his faults and flaws. Witnesses attest to his 'extraordinary force of character' but he is also variously described as callous, selfish, ruthless and manipulative. He often failed to do his share of camp or hut duties, leaving such concerns to his colleagues and companions. He was also a smoker and drinker (he introduced me to the joys of Glenmorangie) and used amphetamines to help meet the prodigious demands he placed upon himself.

He was also notably inattentive to technical details, something he appeared to consider tedious. If that contributed to his image as a non-conformist or free spirit, it also brought his destruction. He was continuing his explorations of the far north-west, in particular its sea stacks, when he targeted the first ascent of The Maiden, off Whiten Head. On 25 May 1970 he and four colleagues, including Paul Nunn, reached the top. They proceeded to make an abseil descent with Patey last in line. He had descended some 15ft when his rope jammed. As Patey tried to shake himself free, the karabiner attached to his harness flew open and he fell 100ft to his death. Dixon makes the stark commentary: 'Crucially, in his typical careless pattern, he was not using a screwgate.' Patey was 38.

The final judgment is accorded to Paul Nunn, who wrote in 1978: 'Tom had exercised an unchallenged hegemony over the North-West, and his going left a void in his fief which could never be so adroitly filled.' It was, in summary, 'the end of an era'. For me, it is astonishing, and unsettling, to realise the era in question ended more than 50 years ago, as the events I witnessed seem so fresh in my memory.

Dixon's writing is strong and clear. For all its magnificent qualities, however, the book has occasional flaws. There is sometimes a lack of chronological rigour, as for example over the dates of the births of the Pateys' three children that go unstated. Nor is the precise date of Patey's death recorded. Dixon makes copious use of footnotes, consigning material there which I felt could have been incorporated into the text with some judicious splicing. This can leave us to patch information together for ourselves, as with the story of Patey's older half-brother Michael, where the details are spread between the text, the footnotes and a picture caption. Perhaps Dixon did not trust his own ability as storyteller but in that event he misjudged himself.
Dixon received invaluable help from Patey's son Ian, who shared the voluminous archive devoted to his father. There are numerous photographs, many of the finest taken by Cleare. Like all good books, this one leaves you with questions as well as answers, as you ponder the character of this colossus of Scottish mountaineering, as well as savour the era and the milieu that Patey did so much to define.

Peter Gillman

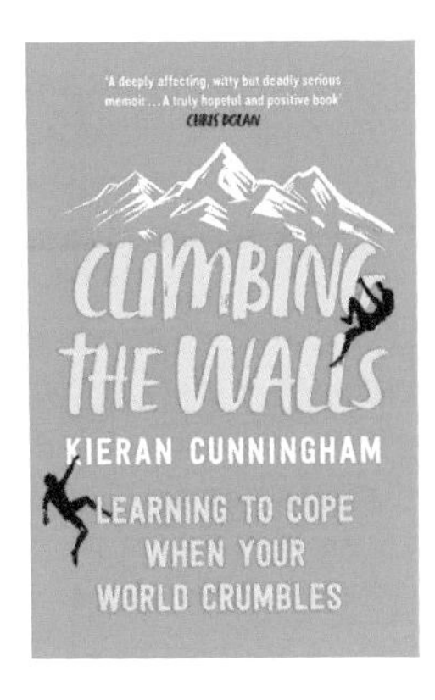

Climbing the Walls
Learning To Cope When Your World Crumbles
Kieran Cunningham
Simon & Schuster UK, 313pp, £10

There's something like an anxiety or resistance in starting to read someone else's lockdown journal. Every one of us has our own unique and painful recollections of that time and a perhaps low appetite for getting to grips with someone else's. But Kieran Cunningham is an exceptional writer (and climber) and within a few pages of *Climbing the Walls* he wins an investment from you in his story. By the end of the book he's paid you back with a depth of wisdom and empathy that sheds gratifying light on your own quarantine entrapment and post-pandemic recovery. And on your climbing, too.

There's surprisingly little actual climbing in this book that so wonderfully penetrates the mystery of why we do it. And much of the climbing Cunningham writes about is just the scrappy lockdown contingency of buildering on the property of his 90-year-old landlady in Sondrio, northern Italy. There, in the province neighbouring Bergamo, the epicentre of the European pandemic, he traverses the pain away on a cocktail of schist, serpentine, granite and gneiss making up the walls of her house and the retaining walls of neighbouring vineyards. It's all he can get his hands and feet on without falling foul of Italy's 2020 lockdown, which preceded our own numb torment in the UK by about two weeks. It's day 11 of his confinement when he hits on this solution, suddenly 'finding more pleasure than I ever thought possible from something so banal.'

Halfway through this diary, in good old fashioned technical language, he drafts a 'Guide To The Walls Of No3 Via Aurelio Fracassetti' in loving detail, delineating the crimps and pockets of the Dusk Wall (an ironic reversal of Yosemite's Dawn Wall), the Dirty Wall and an airy, physical pitch around the exterior of the house called *Indecent Exposure*. The Scorpion Wall gets its name from the 'fist-jam pocket just past the bedroom dihedral (which) has a scorpion inside.' He's discovered this feature a few days earlier, taking a sting that swells his hand to double its normal size and potentially threatens the integrity of his quarantine.

Something else exceptional about Cunningham is the extremity of his mental health. All his adult life he's been managing bipolar disorder, surviving manic episodes and suicidal near misses and spontaneous midnight solos of hazardous mountain routes. The reader learns a great deal about the condition, and the day-to-day reality of living with it. It's a nakedly honest account; the experience of his directness feels almost voyeuristic to the reader. But the discussion of his bipolar disorder becomes a prism through which the wordless secret of climbing, what it means and why we do it, is clearly refracted.

One of the disquieting reactions he's got used to when revealing his condition to people he's becoming close to is 'Well, we're all a little bit like that, aren't we?' So I hesitate to say how much we climbers can see of ourselves in this account of his relationship with climbing as an antidote to the suffering his bipolar regularly inflicts. But his depiction of movement in the mountains as a coping tool for the 'excessive physiological and intracranial tension' he periodically endures will be a familiar concept to us all, even if our own mental fugues are not so profound. And he has the wisdom and self-knowledge to upend this paradigm near the end of the book. It's an insight he offers on bipolar rather than on climbing but we all know it deep down as one of the most baffling open secrets of what we do: 'Often the joy is more agonising than the despair, and the despair spangled with exquisitely raw, visceral beauty.' In fact, the book is shot through with this duality. A theme he returns to more than once is his friend Luigi's assertion that *l'alpinismo è sofferenza* (mountaineering is suffering).

It's not all reflection. The story is told with drive and tension. You genuinely worry as he slowly runs out of the crucial meds he needs to help fend off a crisis. There's humour and politics: a local bank clerk tells him: 'Your new Prime Minister makes even Berlusconi look good.' The main characters around him, either in Sondrio or at the painful remove of Zooms and phone calls, are all compellingly drawn, especially his parents up in Fife, his girlfriend Aiyla over in Istanbul and Giuseppina the nonagenarian landlady upstairs. Luigi, the climbing friend who understands about *sofferenza*, reappears in a footnote with a lighter-hearted assessment of what climbers are: 'Boulderers are problem-solving technicians, sport climbers are gymnasts, trad climbers are engineers, alpine climbers are adventurers. All of us are madmen and poets.' And when he lets the memory or reality of actual climbing into the narrative he renders it with unflashy but exciting clarity.

One remembered mountain moment comes to him in a dream and provides my favourite passage in the book, a poet climber's capture of the perfect condition of stillness and completeness. The recollection is of an epic on a 300m multi-pitch route in Val di Mello. Near the top, as daylight fades, his partner has revealed herself to be less experienced than she professed. She's never abseiled before but the night will be too cold to bivy. There's only one head torch between them and that gets dropped at one of the anchors on the way down. They plough on with only their phones for emergency lighting. Then Cunningham has to descend over an overhang into space. In the pitch blackness and 1,000ft above the valley floor, he promises to give a tug when it's safe for her to follow. Inexplicably, he locks off and dangles in the night air for 15 minutes. They make it down at 3am, exhausted and dehydrated, but 'in the dream ... I remained on the rope, dangling in space, snug in the womb-like embrace of the darkness and emptiness. I understood I would stay there for ever and, rather than panic or despair, felt myself suffused with an all-encompassing warmth and peace the like of which I've never known.'

Nick Simons

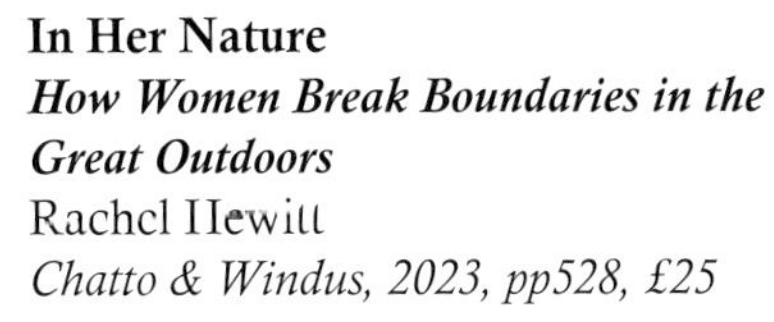

In Her Nature
How Women Break Boundaries in the Great Outdoors
Rachel Hewitt
Chatto & Windus, 2023, pp528, £25

Valley of Giants
Stories from Women at the Heart of Yosemite Climbing
Lauren DeLaunay Miller
Mountaineers Books, 2022, pp240, £19

A few summers ago, with my friend MJ, I took a two-day mountain bike ride along a 70-mile section of the Pennine Bridleway. Starting in Hebden Bridge, we headed north towards Kirkby Stephen on the northern edge of the Yorkshire Dales, enjoying the climbs and descents of the Pennine trails in between, along with café and pub stops, and a bivy on Ingleborough Common on a perfect midsummer night.

As two women, MJ and I did not think twice doing this on our own. We have grown up and spent our adult lives around friendship groups in which it is normalised for women go to the outdoors, either alone or in small female groups. It's perhaps not a coincidence that we both started to do this at university: each of us spent time in university climbing clubs, MJ at Southampton and myself at Leeds.

I took to the Leeds University climbing scene as soon as I arrived. I didn't even think about it at the time, but in this club strong women abounded, both in their presence and abilities at the crag and in the mountains. I had found a group of like-minded people and thrived, loving my time spent with them climbing in the UK and beyond.

These were formative years, after which I threw myself into much more climbing, along with fell running and cycling in mountainous places, activities I continue with today in my mid 40s. Halcyon days? Certainly, in many ways. Looking back now however, at the climbing culture and mindset back then, those days were also of their time. For example, while the climbing and mountaineering books and magazines of the era were inspiring, exciting, funny and entertaining, they carried a strong bias towards a particular perspective, dominated as they were by male stories. It was unusual to see a book or journal in this genre that told of the female experience, or a woman's point of view.

This was of course nothing new. Since the establishment of the *Alpine Journal* in the mid 19th century, men have dominated stories of climbing mountains. You could argue of course that this was reflective of society then and through the 20th century to today. But that argument quickly falls down. As most history was written by men, many of the stories of female protagonists went unrecorded or disappeared. Women may have been present in fewer numbers than men but they were certainly there, pushing themselves and their boundaries in the same ways as their male counterparts.

In recent years this issue has been increasingly recognised, questioned and pathways of correction sought. Published in 2022 and 2023 respectively, two books that seek to do this are *Valley Of Giants* and *In Her Nature*. Both these books address the historic imbalance by bringing forward the female voice and their experience of rock climbing, mountaineering and mountain-going in general.

Edited by Lauren DeLaunay Miller, California resident and regional editor of the *American Alpine Journal, Valley of Giants* is an anthology of nearly 40 pieces written or narrated by women. The book spans the history of Yosemite climbing: Marjory Farquhar's experiences with the Sierra Club in the 1930s, through the golden era of the latter half of the 20th century, to the modern day, featuring well-known climbers such as Liz Robbins and Lynn Hill. Yosemite was of course one of the (if not *the*) global hotbed of rock climbing during this time, famous for the hard-climbing dirtbag lifestyles of the protagonists of the day.

The written pieces in *Valley of Giants* are a mixture of previously published articles (in magazines and journals such as *Alpinist* and the *American Alpine Journal*), book extracts, new prose pieces and interviews. Curating in this way collects into one place, articles with the shared theme of women's climbing in Yosemite, showing us that such women's writing has been present for a long time.

One of the articles from the *AAJ* was first published in 1974. An account of women climbers and notable first all-female ascents in Yosemite and beyond, the author Sibylle Hechtel wanted the piece to be named 'Walls Without Balls'. The *AAJ* editorial team refused, declaring the title too coarse and so Hechtel insisted the piece was published untitled. This anthology reverts to the original title, a fitting name for an article written in the era of the Stonemasters that tells of multi-day epics on the big walls: women climbing for themselves and by themselves.

Not surprisingly, common themes within the pieces are self-discovery, a determination to show what women can climb and the style in which they can do it. But the ways in which the contributors write about their climbing, friendships and how they explore themselves makes for a collection that differs from the standard rock-climbing anthology. As Mari Gingery notes in her foreword:

> *Narratives by women offer fresh perspectives on the aspirations, situations, and resolutions encountered in rock climbing. While chasing the basic goal of ascent, they often differ in their motivations, their approaches to the climbing life and their perceptions of the climbing experience.*

Rachel Hewitt.

Yosemite legend Nancy Bickford Miller rappels after climbing the Lower Brother in 1955 *(Bob and Ira Spring)*

There is a far greater willingness to explore emotions and the ways they impact the relationship between climbers as they push themselves on the rock. In the collection this is frequently expressed in the tenacity of women, showing the men they can do it too. That's no surprise given the egos of the majority male environment these women were climbing in. Inspiring in itself this tenacity combines with a willingness to write of weakness and doubt and how these were often overcome with the support and determination of female climbing friendships.

Probably the most renowned female rock-climbing achievement in the Valley is Lynn Hill's first free ascent of *The Nose* on El Capitan. While this achievement is of course referenced in the anthology, Hill's contribution (taken from her memoir *Climbing Free*) focusses on her first female team ascent of El Capitan's Shield, climbed over six days with Mari Gingery.

One of my favourites in this collection was 'Like Mother Like Daughter', co-authored by Jane Jackson and her mother Catherine Cullinane. A piece written in the first person by Jackson and interspaced with Cullinane's memories of the hard climbing she did in the Valley 30 years previously, we follow Jackson as she pushes her own climbing grades, often followed on the rope by Cuillinane, who then tells her daughter her story of climbing the given route (or something more difficult) a generation before. The younger woman's eyes are opened with respect, appreciation and pride, leaving her wanting to learn more and more of her mom's past life on the Yosemite granite. In reading this piece I felt the two of them bond in new ways and felt pleasure for them in the joys they find climbing together.

Valley of Giants sets out to redress the balance of the recorded history of rock climbing in the Valley. *In Her Nature* author Rachel Hewitt has the same aims but they are wider. While she focusses on Britain and in particular England, Hewitt traces a history (I so want to write *her* story) from the times when mountains were first being conquered by European and American society figures through to the present day. She takes a two-pronged approach to this: her own contemporary experiences as a female trail runner and, through her research, she finds and tells women's stories, notably Ladies' Alpine Club founder Lizzie Le Blond and a number of her contemporaries.

An academic by background, Hewitt takes a scholarly approach to her writing. It is forensic in the ways in which she uncovers and explores the forgotten stories of women and how they were forgotten. There is depth and authority in this approach and, although academic, Hewitt's writing style is far from dry. This is an impassioned, at times poetic investigation. Hewitt shows her anger and sadness at the ways in which women's experiences and achievements have gone unrecorded in the mountaineering canon, making an important point that it seems the establishment of clubs and governing bodies played a significant part in this. They were literally always men-only groups: women's interests and points of view were dismissed and quashed by the patriarchy.

Along with anger at the imbalances and unfairness, grief was also a powerful driver for Hewitt to write this book. Early in *In Her Nature*, she writes of the intensity of recently losing several close family relatives. Hewitt started to increase her running miles because she found it a source of healing (or at least a mind-calmer). That and the fact that it is probably the most practical way for a mother of young children (as Hewitt was at the time) to get short stints of time to herself in a way conducive to getting fitter. I could more than relate to both of these.

As she increases her time spent running, Hewitt observes the inherent sexisms there are within it. The bias of cut-offs in ultra-running races that always favour men and how for decades trail-running shoes, rucksacks and similar have been designed to fit the male foot and frame. And of always having to think about the risks of being a lone female runner, along with the jeers from men in vans were disturbing experiences of men who either followed her or seemed to go out of their way to intimidate her in other ways.

In similar ways to Caroline Criado-Perez's ground-breaking work *Invisible Women*, which exposes the inherent male bias and the impact of this in all parts of society, Hewitt shows us how the great outdoors has carried male bias for generations in ways that have accepted for far too long. Reading *In Her Nature* made me angry and also glad that Hewitt has written this book highlighting these gaps and problems in society.

At the same time, I questioned Hewitt's perception of risk (as she herself does in the concluding sections of the book). Perhaps because I personally run or walk on moors, mountains and in forests by myself, not uncommonly at night, my own perception of the inherent dangers of risks due to threatening and violent behaviour by men is that it is actually very low. Of course, the problem here is when such violence does occur it is an awful, awful thing. Even though they're rare, such events perpetuate women's fears, heightens our general perception of risk and Hewitt discusses how in itself this is very much a form of male control over women.

This brings me back to my bike ride with MJ along the Pennine Bridleway. During the afternoon of our first day's ride, we dropped off Weets Hill to Gisburn, where we stopped for a while at a café. While we were there, I got talking to a woman who was probably a decade or so younger than me, who had a toddler and six-month old baby with her. She told me how much she loved to go mountain biking on the moors but that she hadn't been for a long time because it's 'too dangerous': her husband was not keen on her going out alone and she was clearly fearful of it herself. After speaking some more, she told me her husband went out biking by himself all the time while she stayed at home and literally held the baby.

I left the café feeling angry and sad for this woman, that the freedoms I cherish were out of her reach. Reading Hewitt's book made me remember this encounter in Gisburn. It also showed me I have a privilege I've never even considered. Yes, of course I consider the potential dangers when I head outside alone. But I am so used to doing so I have long since realised that my risk of harm at the hands of a man is actually extremely small. In today's society I think it likely women like MJ and I, and hopefully now Hewitt, are still in the minority.

Valley of Giants and *In Her Nature* are two complementary books. In different ways they show the same things. *Valley of Giants* is very much of its genre: dirt-bag climbers and visceral descriptions of the rock and the women climbing it. We feel their struggles, pain and the exaltation of achievement, interspaced with deeper explorations of the associated feelings and emotion than perhaps we are used to. *In Her Nature* is more of a mainstream book than many about mountaineering and trail running have been. This extended reach is much needed. If Hewitt's words achieve in running and mountaineering what Criado-Perez did with perceptions of how society is generally structured to fit a male, then it can go some way to addressing the male bias and gender imbalance still inherent in outdoor activities today.

Heather Dawe

High Risk
Climbing to Extinction
Brian Hall
Sandstone Press, 2022, 380pp, £25

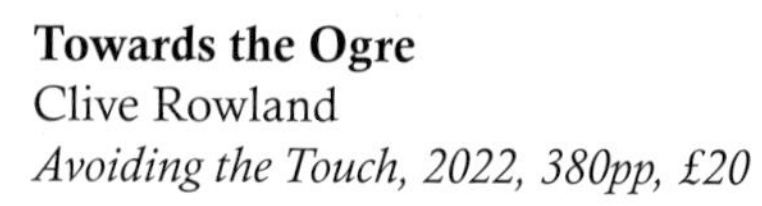

Towards the Ogre
Clive Rowland
Avoiding the Touch, 2022, 380pp, £20

There are plenty of reasons for reviewing these two books together. Both are overdue. Both authors tell the stories of their lives. Both try to give honest accounts of dangerous adventures. Neither shies away from the terrible human cost of those adventures. And while they go about their subject matter in very different ways, both approaches have their merits.

Clive Rowland was one of the participants in the 1977 epic on the Ogre, an unlikely survival story that went straight into mountaineering folklore, not least because two of the main protagonists were household names. He tells his version in a straightforward, low-key, unaffected way. ('What would you have done youth, if I had been unable to crawl?' Doug Scott asks him, when Rowland and Mo Anthoine have brought him and Chris Bonington safely down. 'I would have left you Doug. One dead hero is better than two, especially when the other one is me!') The bonus with this book is the rest of his climbing career; I doubt many will know the scale of what he achieved.

Then there is Brian Hall's intriguingly imaginative account of 12 of his mates who for a variety of reasons that are obvious from the title are no longer with us. How Hall remained alive to write *High Risk: Climbing to Extinction* is a mystery that even he doesn't attempt to explain but he doesn't shy away from the hard truth that is all too apparent to the great majority of us: that climbing is dangerous. He starts with a quotation from what is called in the West the *Tibetan Book of the Dead*, exhorting us to keep in mind our own mortality. One wonders to what extent the 12 subjects of his book had this in mind as they went about their climbing lives.

Some more than others you suspect. Hall himself says: 'I look back on many of our actions as idiotic and unjustifiable. But viewing those pictures and unpacking those old boxes in my office took me back to an exhilarating and happy part of my life.' It was, he says correctly, 'a significant time in climbing and mountaineering' and his 'outrageously talented companions' and their legacy 'deserve to be remembered.'

So who were these 12? Some I knew, some only by reputation, one or two not at all. There's his climbing pal from youth Sam Cochrane, who dies unexpectedly of a heart attack shortly before a long delayed reunion. After school in Kendal they went to Leeds University together, in the late 1960s a hotbed of climbing talent. There he met the rock-climbing wunderkind John Syrett, whose tragically short life and suicide was the subject of a recent biography. Also at Leeds was legendary alpinist Alex MacIntyre. In 1971, he opens his student house door to Mick Geddes, then at Cambridge with Al Rouse, another of his 12 subjects. Geddes was 'a magician when ice climbing', Hall writes, and his death from cancer at 34 is a reminder that fate may not choose the mountains to come for you. There's old friend John Whittle, whose talent for pub-time story-telling became a kind of curse, as his health collapsed from too much drinking. There is of course a litany of climbing accidents: Roger Baxter-Jones, Georges Bettembourg, Pete Thexton, dying high on Broad Peak from pulmonary oedema, driven, obsessed Joe Tasker, avuncular, big-hearted Paul Nunn. The last of the 12 is Andy Parkin, who very nearly wasn't with us, but continues to explore the mountains through his art as well as his climbing.

It was interesting reading each portrait of the outrageous characters that inhabited our psyche during climbing's 'lost decade' as he names it: a long decade from the early 1970s to the 1980s. I felt at times those portraits were too short. He offers an honest account and tries to address the complexity of their motivation, in life as well as the mountains, their different personalities, their weak spots and fears. Are they're common answers here? What can we say about their histories when motivations can be so different? When trying to fathom the reasons for why Peter Boardman and Joe Tasker pushed so hard on the north-east ridge of Everest in 1982, he wonders if they were addicted to risk. 'Joe's ambition and drive were unbounded, ultimately killing him.' Hall tries to dig into these questions, without ever excusing himself from a similar charge, honestly acknowledging where he lacks understanding, and he turns to experts for help. Yet at the end of the book his conclusions are straightforward: 'I chose to be a mountaineer because I wanted adventure,' he writes. Trying to explain why he's alive and so many friends aren't, he often reaches for the same word: fate. Yet in telling their stories, he takes great pleasure in spending time with his old pals, 'forever … vibrant and young.'

Clive Rowland's conclusions are rather similar but his book is very different. Hall won the Boardman Tasker Award for *High Risk* and it's well published. *Towards the Ogre*, I felt, is more like a diary spanning the whole of Rowland's long climbing career, worth reading for the sheer breadth of expeditions he went on. I suspect these are largely unknown by the wider mountaineering audience. But he doesn't delve into the personalities or motivations of his companions in the same way Hall does.

It starts in his native Sheffield. Rowland came from a time and place that is starting to fade from memory. He opens with the story of being fascinated by snow falling on his street in Crookes and how he got sick eating a snowball. That's the industrial north for you. His parents were keen cyclists and clearly devoted to family life and gave him a stable upbringing and a love of the outdoors. From the start he clearly had a sense of natural justice, standing up to bullies on behalf of the weak. Ordinarily quiet and easy going, when he sees something wrong or foolish, he doesn't hesitate.

Rowland serves a familiar apprenticeship, from hillwalking and climbing in the Peak, to north Wales, Scotland, the Alps and the Himalaya. Along the way he meets a cast of interesting characters, like Hall did, which is where you feel he thinks the value of adventure lies. 'We had fun, didn't we Clive?' Joe Brown tells him towards the end of his life. 'Yes we did,' Rowland concludes. 'Maybe some summits were not reached, but the shared endeavour and camaraderie made it all worthwhile.' He had his share of tragedy. It was Rowland who turned over the body of Tom Patey at the bottom of the Maiden following his abseiling accident. He was in the Pamirs in 1974 for the tragic events that saw 13 climbers perish on a doomed international expedition. And he watched in despair as the young and newly married Graham Evans asphyxiated having got into difficulties on the *Yellow Edge* of the Tre Cime. Paul Nunn is a presence in both books and he proved one of Rowland's great friends.

For climbing historians, there will be particular interest in Rowland's story of the Ogre, or Baintha Brakk to give it its proper name. In Hall's book, I knew perhaps half the cast. In the legend of the Ogre I knew three of the four key players excepting Rowland. This was corrected in 1993 when I made a film about Doug's epic crawl down the mountain. The story is well known. After reaching the summit Doug slipped and broke both his legs while Chris, not wishing to be left out, later fell and broke a couple of ribs, contracting pneumonia as a consequence. It's most likely that Rowland's actions stopped him from dying in the fall, as well as sharing the burden of rescue with Mo.

Over three days I interviewed Chris, Doug and Clive who seemed the most relaxed despite the presence of our two superstars. (Mo had sadly died by this point.) The reason I deduced was simple: he had no public profile to protect. Now Clive has searched his memory to give us a wonderfully descriptive memory of an epic survival story that could have so easily given Brian Hall two more chapters on extinction.

In my opinion it's alpinism's answer to Shackleton's epic retreat from Elephant Island to South Georgia after Endurance had slipped beneath the ice in Antarctica back in 1914. True, none of Ernest's 27 men were injured whereas on the Ogre everyone apart from the heroes wanted part of the action. The personal cost for Rowland is shown in a photo taken shortly after they reached the safety of base camp. It shows Clive emaciated and sunburned, like the survivor of an overexposed concentration camp. 'What the **** happened to you?' Jim Curran asks when they run into each other at Skardu airport. Back in Islamabad, he's asked to come to the morgue to identify Bonington's body, only to discover a mistake has been made and it's an unknown American.

Even then it wasn't over for Clive Rowland. After two weeks rest and recuperation fishing in the Swat valley, he set off to drive home with a young British embassy official but was unable to avoid hitting a boy playing chicken with the traffic across the border in Afghanistan. The aftermath of that accident must have been a nightmare and how Rowland dealt with it shows the measure of the man.

Both these books, like the best mountain stories, have much to tell us about the risks and rewards of the climbing life. Despite it all, neither of these authors seem to regret the path they chose, just the pitfalls along the way.

Leo Dickinson

Closer to the Edge
Leo Houlding
Headline, 2022, 337pp, £20

Maybe I live a cloistered existence and belong to the wrong generation, but though I'd heard his name, I had little idea what exactly is the author's claim to fame. Now, having read his autobiography, I know. Leo Houlding is an exceptionally gifted rock climber who has grown up to become an adventurer. No longer a youngster but a family man with small children, it seems he is still addicted to extreme adventure. In the book he recounts important episodes and events in his life story to date, coming over as rather full of himself, which is tiresome, if perhaps justified.

Leo was lucky, not only to spend his childhood in the Lake District but also to have a father and grown-up friends who were serious hill walkers and scramblers. When hardly more than a toddler he was encouraged to scramble around on small rocks and outcrops accessible from home. He was only seven when he accompanied his father and a friend to the summit of a snowy 3,000m peak in the Taurus of southern Turkey. In such company he met serious adult climbers, was introduced to the technicalities of rock climbing on real Lakeland crags and rapidly became obsessed, encouraged enthusiastically by his father who even took up the game himself. At the age of 11, after an ascent of the Old Man of Hoy with adult friends, Leo never looked back.

Winning climbing competitions as a child prodigy he established a name for himself but he abandoned such things as 'boring in format and completely lacking in adventure', an ethos which has governed his life ever since. An impressionable kid, for a while he became 'apprentice' to some of the leading rock jocks of the 1990s before dropping out of education with his parents' agreement on the promise of making a go of it as a professional climber. Indeed, by the age of 16 he was actually attracting sponsorship and earning money from his climbing. Graduating to the infamously hedonistic Llanberis climbing scene in its final years, he was able to burn off the hardest routes on Cloggy and Gogarth, often solo, and out-neck the best of his rather older mentors. Before long, fully sponsored and a television personality of sorts, it appeared that he'd already made a go of it; at the age of only 17 he was a professional climber.

Captivated as a child by Ansel Adams' photographs, Yosemite was the obvious next stop. The Valley became Leo's promised land. Aged 18 when he arrived to join the Camp 4 scene, becoming the youngest of the so-called Stone Monkeys, one of the hard climbing, hard drinking, dope smoking, squalor living, fulltime tearaway climbers who were also into the illegal and extremely dangerous thrills of base jumping and wing-suit flying, in both of which 'diversions' the young Leo also took great delight.

A large part of the book is devoted to the Valley and what he achieved there with his like-minded colleagues; he hoped to concentrate on big-wall free climbing but also found himself breaking speed records on the hardest routes, putting up new ones and surviving storms. Everything in these chapters seemed to be 'outrageous', 'terrifying' or 'horrific'; it proved tedious and left me rather cold. I'm no stranger to Yosemite myself and am well aware of its climbing history but I soon lost track of move after move, crack after crack, roof after roof, haul-bags full of fear and the frequent falls, spread over a number of years and dozens of pages.

Adventure eventually rears its head with an expedition to the Paine and Fitzroy massifs and an all but disastrous attempt on Cerro Torre. I could follow the action because I know both areas so I found this chapter quite interesting. Later chapters cover an expeditionary climb on Mount Asgard in Baffin Island, described in repetitive detail, and another to Cerro Autuna, an iconic tepui or mesa monolith in the Venezuelan jungle, a sort of re-hash of Hamish MacInnes' *Climb to the Lost World.*

By the age of 32 Leo is married and making serious money by organising and appearing in way-out adventure films and still capable of leading top-end rock climbs, if rather more responsibly than in his youth. Two good chapters cover expeditions to the Antarctic, the first to Ulvetanna, the Wolf's Fang, a spectacular granite spire rising some 900m from the ice of eastern Antarctica. Located only in 1994 and no longer virgin, the first ascent of the spectacular mile long north-east ridge presented a worthy subject for an exciting and exceedingly expensive movie.

The other Antarctic adventure was aimed at Spectre, an upstanding granite molar in the remote Gothic range, only 270 miles from the pole and thus out of range of the usual polar aircraft. This time the three-man team made the 17-day approach and return by kite ski, towing some 1,400lb of food and gear on pulks. This surely was a serious and necky adventure.

Yet to my mind the most illuminating chapter describes Leo's ascent of Everest's north ridge in 2007 for an IMAX movie, acting the part of Irvine for a short stretch of the climb while (at least to start) wearing contemporary clothing and using the appropriate equipment alongside Conrad Anker playing Mallory. Particularly intriguing was how Anker, having removed the Chinese ladder, climbed the enigmatic Second Step with a couple of crampon moves and a single hand jam. This was exactly how Everest climber Chu Yin-hua, then my expedition liaison officer, told me he himself had climbed the Second Step in 1960, his ascent being discounted by the establishment. Chu believed Mallory might well have reached the summit.

There are two folios of good photographs, 46 images in all, very well reproduced on glossy paper but often of the snapshot variety and used too small to make much impact. Several of the best images reproduced full page would have added much to the book.

The concluding chapter tells how Leo and his wife Jess introduced their two very small children to climbing, not merely on outcrops or Lakeland crags but on full blown, serious alpine peaks. No doubt many will castigate them for this, but the Houldings feel that 'Learning to manage fear is an invaluable life skill,' adding that adventure is important to nurture a child's confidence and unleash his or her capabilities. I think we will all agree with that, and I'd hazard a guess that Leo and Jess know what they're doing.

John Cleare

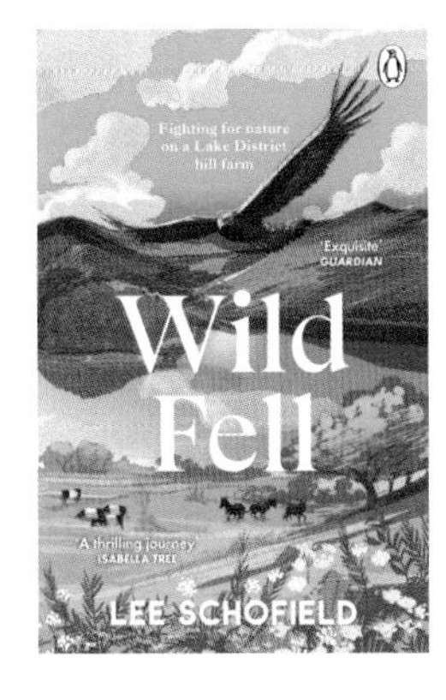

Wild Fell
Fighting for Nature on a Lake District Farm
Lee Schofield
Penguin, 2023, 368pp, £11

Halfway through Lee Schofield's engaging and hopeful book, I got so excited I put it down and took a trip to where the book is largely set, the Naddle Forest and the stretch of land between Haweswater and Swindale. Much of this is owned by United Utilities, one of our beleaguered water companies, and in recent years managed for nature by the Royal Society for the Protection of Birds (RSPB). The Naddle Forest is ancient and surrounded by a high wall constructed in the 1300s to create a hunting preserve for the elite. At that time, there were still wolves in the Lake District, beavers too, and cranes, doing their delightful, dipping courtship dance in the spring. Eagles too, and Schofield opens his account with the sad tale of the last golden eagle to disappear from the Lake District, a lonely male which presumably died in 2015 after a decade on its own. All these melancholic absences are part of a long process that has left Britain as one of the most nature-depleted countries on earth. Beavers and cranes are making a small comeback, wolves not so much. Fingers crossed for the eagles, since both golden and white-tailed eagles were there in Wordsworth's day.

The Naddle Forest is a magical place, unsurprisingly perhaps given its great age. It's a tiny fragment of the temperate rain forest that once ran the length of western Britain, its old oaks moistened with warm and wet Atlantic air, sewn through with mosses and ferns, patched with lichens. The bird life is delightful: pied and spotted flycatchers, several species of warbler, redstarts and tree creepers. Yet only around 12% of the Lake District is wooded and half of that is conifer plantation where there is only a small fraction of the biodiversity of somewhere like Naddle. Most of the Lake District, of course, has for centuries been sheep walks, where, more recently, historically high stocking levels have left little apart from grasses tough enough to survive constant grazing.

If anything, the situation has worsened since the Lake District became a national park. As Schofield reminds us, in 1951 'its streams and ditches were busy with water voles, corncrakes rasped from the meadows, black grouse lekked on scruffy fellsides and corn buntings perched on fences around little arable plots.' A large part of his story is about what ecologists often call 'shifting baselines'. An obvious example is the experience of the the curmudgeonly Alfred Wainwright, whose discovery of the Lake District before the war introduced him to a paradise that he watched become gradually 'overrun' with visitors, many of whom were inspired by Wainwright's popular guidebooks. Quite what he would make of the current scene you can only imagine. In 2018, the Lakes had 19.38m visitors, a figure to set against the 42,000 who actually live there. Those visitors, outnumbering inhabitants by more than 450 to one, spent £1.48bn. That's roughly what the sheep-farming industry turned over nationally. Of course, tourism and sheep farming are often intertwined. Many of the Lake District's 1,200 farms rely on tourists to boost their incomes. Much of the farming income on hill farms comes from the taxpayer in the form of government support payments.

So the framing of Schofield's book seems pretty dismal. An unprofitable industry with deep cultural roots that has caused long-term impacts on a region of a nature-depleted country that is often thronged with visitors. Many of those visitors, inspired by best-selling writers like George Monbiot and his warnings of a 'sheepwrecked' landscape, make loud demands for change. Farmers, whose families have worked on the fells for generations, feel understandably aggrieved. The idea of rewilding, in all its several definitions, becomes a new battleground in the culture wars fought daily on social media.

Schofield tacks through these stormy seas with remarkable patience and considerable self-knowledge. It's quite clear in recounting his experience that he's had to face a great deal of opposition, some of it unpleasantly aggressive, and in doing so addressed some aspects of his personality that made that process more difficult. He took over the running of Naddle and Swindale farms soon after the RSPB started managing them in 2012. The prospect of one of the big conservation charities getting their hands on traditional sheep farms, with all that implied for their neighbours, raised hackles. The RSPB was now sharing common land with a group of farmers who resented their presence. Schofield was regularly told he was an idiot and that he didn't know what he was doing.

At public meetings he was accused of dismantling a thousand years of custom and practice, of abandoning land and of removing sheep whose lineage dated back to the Vikings. All he'd done is halve the flock on the properties he was managing, give more space to nature and a bit less to food production. He could have become angry and resentful but instead he examines himself for not explaining the arguments better. The uncomfortable truth is that the Vikings didn't have access to the kinds of public subsidy that almost every sheep farmer in Britain relies on to stay in business. That financial support cannot be unconditional, not when our mountains are so poor in biodiversity, shorn of native forests and even now sometimes restricted in access.

It's an uncomfortable truth that tourism in the British uplands has made a purse from a sow's ear, or perhaps in this case a sheep's ear. Travel to many other European mountain ranges and you cannot fail to notice this. There's more of everything: birds, mammals, flowers and trees. Somehow we have managed to turn the upland environment into an issue in the ever-decreasing circle of our times: the culture war. Schofield shows remarkable patience and forbearance in trying to lift the argument out of this binary dead end. He says he loathes the 'toxic polarization' of the debate. He draws a neat distinction between farming policy and farmers. There are an increasing number of sheep farmers in England who are beginning to see that another way is possible. And Schofield takes a trip to Norway to illustrate how a country once almost as denuded as Britain changed its ways and allowed the mountain environment to recover.

The aspect of this discursive, uplifting and thought-provoking book I liked best was Schofield's attention to flowers. His knowledge is both broad and deep; he sees their beauty but also understands what their presence or more often in the case of Britain's mountains their absence tells us.

> *A deflowering has happened across vast tracts of our countryside, both in the intensive farmland and in the seemingly wilder hills above. Over time, we've come to accept a landscape in which wildflowers survive only in the liminal spaces as normal. Yet without them, the rest of life has little chance.*

Walking across a patch of boggy ground at Naddle Farm, I found myself thinking of these words. In front of me was a large patch of spiky yellow bog asphodel and some marsh valerian, bright white against the reedy grasses. The whole scene had a richness and complexity I've rarely experienced in England or Wales. This was much more the Lake District of a few centuries ago, not the battered relic we've inherited. Seeing this place was a revelation, Schofield's book even more so.

Ed Douglas

Native Air
Jonathan Howland
Green Writers Press, 2022, 380pp, £23

'Nothing ever happens once and is finished.' These words from William Faulkner on the frontispiece of Jonathan Howland's award-winning novel contain a tension echoed in the vehemence of the book's first word: 'No.' It is 2013 and Joe, a former climber, receives a letter from Will, son of his dead climbing partner Pete, inviting him to finish a climb of extreme difficulty on the fictitious Mount Moriah that the pair hadn't been able to complete. Joe's reaction is understandable; he has climbed only twice in the last 24 years. Yet despite his initial misgivings, he recognises Will's communication is 'less an invitation than a summons' and decides to accept it, acknowledging that he misses the cocktail of emotions that had so potently fuelled his climbing days and had long been absent during his ill-fated Christian ministry.

The narrative circles back to the 1980s, when Pete and Joe were joyously living the archetypal hand-to-mouth climbers' existence with nothing more urgent on their immediate horizon than the next project. Theirs was a climbing marriage: sharing not only what few possessions they had but also the essential trust and intimacy of a relationship on rock. Howland illustrates this perfectly as the pair find themselves confronted by a chimney, its narrowness seemingly un-climbable until Pete manoeuvres them both into a chest-to-chest position in order to ascend: 'One animal, two sets of lungs.' They build their lives, navigating both the unspoken intensity of their friendship and their partnership on the rock, by not dwelling on either aspect. They shared an unspoken confidence in each other, enjoying an impressively successful partnership that other climbers envied.

Pete was the stronger partner: bolder in vision, fitter and with a seemingly limitless imagination that fed on the increasing difficulty of the climbs he planned so meticulously. This, coupled with his generosity of spirit, charmed and inspired Joe for a decade but then the 'seethe I felt about his ever-expanding chart of enthusiasms' started to erode his own. He saw Pete's ideas were obsessions whose powerful hold seductively stripped away the norms of everyday living, which had simply lost their meaning for him. Yet there was still the irresistible call of the rhythms of their existence, its routines unhitched from conformity, its closeness and what Pete referred to as 'its aliveness' making Joe's un-crystallised ambitions of studying in a seminary and entering the ministry seem to lack truth, substance and vitality. Climbing with Pete, Joe could see solutions to the physical problems rock presented them and simultaneously feel the proximity of risk that both threatened and enlivened them. His rationale for becoming a minister was rooted not in his need to help others but to discover the same juxtaposition he found in

Jonathan Howland.

climbing within religious belief: a flawed premise. Would his tenuous hold on faith pay the price of what Pete felt to be his betrayal of all that they held so dear, not least their partnership?

Pete's death, nine years later, caused by an inexplicable 700ft fall from a route he had soloed with ease on countless occasions, brought Joe a double grief: both for his friend and for the way of life that had still taken him to the mountains, despite his family commitments, and allowed him to be wholly present in the vertical world in which he so obviously thrived. Joe felt anew the loss of colour and challenge in his life, dislocated from the urge of appetite, with memories his most vividly immediate companions. He had only the irreconcilable loss of the man who had given him the compulsion to climb, the source of all his vitality: 'It's all there is, a deep and true and unshakeable communion of grief.'

Will's invitation to finish the Mount Moriah route has come at a timely moment for both of them. Will's life has been drenched in the past, awash with the mythology of a father who was simultaneously 'everywhere and nowhere', often poetically and heroically alive to the climbers who knew and admired him, but a barely remembered presence to his son, who wanted only to have an honest understanding of the father he had never really known and whose prodigious talent he had inherited.

Howland narrates the eventual completion of the climb with a tenderness that never slides into the maudlin. The scattering of Pete's ashes both revives but redefines Joe's grief: this time his sadness is for Pete, the consummate lover of life and for all the living he would never do. As Joe and Will wrap around each other all night in order to endure the bitter cold at the top of the route the steady beat of Will's heart reassures Joe that this is a life that will continue what Pete was, what he began and what he never had the chance to finish. This will be no mere imitation: Will is invested in a future and a family with his partner Alison. Pete, on the other hand, while loyal to Will's mother, found nothing compared with his love of climbing. Ties to home came second to an uncontrollable need to construct his life around the truths of existence that he felt climbing and understood nowhere else.

Native Air, which won the grand prize at the Banff Mountain Book Festival last year, is very far from simply a narrative for and about climbers. The fluid and compelling descriptions of the technicalities of the various routes within it beautifully convey the essence of experiences on rock and, with the inclusion of two glossaries of climbing terms, bring clarity to climber and non-climber alike. Howland has, with consummate skill, succeeded in weaving together stories of a heart-and-soul commitment to the beautiful danger of climbing and two people trying to make sense of the most profound loss of their lives.

Val Johnson

Through Dangerous Doors
A Life At Risk
Robert Charles Lee
E L Marker, 2021, 213pp, £19.95

There are two life stories told in this fascinating book, both of them beset with risk and enlivened by adventure, but Robert Charles Lee's two lives couldn't be more different. They're delineated under two headings, 'Solo' and 'Duet', though it feels like the lived experience of pivoting from one to the other may not have been as sharply defined as it is on paper. The duet is played with Linda, who emerges from Kenya after three years in the Peace Corps to become Lee's wife and climbing partner, more or less saving his life.

The wild solo he's been playing until then evolves out of a troubled childhood in a racist backwater in North Carolina and develops into a long and very trippy passage of drug abuse and either surveying or logging in Oregon and Alaska. Orthodox climbing barely intrudes. Adventure comes from high-speed drunk driving or solitary multi-day explorations of desert canyons.

Lee describes both his lives with unselfconscious honesty, barring the occasional and troubling ambiguity. ('I don't recall any lynchings,' he writes.) It's a clear, individual voice, as if you were sharing a tent on a mountainside and hearing his story face to face. And in his unguarded vividness, you wonder (as you sometimes do of any climbing partner you're stuck in a tent with) whether you actually like him or not. The dazzling adventure anecdotes, the careless tales of rolling 'joints with one hand while driving, chain-smoking weed along the way', the precisely recalled macho ripostes to threatening interlopers. ('Bring it on. I'll wrap this fucking bike around both your fucking red necks.') Yet you can't help allowing for his faults and fallibilities in the frank account he gives of himself. Just as you see the truest version of a climbing partner in the extremes of exhaustion or weather, you accept and admire Lee for the humanity his exceptional life story reveals.

After turning away from a life of using and into one of proper climbing, his working life takes him into a graduate course in environmental risk assessment. Over the following quarter of a century he evolves into a respected and substantial risk scientist. The word risk is in the subtitle to the book, and often he mentions the managing of risk or alludes to its rewards. But this is not an academic treatise and, perhaps disappointingly, he doesn't make space for a detailed analysis of the science of risk. Sometimes the subject is dovetailed into a poetic equivalence with something intangible, maybe a connection to William Blake or Aldous Huxley, dating from his psychedelic days, a deliberate abandonment of science and exactness in a committed reach for the heart of the matter. The whole book is a meditation on the drive to go through the doors of perception. And yet the reader is left hungry for an earthier, more rooted investigation of the 'complex and dynamic set of risks' that climbing involves. He mentions a paper that he and Linda once wrote on rational risk management approaches in mountaineering, which I would have welcomed as an appendix.

Towards the end, he confesses a regret that he 'didn't study risk psychology.' And yet it's a psychology he's been inhabiting all his life, whether blasting away with boyhood firearms or stoned and adrift with the US Forest Service or climbing with the best in the Canadian Rockies. The answer to the riddle is tantalisingly close.

Last year in this country Bangor University sports psychologists Dr Marley Willegers and Prof Tim Woodman published research on how climbing and mountaineering regulate our emotions, giving us a sense of control over our inner lives. I would love to hear Lee's take on their conclusions. Like him they agree that those taking part in high-risk sports 'are not "sensation-seeking" and don't crave the adrenaline rush. There's something else taking place.' It's that elusive something else which Lee circles throughout his memoir, using for instance the expression 'I maintained' to describe staying rooted in the extremes of both colossal LSD doses or disproportionately hazardous climbs.

Willegers and Woodman say, 'People who feel that they have little control over their daily lives, who feel like a "pawn", can be drawn to high-risk sports where they are able to exercise control over strong emotions, such as fear, and take actions that dictate whether they succeed or die. The benefits of this emotional control in high-risk situations are then transferred back into daily life.' I recognise something in that and feel sure Lee would too.

Lee doesn't turn his back on the question, far from it. Peppered throughout the book are cold-bloodedly clear axioms that we all know are true. Fundamentals like 'Risk is cumulative ... the more I climbed the more likely it was I'd be involved in a serious accident.' Or: 'Sometimes it's just more efficient and safer to climb without pro and get it over with.' Or the one prized by loved ones who don't understand the great care with which we undertake our climbing: 'there's only so much that can be done to prevent incidents like this ... aside from *not climbing* [my italics]'.

There are thrilling passages of climbing narrative, especially in the 10 years when work takes Linda and him to Calgary and his American climbing experience takes a Canadian quantum leap: 'The Rockies are snarling Pitbulls compared to the Golden Retrievers of the Cascades.' He's the kind of climber who, on a work visit to the UK, can bowl up to see what the Ben is all about and settle for a winter solo of Tower Ridge in 'what Scots climbers sportingly call "full conditions", or "a bit fresh."'

Flow state is the condition he's striven to achieve all his life, in all his risky undertakings, stepping boldly through the doors of perception, and again and again there are rich and satisfying traces of it in this very enjoyable memoir. Recommended.

Nick Simons

An Expedition Handbook
with Mountaineering Case Studies
Dave Wynne-Jones
Whittles Publishing, 2023, 256pp, £15

There have been a few books published before with similar titles aiming to show how to organise climbing expeditions to remote locations. This book is a little different. It is an account of the author's experiences over several decades of mountaineering and ski expeditions, presented with the benefits of hindsight, aiming to examine successes, mistakes and lessons learnt. The first third of the book is organised thematically considering the various aspects of expedition planning and management. The larger section is made up of entertaining and well-written accounts covering over a dozen trips worldwide between 1997 and 2013. Dave was heavily involved in both the Alpine Club and Eagle Ski Club during this period and the majority of the trips described were either club meets or more informal projects involving a combination of club members and friends.

Reports and articles covering several of these trips, written by Dave or other team members, have already been published elsewhere, not least in the *Alpine Journal* or the Eagle Ski Club's yearbook. There are also several reports lodged with the MEF and held in the Alpine Club Library available for consultation. What makes the accounts different here is that they have been written to highlight the multitude of issues that can make the difference between a harmonious and well-organised expedition and trips that are less successful or enjoyable. In doing so, Dave succeeds in giving a snapshot of a particular type of expedition at a particular point in time.

Club-based trips and peer-to-peer expeditions have their pros and cons. In the decades since the start of low-cost long-haul travel, these have been the traditional entry routes for many UK climbers to mountaineering beyond Europe. In more recent decades, with the increasing prevalence of commercial operators offering guided trips to popular and less well-known peaks worldwide, this has been changing. Climbers wishing to travel to the Greater Ranges now have a variety of options to choose from.

Anyone wanting an insight into how the peer-to-peer option works would be well advised to read this book. Along with several successes there are a few damp squibs and an alarming number of near misses. Perhaps Dave's teams just had more than their share of bad luck. From the examples described it would appear that this style of expedition is best suited to small independent groups climbing different objectives from a shared base camp. It is much harder to harmonise the strengths and abilities of a disparate group of climbers on a single large peak, as shown by Dave's experiences attempting Saraghrar (7340m) in the Hindu Kush.

There will always be a place for this type of trip. Some are attracted by the obvious cost savings when compared to guided trips. Others will have a strong preference for the ethos of self-organised expeditions. Without the chance to lead a low-cost self-organised trip I would never have had an opportunity to visit the Himalaya. That first trip in 1987 also inspired me to embark on a 35-year career that is only now drawing to a close. I am fairly sure that most British guides of my generation working in the Himalaya started in the same way.

Commercial expeditions are now a more popular gateway to climbing in the Greater Ranges. Increasingly, people are drawn to short duration trips to popular peaks. While these lack the exploratory aspect of the trips described in this book they appeal to many of today's climbers who are more risk averse and who are prepared to pay a higher cost for a higher chance of summit success.

There are other ways in which the expeditions of the future will differ from the projects described here. Environmental considerations will make it difficult to justify regular long-haul travel in the future. On a practical level climate change is now rapidly destroying the world's glaciers. Diminishing snow cover is making traditional snow and ice routes unviable in many mountain ranges. On the more positive side there are now good local agents in many countries who can provide quality equipment like tents making for more comfortable trips and reducing the need to struggle with excess baggage on flights from home. Communications technology is also advancing and there are now lightweight affordable options that enable teams to communicate effectively both on the mountain and with the outside world. In regions with an adequate rescue system these can save lives.

There is however one constant that links the expeditions of the past with those of the future, applying equally to self-led and guided groups. The single most important aspect of any trip is the relationships formed between the participants. Team dynamics and interpersonal considerations are the key to any successful trip in the mountains. No group sets out to become dysfunctional but it can happen. Dave gives many examples of teams that have worked well together and a few of teams that have not. For anyone considering organising or joining a first expedition to the Greater Ranges these should be studied carefully. There is as much to learn from Dave's examples of group interactions as from his information on planning, equipment, logistics and medical kits.

Dave Hamilton

We Can't Run Away From This
Racing to Improve Running's Footprint in our Climate Emergency
Damian Hall
Vertebrate Publishing, 2022, 215pp, £15

This is a difficult book to read. That's not a criticism: it's meant to be, as Damian Hall acknowledges from the start: 'Stop! Please, for your own sake, put this book down right now. There's a very good chance you'll regret reading it … you'll probably never think of your running in the same way again.' We can't say we weren't warned.

As Kilian Jornet, no mean runner himself, puts it in his foreword, 'Runners like myself often think that because we run in the outdoors we have a special relation with earth and nature, and that we're more aware of the problems we're facing, but unfortunately that awareness isn't really that great when we dig deep, and it isn't doing much to solve the issues.'

Although this is a book primarily aimed at runners, especially those who compete, it also holds up a mirror to the embedded environmental consequences of mountaineering (kit, travel, fuel and so on). On those grounds, it merits reading by those of us who traverse our mountains more slowly.

Hall, an ultra runner perhaps best known for his record breaking FKTs (fastest known times), was spurred by the mainstreaming of the climate emergency in the last decade to examine his own impact. His first response was 'low carbon' record attempts, using public transport and 'ethical fuelling' (his vegan diet) with some 'plogging' (picking up litter whilst jogging) thrown in. He soon became regarded as a de facto activist though he felt 'more eco-worrier than warrior'. He was also asked to help advise on the sustainability of races. This book traces his three-year journey towards understanding running's impact on the planet and what can be done to improve it.

Clearly, this could have been a very dry book. But, despite the 89 footnotes, eight pages of endnotes and five pages of further reading, he's made it very accessible. That's not to say you don't reel sometimes from the relentlessly depressing facts and figures but Hall does his best to dress this up with black humour and some fabulously bad puns and bants. Indeed, in 'Hall-speak' climate change is usually referred to as the 'Big Kerfufflefuck', which pretty well sums up the situation we find ourselves in. As the title aptly proclaims: 'We Can't Run Away From This'. He's not wrong but ploughing through the book in one go will be beyond most people's endurance, despite his engaging writing and wry commentary: definitely a dip-in and dip-out of book.

His scope is certainly comprehensive and takes a holistic look across all of running's specific impacts before segueing into how our home lifestyles are part of the problem. Chapters address footwear ('Shoespiracy'), running clothes ('Getting T-shirty'), the role of the sportswear industry ('Industry Illusions'), events ('Racing Away from Net Zero'), transport to events

('Great Training'), food ('The Planet-based Diet'), plastics ('Fossil Fuelling'), consumerism ('Well Stuffed') and agency ('Little Bit Activism'), all sandwiched between a very on-point intro ('How Bad is Running?') and a more upbeat outro ('How Good is Running!').

Each chapter wraps up on a positive note with a 'Yeah, but what we can we do about it?' set of suggestions. Whilst this often provides welcome advice on options and next steps, the list of points or asks are sometimes pretty long and daunting. Perhaps anticipating the lift in mood we need before reading that list, all chapters end on a joke. As a signed-up member of the tofu-eating, Guardian-reading wokerati my favourite was 'What's the difference between Greta Thunberg and Donald Trump? One is an angry attention-seeking child who yells at foreign leaders at international conferences and never does anything that actually helps. The other one is a Swedish climate activist'.

Although each chapter does, depressingly, include a long litany of negatives, there is plenty of balance and he aptly weaves in many other voices of those engaged in the issues to provide a wider perspective. Sometimes it's difficult to judge if he's a bit too close to the problem, or too wedded to his sport, to have a properly balanced view but he's honest about that, often to the point of self-flagellation. He's also upfront about his closeness with the industry (the companies that support him are listed at the outset), although he has now narrowed his brand sponsors by dint of their ethical outlook. Whilst I do have a high regard for inov-8 shoes and the brand itself (who sponsor Hall), I did find them rather over-quoted in the early part of the book. But it's a minor quibble that doesn't detract from what is a unique and impactful book. I, for one, learnt a lot and realised there's a lot the ordinary Joe like me can do to tread a bit more lightly.

Andy Tickle

A Path of Shadows
John Porter
Little Peak Press, 2022, 80pp, £17

'Climbing takes us to a place where we've never been before,' says John Porter at his poetry reading for the Alpine Club's Bristol group. Actually this is the second mountaineering poetry reading that the AC has boldly belayed up the twisting stairs of the Nova Scotia pub recently. As was the case for Dave Wynne-Jones' exhilarating evening of local climbing poets, the room is full. What is going on? It is three decades since Ken Wilson barked at me, 'Poetry isn't where climbers are at.' At that time the late Al Steck reported to me the frank commercial judgement of Michael Kennedy, editor of *Climbing*: 'There is no demand for poetry.' Indeed, in my elevated position as poetry editor of *High* magazine it was clear that my job was to be making gracious rejections. And over all that time, for the last 50 years in fact, John Porter, alpine-style pioneer in the Greater Ranges, was writing the poems now collected in this first (and, I hope, not last) collection of poetic meditations on that path of shadows. 'That place,' John continues quietly, in the exposure of his solo platform, 'is beyond the comfort zone.' We all know what he means. But now he lets slip the clue as to why we are all here: 'I just wanted to be somewhere different inside myself.' John's English father met his Canadian mother in Nova Scotia. And here we are, full circle, and experiencing somewhere different inside ourselves.

There are brief prose introductions to each of the six sections of poems in this book and they illuminate and elaborate an original conception of poetry. John is a scientist, his background, before joining that legendary Leeds University climbing cohort, was in geophysics. For him poetry is a symbolic equation in which juxtapositions of atoms attempt to explore 'the dark matter and dark energies' that science cannot articulate. But make no mistake, these are real poems, playful with form and space and thought:

Above these peaks
Imagination gathers
Takes what it can
Leaves
A blank wall

So we have sections titled, 'Equations', 'Addition', 'Subtraction', 'Divisions', 'Mountains' and 'Abstractions'. Of course, divisions and additions infuse poems in the section 'Mountains', not least in the poem 'Leaving the Mountains' where the three-line stanzas each expand the accumulating exploratory 'equation' of the poem whilst not avoiding the hard physicality of shared climbing that is both uncertain and connecting:

Those hard uncertainties shared so steeply
Gathered divisions of our lives together
No luxury of fate fixed in stars.

Yet still that touch of the mountain made,
The hard connections to a way above
Created a link, what we had to do just to be.

At his reading John referred to these poems as 'meditations' made at moments over decades. They are accomplished poems that do not come from poetry workshops or regular participation in a poetry group. Most significantly, they arise, in notebooks and diaries, from a mountaineer, as John said, 'Giving myself permission to write without readers.' Now is the time for these thoughtful, probing, strangely affecting poems to find readers who will gain pleasures and insights from this particular path of shadows. 'We grasp moments in the mountains / to invent the rest of a lifetime'.

Terry Gifford

• Also received are two books from micro-publisher Little Peak Press, one of poetry and the other an illustrated travelogue. Faye Latham's ***British Mountaineers*** is a paperback collection of over 60 erasure poems, each printed in full colour. The book is as much artwork as it is a collection of poetry. It takes as its starting point F S Smythe's *British Mountaineers*, published in 1942 at a moment of national crisis to tell the history of our alpinism, with stories of courage, triumph and sacrifice, and not a little jingoism. Using the process of erasure, Faye Latham reshapes Smythe's text into a dreamlike tale told from the perspective of an avalanche victim. Words are painted over and 'buried beneath the snow', with Tippex standing in for actual snow. 'Fragments of conversation tumble down like sentences cut off in the wind,' the publisher writes. 'The narrative voice is as changeable and combative as the weather, momentarily strong then filled with doubt, transiently still then bursting with life. Holding onto language, the original text resists its complete erasure. A voice speaks to the reader from beneath.' There are images grabbed from Ron James' Snowdonia guidebook as well as Latham's family pictures and the whole montage is both haunting and fragmentary, as you might expect from an avalanche victim, but also at times quite witty. 'What happens when we bury ourselves within a landscape? What do we become, and who will remember us? At the brink of losing everything, what stories are we left with? What do we leave behind?'

The travelogue is from Little Peak publisher Heather Dawe, artist and co-editor of the award-winning anthology *Waymarking*. ***Mountain Stories*** is an illustrated memoir of journeys through some of Scotland's most beautiful landscapes, including Skye's Cuillin, Knoydart, Assynt and the Far North. Writing during lockdown, author and artist Heather Dawe finds telling these stories a powerful means of reconnection with the mountains when they are physically inaccessible. Dawe's journeys are made by walking, running, cycling or sea-kayak. These stories are a reflection of the importance of wild places and the inspiration, art and culture associated with them.

Return to the Scene of the Climb
A Story of the First American Ascent of Everest
James T Lester
Bench Press, 2023, 273pp, £25

As his daughter freely admits, Jim Lester, 'wasn't any sort of an athlete, or even a hobbyist sportsman. He liked to sit, and especially to lie down.' Nevertheless, for a few months in the spring of 1963, he was part of one of the most successful expeditions to visit the Himalaya. The American Expedition to Mount Everest (AMEE) placed no fewer than six mountaineers on the summit, including Tom Hornbein and Willi Unsoeld, pioneers of a new route on the west ridge.

Sherpas on their American road trip after the 1963 Everest expedition. Left to right: Girmi Dorje, Ila Tsering, Nawang Gombu, Capt Noddy Rana, Ang Dawa, Nima Tenzing.

On their return, President Kennedy famously declared that AMEE members had pushed 'human endurance and experience to their farthest frontiers'. As a psychologist, Jim's role on the expedition was to identify the personality traits of those most likely to succeed in such a challenging environment. Over the course of a month at advance base he conducted a series of lengthy interviews with those who passed through. However, as Hornbein later observed, he offered so much more. 'He was a caring presence who provided counsel to various members of the team in addition to his research pursuits.'

Caught up in expedition life, Jim paid little attention to those local porters and climbing staff that made such an extraordinary expedition possible. He would correct this oversight later: 'Within the stories of expeditions, one can often glimpse a crowd of obscure figures, mostly in the shadows of the climbers and of the mountain, figures who are absolutely essential to the plot but who seldom get more than a few sentences in expedition narratives. These are the Sherpas, and they deserve more.' And 'more' is what Jim provided. On returning from Nepal, the US government invited five Sherpas, along with AMEE's liaison officer to visit on an all-expenses-paid trip. Jim volunteered as guide and driver and spent two months crisscrossing the country. Whether it was a visit to a ranch or a tour of a coalmine, the group received nothing less than red-carpet treatment. However, Jim quickly learnt that what impressed his guests most was something far simpler. 'They were wild about window shopping, just strolling down the avenue – any avenue – and observing the really fantastic variety of objects offered in the windows. I could make our stay in any town a success by giving them an afternoon on their own for this kind of strolling.'

By the end of their trip, Jim's respect and affection for his charges had grown immeasurably. Later, he would describe their time together as a 'joyful and unexpected bonus, a wonderful dessert after the main meal of Everest.' A further course would be added some 30 years later, when armed with just a group photograph, Jim set off for Kathmandu with the intention of seeking out those Sherpas he first met on AMEE. With the help of guide and interpreter Sherap Zangbu, he was able to meet 10 Sherpas including three who visited the US after the expedition. Their conversations were wide-ranging, from their memories of the past through to plans for the future. From each meeting it was clear that the mountains had played only a small part. What really mattered was the life led in between. Above all it was the relationships formed with family and friends that counted, something Jim wholeheartedly agreed with.

Jim's account of AMEE, the road trip through the US, and his eventual return to the Himalaya have been brought together in *Returning to the Scene of the Climb*. Edited expertly by Jim's daughter Alison Jean Lester, it is a moving account of a life that was enriched by contact with the Himalayas and it's people. It's a book that I would highly recommend.

Jeremy Windsor

Seeking The Light
Climbing All 24 Of New Zealand's Highest Mountains
Gavin Lang
Potton & Burton, 2022, 192pp, NZ$89

Sitting here in south-east London, the Southern Alps of New Zealand feel a long way away. At least, that's how I remember feeling 15 years ago when I was actually in that country, anxious that my first (and in fact only) child's imminent birth might come sooner than expected while I was still far from home, powerless if required to dash to the maternal bedside. Compartmentalising that anxiety, I remember gawping into the emptiness of the Cook Strait from Wellington, wishing my short-term assignment would take me across it and closer to the legendary Aoraki/Mount Cook over on South Island. I came home with the New Zealand Alpine Club's 2001 guidebook, a map of the two national parks it covers and an aching appetite to return, which has never let me go.

That sharp appetite has been whetted again by Gavin Lang's mouth-wateringly beautiful photographic book documenting his project to climb New Zealand's 24 3,000ers. It really has ignited a whole renewal of my passion and planning to get back to the other side of the world and onto these sensational mountains.

Comparison is odious (or odorous, as Shakespeare's Dogberry would have it), but I cannot help likening Lang's work in the Southern Alps to

Spreads from *Seeking the Light*, New Zealand's sumptuous answer to Ben Tibbetts' *Alpenglow*.

Ben Tibbetts' in the European Alps. Tibbetts has been working on his own book of northern hemisphere 3,000ers which is yet to be published, but it's his signature 2019 book *Alpenglow* (a photographic and literary journey over the 82 peaks on the UIAA list of European 4,000ers) that I'm thinking of. *Seeking The Light* is its New Zealand cousin.

There's a kilometre's difference between the familiar 4,000m benchmark covered in *Alpenglow* and the 3,000m that delineate Lang's 24 peaks. Yet even if you've never set foot on them yourself, it's not difficult to accept that discrepancy as being inconsequential when you consider the Southern Alps' orography and proximity to the south-west Pacific Ocean with its moisture-laden airflows plastering them with snow and ice. Lang reminds us that, 'Climbing in New Zealand's Southern Alps is often referred to as a training ground for the Himalaya. The vertical relief is the same from the valley floor to the summit, but without the issues related to breathing thin air at 8000 metres.' They certainly made Edmund Hillary into a worthy partner to the experienced Tenzing Norgay in 1953. Hillary's son Peter, himself a prominent pioneer in the Southern Alps, provides a deeply felt foreword to *Seeking The Light*.

Chapter by chapter and with a variety of strong partners Lang ticks off his peaks, often enchaining more than one into a single multi-day outing, most notably with an ultra grand traverse of Aoraki/Mt Cook, Rakiroa/Mt Dampier, Vancouver and Malaspina and, perhaps even more impressively, with the first winter traverse of Torres Peak and Horokoau/Mt Tasman.

It isn't only toponyms that are rendered into *te reo* Māori. The book is studded with motifs and dual language passages honouring indigenous culture. To Ngāi Tahu (the South Island's principal *iwi* or tribe), Aoraki represents the most sacred of ancestors, from whom they are all descended. Standing at the very top of the mountain denigrates its status and climbers are encouraged to stay off the true summit.

Lang, originally from Ireland, found his true mountain range in 2004 and has lived and guided there ever since. In the book, the partner he ties on with most frequently is Ruairi Macfarlane, another mountain guide, raised on New Zealand climbing and snowboarding and now based mostly in the Canadian Rockies. The Southern Alps are notable for their long, difficult and fast-changing approaches, and for the custom of leapfrogging over those approaches by helicopter. Many of the chapters begin with an environmentally dubious but locally normalised chopper ride. Macfarlane, however, is a stickler, 'not keen to truncate the approach with a helicopter flight.' As he and Lang walk in to their sensational winter Torres-Tasman traverse, their packs are 'a sobering reminder that walk in/walk out affairs are for purists, requiring a fair amount of sweat. But it helped us acclimatise.'

From the comfort of my home in Peckham, it's hard to guess how taxing these approaches and exits really are. Certainly, the wasting of glaciers and erosion of moraine walls is a fast-moving story. The modern NZAC guidebook that Lang recommends more than once (*Aoraki Tai Poutini* by Rob Frost, 2022) is very good on all this, warning where customary approaches have become unviable, forecasting changes yet to come and even in one instance cautioning readers to ignore the map entirely. Having followed Lang's prompt and ordered my own copy, I too (as an armchair daydreamer at least), strongly recommend Frost's very clear, thorough and thoughtful guidebook.

Something else that's hard to interpret from the northern hemisphere is New Zealand's alpine grading. These are grades that have evolved since I first got my hands on the predecessor guidebook in Wellington 15 years ago. Now there are two sets of numbers to baffle the grockle on the other side of the world: an unfamiliar seriousness grade in Roman numerals and another technical grade in Arabic ones. *Assez Difficile* never felt so foreign. For added interest, where Lang writes about pure rock climbing on Magellan, there's the equally exotic (to my ear) Australian Ewbank grading to contend with. (Although neither Lang nor Frost says so in their respective books, the new NZ grades are known as the Frost grading system.) The lasting impression is one of having to travel to Southern Alps to prove the puddings in person.

Lang's stunning photography provides a powerful incentive to do exactly that. Frequently his frames cover whole pages and often stretch across two, inviting not only a rich imaginative diving pool for the far-flung foreigner but also immense detail and visual data for those operating locally. Conditions vary, of course, but each photo is dated for seasonal context.

Outsiders like me, unused to the range's complexity, will benefit from opening Google Earth or having a local map to hand. A very interesting appendix details the camera equipment he carries but the truest photographic insight he reveals is during his account of climbing the south face of his favourite mountain Tititea/Mt Aspiring (in a first ascent achieved in winter with Sooji Clarkson which, like the book, is called *Seeking The Light*): he has the humility and self-knowledge to understand, notwithstanding the excellence and beauty of his results, that 'despite shooting hundreds of images on each trip, they never fully capture the range of experiences I've had.'

Any of us who commits to handling a camera in the high mountains understands that conundrum.

The writing that accompanies the photography brims with vividly rendered action, fascinating technical detail and indispensable local knowledge. And there's a current of personal reflection that shows through repeatedly. The impressive Torres-Tasman traverse unfolds, for instance, while a friend in hospital who looks to be rallying sadly loses her life to cancer, and from the beginning of the book the questions of loss, change and recovery. Lang's own battle with burn-out and the promise of the healing power of climbing ripple across the surface: 'You may have come here for information about the mountains, but what permeates these pages is their value as an element of nature and adventure, in freeing us from mental-health shackles and helping us to lead healthy lives.'

The Southern Alps have a rich climbing heritage and I sometimes wished that editorial prerogatives had allowed greater scope for Lang to tell the reader more of the range's history. The name Freda du Faur comes up a couple of times, for instance. She was one of the party of three who made the first Grand Traverse of Aoraki/Mt Cook in 1913, a globally significant climbing achievement in its time. Lang names her 1915 book *The Conquest of Mount Cook* in his bibliography and maybe I'll read that next. I'd love to know more about her.

When Lang returns to Aoraki/Mt Cook for a second chapter so that he can describe his incredibly bold solo of its (south-east) Caroline face, I was reminded of a tragedy that is genuinely the stuff of climbing legend. He rightly quotes John Glasgow claiming 'a victory for hippies' when he and Peter Gough made the first ascent of the Caroline Face in 1970. Seven years before, John Cousins and Michael Goldsmith had left the Ball hut for a reconnaissance or attempt on this very hazardous aspect and had disappeared. In a rhyme or echo of the mystery surrounding Mallory and Irvine vanishing high on Everest in 1924, the bodies of Cousins and Goldsmith were discovered in 1999. Film in their camera was too damaged to develop, but the fact that they were found *on the other side of the mountain* strongly implies that the first ascent may have been theirs.

Buy this book. Treat yourself to the expert wisdom of a climber who knows the Southern Alps like the back of his hand and who captures them with an exceptional eye. If, like me, you're trapped in a dream of making it back across the world and onto those mountains you'll find yourself already there, where 'warmer air wafts up from the valley below, bringing the scent of lush green rainforest.'

Nick Simons

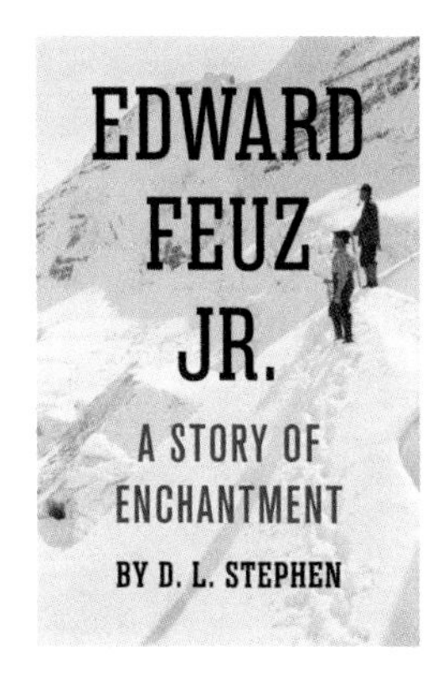

Edward Feuz Jr
A Story of Enchantment
D L Stephen
Rocky Mountain Books, 2021, 320pp, $28.00

The Canadian mountaineering tradition has its layered origins in the role of the Canadian Pacific Railway (CPR) and its employment of Swiss guides, of whom Edward Feuz Jr (1884-1981, originally Eduard) was, without much doubt, one of the most significant of the first generation of Canadian mountaineering. The beauty and joy of Donna Stephen's biography of Feuz is the way she intricately threads together both Feuz's compelling mountaineering life and her own journey of sorts with Feuz and his wife. *Edward Feuz Jr* is both a biography of Feuz and a memoir of Stephen's journey into the enchantment and magic of mountaineering and mountain life and culture via Feuz's Sherpa-like leadership.

Edward Feuz Jr is a companion book and yet takes deeper dives into the Swiss Guide ethos than the path-breaking *The Guiding Spirit* (1986), by Andrew Kauffman and William Putnam. Many of the first-generation guides are aptly mentioned in this admirably personal and focused biography of one the legends in Canadian mountaineering culture. But its evocative beauty is revealed in the way Stephens highlights Feuz's multiple first ascents, significant guiding skills and legendary status along with his personal, private and family character, and his distinctive personality.

Stephens had access to this latter aspect of Edward Feuz because her American family, for decades, had a maturing relationship with Swiss guides and in particular Feuz and his wife, Martha. The history of the Swiss Edelweiss Village in Golden, a heritage site presently threatened by developers, is told in tender detail, while the tensions between the Swiss guides and the CPR are recounted in an equally candid manner. The early years of the Swiss guides and their families was a most difficult one: the British Columbia interior lacked basic amenities and the frigid Canadian winters were in stark contrast to the more temperate and urbanised Alpine life in Switzerland.

Stephen is certainly not shy about sharing in poignant detail many of the challenges faced by Feuz and other Swiss guides in Golden in the early decades of the 20th century. The ample collection of photographs of Feuz and friends, including many with Donna Stephen's friends and family, provide a generous contrast to the text. The photos offer a journey into the emerging generations of the Canadian mountaineering ethos in BC, with the Golden, Rogers Pass, Yoho, O'Hara and Lake Louise mountain paradises worthy of many a repeated trip and trek.

I enjoyed the bounty of this book on several levels. I lived in Alpine Switzerland from 1972-4 and spent much of my time near Interlaken, where the Feuz family is from, and I trekked many of the trails and climbed many of the peaks that Stephen mentions and that Feuz led trips to. Many of the mountaineering legends in the Canadian Rockies including Bruno Engler, Lizzie Rummel, Georgia Engelhard, Conrad Kain, Seppi Renner and Ruthie Oltmann, to name a few, have since whispered mountain lore and wisdom to my soul. I have also spent time at the Swiss Edelweiss Village in Golden and chatted with Jean Feuz Vaughan when she was alive. She kindly invited my wife Karin and me to spend an evening in the standard and much decorated Feuz mountaineering home.

Many BC climbs led by Feuz feature in this keeper and charmer of a book. Legendary trips include Assiniboine on the Great Divide between BC and Alberta. In December 1976 I did a five-day ski trip into Assiniboine under a full moon. Small wooden cabins and crackling fires kept us warm on frigid nights. Feuz did multiple trips into the Lake O'Hara area, which is certainly one of the must-do trips of the Rockies and the crown jewel, in many ways, of high alpine trips, with the Alpine Club of Canada's Elizabeth Parker hut to nest in. Feuz played a leading and significant role in the building of Abbot hut, once a delight of a rock-solid shelter to bunk in at night before climbing Lefroy or Victoria, sadly now torn down because of the vagaries of climate change. Stephen recounts the many trips she, her sister Cindy and her family went on with Feuz and records the multiple comments left by patrons and clients who honoured and celebrated Feuz's guiding skills.

As the book inches towards its inevitable end, Feuz's wife has died and increasingly he is alone and lonely. Donna and Cindy become not only Feuz's daughters but 'Edward's Girls', as the final chapter is titled, making this a touching and telling tale of lives knit together through the enchantment of the mountains.

This final chapter lingers on the climb that Donna, Cindy and Seppi Renner did to the summit of BC's Mount Tupper in 2005 to celebrate Feuz's first ascent of the peak decades before. It was a pleasure to me to relive the animated moments as step by step, rock by rock, photo by photo the group made the lengthy trek to the demanding peak. Seppi, faithful guide and mentor, was in many ways the younger version of Edward Feuz.

There is ample reason for a pleasurable read or browse of *Edward Feuz Jr*, a story about the enchanting world of mountaineering culture and mountains. Feuz is a true guide into such a reality.

Ron Dart

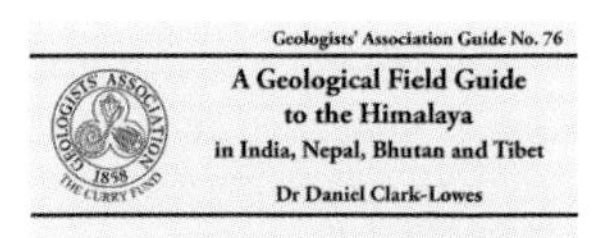

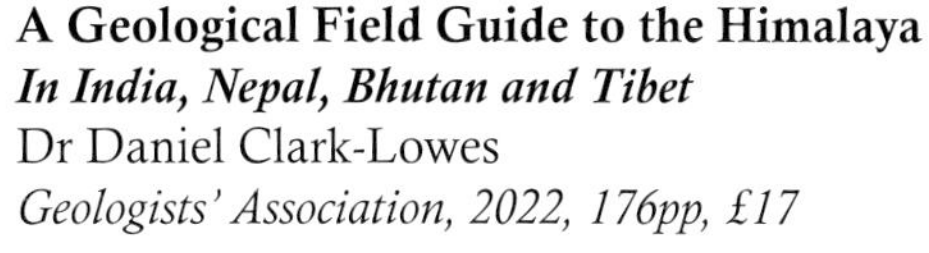

A Geological Field Guide to the Himalaya
In India, Nepal, Bhutan and Tibet
Dr Daniel Clark-Lowes
Geologists' Association, 2022, 176pp, £17

Collisions of continent-bearing plates are among the most spectacular manifestations of plate tectonics, yielding awe-inspiring mountain ranges and playing an important role in modulating climate, controlling seismic hazards and influencing the global carbon cycle. And with the 14 highest mountains in the world, all over 8,000m in elevation, the Himalaya comprise the largest active collisional mountain belt on Earth stretching from the Karakoram mountains of the Kashmir region in the north-west to Myanmar in the east, over a distance of no less than 2,300km.

A Geological Field Guide to the Himalaya in India, Nepal, Bhutan and Tibet is the fascinating story of how the Himalayan mountain belt evolved, piece by piece, from the convergence and collision of the Indian and Eurasian plates beginning approximately 60 to 50 million years ago, to the closing of the ancient Tethys Ocean and formation of one of the most spectacular and geologically significant areas on Earth.

This elegantly written and produced field guidebook covers every segment of the mountain belt from the southernmost foothills of the Himalaya, the Siwalik Hills that were derived from the uplifting mountain chain to the north, through the old, yet low-metamorphic grade Proterozoic sedimentary rocks of the Lesser Himalayan Series, across the spectacular crystalline core of the high-grade Greater Himalayan Series, through the surprisingly un-metamorphosed sedimentary rocks of the Tethyan Himalayan Series that form the backside of the mountain range and cap Mount Everest, to the Indus suture zone and the collisional boundary with the Eurasian plate. The book also includes historical snapshots on some of the early geologists who shaped our understanding of Himalayan geology, succinct and clear explanations of the fundamental concepts of metamorphism and the partial melting of rocks, igneous terminology and volcanism, a review of the vexing question of dating the onset of the India-Eurasia collision, an overview of the last glacial cycle in the Himalaya and younger post-glacial features, a description of the four sacred rivers that have their source near Kailas, Tibet's holy mountain, information on the catastrophic Gorkha earthquake of 2015, and more.

This is one of very few guidebooks that present the entire sweep of Himalayan geology for both the expert and the general reader. It is profusely illustrated with full-colour photographs, figures, geological maps and sketches. It also includes contemporary and classic images that capture some of the region's notable cultural and geological features. And true to its title, one of the guidebook's main appeals resides in the careful geological description of localities, road itineraries, trekking routes and excursions known to the author. Much to the reader's benefit, each of these is placed in a proper geospatial and temporal context using maps, schematic cross-sections, time charts and numerous magnificent photographs of mountains, outcrops and rock samples as taken by Dr Clark-Lowes. Finally, the guidebook also features suggested titles (including tourist and trekking guidebooks) for future reading, select key references in leading scientific journals that are keyed to the text and a comprehensive listing of recommended small and large-scale maps for excursions in the Himalayan region.

In short, this is an essential reference for travellers, hikers, climbers, naturalists, rock hounds, students and academics: indeed, for anyone curious about the Himalayan mountain belt. Importantly, the book showcases many sites that are easily accessible from roads and paths making it an invaluable field guide in a land of superlatives. Every page of the guide sparkles with information and knowledge. Just reading the captions in this profusely illustrated book provides an education in the geological forces that have shaped the highest mountains in the world. It presents the science of geology and the geology of the Himalaya in a very colourful and easy to understand fashion. I have no doubt that any geologist who flips through the book will not be able to resist the urge to purchase it. It is the ideal source book for a basic understanding of the geology of every segment of what is considered the archetypical collisional mountain belt and it may well inspire young people to pursue a career in the study of geology.

Prof Marc St-Onge

Photographic Books

Here is a book to immerse oneself in. To look at **Thomas Crauwels**' images in ***Above*** (Hemeria, 2021, 200pp, £82) is to revel in the mountainous sublime, and the beauty of sumptuous and subtle tones of grey. These photos are exquisitely printed. And one would hope so, given this book comes with such a hefty price tag.

Though he began 15 years ago photographing from terrestrial viewpoints, Crauwels now does much of his work from helicopters. He's a master of the craft of aerial photography, timing his photographic missions at the most majestic moments, often just after the epic snowstorms of winter and spring. These photos, mostly taken in conditions when it would be extremely hard to be in the high mountains, are also a testament to the expertise of the helicopter pilots.

Crauwels is also a skilled image editor. He prints his images at an often monumental scale and since first taking up a camera just as the digital revolution was just getting underway, he has been on a continual hunt for better image quality. He admitted to me a certain geekiness, keeping up with each development of camera technology and moving from Nikon to Sony to Fuji as each generation advanced. When looking into the details you can see Crauwels is exploring and exploiting everything that a modern sensor can capture. He sometimes pushes the images to the brink of collapse.

Nowadays this is, thankfully, rather quicker with processing software like Lightroom than it was 20 years ago in the wet laboratory, where one would pull endless proofs and carry out meticulous dodging and burning by hand. Yet in the search for the dramatic and sublime, it is now very easy to over-edit photos. Contemporary photography is rife with examples. Most of the time Crauwels has the tact and judgment to remain the right side of gaudy, and cover his editing tracks behind him.

A minor gripe I have with this book, and most vertical format photography books, is the abundance of images that are cut in half by the crease of the book. I find this rather undermines the effort Crauwels has made to keep the pages clean: six pages of thumbnails are dedicated to this at the back of the book so as not to obscure the page with the text!

Positioned somewhere between Balthasar Burkhard and Mario Colonel, the notes of the former in Crauwels work make me yearn for the days of celluloid film, the hours and days of the magic dark room, and the subtle fumes of selenium toner. Crauwels work is clearly a product of the digital age;

his crisp image quality speaks of how good the current cameras are. Yet his work strives for the kind of grand gestures that we typically associate with large-format analogue photography. The rich blacks and subtle highlight tones are deceptively difficult to bring out in digital printing compared with in silver-gelatin printing and Crauwels has obviously worked closely with his printers. The result is stunning.

Rather than a book of photography, ***There and Back*** (Ten Speed Press, 2021, 320pp, £38) from **Jimmy Chin** is a chronological chart of Chin's adventurous life with a camera. The years 1999 to 2017 are illustrated by hundreds of photos, and each chapter or adventure is introduced with a short essay. The book travels in time from a pre-digital era where Chin was cutting his teeth as a North Face athlete to more recent projects, images from which many of us will have already seen. In the last decade Oscar-winner Chin has become a notable figure in popular culture through his acclaimed films and his association with some of the legends of climbing, notably Conrad Anker and Alex Honnold. His creative output has landed him firmly on the world stage.

Apart from his story of waiting in Galen Rowell's studio for five days until the legendary photographer would deign to speak to him, this book leaves us wondering how he went from the humble background of son to two librarians in Minnesota, to doing several expeditions each year as a North Face athlete? I can't help but admire and envy the diverse and magnificent journeys Chin has been on. His skills as a professional adventurer – of earning a living from a life lived outdoors – are second to none. Given the diversity of roles he has filled, from alpinist and climber, to skier, photographer and cameraman, Chin seems as much an entrepreneur and businessman as photographer.

Though much of the book is gritty documentary photography that shows us the work going on behind the scenes of big, ambitious mountain projects, a handful or so of these photographs are truly stunning, show-stopping images. There are moments here that epitomise the magic that can occur when a skilled photographer collides with a world-class athlete. Some of the photos of Honnold, for example on the Thank God Ledge on Half Dome (p178) or the Enduro Corner on *Freerider* (p279), are epic images and defining cultural moments for the sport of climbing. You've got to be trusted by the right people, to be in the right place at the right time and have the right skills to get images like these. Chin has also clearly been willing to put in the thousands of hours of work necessary to craft such complex and ambitious stories. Having now created several highly acclaimed documentaries, Chin is at the pinnacle of his career. We wait to see what he does next.

Alex Buisse spent over 10 years collecting images of the Mont Blanc massif for ***Mont Blanc Lines*** (Vertebrate Publishing, 2022, 176pp, £40), setting himself the mission of harvesting images of the steep mountain faces of Mont Blanc and then more recently, iconic mountains and cliffs across the world, under the most magnificent light of sunset and sunrise. The book itself is a novel hybrid of photographic coffee-table book and Alpine climbing topo. The photographs stand on their own as landscape image, but on top of these Buisse has painstakingly drawn on nearly all the existing climbing routes, as detailed in François Damilano's guidebook series to the Mont Blanc massif *Snow, Ice and Mixed* or the ski lines in Volodia Shahshahani's Toponeige.

During the 2020 lockdown, a friend and pilot (who, as a professional, was authorised to take to the air), invited Buisse to fly in the high mountains. Buisse used this unique opportunity to pull together a more comprehensive overview of most of the faces of the Mont Blanc range in ultra-high resolution. The topo aspect of the book shows the routes that already exist, with their difficulty and date of first ascent. (There isn't any more detailed information, as these can be found in the comprehensive guidebooks.) Moreover, assiduous alpinists can use this book to spot the spaces that are still bare, where opportunities exist for first ascents.

On top of all this, the book is packed with fascinating texts by prominent (or less prominent) alpinists, recounting ascents of some of the featured lines, as well as extracts of historical information. This book does a lot of things well. Perhaps it's the book version of a Swiss army knife. That said though, it's far too heavy a tome to put in your mountain backpack.

Ben Tibbetts

Guidebook Notes

There have been relatively few new guides to alpine destinations published in the last 12 months but revised editions of some important volumes have arrived on our shelves. On this front, Ben Silvestre and Philip Jardine examine the updates to *Patagonia Vertical and Rockfax Chamonix* later in this section. Also of likely interest to alpinists is the new release from Mountaineers Books: ***Climbing Colorado's San Juans*** by Matt Payne and Bob Rosebrough.

Closer to home, Italian publisher Versante Sud, who have an impressive range of guides in both Italian and English, have released the first volume of ***Easy Alpinism in Trentino-South-Tyrol***. This selective guide provides descriptions for 133 climbs in the lower grades for the area west of the Adige valley in northern Italy. Most of the lines included are classic routes, primarily selected for their low difficulty and spectacular surroundings.

In 2023, Versante also released an update to 2003's ***Innsbruck Rock***. This guide to sport climbing around the Austrian Alpine mecca is a useful addition to visitors' libraries, providing information on a host of worthwhile venues.

In the UK, publishing activity has been focused on Scotland, with the Scottish Mountaineering Club (SMC) enlisting Iain Thow to produce the new issue of ***Highland Scrambles North***. This title complements 2017's *Highland Scrambles South* (also by Thow) to provide coverage of the best scrambles and low-grade rock routes in most of Scotland. The guide is produced in the new SMC style, with larger proportions, no plastic cover and the addition of photo topos in place of traditional illustrations. Also in this new house style is ***Scottish Winter Climbs West*** by Neil Adams. Covering not just Glen Coe and Ben Nevis, but many other less well-travelled venues as well, the guide includes more than 1,300 routes and has a significant focus on conditions, offering advice on the best venues for particular weather cycles. Profits from

both of these titles go to the Scottish Mountaineering Trust, which provides funding for mountain education, access and the maintenance of mountain infrastructure such as paths and huts.

Scottish Winter Climbs West is not the only new guide covering Scotland's most famous honeypot venues. Mike Pescod has produced the eighth edition of Cicerone's ***Winter Climbs: Ben Nevis and Glen Coe***, an update to the 2010 edition. The title is split into two volumes: the first covering Glen Coe and Ben Udlaidh; the second Ben Nevis, Mamores and the Grey Corries. Both books are pocket-sized guides that can be carried separately or stored in a larger joint sleeve. The two-volume set covers the most popular routes at the included venues with a wide grade spread from introductory snow plods to hard mixed and ice lines. Each venue comes with an overview of the route types, approach details and a photo topo. While the small size of the guide is undoubtedly an asset when carrying it on the hill, it also means that photo topos are smaller than would be ideal and route descriptions shorter. While not a problem for the experienced Scottish winter climber, route finding with this guide would likely prove challenging for the uninitiated.

Lastly for Scotland, 2022 also saw the release, under the Wired banner, of a new version of ***Scottish Rock Climbs***. Compiled by Kevin Howett, the guide covers both trad and sport climbs, at all grades, throughout the entirety of the country.

Other updated titles for the UK include new editions of ***North Wales Climbs*** and ***West Country Climbs*** from Rockfax, ***North Wales Limestone: The Definitive Guide*** from On Sight Publishing and a revised edition of Cicerone's ***Scrambles in Snowdonia*** which covers selected lines in the national park from grade I to III.

Patagonia Vertical
Rolando Garibotti & Dorte Pietron
Sidatra D O O, 2022, pp416, £40

Whilst leafing through this new, second edition of *Patagonia Vertical*, it is hard to be anything other than impressed at how much effort has gone into documenting the climbing in these mountains. This not only makes the book a fantastic resource but also renders it rather difficult to review. Climbing somewhere like the Chaltén massif isn't something a climber usually takes on without some expectation of having a serious adventure. But that sort of adventure isn't usually accompanied by first-class topos and route descriptions of which even the Alps would be envious. Therefore I must emphasise that any criticisms come with an important footnote: that having this guidebook available at all is incredibly good fortune.

I've been lucky enough to travel to El Chaltén twice, both times equipped with the first edition of this guide. Even in the first edition the knowledge contained in the book was incredibly useful, with the layout designed both to inspire and to make finding suitable objectives as simple as possible. The first edition was always straightforward to use but it is clear that great effort has gone into streamlining the new edition, making it a pleasure to read through and easy to navigate.

The photos are wonderfully selected, with the front cover immediately capturing the grandiose essence of climbing in the range. Glancing at the book sat on my table is enough to give me the strong urge to return. But it's not just the front cover. Inspiring photos are peppered throughout, which I always feel adds a lot to a guidebook. In terms of the actual climbing, it's hard to overstate just how useful it is to have high-resolution photographs of most of the faces with the routes marked and often a detailed topo to boot. Given the sheer number of routes in the massif, it would have been easy for this book to become an arduous tome but the balance between information and history is just right, with the descriptions kept brief on all but the most classic routes (or those most in need of either completion or repeat ascents). Nonetheless there is enough history to make reading the guidebook enjoyable in its own right.

One element that would have benefited from more detail is in the approach descriptions, as this seems to be one of the areas where first-time visitors come a little unstuck. The approaches to the Torre valley for instance seem to change year on year, with the north side approach being both notoriously hard to do on sight and having significant objective danger. More reference to the evolving nature of these approaches would have been welcome but it's possible these descriptions have been kept to the minimum to encourage discussion amongst climbers about the best approaches during a given season. That being said this section doesn't seem to have changed much since the first edition.

Finding the correct level of detail is one of the most difficult parts of guidebook writing, particularly when the availability of information inevitably contributes to the growing number of inexperienced climbers who are venturing into the massif. Not everyone has the Alps on their doorstep to help them develop the necessary skillset and these mountains are perhaps mistakenly seen by some as a place to learn the art of alpinism. This issue is compounded by the fact that whilst staying in El Chaltén it is easy to get caught up in the hype of looking at forecasts and 'going big' during the rare weather windows. I don't remember if the first edition addressed this issue much but it is a relief to see that this new edition has a fairly extensive section dealing with risk assessment. This is an absolutely vital read for novices and a worthwhile refresher for experienced alpinists.

All in all, reading *Patagonia Vertical* is an unalloyed pleasure and as well as imparting his immense knowledge of the range, the author's passion for the area is also evident on every page. Whilst hanging out in El Chaltén it is not uncommon to find oneself at a bar or party, only to find the author, Rolando Garibotti, holding court over a crowd of onlookers who are all desperate to glean as much precious information from him as possible. To have that well of information neatly summed up in a mere 400 pages is absolutely priceless.

Ben Silvestre

Chamonix
Charlie Boscoe & Luke Davies
Rockfax, 2022, pp512, £35

The first edition of this book (led by Charlie Boscoe) came out in 2016. Luke Davies is now at the helm and has edited the second edition into an enthusiastic and modern young adulthood. Luke came to live in Chamonix in 2016 and is now on the British guide scheme, so it's not fanciful to imagine both he and the guidebook coming of age together.

Just like a member of the Alpine Club, a good guidebook improves with age (and puts on a little weight). This new edition has grown in size to more than 500 pages and covers the main Mont Blanc massif from Le Tour to the Conscrits hut, as well as the Aiguilles Rouges (extending just into Switzerland) and valley crags from Servoz to Barberine. There are several completely new sections in this edition, including the addition of Charpoua and Nant Blanc.

The route descriptions are the meat of any guide. These follow the familiar Rockfax format with complementary topo photographs. Many of these have been improved (for instance the south face of the Moine) but I am left wondering whether a good drawing would be even better. Am I the only AC member to have wandered aimlessly on this face, hopelessly lost?

Subtle improvements have also been made to many of the route descriptions. For instance, you now know where to go at the top of the Lépiney crack: left if you were wondering.

Yet guidebooks are not just for facts, they are also for inspiration. The action photographs in this guide certainly inspire. Davies is pretty handy behind the camera and most of the superb action photographs in this edition are new. A generation of young, mainly British climbers who came to Chamonix to live and work before Brexit are here in multi-coloured glory.

These improvements are to be commended, but in alpine terrain even the best guidebook descriptions and photographs can soon find themselves out of date. This problem has only been exacerbated in recent years as climate change has ravaged the Alps. In those areas where summer heat waves have begun to melt the permafrost, not only are formations changing, but the risk of accidents from instability and rockfall is also increasing. Nowhere is this more obvious than on the Grand Couloir below the Goûter hut that sees fatalities due to stone fall every year. This guide helpfully tells you how to pronounce the French for stone fall (p340) 'but any loud expletives should work.' The *Cosmiques* also changes frequently due to its altitude and geology, as do huts: no Fourche bivouac hut anymore. No written guide can hope to keep up with these changes and therefore any description needs to be supplemented by online resources, particularly *Camp to Camp*.

For some climbers this book may act as a catalogue of possibilities. Further information can then be sought either online or in the various specialist guidebooks. To their credit, Rockfax lists many of the other specialist guides in a full-page photograph. It seems unlikely you will head off for one of the hard multi-day routes in this guide without supplementary information from online sources. Rockfax has its own digital resource, complete with imported UKC comments in the form of their excellent app. I find the route photographs (especially of multi-pitch rock climbs) display very well in this format.

As a directory to the routes and peaks of this historic range, this updated guide has much to recommend it but I would not be earning my salt as a reviewer if I did not highlight a minor flaw: the *Perrons Traverse* a 'half day'? No: not for most people climbing on sight. My humble apologies to Paul Fairburn, with whom I completed it in five and half hours to prove it could be done, but it's better to allow eight or nine.

Very minor errors aside, if you're an Anglophone on your first visit to Chamonix and keen to sample the range of climbing styles the massif has to offer, this guide is an essential buy. Many AC members who already know Chamonix will also enjoy it and it would be a brilliant gift for any budding young alpinist. I look forward to seeing the guide reach middle age under Luke's expert direction.

Philip Jardine

Obituaries

'La Montant sur la Pitz Val Rhein et Glacier du Rheinwald', Johann Ludwig Bleuler, 1820-40, body-colour, 56.7cm × 43cm. *(British Museum)*

In Memoriam

The Alpine Club Obituary	Year of Election (including to ACG)
Derek Fordham	1972
Denis Bertholet	1968
Mark Bricknell	1957
Lizbet Fairley	1975
Tom Hornbein	Hon 2010
Barry Imeson	2005
Ron James	1974
Robert Langford	1960
Denis Mitchell	2009
Graeme Nicol	1959
Bill Norton	1992
David Pownall	Asp 1975, 1979
Bill Roberts	2019
Fred Smith	1976
Maryke Tilman-Deelen	LAC 1947
Alan Wedgwood	1962

The editor will be pleased to receive obituaries for any of those above not included in the following pages.

Denis Bertholet
1929 - 2022

Denis Bertholet

Denis Bertholet, who died in August 2022 aged 92, was born in Montreux and spent much of his life in Verbier as a guide and ski instructor where he founded the ski school. He was member of the AC from 1968. A pioneer of off-piste skiing when other instructors preferred keeping to the marked routes, during his life he was a potholing, parachuting and diving instructor as well as a high-altitude mountain guide.

Denis had a life-long passion for the mountains and travelled to the Himalaya on many occasions. A photographer and cameraman, he was a graduate of the School of Applied Arts of Vevey. He was the author of several books as well as director of a couple of films. He shot his last film *Kanchenjunga* following the 1983 Swiss expedition to the Himalaya. Because of avalanche and rockfall May and Bruchez climbed the first ice barrier by the 1980 Japanese route. They established camp four in an ice cave and eventually got to the summit in 10 hours by the British route, returning by moonlight. He also directed *Spedizione al Nevado Taulliraju* a documentary about alpinism that takes place in Taulliraju.

Denis loved the Sherpa people and dedicated much of his later life to Nepal where he built a school.

Robin Quine

Elizabeth Diana Fairley
1940 - 2022

Lizbet Fairley

Lizbet was born in Oxford, the second of four children, to Robert and Lettice Strickland-Constable but home until marriage was in the village of Brasted near Westerham in Kent. She was educated at Walthamstow Hall School, Sevenoaks (known affectionately as Wally Hall) and won a scholarship to study cello at the Royal College of Music. She continued her studies at the Staatliche Hochschule für Musik, in Köln, under Gaspar Cassadó. She was a talented cellist and had a passion for teaching cello in schools and several of her students went on to play professionally. Lizbet played with a variety of chamber music groups in south Buckinghamshire, Berkshire and Ealing until well past retirement age when advancing Alzheimer's disease curtailed her activity. Music was to punctuate our climbing and skiing visits to the Alps when we would always attend concerts in the locality.

She came from a mountaineering family. Her father was a member of the AC, which he had joined whilst still a student at Oxford. Mountain holidays were common, and two summer holidays based at Saas Fee with Lesley Letts, Neil Ker and Hugh Pasteur (all AC members) and their families introduced her to the Alps. By age 17 she had climbed 12 summits including the Tête Blanche, Pigne d'Arolla, Alphubel and the Nadelhorn. A cousin recently commented that Lizbet was the first woman she had ever seen who wore boots.

We met at Hywel Lloyd's cottage in Brecon. By then she had already completed four more Alpine seasons including a summer traverse of the Haute Route and an unguided ascent of the Hörnligrat on the Matterhorn. Many climbs had been in all-female ropes with, among others, Dorothea Gravina, Heather Wheeler and Sylvia Yates with whom she did the traverse of the Barre des Écrins.

Our first summer together was based at the campsite in Zermatt where we made many lifelong Alpine friends. Two years later we were back again with big ambitions. After a warm-up climbing the Zinal Rothorn via the Rothorngrat we went up to traverse the Wellenkuppe and Obergabelhorn but on the descent of the Arbengrat we were delayed by bad weather and spent the night in a snowhole. Next morning, none the worse, we descended to the path towards Zermatt. Having breakfasted at Biel we continued in a leisurely fashion towards Zermatt to be met at Zmutt by a flurry of concerned friends alarmed at our non-appearance at the campsite the previous evening. Slightly chastened, the following day we went up to the Bétemps Hut intending to climb Monte Rosa by the ordinary route. Instead, on hearing of our adventures, the guardian sent us up the Cresta Rey: steeply direct to the summit of the Dufourspitze. This, he said, was the dry and sunny way, adding that he would rather climb it twice than trudge along the ordinary route with everyone else. We had the route to ourselves.

We married in the summer of 1972 and spent a glorious four-week Alpine honeymoon climbing, amongst many others, the Lenzspitze-Nadelhorn-Ulrichshorn traverse, the Aiguille du Purtscheller south ridge and the traverse of the Aiguilles Dorées. In those days we thought we could achieve anything. We climbed regularly in Wales and Scotland and our summers would be spent in the Alps on classic routes such as the north ridge of Piz Badile, the Dent Blanche, the Biancograt to Piz Bernina, the *Forbes Arête* of the Aiguille du Chardonnet and the *Éperon Renaudie* on the east face of the Dent du Requin. We always shared the lead.

For six years we lived in south-west Germany near Villingen on the eastern edge of the Black Forest and just three to four hours' drive from the Alps. This proved to be an ideal place for mountaineering parents to bring up a young family and enabled us to explore many corners of the Alps that are relatively unknown to most British mountaineers, such as Montafon, the Alpstein, Filisur, the Swiss Val Ferret, the Oberengadin and the Swiss National Park. Lizbet developed a strong interest in geology with many field trips in the surrounding region, the Schwarzwald, the Wutachschlucht, the Schwäbishe Alb and throughout the Alps, an interest that passed on to our younger daughter. We learnt to ski here.

On returning to the UK we made our home in Gerrards Cross where we lived for 40 years. Holiday weekends, half terms and school holidays spent at her cottage at Gwastadnant, Nant Peris, were a regular occurrence. North Wales was an ideal base to get out into the mountains and she encouraged our children to explore from an early age. She was always more at home in the outdoors and camping than staying in a fancy hotel. It always felt like she could always rustle up a feast out of whatever was available ('nosh' and pasta being the most memorable) after a long day out in the mountains. And every year without fail we made the pilgrimage to Tschagguns in Montafon, Austria, to ski.

In 1975 Lizbet became one of the first women to join the AC by direct application rather than through membership of the Ladies' Alpine Club. She was always interested in the AC. It was important to her and she derived great pleasure from all its activities. She was elected to serve on the Committee and ran the publicity for the 1982 *Treasures of the Alpine Club* exhibition at South Audley Street. She trekked in the Garhwal Himalaya and climbed in Mongolia with other AC members and few London lectures, dinners or Alpine meets passed by without her presence. Her collection of alpine plants is a constant reminder of our many Alpine starts, walks and climbs in the mountains.

Friends and family were special to Lizbet. She always paid great attention to maintaining relationships and friendships, organising celebrations for every significant anniversary. So it was a great joy to her that we were able to celebrate our golden wedding anniversary together with the family at home just two months before her death. She died peacefully in her sleep at dawn on 22 August. Apart from myself, her daughters, Lucy and Alice, her granddaughters, Hannah, Charlotte and Sophie and her brothers, Fred and Bob survive her.

John Fairley

Derek Fordham
1939 - 2022

Derek Fordham

Few Arctic travellers were able to convey so brilliantly the mesmerising effect of that landscape as Derek Fordham, who has died just shy of his 83rd birthday. Over the course of almost 50 years he led dozens of expeditions to Greenland, Svalbard, Iceland and northern Canada, first for the climbing and then later for the epic journeys. In this article entitled 'Arctic Voices' (*AJ* 1997, pp32-8), he reflected on his travels:

I was drawn by the two voices of the Arctic: that of the hauntingly beautiful, cold, silent landscape and that of the Inuit, descendants of Peary's Eskimos, a people whose degree of warmth, friendliness and total adaptation to their environment seemed in inverse proportion to the comfort of their homeland.

On the first expedition I shared with the Inuit we dog-sledged north-wards up the East Greenland coast. … We cooked with them on the very oldest and most potentially explosive-looking Primus stoves. We hunted seals in the pastel light of the Arctic night, and cut them up back in our happy camp on the pack ice surrounded by a vast number of hungry dogs giving vent to their coda of the Arctic. We had an insight into a world little changed since Peary's time.

The expedition was the 1971 Anglo-Danish Trans-Greenland Expedition, a 49-day 800km traverse from the east coast, over the icecap which rises to 3,000m, to the west coast. The journey began from the airstrip at Kulusuk with a 125-mile dog-sledge journey with 10 dog teams northwards over the frozen Denmark Strait to the head of the fjord, Kangerdlugssuatsiaq. The dog drivers returned to Kungmiut while Fordham, John Anderson, Erik Hjelmar and Sven Poulsson began a 55-mile man-hauling sledge trip up the Glacier de France and Paris glacier to the Inland Ice. Derek navigated using a sextant.

Considerable difficulties were encountered on the lower section of the glacier, but Camp 12 was established on the margin of the Inland Ice three weeks after leaving Kangerdlugssuatsiaq. We headed northwest across the Inland Ice on the 435-mile traverse to Nuuqaaq on the west coast, which was reached 30 days later, thus completing the longest man-hauled sledge traverse ever made across the Inland Ice.

Theirs was the fifth crossing after Nansen. It wasn't exploration in the sense of discovering new land already known to the Inuit but as he put it 'the purpose was to explore'. As he later elaborated:

… not to find new land … but to climb a mountain as well as make a very long ice cap crossing and, in so doing, explore our reactions to life in the Arctic and with each other. It was the journey that was important.

Derek's first expedition to Greenland was in 1968 where, as leader of the London University Graduate Mountaineering Club expedition, he led a team of five with the first ascent of Ingolfsfjeld as the main objective (*AJ* 1969, pp282-4). Although the summit eluded them, it was a great success with long-term friendships and a passion for the region forged. The team had travelled by boat driven by local hunters from Tasiilaq to the base camp at the head of Kangerdlugssuatsiaq fjord. Two team members found a way onto the long, difficult summit ridge from the south-east before being weathered off the mountain without making the final ascent. In the interim, Derek and other members of the team managed the first ascent of a peak they

Fordham at home in the Arctic. *(Derek Fordham)*

named Pinderbjerg. (His wife Jeni's maiden name was Pinder.) There were also first ascents of three other peaks, Semberg, Pt 1600 and Pt 1400. Ingolfsfjeld, with its then challenging access, was not climbed until 1975.

Some 23 expeditions to Greenland followed, often with his wife Jeni. He kept detailed records of each of his journeys, regularly pored over maps of Greenland in his house in Greenwich with those who visited him to learn from his vast knowledge of the country. In 2016 he received the Polar Medal 'for outstanding achievement and service to the United Kingdom in the field of polar research as Arctic expedition leader, mountaineer and ambassador.'

The penultimate visit to Greenland was in 2015 to the northern part of Disko Bay, with fellow Arctic Club member and partner, Dr Lorraine Craig. Travelling by small motorboat, they revisited Saqqaq, the place where his Trans-Greenland expedition ended in 1971. He returned to Saqqaq for the last time in 2017. Although not as physically able as in earlier days, he visited Camp Eqi, where he had arranged for one of the huts, Hut 10, to be named after Col Andrew Croft to recognise his significant polar expeditions, and see old Greenlander friends for the last time.

Derek Ernest Fordham was born in Lewisham on 9 August 1939, the son of a carpenter. He was an Alleyn's scholar before studying architecture at the Northern Polytechnic, Holloway. Remarkably, he managed to combine his forays to the Arctic with the professional life of an architect, working on large-scale public projects such as social housing schemes for the Greater London Council and the Thames Barrier.

Over the years, Derek built up an enviable expertise – as well as photo and book libraries – on all things Arctic, and he enjoyed passing that encyclopaedic knowledge on. He wrote the Arctic notes for the *Alpine Journal* from 1969 to 2010, which stopped when Greenlandic home rule was estabished and expeditions were no longer required to register in either Denmark or Greenland. He wrote reviews of polar books for the science journal *Nature* and authored a 48-page book, aimed at younger people, entitled *Eskimos* (Macdonald Educational, 1979). He had two letters published in *The Times*, on lead poisoning and Franklin in 1984 and more recently to correct the claims of a British adventurer to have broken a west-to-east Greenland speed record.

A dedicated committee man, he served on the Alpine Club Committee from 1977 until 1979, was on the Mount Everest Foundation screening committee from 1982 until 1994, then a member of its management committee from 1995 to 2001. He was involved in organising various events through the Alpine Club and the ski-mountaineering symposia that run every five to 10 years organised jointly by the Alpine Club, Eagle Ski Club and Alpine Ski Club. But it was as honorary secretary of the Arctic Club, a post he held for 32 years, where Derek's idiosyncratic style will perhaps be missed most.

Derek's other skill was in organising expeditions. He was a meticulous planner, able to organise complicated logistics, whether liaising drop-offs with Inuit or sourcing classified US maps. This talent was paired with dogged determination. Whatever the situation, he had an ability to keep going day after day. Above all, he just loved the sheer remoteness and beauty of the Arctic. In an article for the Alpine Ski Club, he reflected poignantly on a lifetime spent venturing north.

> *Those who have experienced the icy deserts often fall under a spell similar to that which Wilfred Thesiger ascribed to the sand desert: 'no man can live this life and emerge unchanged'. Perhaps, if you have the chance to ski for endless untracked kilometres under the pastel skies of the Arctic night, you too will lose yourself to that special magic of the Arctic and a part of your heart will lie forever in that hauntingly beautiful land.*

His wife the molecular biologist Dr Jeni Pinder died in 2009. Their son Charles and his partner of the past 13 years, Dr Lorraine Craig, also a past president of Arctic Club, survive him.

Lorraine Craig and Tarquin Cooper

Graham Elson writes: We were young architects when we met in 1964, before becoming lifelong friends, walking, climbing and skiing in the UK, Europe, Russia, North Africa and Greenland. His early climbing experience was with the University of London Mountaineering Club, where he met his future wife, Jeni. His climbing and ski-touring trips took him to Greece and Spain as well as more travelled destinations such as Chamonix and the Verwall and Silvretta in the Austrian Alps. One of the early trips Derek took was to Morocco where he and three university friends drove down to explore the Atlas mountains in an old Ford, which provided many tails of mirth before the climbing even started. Derek's is a sad loss, and his passion and knowledge of the Arctic as well as his lighthearted and dry humour will be greatly missed.

David Drewry writes: I knew Derek for over four decades through our shared Arctic interests. He was a frequent visitor to the Scott Polar Research Institute in Cambridge, where I was on the research staff. It was quite clear from our earliest encounters that Derek was a serious expeditioner and mountaineer. When we first met, he had just completed the impressive crossing of Greenland in 1971. It was an inspiring expedition that deserves to be better known, perhaps because the telling of its story was a little delayed. Derek sent me a copy of the expedition report in September 2011 with the words: 'Here is the expedition report I talked of – 40 years late!'

He went on to make many further and challenging visits to remote parts of Greenland and Arctic Canada, several with his engaging wife, Jeni, often living with Inuit communities. She shared Derek's enthusiasm for the polar world but died tragically of cancer in 2009. They were a formidable team.

During our varied meetings and discussions I was grateful for his interest in the Arctic Club. I was the secretary of the club for a number of years and when I looked to hand over the baton, I was delighted that Derek showed himself willing to take it on – a role he fulfilled for two decades with great diligence. Notwithstanding his impressive achievements, recognised by the award of the Polar Medal, Derek remained a man of considerable modesty, almost diffident about his accomplishments, but ever eager to assist others in gaining their expedition goals.

Tom Hornbein
1930 - 2023

Tom Hornbein

In the early hours of 23 May 1963, Tom Hornbein found himself enduring a bivouac at 8,500m on the south-east ridge of Everest. 'The night was overpoweringly empty,' he wrote in his classic account *Everest: The West Ridge*. 'Stars shed cold un-shimmering light. … Mostly there was nothing. We hung suspended in a timeless void. … Unsignalled, unembellished, the hours passed. Intense cold penetrated, carrying with it the realization that each of us was completely alone. Nothing Willi could do for me or I for him. No team now, just each of us, imprisoned with his own discomfort, his own thoughts, his own will to survive.'

That isolation from his three companions was ironic for a man who set the greatest store by human connection. Beyond his exceptional new route on Everest, his distinguished medical career, his research into high-altitude physiology and his passion for literature, Tom had a genius for friendship: humorous, caring and engaged, talking with him was a delight. I recall a lunch with him and his old friend Nick Clinch, who he had met cleaning out the latrines on a summer camp in Colorado when they were still students. The richness of their conversation, their sense of fun, the absence of grandeur all left a deep impression on me. Yet, as the Canadian explorer and writer Jerry Kobalenko put it: 'Though kind and loving, Tom was far from a pushover.'

'My mom and my sister used to call me "Tom Mule",' he once confessed, although looking back at his life he could see moments when that 'stubborn persistence' paid off. He could also see moments when he might have more profitably backed down. A willingness to reflect with an open mind on his own nature was one of the many appealing things about Tom. 'When my parents sent me to summer camp, I fell in love with the natural environment. But the enduring foundation is not the mountains; it's the people I've shared them with. Over the long haul it's the enduring friendships. With Everest, for me, the best part was these relationships as they unfolded in the years after the expedition.'

Thomas Frederic Hornbein was born the second of three children in St Louis, Missouri, on 6 November 1930. His father was an advertising executive while his mother focussed on raising their family. As a boy, Tom was climbing trees and onto the roof of his home. Aged 13 his parents had sent him to summer camp in Estes Park, Colorado, near Rocky Mountain National Park. Discovering the mountains, he would say, was 'the major pivotal event of my life. Those high hills became my spiritual home, underpinning all that followed.'

It was, therefore, predictable that he would end up returning to study geology at the University of Colorado Boulder. It was also predictable that he would spend a lot of his time rock climbing, sometime cutting classes to do so. He did a number of impressive first ascents at this time, notably *Chasm View Crack* with Bill Eubank and Brad Van Driver, to the right of the Diamond on Longs Peak. This was in 1950, before the Diamond itself had been climbed. The route included a 60ft layback crack too wide to protect with what was then available, a pitch Tom led. It still gets 5.9+ but is avoided by many parties, despite improvements in gear. Another 5.9 from this period was *Zumie's Thumb*, left of the upper east face on Longs Peak.

While at Boulder Tom was an early volunteer with the Rocky Mountain Rescue Group, which fired an interest in first response. During the summer, he worked at the same summer camp he'd gone to as a boy, which is how he met Clinch, who would be instrumental in taking Tom to Asia. The pieces of his life were coming together. Having gone to Boulder as a geology major, he switched to pre-med and having graduated returned to St Louis to study medicine at Washington University. There he began to ask questions about how humans adapt to altitude and his idea of becoming a general practitioner in a small mountain town gave way to curiosity about acclimatisation.

Graduating from medical school in 1956, the following year he went to Alaska on an expedition led by Fred Beckey, flown onto the west fork of the Ruth glacier by the legendary Don Sheldon. The team made a spirited attempt on Mount Huntington, which finally succumbed to Lionel Terray in 1964,

The iconic image of Hornbein and Unsoeld on the west ridge of Everest used on the cover of Hornbein's classic account of the ascent.

and made the second ascent of Mount Barrille. In 1960, Nick Clinch invited on an expedition to Masherbrum, so nearly climbed in 1957 by Joe Walmsley and a team that included Don Whillans. Tom took a fall of over 200ft following an avalanche and on the first summit attempt held Jawed Akhter, who cartwheeled off down the slope having slipped out of his steps. Tom grabbed the rope with one hand and wrapped his other around a fixed line. Akhter had gone more than a hundred feet by this point and Tom's teammate Dick Emerson, as teammate Willi Unsoeld recalled, 'asked with some interest, "Are your arms going to be strong enough, Tom?" The reply was, naturally enough, "Well, they'd better be." And they were.'

Emerson was himself unwell and in the aftermath of this fall, Tom descended to perform his role as expedition doctor, missing out on the successful summit climb. Yet his performance and understanding of oxygen equipment and its shortcomings made him an obvious choice for the 1963 American Everest expedition. By then he had finished a research fellowship in St Louis and was was now obliged to work as an anaesthesiologist for the American navy. Connections in the Kennedy administration sprung him from that.

The Americans, ably and democratically led, had two objectives, the most pressing of which was the first American ascent. That didn't suit everyone. 'We wanted more uncertainty in our diet,' Tom recalled. 'If getting to the summit was the only goal, then you would choose the route most likely to get you there, which the team also achieved. But there was a subset of us who had a dream to pursue the West Ridge.' On the approach and at base camp, there was much group discussion about how the large expedition should apply its resources. 'Willi and I complemented each other handsomely,' Tom said. 'As we made the case for the West Ridge to the other men on the expedition, I took on the role of being very outspoken, even a bit extreme at times. He felt exactly the same way as me, but he was able to come across as the guiding force that helped everyone reach common ground.'

After Jim Whitaker and Nawang Gombu reached the summit on 1 May, the pressure was off and the team on the west ridge was given the full support of the expedition. A strong Sherpa team along with Dick Emerson, Al Auten and Barry Corbet worked to get Unsoeld and Hornbein to a high camp at 27,200ft at the base of the couloir that now bears Tom's name, since it was he spotted the line on an Indian air force aerial photograph. (Tom used to dine out on the story of how, in a climbing shop in Copenhagen, the assistant had looked at his credit card and said: 'Hornbein? As in the couloir.') Climbing without the security of fixed ropes, the pair was slowed by technical challenges, including a 60ft rock pitch on crumbling limestone, and didn't reach the summit until 6.15pm. The plan was to descend in the boot-prints of Barry Bishop and Lute Jerstad, who had also been to the summit that day. Unsoeld and Hornbein caught them up on the way down and when it grew too dark to see, they bivouacked. Unsoeld and Bishop suffered terrible frostbite injuries but Tom escaped, perhaps because he had warmed his feet on Willi's stomach.

Tom Hornbein would live another 60 years, give or take a few days, after his Everest ascent. He was the last of the four who suffered on Everest that night, by some margin. The climb itself is now widely regarded as one of the great ascents in Himalayan history, achieved of course with commitment and imagination, but also integrity and as Tom himself would say, a lot of luck. He was content that Jim Whitaker, thanks to his primacy, got all the attention, which, in Tom's phrase, 'he carried magnificently.' All Tom wanted to do was get home, forget about Everest and start his career in medicine. He didn't want to be know as simply the doctor who climbed Everest.

Back in the United States, Tom was appointed assistant professor in the anaesthesiology department of the University of Washington and he and his first wife Gene Swartz moved with their children to Seattle. Tom described the appointment as a 'professional candy store' mixing intensive care, research and shaping how the next generation were trained. He published scores of papers, went on to run the department and retired as professor emeritus in 2002. His one climbing book, published in 1965, turned out to be a classic and is still in print, with the most recent edition appearing in 2013 for the 50th anniversary. It was typical of Tom to award the royalties to the Seattle-based publisher The Mountaineers.

Everest was not the end to his expedition life. In 1985 he joined old friend Nick Clinch on a joint Sino-American trip that made the first ascent of Ulugh Muztagh and he returned to China four years later with his son Bob and his friend Charlie Houston's son Robin. Ten years later, and four after a hip replacement, he achieved a long-held ambition to climb the *Casual Route* on the Diamond. After his retirement, he returned to Estes Park with his second wife Kathryn Mikesell, a paediatrician, whom he married in 1978. She survives him, along with his five children with Gene, Lia Scavotto and Lynn, Cari, Andrea and Bob Hornbein, and his daughter with Kathy, Melissa Hornbein.

Tom had great admiration for his teammates on Everest but held Barry Corbet in particular regard. Corbet became a paraplegic after Everest in a helicopter accident and after that a champion for those like him who had suffered a spinal injury. Tom often reflected that 'if he hadn't been paralyzed, there's no way he could have touched so many lives. He was a real hero to me.' A lot of people felt the same way about Tom Hornbein.

Ed Douglas

Dr Jeremy Windsor writes: During Tom's time at medical school he became fascinated with the process of high altitude adaptation. Like other researchers at the time, his attention was particularly drawn to how the body sensed low levels of oxygen and communicated this information to the brain. During his final year, Tom was able to conduct his own experiment. Using himself as the only subject, he pedalled a static bicycle and measured his ventilation across a series of different work rates. This was then repeated whilst breathing a hypoxic gas mixture. Over the course of the next few days Tom then prescribed himself a series of blood transfusions. This had the effect of increasing the number of red cells in his circulation by more than 30%. Consistent with Tom's predictions, his levels of ventilation fell significantly when the tests were repeated, especially in hypoxic conditions. For the first time, it had been shown that the concentration of red blood cells could play a key part in controlling breathing at high altitude. A publication in a prestigious medical journal soon followed. So too did several opportunities to further his research career. Over the next two decades he conducted a series of studies on the control of breathing in a hypoxic environment. His appointment as chair of the anaesthetics department at the University of Washington meant that by the late 1970s his opportunities for research had dwindled dramatically. Nevertheless, research remained a lifelong interest and he did much to support the work of others.

Barry Imeson
1937 - 2022

Barry Imeson

Seasoned mountaineers were saddened to learn that the journal *Loose Scree* had finally slipped downhill. Published six times a year for nearly 20 years before its final issue in September 2019, *Loose Scree* was the creation of Barry Imeson, its founding editor, and contained articles, letters, poems and short stories but no photographs. Written by and for the older climber, contributors received a free copy and, according to Barry, an immediate surge of wellbeing. Barry was not interested in fame or personal fortune: he was a true socialist much admired by all he came in contact with.

The final edition of *Loose Scree*, Imeson's labour of love.

Apprenticed first with engineers Reyrolle's at Hebburn on Tyneside, after his national service Barry trained as a teacher at Trent Hall, Middlesex. He returned to the north-east as a teacher and coordinator of outdoor activities, developing his skills and starting youth groups in Bellingham and surrounding schools. He took parties of students on novice climbing courses, camping in the Lake District and abroad to Italy in a vehicle that turned out to be very unreliable. He was a keen cyclist, regularly doing long-distance tours.

His next job, as a youth officer for the Inner London Education Authority (ILEA), gave him the chance to start a training course for youth workers to take groups on climbing expeditions. A keen photographer, Barry left boxes and boxes of slides, images taken at these meetings in Wales and Scotland. During this period, Barry was in the first cohort to gain his degree through the Open University. The demise of the ILEA prompted Barry to work briefly for Derbyshire County Council and then came his return to the north, to Highgreen in Tarset.

Without doubt his favourite area was the Cuillin hills on the Isle of Skye to which he made an annual pilgrimage for something like 40 years, usually in June when the days were long. He liked to go late into the hills 'because it was more sporting' and often finished after dark. A colleague, Bill Burlton, remembers climbing *Collie's Route* on Sgurr Mhic Coinnich with him, starting rather late in the day. 'This is a 1,000ft (300m) ridge finishing right at the summit where we arrived about 11pm. The descent, scrambling along the main Cuillin ridge in the gathering dark, and then down Coire Lagan at 1am, was truly memorable.'

Barry was fascinated by the early climbing pioneers with their tweed jackets, nailed boots and hemp ropes whose expeditions required fortitude and stoicism, unlike modern-day climbers who have state-of-the-art gear, maps, guidebooks and GPS to help them. He had a very impressive library of mountaineering literature. At a guess, over 3,000 books, and without doubt one of the largest private collections of such books in the country. It included first editions, signed copies and sets of climbing club journals and it spanned the whole age of British mountaineering from the mid 1800s right up to date. Some of the books were bought as new but he spent a lot of time at second-hand sales venues, looking for 'treasure'. No matter to what part of the country his travels took him, Barry wouldn't miss the opportunity to browse bookshops and local jumble sales. Not surprisingly he was very knowledgeable about the mountaineering world and entertaining to talk to.

In 2001 Barry began his great effort with *Loose Scree*. A number of the contributors were well known writers in the mountaineering world: David Craig, Harold Drasdo, Terry Gifford, Colin Wells, Dave Gregory, Robin Campbell, Dennis Gray and Hamish Brown. Barry also dug out old articles and poems from books and journals to flavour each issue. The magazine was distributed free to anyone interested and ran for 111 issues, the final one appearing in September 2019. Recipients looked forward to Barry's editorial, which appeared under the title 'Flatus Decrepitus', which was always full of wit and pawky humour and often took a dig at modern mountaineers and the mountaineering establishment.

He was elected to the Alpine Club in 2005 whilst engaged in researching and writing a biography of the noted late Victorian mountaineer John Percy Farrar, editor of the *Alpine Journal* and later president of the Club. This was published by *Loose Scree* in 2010 as *Playing The Man: A Biography of the Mountaineer, Captain John Percy Farrer DSO*. In a generous review, (*AJ* 2010, pp378-9), Stephen Goodwin quoted Geoffrey Winthrop Young: 'Farrar's was probably the strongest single influence modern mountaineering had known, and as editor of the Alpine Journal he had kept it at a level of literary and scholarly excellence that could challenge comparison with any more celebrated quarterly.'

Barry was twice married and had five children of whom he was very proud. 'They have all grown up to be respectable adults,' he said, 'without any input from me, a tribute to their respective mothers.' For the last 25 years, Dorothy Bell was his partner. She writes:

On the Tarset Parish Council, Barry served first as a member, then as Chairman. His style was inclusive and all-encompassing; instigating regular public meetings when anything controversial arose; dealing with difficult situations with equanimity and grace. A complex and complicated character, he made a valuable and varied contribution during his life on this earth.

Roderick A Smith

Ron James MBE
1933 - 2023

Ron James richly deserves the epitaph of 'influencer'. During his long life he was a powerful and safe rock climber, an instructor and mountain guide, leader of an innovative mountain rescue team, director of a pioneering course in outdoor studies and the environment, author of a significant selected guidebook and, on his retirement, a golfer of merit and a warm family man. The esteem in which he is held by so many people can be judged by the enthusiasm for him and his activities that an internet search for 'Ron James, mountaineer' will reveal.

Ron was a science teacher in Birmingham before he moved to north Wales and started climbing in earnest in 1956. In 1959 the opportunity arose to buy Ogwen Cottage to use as a mountaineering school, beating off competition from a major brewery that wanted to turn the property into a pub. He prided himself in being a neat, precise and safe climber, skills gained from early days wearing Tricouni nailed boots, where it was important to

Ron James and his celebrated guidebook.

Ginny and Ron James in 2009 at Buckingham Palace, where Ron was awarded the MBE.

accurately place the toe on the hold. He often wore nailed boots when taking students on climbs. His philosophy was: 'If I can't down climb a route in the wet wearing nailed boots then I shouldn't be taking students on it.' Ian Campbell, an instructor at Ogwen Cottage with Ron in the early 1960s recalled:

> *Ron was the guru and he influenced us all. He was the master of rope technique and placing protection. He would climb with people of all abilities and always made sure they enjoyed the climb and did it properly. As a Guide he was unique in that he would take clients up routes that were near to his own top standard; there was nobody else guiding climbs like Cenotaph Corner and White Slab. Ron was one of the best climbers of his time.*

With companions like Ian Campbell, Mo Anthoine, Davy Jones, Dave Potts and Dave Yates, Ron pioneered more than 80 new climbs, including *Mean Feet* (HVS) and *Inverted Staircase* (VS) in the Moelwyns, *Grey Arete* (HVS) on Glyder Fawr, *Meshach* (HVS), *The Plum* (E1) and *Falcon* (E1) at Tremadog and *Lavaredo* (VS) on Carreg Alltrem. He had snatched *The Plum* from under the nose of Joe Brown. The pair had been standing under Tremadog one evening and nodded towards the crag. 'There's one plum left,' he told Ron, who could see exactly where he meant. Ron was back next day to grab it.

In 1964 Ogwen Cottage was taken over by the city of Birmingham, with James remaining as head of centre for a further five years at the end of which he was appointed principal lecturer and head of outdoor education at I M Marsh College of Physical Education. As Ron's work at I M Marsh matured over two decades, the course morphed into a degree and its reputation flourished. Over the years hundreds, perhaps thousands of teachers came under Ron's influence, his ideas and his enthusiasm for the great outdoors. As a qualified guide, from 1996 to 1999 president of the British Mountain Guides, he had the technical skills to back it up.

Shortly after this move, his book, *Rock Climbing in Wales* (1970, Constable) was published, although its real scope was Snowdonia. This was probably the first and certainly best known, independent selected guide to a specific area. It became a tick list for the 1970s generation, describing 'some 200 climbs I have found during the last eighteen years of climbing to be the most enjoyable on any particular cliff or in any one valley.' By the time the second edition was produced in 1975, James had become a well-known figure and his guidebook a bible for many. He was also the author of *Rock Face* (1974), an instructional book to accompany the BBC TV series.

Back in 1964, Ron had co-founded the Ogwen Valley Mountain Rescue Organisation. (He cut his teeth early in rescue work, helping a teenage Chris Bonington off Tryfan in the early 1950s.) His work was influential and innovative. He enlisted the assistance of the RAF helicopter teams from Valley, visited Austria to observe developments there and imported specialist equipment, such as a Mariner stretcher, the Tragsitz rescue harness and reels of steel cable and a winch for use on the big cliffs.

Throughout his career in north Wales, Ron was also climbing in the Alps, particularly in the Dolomites, his favourite area, where he climbed for 40 years. He was elected to the Alpine Club in 1974, and the Club published his *Selected Climbs in the Dolomites* in 1988. In 2005 he fully updated this work, the Alpine Club publishing *Dolomites East and West* in two volumes, based on his deep experience of these mountains.

Although he retired from I M Marsh 1985, he remained extremely active in climbing, cycling and golf, passions he shared with his wife second wife Ginny. (He had been married previously to Barbara James.) He became a competent golfer at the Maesdu Club near his home in Llandudno. He brought his organisational skills, particularly with computer and spreadsheet, to the club and became captain in 1992. In 2009 his work with mountain rescue was recognised with the award of the MBE. He suffered a debilitating stroke five years before his death greatly restricting his mobility, and making his final years difficult, but the spark remained until his passing.

Roderick A Smith

John Wilkinson writes: Ron not only taught me to climb but also to get out in all conditions. He revelled in doing routes in foul, cold weather, my initiation coming on *Munich, Main Wall* and first sorties on Cloggy, all in winter. Likewise in his favourite stomping ground, the Dolomites, where I did many of the big climbs of the day (many of which still are) behind him as a beginner, even when in snow. The experience was usually lightened by his fund of improper stories, recounted in his Brummie accent. Thanks Ron. I owe you a lot.

Robert Endean Langford
1938 - 2022

Langford leading the North Ridge of Ramchukor Peak in Kulu.

Robert Langford graduating just before his death.

Robert Langford was born in Bromley, Kent, the son of Ernest and Cora. His father died when Robert was 10. He attended Eastbourne College and then Sandhurst, before going up to King's College, Cambridge in 1959 to read mechanical sciences, already an officer in the Royal Engineers.

Early mountaineering interest is evidenced by several trips with Sandhurst Mountaineering Club, the Royal Navy to Folgefonna glacier in Norway for surveying and meteorology, and with the Army Mountaineering Association (AMA) to the Alps, all of which combined to support his election to the Alpine Club in 1960.

In 1961, while at Cambridge, Robert led an undergraduate expedition to the Cumberland Peninsula and Baffin Island in Arctic Canada, authoring an enthusiastic account in *AJ* 1962, available online. At the time of this expedition Baffin Island was little explored and few mountains had been climbed. Spirited attempts at the spectacular peaks of Asgard and Friga reached the col that separates them. Many years later Robert contributed to the booklet published to mark 100 years of the CUMC, *A Century of Cambridge Mountaineering* (2019), an interesting update of subsequent climbing in Baffin Island, including the opening sequence of the Bond film *The Spy who loved Me*, which involved Rick Sylvester skiing off the summit snows of Asgard.

In 1965, and now a captain, Robert was one of a small party of the AMA led by Bob Pettigrew to the Kulu Himalaya. Exploration led to the first ascent of Ramchukor Peak (5200m) and the crossing of the Sara Umga La, (*AJ* 1966, pp236-48). He married Susan in 1966 and had three children, Jonathan, Louise and James. After further service in the Paras and Commandos, Robert left the Army in 1972, becoming a chartered accountant occupying increasingly senior positions with Coopers and Lybrand, Lloyds Bank and the Institute of Chartered Accountants. He was the principal author of *Sustainablility: The Role of the Accountant* in 2003.

He took up skiing, and ski touring in the Alps, Finland and Canada, and sailing, in a small boat he kept in Cornwall. His son, Jonathan, recalls:

Dad's two favourite hobbies were sailing and skiing. He was also a keen walker. My happiest memories of dad besides family skiing and sailing holidays are our times together in St Mawes, Cornwall. He was very interested in geography and in particular the environment and further pursued this, completing a geography degree at Winchester University and graduating in October 2022, shortly before he died.

In 2020 Robert married Cheng, who survives him together with his three children.

Roderick A Smith

Denis Mitchell
1948 - 2023

Denis was born into a coal-mining family in Durham, where later he went to university to read biology, which he taught during his career as a teacher.

We met in the early 1970s through the Shropshire Mountaineering Club. We were then in our 20s and just starting our teaching careers near Wellington in what is now Telford. He had tremendous energy and enthusiasm for the mountains and wild places and was already in possession of the Mountain Leaders Certificate. It didn't take us long to get together and bond as climbers, nature lovers and committed country dwellers. We did much voluntary work together with young people from his school, taking them on the hills and introducing them to camping and climbing, as well as being volunteer instructors at centres in north Wales.

Denis was rather shy and quiet in those days but eventually he popped the question, on the Munro top of Meikle Pap on a freezing winter's day when we'd already climbed a snow gully on nearby Lochnagar. We had a honeymoon in Benidorm but regretted not taking climbing gear and after one interminably boring morning on a beach trying to be ordinary tourists, we gave up sunbathing and caught a bus most days into the rugged Spanish hills, seeking out scorpions and praying mantises, and enjoying the wildflowers and unusual birds.

Denis and I had a wonderful few years together living in Treuddyn in the Welsh borders, climbing in the Alps in our summer holidays and rushing off to climb rock in the Lake District, north Wales and Scotland for all our school holidays. By then we were keen members of the Chester Mountaineering Club. Our first Alpine trip was a backpacking expedition from Montreux to Interlaken, over high passes. This was over the Whit holidays and there was a lot of soggy snow covering the footpath with its security chains and ropes all completely hidden. Denis decided it was great fun to jump hard onto the mass of snow at the top of the pass, so it began to slide and carried us down

Denis Mitchell on the summit of the Zinal Rothorn.

the other side. He would squeal with glee. I was absolutely sure we were about to die. It was great character-building stuff and we did well to survive. Our very next Alpine efforts were climbing 4,000m peaks around Chamonix. Denis was bold and strong and soon developed into a safe and confident mountaineer on rock and snow. Eventually, in 2009, he joined the Alpine Club, and completed climbing all the Alpine 4,000ers, which is a considerable feat.

Sadly, after a few years we ended up drifting apart, mostly due to his perfectly natural urge to further his career by taking a post at a school in Cuddington, in the flat heart of Cheshire, where I absolutely didn't want to live. There he remarried and had a daughter, Laura. However, we remained friends, and continued to meet up at climbing venues at home and abroad. Mutual love and respect continued, through our later relationships, and it was always a pleasure to share a climb, ski, a cuppa or a chat with him as an old friend.

His personality suffered a serious change after a terrible head injury in 1998, when he fell from *Hollybush Crack*, a VS on the Roaches. He lost a chunk of right brain but after emergency treatment, his strength of character really showed as he fought to understand and control his new mental condition and return to some kind of normal life.

He was always so proud of his daughter and grandchildren, and longed to live nearer them, but he had relocated to Kendal, close to the hills that he depended on for mental strength and his dream was never fulfilled. Sadly, in 2021 he was diagnosed with prostate cancer, which spread. After several operations and eventually some weeks in hospital, he passed away in January 2023.

He was truly a man of the mountains.

Marian Parsons

Dave Wynne-Jones writes: I first met Denis in 1984 in Wrexham where we were both teachers and shared a need to get into the hills to counter the inevitably stressful experiences associated with the job.

Snowdonia was just an hour away from Wrexham, ideal for a day out on the Nantlle Ridge or Snowdon Horseshoe but we also stayed at Pen Ceunant Uchaf, the Chester Mountaineering Club hut, rock climbing in the Pass and Ogwen during longer weekends. Denis regarded himself as more of a winter climber and in the 1980s and 1990s Crib y Ddysgl and the Trinity gullies offered far more frequent opportunities for snow and ice work, often soloing for speed during the short winter days. Always up for exploration we once climbed a tenuous line of ice pitches to the right of Cyrn Las that turned out to be quite testing and may well have been, ironically, *Schoolmaster's Gully*. On another gloriously sunny winter day we made a lightweight traverse of Tryfan, Bristly ridge and down Y Gribin ridge in snowier condition than we'd expected.

I was marginally stronger on rock routes, so we made a good team in the Alps, climbing mixed routes in the Chamonix area. Marian, Denis' first wife and herself a climber, encouraged us to join the Alpine Club where we fell in with a motley crew focussed on climbing the 4,000m mountains of the Alps, although none of us was blinkered about that. If there were good routes on lower mountains in the area, we'd be up for those as well. It was a way of exploring the Alps beyond Chamonix together with the likes of Mike Pinney, Jeff Harris and John Mercer. I remember Denis' keenness to take on some of the big traverses like the Alphubel-Täschhorn-Dom and the Bishorn-Weisshorn. He was an utterly reliable alpinist, although on the steep north-west ice face of the Aiguille de Bionnassay, with no natural runners and no time to place and remove ice screws by pitching it, we both opted to un-rope and remove the risk that one of us might slip and drag the other off. Later that season, emerging onto the ridge after similar unprotectable climbing in the Schneider Couloir on the Aiguille Blanche de Peuterey, Denis said, 'I really don't know why we didn't take the rope again off for that, because it was absolutely no use.'

As our skiing developed, Denis and I began to look for new challenges off piste and then in ski mountaineering. In 1991, Ralph Atkinson joined us for our first hut-to-hut ski tour: the classic Haute Route from Chamonix to Zermatt. The following year we were skiing 4,000m peaks including the Strahlhorn, Rimpfischhorn and Allalinhorn from Saas Fee. On the Weissmies, Denis and I pressed on despite negative comments from one of the party, who flatly refused to continue, while we took turns to break trail all the way to a windswept summit that in winter felt Himalayan in scale. There's more on all this in my book *4000m: Climbing the Highest Mountains of the Alps*, but in the later 1990s, with differing Alpine objectives and my increasing interest in expeditions, we climbed less together in the Alps and more often in the UK.

In 1998 Denis suffered a terrible head injury whilst climbing at the Roaches but characteristically fought his way back to fitness, so that in 2001 he finally completed his ascents of the Alpine 4,000ers, becoming one of the small group of British climbers that, in 200 years of climbing history, have actually managed to do so. There were times when the after-effects of that injury put him into hospital again or made him difficult to get on with but sooner or later his characteristic grin let you know that the same old Denis was still there.

His move to Kendal and mine to Bristol meant that we saw much less of each other in recent years, although I always called in on him during a visit to the Lake District, impressed by the way he kept active and sociable through walking and cycling, often in the company of local friends. Even in marginal weather he would insist that we get out on the hill, however briefly. Ill-health limited those activities as he grew older, but only a year before his death I'd found him cheerfully sunbathing with his shirt off in his back garden, oblivious to my knocking at his front door. It was great to see his face brighten with recognition but it was also clear his body was suffering the ravages of illness. Still, it was a shock to hear from him in hospital and a greater shock to hear of his death so soon after an operation on his spine.

Life dealt Denis a hard hand but he played it with a determination to make the best of whatever came his way.

Graeme Nicol
1935 - 2023

Graeme Nicol was one of four British climbers who raised the Union Jack on the summit of Peak Kommunizma (7495m) in Tajikistan in August 1962. Known today as Ismoil Somoni, it was then the highest peak in the former Soviet Union. Nichol started his climbing career while a medical student at the University of Aberdeen and he soon established himself as one of Scotland's leading ice climbers.

Andrew Graeme Nicol was born there in 1935, son of Rosella (née Ewen), a former typist, and her husband Andrew Nicol, who had fought in the First World War trenches and against the Bolsheviks in Murmansk in 1919 before teaching business studies. He had a brother, Donald, a physicist who migrated to Australia. It was a modest upbringing. The brothers shared a room in a two-bedroom ground floor flat until their early twenties. Two spinster aunts and a bachelor uncle lived upstairs.

Encouraged by his fiercely ambitious mother, Nicol was educated at Aberdeen Grammar School, where, with the scouts, he developed a love of hillwalking, rock climbing and the mountains. With a group of friends, he set up the Boor Boys mountaineering club using primitive equipment such as a 'borrowed' washing line for rope. It later became the Corrour Club, which Tom Patey described as 'a motley collection of ex-grammar schoolboys, "brigands of the bothy", who enforced a regular reign of terror on a community where misanthropes and ornithologists were rife.'

His most famous climb from this period was the first winter ascent of *Zero Gully* on Ben Nevis in February 1957 with Tom Patey and Hamish MacInnes, described as 'one of the greatest achievements in Scottish winter climbing.'

The summit of Kommunizma, August 1962. Ovchinikov, Alchutov, Brown, Nicol, Malachov, Gippenreiter, McNaught-Davis. *(Malcom Slesser)*

Graeme Nicol, right, with Norman Tennent. *(Tom Weir)*

It inspired the classic essay, 'The Zero Gully Affair' by Patey in the 1958 *SMC Journal*. During vacations he also made a number of visits to the Alps.

Qualifying as a doctor in 1958, Graeme was of that last generation required to do national service. Following officer training with the Royal Army Medical Core (RAMC) he volunteered for service with airborne forces. Having completed parachute training, he went to Parachute Field Ambulance and then 2 Para. The SAS then asked him to apply, eager to boost their mountaineering resources, and even offered to waive the punishing application process. Graeme insisted that wouldn't be necessary and after passing he became their medical officer. He completed his free-fall course with French special forces at Chalon-sur-Saône and Pau and then served in Oman and Libya.

For the rest of his life Graeme retained a great pride for his service in the airborne forces and strong friendships stemming from his time with them. He continued to hold Territorial Army appointments, reaching the rank of colonel. After military service, Graeme returned to Aberdeen and completed a PhD in hypothermia before holding appointments in the medical school as an academic pathologist.

Following a largely successful visit to the UK by Russian climbers in 1960, both the AC and SMC separately applied to the Soviet authorities to visit the Pamirs. After a lengthy delay, an invitation was received from the Soviet mountaineering federation for a single group of 12 from the two clubs to visit the Pamirs in July and August 1962. Malcom Slesser, the leader of the SMC contingent, described the notion of the joint party as: 'a bit like proposing that North and South Korea should co-operate on making a nuclear bomb.' On arrival in Russia, John Hunt was appointed leader of the whole expedition. Animosities between the various nationalities, ideologies, customs and practices ran deep: Scots against English, both against the Soviet Union, communists against capitalists, competing ideas on fitness,

A medal struck by the Russians to commemorate the 1962 expedition. This remained on Nicol's desk throughout his career.

diet, smoking and drinking, discipline, climbing to a sports plan and so on.

Early in the expedition, Robin Smith, still only 23 but already a force, and the more establishment figure of Wilfrid Noyce, veteran of 1953, were killed descending from the summit of Mount Garmo (6595m). Following a strong debate, Hunt retuned to the UK but the expedition continued. A team of four UK climbers (Nicol, Joe Brown, Slesser and Ian McNaught-Davis) and four Soviets reached the summit of Kommunizma in a sort of strenuous alpine-style push.

Their ascent was wittily described by McNaught-Davis in his article for *AJ* 1963. Graeme suffered from a gut infection but, but as McNaught-Davis explained, he wasn't going to back down. 'Graeme, who looked grey with fatigue, stated emphatically that as long as he could put one foot in front of the other, he was going upwards.' On the way Graeme treated one of the Russians who'd suffered a suspected heart attack, which at least allowed them to catch up with the Soviet contingent, who had gone to the top without them. Graeme had a Saltire tucked in his rucksack that he flew from the summit. If 'the climb was rarely pleasurable,' McNaught-Davis concluded, 'it was nevertheless unforgettable.'

Slesser's book *Red Peak* (Hodder & Stoughton, 1964), chronicled the expedition, warts and all. His account should be weighed against Hunt's more measured tones in, for example, the *Alpine Journal* for 1963; in the Cold War context of the early 1960s any activities that brought men together to tussle with the forces of nature must have been useful bridge building. Kommunizma was the apogee of Nichol's mountain career, although he continued to climb important new routes in Scotland (see below).

At a party in the summer of 1965 he met Christine Walker, a student midwife, and they married the following year, with their first child arriving in 1967. Ten years later, with oil fever gripping Aberdeen and restless in his job, Graeme left academia to become an occupational doctor with BP and was seconded to Abu Dhabi as medical officer for the Abu Dhabi Petroleum Company. In 1983 he joined BP's head office in London, eventually becoming the company's senior medical officer, a role that took him all over the world.

After retiring from the oil industry Nicol became a lecturer in occupational medicine at the University of Al Ain in Abu Dhabi. The post was intended to be for a year but he stayed for seven, during much of which he and Christine lived in the Hilton Hotel. Finally returning to Aberdeen around 2003, he once again sought pleasure in the Scottish mountains as a member of a hillwalking club known as the Galloping Geriatrics. He also reconnected with a couple of the Russians from the Pamir expedition, remembering them at least as fondly as some of his British colleagues. He became an enthusiastic sailor.

Graeme died aged 88 of complications from Alzheimer's disease and bladder cancer. His wife Christine survives him with their three children: Andrew, a barrister, Stuart, a venture capitalist, and Patricia, a *Sunday Times* journalist.

Roderick A Smith

Simon Richardson writes: Graeme Nicol met Tom Patey on a Lairig Club meet during his first term at Aberdeen University in November 1952. Although Nicol was only 17 years old, Patey was quick to recognise Nicol's youthful strength and ambition, and two weeks later they made the first ascent of *Scorpion* (V,5) on Carn Etchachan in the Loch Avon basin with Mike Taylor and Ken Grassick. This challenging mixed climb was at the vanguard of a new era of Cairngorms winter climbing, and the route, with its notorious sting in the tail, is still highly respected today.

In February 1957, Nicol visited Ben Nevis with Patey. Together with Len Lovat they climbed *Cresta* (III) the first route on the Little Brenva Face and nowadays an established classic. Patey and Nicol upped the pace two days later when they joined forces with Hamish MacInnes to make the first ascent of *Zero Gully* (V,4). *Zero* was the first V on the Ben and had been a long sought after objective for over 20 years. Modern ice tools have tamed the route but 65 years ago it was a step-cutting tour de force, heralding a new era of classic ice climbs on the Ben.

That December, Nicol concluded a very successful year by making the first ascent of *Sticil Face* (V,6) on the Shelter Stone with Ken Grassick. It was the first winter route to tackle this awe-inspiring cliff and arguably Nicol's finest mountaineering achievement. Before the building of the Cairn Gorm ski road in the 1960s, climbing on the cliffs in the Loch Avon basin was very serious and entailed a four-hour approach from Derry Lodge to the south.

Other new routes followed such as *The Great Rift* (V,4) on Braeriach with Jerry Light in 1964, but Nicol's technical highlight was the first winter ascent of *Pinnacle Face* (VI,7) on Lochnagar with Light and Grassick in 1966. Climbed wearing nailed boots it was the most difficult mixed route in Scotland at the time but it was to prove to be the 'swansong of the Tricouni Tricksters' with the curved axe revolution just three years away. *Scorpion*, *Zero Gully*, *Sticil Face* and *Pinnacle Face* all feature in the book *Cold Climbs* and Graeme Nicol's Scottish winter legacy will continue to inspire climbers for generations to come.

David Melvin Pownall
1946 - 2023

David Pownall, Kutwal valley Karakoram, 1985 *(Lyn Noble)*

Dave died on 8 January 2023 after many years struggling with increasingly complex and debilitating health conditions. His climbing career and love of wild places started in the scouts and in 1966 he became an enthusiastic member of the Mynydd Climbing Club. One of his climbing partners was a young Pete Boardman who wrote in his famous book *The Shining Mountain*: 'Life has many cruel subtleties that require far more courage to deal with than the obvious dangers of climbing.' This could have been written for Dave, one of the bravest and most determined people you could ever meet; courageous and optimistic to the end, refusing to let his deteriorating health get in the way of the activities he loved.

Dave was born in Chingford, Greater London. The family moved north to Hazel Grove where he attended Hazel Grove Secondary School and joined the scouts. Dave and Pete climbed together at home and abroad until 1977, often with the Mynydd Climbing Club. After leaving school he served an apprenticeship as a stereotyper in Manchester, the start of a long career in printing.

Regular climbing in Snowdonia and the Peak District followed, with early repeats of the test pieces of the day. Horizons widened with a truck-based expedition in 1967 to Cilo Dağı in Turkey and regular trips to the Alps. Dave wasn't just a rock climber; he was a mountaineer and loved an adventure: Scottish winter routes, primarily on the Ben, or long challenging days in the hills.

Dave joined the Alpine Club as an aspirant in 1975 and as a full member in 1979. Night shifts printing the Express and Mirror newspapers in Manchester together with my own weekend work pattern meant that most weekend meets were out of the question. However, midweek days off meant we often had the crags to ourselves.

His pride and joy was a VW camper van that became our mobile base camp for routes on Shelter Stone and Gogarth and also for Scottish skiing (or trying to). By 1980 he had built up an impressive record of climbs including *Red Wall* and *The Sind* on Gogarth and the Brenva spur and north-east face of Les Courtes; all done in a quiet unassuming manner that belied great competence and, gave great confidence to his partners. In 1985 the Buxton branch of the AC, Herbert Hartley, Ted Hanson, Dave and myself, joined an Alpine Club meet in the Karakoram. The joining instructions said 'meet on the left bank of the Chogo Lungma glacier'. We did, and had an exciting traverse of the Haramosh La and out via the Kutwal valley.

The following year was a classic in the Oberland and Valais with traverses of the Fründenhorn and Blümlisalp followed by the north faces of the Doldenhorn and Obergabelhorn and a traverse of the Finsteraarhorn. We always remembered struggling to pitch the tent in torrential rain and being rescued by two Italian families with a giant tarpaulin stretched between their vans and a seemingly endless supply of bread, cheese and wine. Their sons, at the scout jamboree in Kandersteg, would have approved.

As his condition deteriorated, damage to Dave's vocal cords and windpipe caused difficulty breathing and speaking. He described it as trying to breathe through a straw. A climbing friend once told us: 'I can't believe how you two climb together. Dave can't shout and you (i.e. me with hearing aids) can't hear!' Even a tracheotomy didn't stop him; a few days after the operation he insisted on a trial run to Cwm Idwal linking rock climbs from the *Tennis Shoe* to *Grey Wall* and finishing on the Glyders. My son remembers him stopping occasionally to clean out his tube.

Dave was an avid collector of mountaineering books, particularly those shortlisted for the Boardman-Tasker Award. Shelves creaked under the weight of Alpine Club and Rucksack Club journals together with meticulous records of all his adventures ranging from Crafnant to Mont Blanc and the Karakoram. Dave never lost his crystal-clear memory and could always be relied on as a first port of call for dates and details of things I had forgotten. Everything he did was tackled with the same understated energy and enthusiasm, well illustrated during his captaincy of Cavendish Golf Club. He became so involved in course management that some members thought he was the professional green-keeper.

Whatever he did there was always a twinkle in his eye, a little surprise or a self-deprecating comment that could defuse the most gripping situation. I fondly remember a trout meal at the Hotel Engilberge in Ailefroide. At the end Dave scraped all the fish heads and tails onto one plate (we thought he was just being tidy) then poked out the eyes and ate them: consternation, then laughter around the room.

Above all else, Dave was a family man and a dear friend to all who met him. Our children had their first Alpine adventures on joint family holidays. Alpine novices from White Hall Centre were encouraged by his gentle support. In exchange, he received love and unstinting support from his wife Joan, his sisters, brother, daughters and grandchildren. Dave was so proud of them all.

Dave remained a mountaineer until the very end, always wanting to know where the Wednesday walkers had been and, although barely able to walk, always asking: 'Are we off up Kinder then?'

Lyn Noble

W G Roberts
1931 - 2022

Bill Roberts on the Strahlhorn in 1981. *(Gilbert Roberts)*

For Bill Roberts, mountains and mountaineers were an integral part of life. Arriving at Exeter College, Oxford to read English in 1952, Bill had already established a love of hillwalking and climbing during ventures from home in London to the Lake District. It was then as an active member of the Oxford University Mountaineering Club that his climbing took him to overseas ranges. In 1955 he was part of the OUMC expedition to Oksfjord with Ted Norrish (*AJ* 2022, pp361-3), where they ascended many previously unclimbed and indeed unnamed peaks in the far north of Norway. Then in 1958 on an OUMC expedition to Chitral, Pakistan, led by Ted Norrish, he was in a party attempting the unclimbed peak of Saraghrar (7349m) when Peter Nelson fell to his death. The demoralised expedition determined to take no further risks and retreated, leaving Saraghrar to be climbed by Fosco Moraini, who acknowledged 'much helpful information' from the British in his classic book *Where Four Worlds Meet*. He was elected to the Club late in life in 2019. On his application papers, to the question 'How long have you been climbing?' Bill was able to answer: 'Over 60 years.'

In 1960 Bill spent two weeks in a coma before having a major heart operation. It was characteristic of him that a few months later he ascended Mont Blanc with university friend Gilbert Murray to check that the operation had been a success. He had another unnerving experience in 1961 with a fall whilst climbing Mount Assiniboine, again with Ted Norrish. In recent years Bill recounted the incident:

> *I made a careless step and was off, out of control. I started sliding and took some time to get my ice axe into the snow. It started to slow me down, but then I was off again, faster than ever. I bounced on the snow, turned over and shot off down, headfirst. I remember feeling the speed, worrying about hitting the walls of the couloir, thinking of Peter Nelson, and about how he was killed; thinking, incredibly slowly, about what I had to do. There was no sensation of danger…*

He also wrote about his interest in 'what happens as you die. The lack of fear, the slow and careful ratiocination when faced with a problem of how to stay alive.' On a lighter note, he recalled climbing back up 100m to re-join the party with an American companion commenting, 'Gee Bill, that was some fall.' Despite Bill considering giving up climbing they went on to climb Mount Robson.

Tragedy struck in 1963 when climbing partner Gilbert Murray was killed in a rockfall as they slept at the Pioneer hut high in the New Zealand Alps. Bill had an overnight walk down the Fox glacier in search of help for a companion with serious injuries and had to return to bury his best friend in a crevasse: 'That was the tradition then, that you left the dead climber where he had fallen.'

Returning to England, doubtless shaken by the experience of losing climbing friends, Bill settled into teaching at St Bees School. Together with Eskdale Outward Bound, this provided opportunities for him to introduce young people to climbing in the Lake District at venues such as Pillar Rock.

He married Anne at Frizington in 1964 and they had two children, Gilbert and Elizabeth. He wasted little time introducing them to alpine skills: practising cramponing whilst aerating the back lawn, prussiking from a branch of the apple tree and performing ice-axe arrests down snow slopes on High Pike. Now deputy headmaster at Nelson Thomlinson School, Wigton, he gave his family some of the most formative experiences of their lives, leading 12-year-old Gilbert up the Pigne d'Arolla in 1977 followed by several other ascents of F and PD classics such as the Weissmeis and Breithorn. These and a family ascent of the Allalinhorn, I might add, were before the construction of lifts made them into one-day altitude training peaks. A memorable morning on the Pigne de la Lé saw the family caught in a thunderstorm, ice axes 'pinging' from the all too close lightning.

Bill retained a deep respect for mountaineers, characteristically spotting Noel Odell in the streets of Saas Fee en route to the ABMSAC's 75th anniversary at the Britannia hut in 1984 and asking: 'Sir, may I carry your case?' He also retained contact with Outward Bound and OUMC friends, climbing the Petite Dent de Veisivi with Eric Plumpton and the Portjengrat

Following early retirement, Bill devoted himself to academic research, taking an Open University master's degree and then a doctorate from Newcastle University. He became an author, writing several books including *A Dawn of Imaginative Feeling* (1996) and *Thomas Gray's Journal of his Visit to the Lake District in October 1769* (2001). In these, he contributed to our knowledge of how mountains that had been once been considered 'rude and awful' became admired and appreciated. Yet, as he wrote: 'There is an underlying anxiety that we have lost the awe and magic that Gray found, and a belief (that is part hope) that it is still there to be retrieved, if you know where and when to look.' Bill was also a prolific writer of poetry, dedicating many to close friends and family, whilst also taking inspiration from the natural world. Meanwhile he indulged his love of the Northern Fells, a passion shared with distinguished mountaineers, logging over 300 ascents of High Pike.

A diagnosis of heart failure provided a welcome impetus for a solo train journey back to Saas Fee at the age of 86 to walk from the Felskinn to the

Britannia hut. Through 'grit or just cussedness' he battled through wet snow, railing against W H Auden's idea from 'Hymn to St Cecilia': 'That what has been may never be again' and seeking to re-capture the past. As he wrote in a 2018 poem about the outing:

Heart pounds, lungs work overtime, now knowing
This is the spirit's stamina, keep on going!

Gilbert Roberts

F A Smith
1926 - 2022

Fred Smith

Fred Smith, left, climbing at Peñon Ifach in Spain in his 80s.

Few mountaineers, when asked about their achievements, could ignore their considerable successes when climbing and instead say, 'I founded a climbing club.' Yet that, in the years to come, is what the many grateful members of the Merseyside Mountaineering Club will associate with Fred Smith, long after his climbing career has been forgotten.

Fred was born in Bebington, Wirral, to Arthur Smith, a technician at Lever Brothers and Ada (née Peers), a nursing sister. He left Bebington Secondary School at 14 to take up an apprenticeship at the shipbuilders Cammell Laird, the first of several jobs that provided a background in all things practical. Fred had joined the Wayfarers' Club in 1948 and became an active and popular member. He was a strong rock climber and made several new routes in the Llanberis Pass partnered by Peter Harding, Dennis Davis, Johnny Lawton and others. Through the 1950s and 1960s he was a regular visitor to the Alps, and climbed many traditional mixed routes, including the Zmutt ridge of the Matterhorn, the Teufelsgrat on the Tāschhorn and the Kanzelgrat of the Rothorn. He was particularly proud of an ascent of the *Brioschi* route on Monte Rosa's Nordend, in the company of Ray Colledge and Dennis Davis, completed in poor weather.

He was originally a member of Alf Gregory's 1955 expedition to the Menlung glacier area of the Himalaya and had done much of the planning, before a knee injury prevented his participation.

Back in Liverpool, the local education committee, in conjunction with the Mountaineering Association, ran winter evening classes for would-be climbers. Fred became the tutor, teaching novices basic rope work and navigation and leading them on occasional trips to north Wales or the Lakes. Several of these beginners became so enthused that they sought to join a club. But a problem arose because some of Fred's acolytes were young women and the Wayfarers', in common with many clubs in those days, was strictly men only. So, with the cooperation of his new friends, in 1958 the Merseyside Mountaineering Club (MMC) was born with Fred as the first president. A hut, on the rather unlikely wilds of the Denbigh Moors, was acquired, later to be exchanged for the MMC's permanent home Cae'r Fran, situated just above Llanberis. Since then the club has flourished and now boasts over 150 members.

Meanwhile Fred had met, while working as a draughtsman at Liverpool Telephone Exchange, the love of his life, Elizabeth Walker, known as Bett. It was the happiest of marriages, producing a son, Ian, and daughter, Christine, and lasted from 1956 until Bett's death in 2020. With Bett's encouragement, Fred decided to abandon his career in industry and use his undoubted powers of persuasion to become a salesman, initially for the import-export agents McConnells as their man in Malawi, where the family joined him for several years. It is necessary, for an honest assessment of Fred, to touch upon his enthusiasms, sometimes for products on sale, which did tend too often to tip over into exaggeration. Those who knew him best came to accept this trait, realising that no malice was ever intended. We learnt, with good humour, to put the wilder claims through the 'Fred filter'.

On returning to the UK, Fred joined the staff of the BMC and was the initiator of their quest, eventually successful, to supply accident insurance for climbers: a huge benefit to the climbing community ever since. He was also administrator, for a time, of the Mountain Leadership Training Board, responsible for the certification of schoolteachers and the like taking novices into the hills.

In 1975 Fred joined the equipment supplier, Karrimor, as marketing manager. This involved close contact with major retailers and suppliers in the UK and Europe. His experience gave Fred the confidence to leave and set up, with Frank Bennett, a new agency for importing and distributing climbing gear, Sanctuary Mountain Sports. The company enjoyed mixed fortunes until the partnership split and then evolved into a new enterprise called High Places, which Fred ran alone until joined by his son Ian as partner. The modest success of this venture was suddenly enhanced when, after some years of evaluating samples, the MOD suddenly placed an order for no fewer than 245,000 pairs of sand-coloured socks. The government's military adventures in the Middle East remain highly controversial but produced a silver lining for Fred and Ian.

During all this time, Fred never stopped climbing. He was elected to the Alpine Club in 1976 and the following year visited Ladakh as deputy leader of the 1977 Merseyside Himalayan expedition. He led many MMC parties to the newly fashionable Costa Blanca for climbing in the sun, was a habitué of indoor walls and celebrated his 65th and 70th birthdays by climbing the Anglesey classic *Dream of White Horses*. Later, he discovered the joys of climbing via ferrate in Bavaria and in the Dolomites, an activity that had the great benefit of being accessible to his wife Bett and daughter Christine. Across the years Fred continued to go to the mountains whenever he could. He was rock climbing in southern Spain into his eighties and climbed in Austria and the Dolomites when he was 87. At the age of 93 he still enjoyed gentle walking with Christine in Alpine areas he had not previously visited. His short story, 'Well, Now There's Posh for You!' is well worth digging out from *Loose Scree* (see obituary for *Barry Imeson* in this issue).

Eventually, cardiovascular problems curtailed his activities and in August 2022, aged 96, a series of strokes brought him down where gravity had previously failed. After a long life in the mountains, Fred will be remembered warmly by his many friends.

Ben Stroude and Paul Davis

Maryke Tilman-Deelen
1925 - 2022

Maryke Tilman-Deelan

Maryke, my mother, was born in the Netherlands on 6 March 1925 to Frederik Adriaan Josef Deelen and Catharina Leonarda Josepha Deelen (née Jurgens). Both parents were Alpine climbers but her mother, Rini Deelen-Jurgens was one of the first, rather expert female alpinists in the Netherlands. Because my grandparents went to the Alps every year both in summer and winter, my mother was taken along from an early age and so learned about climbing.

The family frequented Zermatt and the Dolomites. As part of her Alpine education Maryke had to walk up to the huts to reserve a bed for her mother's tours. Slowly but surely she was allowed to accompany her mother with her guide and became a good climber herself. She was elected a member of the Ladies' Alpine Club in 1949, whilst in her early twenties.

My mother was a volunteer in the Second World War, driving lorries with food to the north of Holland in the last year of the war. She studied law in Amsterdam but did not finish her studies because of her marriage to Eugène Raymond Tilman in 1949. She remained an ardent climber for some time but with the arrival of four children, time was precious and slowly but surely her climbing diminished.

Her love for the mountains never abated, however, and the whole family went to Switzerland both in summer and winter. Up to a late age my mother went for hiking tours in the east of Switzerland. She instilled a love for the mountains in all of her children and grandchildren and they still all go to Switzerland as often as possible. With her passion for nature, she turned to shooting in her fifties and apart from the Netherlands went shooting quite frequently in the UK as well. This sport she practiced till she was almost 90.

She died on 9 December 2022 at the age of 97 after a long and fulfilling life. Until the end she was mentally alert, played bridge, looking after her garden and drove her car till a few weeks before her death. She read much, inter alia on mountains, and she was very happy with the books from the library from the Alpine Club and the *Alpine Journal*. During her funeral some texts, about the mountains she loved so much, were read and one of her last wishes was that her ashes would be dispersed in the Alps.

Frans Tilman

Francis Alan Wedgwood
1937 - 2002

Alan Wedgwood on the Blinenhorn. *(Janet Wedgewood)*

Dr Alan Wedgwood, a scion of master potter Josiah Wedgwood (1730-85), excelled in everything he applied himself to, as a Harwell physicist, engineer, craftsman, director of Wedgwood Porcelain and all-round mountaineer.

Born on 16 May 1937 at Eccleshall, Staffordshire his early childhood was spent at the family's rambling house at Barlaston Lea, built by his maternal great-grandfather James Rendel (1799-1856), the distinguished hydraulic engineer who constructed numerous canals and the Holyhead and Portland harbours. During the war, the house became a haven for arms engineers working at Swinnerton, naval officers from Canada and New Zealand and peripatetic family members who were all seamlessly catered for by Alan's mother Sally. An inspirational governess Miss Greatorex had encouraged Alan's bent for mathematics before he went to a remote preparatory school on Dartmoor and then to Marlborough and Worcester College, Oxford where he got a first in physics and later his doctorate.

When his father Tom died in 1950, Alan became official head of the Wedgwood family. On leaving Marlborough in 1955 his cousin Josiah Wedgwood V, managing director of Wedgwood, urged him to join the family firm at Barlaston, which he did as a temporary apprentice, turning his hand to potting and decorating. In 1956 he joined the Royal Navy for national service and was commissioned as a submariner: rare for a national serviceman. By then he had decided that science rather than manufacturing was to be his career though in 1965 he joined the board of Wedgwood as a non-executive director, retaining the post after Sir Tony O'Reilly's ill-fated Waterford-Wedgwood merger in 1987 and remaining on the board until early 2009. Alan also played a vital role in saving the Wedgwood Museum at Barlaston from bankruptcy to preserve his family's 200-year artistic heritage.

Alan Wedgwood. *(Janet Wedgewood)*

After graduating from Oxford in 1962, Alan took up an appointment at the Massachusetts Institute of Technology for post-doctoral research. On returning to England in 1965 he joined the Atomic Energy Research Institute, Harwell as a research scientist and in 1966 married an Oxford undergraduate contemporary Janet Merer. They brought up their three children at Blackalls Farmhouse, Cholsey. The rest of Alan's professional working life was spent at Harwell. He became head of the Non-Destructive Testing Centre at AEA Technology from 1988 until his retirement in 1996 when he and Janet moved to Cumbria.

This synopsis does little justice to the wider dimensions of Alan's multi-faceted life in which mountaineering played a crucial part. The family had always enjoyed hillwalking, climbing and the mountains. His father Tom, a former Trinity College 'night climber', had taken him to the Lake District as a child and when Alan was six they climbed Helvellyn and Scafell Pike the following year. There were also family holidays in Switzerland and Scotland though without serious mountaineering as Tom was already suffering from the brain tumour that eventually killed him.

Alan was sent to Marlborough because a distant cousin had financed the school's playing fields. Serendipitously, the school had a proud mountaineering tradition with three members of the 1953 Everest expedition – Hunt, Ward and Wylie – being old boys. In Alan's time it also had an active mountaineering club that included four boys who were to take part in the successful 1957 Pumasillo expedition: Simon Clark, its joint-leader, Kim Meldrum, Mike Gravina and Ronnie Wathen.

Alan was a couple of years younger but found the club cliquey and never became a member. He felt the rebuff keenly and during his national service,

Wedgwood on Heughscarth with a view of Ullswater and the Dodds. *(Janet Wedgewood)*

when his ship docked briefly in Sicily, he persuaded five seaman to join him to climb Etna (3357m): eruptions and a blizzard forced them to turn back at 3,000m. Going up to Oxford in 1958, he was determined to get into 'proper climbing' and joined the Oxford University Mountaineering Club (OUMC), then particularly active with the likes of Pete Crew and Colin Taylor. On an OUMC meet at the Avon Gorge he roped up for the first time and thereafter went climbing most weekends. On one of them he met his future wife and fellow mountaineer Janet. In his last year he became the OUMC's president.

During his four years at Oxford, Alan's climbing record was exceptional for an undergraduate. On his novice Alpine season in 1959 his six climbs included the Dent Blanche and the Badile's north ridge. In 1960 seven routes included the Piz Bernina's Biancograt followed by two grade IV, one grade V and one VI in the Dolomites. The following year he did a TD on the Aiguille de l'M, eight Dolomite classics including three grade IVs, one VI (the *Tissi* on the first Sella Tower) and the Marmolada's south face. His last year at Oxford 1962 was also his most successful alpine season when with Colin Taylor they did three classic Oberland traverses and another four around Zermatt. Moving on to Chamonix they climbed the Peigne north ridge, the Grepon's Mer de Glace face, the Grand Dru traverse and the Petit Dru's north face in a single day to make this its second British ascent (see *AJ* 1962).

Before taking up his MIT appointment in 1963, Alan went to Kenya with his brother Steve and Hamish Nicol. On Kilimanjaro they climbed Mawenzi and Kibo via the Great Notch Wall and on Mount Kenya traversed Tereri and Sendeyo by a new route, put up another on Pt Peter's north-west ridge (V+) and finished with Batian's north face by the *Firmin Hicks*. Arriving at MIT later that year, Alan initially found the mores of its climbing community uncongenial and likened its club's grading system, tests and examinations akin to that employed by the Russians. Nonetheless, he soon qualified as a 'leader' and after teaming up with his roommate and fellow rebel Phil Nelson climbed most weekends, often with John Reppy (whose predilection was for hard routes in extreme winter weather), Sam Streibert and fellow Brits Mike and Sally Westmacott.

Although the Americans headed west to the Rockies, Yosemite and Alaska for serious climbing, there was endless virgin rock within a 600km radius of Boston. The 2,000m White Mountains offered a wealth of granite cliffs; Mount Washington's hazardous winter climbing; Cannon Mountain had a half-mile long 350m cliff; and the Shawangunks an 8km-long escarpment of quartz conglomerate. Alan recorded a bewildering tally of routes including half a dozen new ones mostly graded 5.7-5.9. Memorable was *Sam's Swansong*, a new route done in two stages, first with Alan and Sam Streibert who had to take a break halfway to get married, then the rest with Phil Nelson and the Westmacotts, completing 'the best alpine-style route in Eastern USA'.

In 1964 Alan journeyed out west with Phil Nelson. In the Tetons they climbed both Grand and South Teton before the much harder *Irene's Arete* on Disappointment Peak. At Boulder, home to both Phil and Layton Kor, they climbed the Maiden with its spectacular 30m abseil off the summit. In June the following year, Alan and Phil drove to Yosemite for 16 action-packed days climbing with Sam Streibert and John Reppy. Their 14 routes included El Capitan's 650m *East Buttress* in 12 hours, Chouinard's *MM Slab and Moby Dick*: both 5.9s. On the way back to Boston they nipped up Mount Whitney (4418m) the highest peak in the contiguous United States.

Returning to Europe in 1965, Alan teamed up again with Colin Taylor to do the *Bocalette* on the Aiguille de la Brenva. Moving on to the Vercors they laid siege to Mont Aiguille, chalking up two TDs. He and Colin also climbed the *Fissure en Arc de Cercle* on where, as Colin let slip when they were already fully committed, Lionel Terray had fallen to his death. Tragically, Colin, a fellow physicist who so closely shared Alan's climbing philosophy, was killed on the Obergabelhorn's south face in 1974.

Alan's marriage to Janet and the responsibilities of family life marked the end of serious climbing though in no way curtailed mountaineering. On their first Alpine season together, they traversed the Zinal Rothorn, climbed the Jungfrau's south-west face and traversed the Wetterhorn from Kleine Scheidegg to Rosenlaui. Family holidays were now centred on their cottage in Glencoe with AC family meets at Bosigran and skiing in the Alps. In later years, there were family climbing expeditions to the Wind Rivers range in Wyoming, the Selkirks and Vancouver's Coastal range.

In the mid 1970s Alan and Janet turned their focus to ski mountaineering. In 1976, with the Westmacotts and Jim Milledge, Alan and Janet completed a ski traverse of the Oberland from Andermatt to the Wildhorn climbing the Balhorn en route: a fine achievement. The following year Alan led a party that included Janet, Sally Westmacott, Sarah Baker and Pip Hopkinson for a week's ski touring from Andermatt and back, taking in three peaks en route including the Gross Leckihorn (3065m). In 1978, Alan, his brother Nick and Richard Morgan joined me to attempt a guideless ski traverse through the Central Pyrenees from Urdos to Cauterets. We eventually completed a 12-day epic despite atrocious weather, avalanches and the loss of Richard halfway through from a strained back. Emboldened by success, Alan became the anchorman for three further stages of the Pyrenean High Route in 1980, 1981 and 1983. In between thrills and spills, accident and incident we climbed 10 peaks and pushed the route as far as Luchon. Alan, ever his own man, preferred the Swiss Alps where several attempts to ski from Andermatt to Zermatt (the Tour de Soleil) had been foiled by bad weather and high avalanche risk. Eventually, the weather relented and with Janet, the Westmacotts, Jim Milledge and Sarah Baker the route was completed Zermatt to Andermatt in 1984: Alan's final triumph.

Since 1983, Alan and I had seen all too little of each other but in 2001 I persuaded him to join me for a ski circuit of Monte Viso with Rupert Hoare. This was intended as a Pyrenean High Route reunion (Alan having done four of the early stages and Rupert Hoare the last three) but also to settle the contentious question of where exactly Hannibal had crossed the Alps. It became clear from our first day's strenuous ascent to the the Quinto Sella hut in Rupert's slipstream that Alan was far from fit, yet he insisted on carrying on. Early next morning, 1 April 2001, barely 10 minutes after leaving the hut, I happened to glance round to see Alan lying prone under a rock outcrop. His skis had severed a main artery in a fall that shattered his pelvis, ruptured his rectum and punctured his bowels. Without Rupert's frantic race back to the hut for help, the Italian helicopter rescue service's immediate response and Savigliano Hospital's intensive care unit, Alan would not have survived his terrible injuries and the loss of eight litres of blood. He was flown back to England a week later and had his pelvis reset. Within a year he was skiing black runs but the injuries sustained never fully healed and in 2013 his damaged leg had to be amputated.

It was typical of Alan's courage, determination and stoicism that he adapted to this handicap without remorse or self-pity, busying himself in his workshop and scaling hills in a wheelchair bolstered by Janet's love and unwavering support. He combined a scientist's clarity of mind and an engineer's ingenuity with the creativity of an artist. In the mountains, he was a natural leader whose strength seemed limitless and whose judgement never faltered. Those who had the privilege of knowing Alan will never forget him.

J G R Harding

Andrew M Wilkinson
1976 - 2022

Andrew Wilkinson died on 11 September 2022 when a large boulder being used as an anchor point on the Aiguille Noire de Peuterey gave way, resulting in a considerable fall. It seems likely that Andrew, who had a reputation for safe and secure climbing, was an unfortunate victim of the crumbling of the Alps accelerated by climate change.

Known as Wilki to his friends, Andrew started climbing with Durham University Mountaineering Club. Following five years' service with the Royal Marines, including operational deployments in Afghanistan, Andrew qualified as a secondary schoolteacher. His main role, at various schools, was as a pastoral leader to teenage pupils, looking after their welfare and wellbeing and encouraging positive choices in all areas of their school life and beyond. He taught modern languages and ran a range of Combined

Andrew Wilkinson at Everest Base Camp.

Cadet Force and rock-climbing activities. He took students on many adventurous trips to north Wales, sea-cliff climbing on the south coast and backcountry skiing and snow holing to Arctic Norway.

His mountaineering achievements were impressive. He climbed Cho Oyu with a military team in 2006 and Everest via the south-east ridge the following year. In 2012, he climbed both the classic Matterhorn north face and the north wall of the Eiger by the *1938* route. His partnership with Finn McCann on several of these climbs later led to episodes of speed flying, a hybrid of paragliding and parachuting, although in 2015 Wilki pulled out of a flight from the Aiguille Verte with the explanation that 'I'm getting married in three months time.'

With his wife Sarah he made a nearly 3,000km kayak trip down the Yukon river, then an east to west crossing of Greenland by ski. He left teaching and founded Dynamis Adventures, a charity which delivers mentoring and adventurous outdoor activities for young people to build character, unlock potential, raise aspirations and encourage positive life choices, activities deeply rooted in Wilki's strong Christian faith.

He was elected a member of the Club and the Alpine Climbing Group in 2021. On his application form he wrote: 'most of my climbing partners have lost their mojo or given up because their bones are creaking and family life is demanding, I don't want to give up.'

Writing in *The Spectator* in November 2022, Anthony Seldon, former master of Wellington, wrote how his former pupil had come back from Afghanistan, the north face of the Eiger and Everest, 'but not this time from his beloved Alps. Teacher, soldier, adventurer, he left the comfort of Wellington to set up the charity Dynamis Adventures, to help underprivileged children develop and flourish through outdoor adventure. Magnificently brave and tirelessly loving, his Christian faith was his core. Most saw his selfless service, but few its wellsprings.'

The Club offers its deepest sympathy to Sarah and their three young daughters.

Roderick A Smith

OFFICERS AND COMMITTEE FOR 2022

President	*Simon Richardson*
Vice-presidents	*Adèle Long, Nick Kekus*
Honorary Secretary	*Sherry Macliver*
Honorary Treasurer	*Alan Henderson*
Honorary Editor of the Alpine Journal	*Ed Douglas*
Honorary Librarian	*Barbara Grigor-Taylor*

CHAIRS OF SUB-COMMITTEES:

Climbing	*Nicholas Hurndall Smith*
Information Technology	*Vacant*
Marketing, Communications & Publications	*Ed Douglas*
Chair of the Alpine Club Library Council	*Philip Meredith*
Committee, *Elected*	*Richard Nadin, John Porter, Giles Robertson*
Committee, *Co-opted*	*Paul Ramsden*

OFFICE BEARERS

Membership Secretary	*Sherry Macliver*
London Lecture Organiser	*Derek Buckle*
South-west Lecture Organiser	*Tony Westcott, Chris Storie*
Peak Lecture Organiser	*Martin Wragg*
Lakes Lecture Organiser	*Anna Lawford*
Edinburgh Lecture Organiser	*Tim Elson, Zoe Strong*
North Wales Lecture Organiser	*Peter Frost*
Winter Dinner Convenor	*William Newsom*
Chair of the Climbing Fund Sub-committee	*Paul Ramsden*
Chair of the Finance Sub-committee	*Trevor Campbell Davis*
Chair of the Membership Applications Sub-committee	*Richard Nadin*
Chair of the Property Sub-committee	*Vacant*
Chair of the Exhibitions Sub-committee	*John Porter*
Chair of the Environmental Panel	*Tito Arosio*
UIAA Representative	*Richard Nadin*
Honorary Archivist	*Glyn Hughes*
Honorary Keeper of the Club's Artefacts	*Nigel Buckley*
Honorary Keeper of the Club's Monuments	*Charlie Burbridge*
Acting Honorary Keeper of the Club's Paintings	*William Mitchell*
Honorary Keeper of the Club's Photographs	*Bernie Ingrams*
Assistant Editor of the Alpine Journal (obituaries)	*Rod Smith*
Newsletter Editor	*Office Manager*
Social Media and E-newsletter Editor	*Adam Butterworth*
Website Editors	*Adam Butterworth, Jeremy Gould, David Lund*
IT Techincal Support Officer	*David Lund*
Trustees	*Mike Baker, Adam Roberts, Philip Sanders*

Alpine Club Notes

'East Side of Monte Rosa, and Jägerhorn', Elijah Walton, undated, watercolour touched with white, 24.8cm × 34.9cm. *(British Museum)*

VICTOR SAUNDERS

Valedictory Address

Read Before the Alpine Club, 27 November 2022

In 1961 George Finch gave his valedictory address, which began, more or less, thus:

> *It is indeed a privilege to address this, the Alpine Club, the first of the many associations of men [and women] drawn together by a love of mountains and mountaineering. How comes this? How find happiness in such lunacy as scrambling about on the most disturbed, inhospitable and dangerous surfaces of the earth's crust? How can men be such fools?*

Club members will appreciate the particular placc mountaineering and the ascent of Everest had in the late Queen's reign. She is pictured here being shown oxygen equipment by John Hunt at the premiere of The Conquest of Everest at the Odeon, Leicester Square, on 21 October 1953. *(Alpine Club Photo Library)*

Before we try to answer this question, which I believe will be best done propping up the bar after this meeting, I will open my remarks on the last three years (my term serving on your Committee) by remembering some of our members who have died. All of them are deserving of mention, but for today I am going to focus, with a couple of digressions, on those who have contributed to the Club.

To begin with, I would like to mention two personal friends of mine, Julian Davey and Neil Sawyer. It was 20 years ago that Julian called to ask if I was free to do some ice climbing in Chamonix and Cogne. I was so slow to answer that by the time I got round to it, I was double booked with Prof Vernon Gayle. The week was such fun that the experience had to be repeated over the following years. Julian was warm-hearted, talkative, oddly addicted to cheese and secretive about his past, leading to a general suspicion that he had a background in espionage. He was important to other presidents too, as chair of the co-op that brewed beer in Hesket Newmarket. This brewery supplied the Old Crown, the local pub for three past presidents Chris Bonington, Doug Scott and John Porter.

Neil Sawyer joined the Club in 2020 in spite of being a near neighbour of mine in Les Houches. Tragically he died a year later, possibly as the result of a heart attack, while cycling between Chamonix and his home. He had just completed the last of the Alpine 4,000ers. During the lockdown, Neil and Gus Morton introduced me to the rocks in the woods behind our village and in 2020 we had a delightful summer evading gendarmes while illicitly bouldering in those woods.

We all know that Rick Allen won a prestigious and totally uncontroversial Piolet d'Or with Sandy Allan for the magnificent Mazeno traverse and we all know that he perished on K2 in an avalanche. Perhaps less well known was his generosity of spirit and his deep religious conviction. To my regret I only shared one Alpine outing with him, along with our then librarian Nigel Buckley. He was an alumni of Birmingham University and in in that context we have their climbing club here.

At the end of 2020 we lost past president Doug Scott, a giant of Himalayan climbing. In 1988 I was privileged to be with him and Lindsay Griffin (that past president sitting over there) in Bhutan. About Doug, I would say there are three of his dates that were transformative for Himalayan climbing: 1975, 1979 and 1982. The first marks the high point of big team siege-style Himalayan expeditions, the silver age if you like, the golden age being the decade of 8,000m first ascents. The second date marks the beginning of something new: a small team, lightweight, no oxygen, no Sherpas and a difficult new route to extreme altitude. The third date marks the beginning of the new age of pure alpine style new routing at very high altitude. Doug was well known as a complex individual. Lindsay will remember that when he had a chest infection in Bhutan he treated it with homeopathic drugs but both of us couldn't help noticing he was backing that up with amoxycillin. When the infection receded he announced to the world: 'See youth, the homeopathic medicine works every time!' Lindsay and I just said, 'Yes Doug!'

Earlier in 2020, we lost Hamish MacInnes and Joe Brown. It's hard to know where to start with such immense names. But that year we also lost Geoffrey Templeman, who assisted on the *Alpine Journal* in varying roles for 30 years from 1977 to 2006, produced the Club Newsletter and chaired the House Committee during the move from South Audley Street. Here I could do no better than to quote Mike Esten: 'In short, Geoff was the sort of member which every club needs and treasures.'

In 2021 we lost Malcolm Howells who was part of the Trango Tower trip in 1976, probably the hardest rock climb at altitude at the time. Also in 2021, Jim Milledge, who will be remembered for the pioneering medical work during the 1961 Silver Hut expedition under Ama Dablam and his authoritative *Mountain Medicine* which he co-authored with Mike Ward. The same year we lost long-term contributor Evelio Echevarría who wrote the South America notes for as long as anyone can remember. A year later, in 2022, we lost Derek Fordham, the Arctic explorer who contributed to the *Alpine Journal* with many articles and the area notes. That same year we lost John Brailsford, a prominent member of the guiding fraternity who was the most vociferous advocate of the Écrins and inventor of the Moac. Some of us are old enough to remember that, though I didn't know that it was also known as the Great British Nut. He was also an early advocate of the French prussik, which the French at that time called the 'Johnny knot' after him.

I'll end this list with Trevor Braham who died in 2020. Those of us who are old enough will have been weaned on *Himalayan Odyssey* as well as *When the Alps Cast Their Spell* his 2006 Boardman-Tasker prize-winning book. Braham's numerous travels and explorations in little-known, isolated Himalayan regions included parts of Sikkim that Fowler and I were to visit in 2021 and 2022, meaning we trod in his footsteps, which I rather think would have horrified him. Why would that be I hear you ask? Because on reading in the 1985 *Alpine Journal* Mick's comic description of our antics on Bojohagur the year before, Braham wrote to the future president and multiple Piolets d'Or winner. I think he rather missed the humour of the piece because Braham wrote: 'Mr Fowler, you are a disgrace to British Alpinism.' To Mick's undying regret he didn't keep and frame that letter. We have to thank Richard Nadin as membership secretary for his tireless and successful efforts to replace those who have retired or died with new, young and active members.

Looking over the list of past presidents the list reads like a role call of the great and good of climbing history. Many of them were notable writers, including all the living ones. Most of them had an enviable climbing record. Usually they were highly respectable, although Trevor Braham may have dissented from that view. The early presidents tended to be wealthy and sometimes even aristocrats. Later they were drawn from all walks of life. Even so, I do think I am the first lowly working mountain guide in the role. As a guide I bring many of the overcautious, risk-averse principles of that profession to new projects. Three years ago, faced with the frightening prospect of chairing the Committee, I was strongly reminded of the first rule of mountain first aid: don't make it worse.

The previous Committee had done a solid job of putting the club structures on a firm footing. The club organisation that my Committee inherited was already a well-oiled and functioning machine thanks to John, Lindsay and Mick. This Committee took over from John Porter's on 1 January 2022. Three days later the BBC reported a mystery virus causing pneumonia-like symptoms had broken out in Wuhan with 44 cases reported, of which 11 were already serious. Not to worry though, China was at the other end of the world. Except it wasn't. We didn't know it then, but Covid-19 was going to rule our world for the rest of the year and well into the next year too. We were going to be seriously constrained.

Now I am going to take you on a wee diversion so please bear with me for a minute. On the evening of 24 January 1975, in the German town of Cologne, 17-year-old Vera Brand was in tears. The concert she had organised was due to start and the musician had just told her the piano was unplayable. The concert hall had mixed up their instruments. The piano had jangly high notes, inconsistent bass and dysfunctional pedals and the audience was waiting. Jazz supremo Keith Jarrett was on the point of walking out. The tears of Vera Brand did the trick. He decided to work within the limits of the dilapidated machine and produced music that lasts to this day. Forty-seven years later, the Köln Concert remains Keith Jarrett's solo masterpiece. It has sold millions and is the biggest-selling solo jazz album in history.

Sometimes constraints help us to break from the tramlines of our past and look at the future in new ways. The lockdowns were the broken piano your Committee faced in 2020. We had to adapt and did so remarkably well. There were the club-casts and the team of Nick, Nigel and Michael to thank for that. That in turn led to the beginning of a digital lecture archive to add to the *Alpine Journal*, which is now digitised for the last one hundred years. If you haven't dipped into that trove of treasure yet you have a wonderful treat waiting for you. The Club lectures are now being recorded for posterity. (Those who have delved into the old journals will know we used to record lectures as papers read before the Club, a practice that will now be revived through the digital archive.) Our website has a much improved interface making it much more user friendly than it was before Covid-19. It is great, at least in my opinion.

Remote meetings were forced on us and they have been a real success. It seems I am not the only person to think that people behave exceptionally well, making fewer unnecessary interruptions on screen than they do across the table. The remote meetings work well when everyone is on their own device, but we found hybrid meetings are a little more difficult organise, though the last hybrid Committee meeting in October was greatly aided by new technology. Remote meeting has not only saved us a considerable amount of time (with the opportunity cost that entails) but also reduces our carbon footprint in line with the principles of our increasingly important Green Group (thank you Grace Hurford and the team) as well as travel costs which previously came to between £4,000 and £6,000 just for Committee meetings.

The treasurers past and present (thank you Trevor and Alan) managed to see the Club through some trying periods while we were without tenants. Towards the end of the lockdown the Committee set up the AC WhatsApp groups that have turned out to be excellent channels of communication. I use the Haute Savoie group: a real boon to our community. Throughout this period we have our *Alpine Journal*, which excels itself every year.

With the end of the lockdowns there was the Women Rise Up meet to celebrate Lucy Walker and help improve the gender balance in the Club. After all, balance is what climbing is about. In maintaining balance, we have had one man and one woman vice president since 2020 and I hope this will become a tradition. And in this context our guests this year include extraordinary mountaineer and honorary member Gerlinde Kaltenbrunner who will speak at the dinner. We also have dinner guest Masha Gordon, who created the Grit and Rock award to promote women climbing in the Greater Ranges, an immensely important part of sending out the message that alpine climbing is not only for the bearded ones.

Of course we have not achieved all the goals we set out for ourselves. For example, we have been in Hackney 25 years and while it did seem time for a bit of outreach to local schools and community, that was put on hold by the first lockdown. This is work in progress, as is the Himalayan Index project. Adèle Long is working on the evolution of that database.

Things did return towards the new normal a bit after the lockdowns with a superb series of meets, thanks in large part to Nick Hurndall Smith who cannot be here to hear us sing his praises. I understand he is singing somewhere else. There were the excellent exhibitions, including 'Everest by Those Who Were There', thanks largely to the efforts of our hon librarian Barbara Grigor-Taylor. John Porter organised and produced the film of the exhibition, which was shown recently in Slovenia. Looking to the future, your Committee has brought reciprocal rights back the Club and we are now part of the hut exchange scheme officially. Thank you Giles Robertson for your excellent work there. You will see from this that this was a dutiful hard-working committee, to be thanked for their effort over the last few years.

To borrow again from George Finch, whose valedictory speech opened with this truth:

> *Let us not delude ourselves; it is the Honorary Secretary who sees to it that your President keeps to the narrow crest and surmounts or steers round the occasional gendarme in the approved manner. So when, with a note of challenge in his voice, he asked if I intended to give the customary valedictory address, he had really left me with no choice, for by then I had learnt my lesson.*

Plus ça change. We have all been kept in place by the honorary secretary who has worked tirelessly, *tirelessly* for your benefit. Thank you Sherry Macliver.

The Club consists of three assets: its properties, its collections and its membership. And the greatest of these is the membership. Membership. Community: that most important and intangible asset. I believe the sense of community has been increased by this Committee and I do believe that at the very least, in spite of the difficult years they have had to face, they have, like all good first-aiders, not made it worse.

Allen Steck: 1926-2023

How did they do it, Allen Steck and Steve Roper? How did they get such stunningly original writing out of the climbing community with such regularity in their Sierra Club mountaineering journal *Ascent*? When I asked this question of Steck and Roper over the last lunch I had with them in the tiny kitchen of Steck's shingled house on the hill in Berkeley, Steck gave me an eloquent answer. He disappeared and then produced a wine bottle boasting a label that declared, 'Incubus Hills'. Beside the words was the famous Gustave Doré image of climbers falling to their deaths from the Matterhorn. Being Californians they had their own *Ascent* wine label for their daily lunch editorial meetings in Steck's kitchen. Steck claimed it was their last bottle. They could say no more in answer to my question and seemed as mystified as I was.

For 14 issues over 25 years they worked hard at editing the work they received and the wine helped lubricate the spirit of fun and wit that characterised their conversations together in that kitchen, at the crag and round the campfire. They were a double act that spurred each other on to ironic invention. Steck was slow and laconic, Roper jumpy with fast-talking nervous

Allen Steck rappelling at Yosemite in the late 1950s. *(Courtesy T Adler Books)*

Allen Steck (1926–2023) in Peru, 1952. *(Allen Steck)*

Steck used this image of crystals of chemicals used in mothballs on the cover of one edition of Ascent.

energy. Roper was much younger ('Look at that old man climb!' he once said to me at Joshua Tree, where Steck, leading, had forgotten to tie the laces of one shoe. 'El Vago', they called him after he forgot his sleeping bag on a previous early season trip to Joshua Tree.) Roper was shy and reluctant to appear at gatherings. It was Steck who came to speak at the International Festival of Mountaineering Literature at Bretton Hall in 1993. (Jim Curran convinced Steck that it was a religious observance to climb every Sunday, whatever the weather, so that we got pictures of the old Californian Silver Fox brushing snow off the holds whilst climbing at Froggatt.) The 'Slim Fox', as he had originally called himself, had become the 'Silver Fox' when I knew him. He called me 'Fat Badger'. Fair enough. Roper's reply to my recent conciliatory email was, 'As expected. He was 96.' Fair enough.

So I've come to the rather obvious conclusion that the success of *Ascent* ('Ahead of its time,' as John Porter put it to me recently) was built on its success. When they published originality, more originality would follow. They set a challenge to writers by what they published: who could be more imaginatively outrageous than what had gone before? When Ken Wilson was looking for the most interesting climbing writing around as he edited *The Games Climbers Play* (1978) he took his title from an article published in the very first issue of *Ascent* in 1967. With his first two articles Ken set his stall out before beginning the anthology proper. So it is significant that the second article also came from *Ascent*. Ed Drummond's 'Mirror, Mirror' (1973) was typical of what Steck and Roper sought for *Ascent* and it was probably the only place at the time where such outrageously imaginative writing could have been published in the climbing press. Of course, the wine label bore the title of an article by Drummond, his 'rather bland title' having been replaced by one plucked from the opening sentence by the editors. Ed Drummond was encouraged and supported by Steck and Roper at a personal as well as literary level.

'In 1967 we weren't thinking of nurturing writers', wrote the editors in *The Best of Ascent* (1993), still published by the loyal Sierra Club Books. But, along with Drummond, they gave early breaks to some of the giants of the field: Jeff Long, David Roberts and Galen Rowell. 'We simply wanted to publish dramatic pictures and soulful articles,' they added. But from the beginning they knew that they wanted to publish, again ahead of their time, what they called 'photo essays'. When new magazines arrived in the 1980s, *Ascent* switched its focus to climbing fiction, taking a risk, 'quirky' as ever, the editors admit.

Ken Wilson's *The Games Climbers Play* contains seven *Ascent* essays from writers including Tom Higgins, Chuck Pratt, Chris Jones, Royal Robbins and Yvon Chouinard: pioneering climbers who might not have first thought of themselves as writers of pieces worthy of anthologising. Literary nurturing had taken place. In his autobiography, *A Mountaineer's Life* (2017), Steck has a chapter on *Ascent* in which he characterises the first issue as demonstrating 'our desire for innovation and whimsy'. He admits that one of the long gaps between issues was due to himself and Roper researching and writing *Fifty Classic Climbs of North America* (1979), later referred to in an *Ascent* article titled 'Fifty Crowded Classics'. But he also claims, quite rightly, to have influenced later publications and *Alpinist* is a good example. David Roberts has paid tribute to the 'care and craft' of Steck and Roper at Steck's kitchen table. Now there will be no more kitchen meetings with the Silver Fox and, in Steck's immortal words, 'putting empty wine bottles to rest'.

Terry Gifford

Demounting Louis Agassiz

In early 2023, diversity-championing gallery Autograph (just around the corner from the AC in Rivington Place) staged what amounted to a decadal retrospective of Swiss-Haitian-Finnish artist Sasha Huber. The primary relevance to the Club is her long campaign to have the Agassizhorn (3946m), spanning Valais and Berne cantons, re-named Rentyhorn in honour of the American slave Renty, whose image the 19th century Swiss-American 'scientist' Louis Agassiz had illegally expropriated as 'evidence' of inferior racial characteristics.

It's a thought-provoking proposition and part of Huber's work interrogating how history is imprinted onto landscapes through memorialised placenames and monuments. With the current arguments about statues in the UK (Rhodes and Colston, to name but two), this is a timely reminder to rethink our relationship with the past. Unsurprisingly, responses from the Swiss

Sasha Huber on the summit of the 'Rentyhorn'. *(Autograph)*

Huber's portrait of the African-American Arctic explorer Matthew Henson. *(Autograph)*

authorities ranged from a tactful 'inability to comment' to incredulity at renaming a mountain to suit 'societal trends and fashions'.

The charge sheet is that Louis Agassiz, traditionally known as a pioneering natural scientist in the field of glaciology, geology and palaeontology (some of his books are held by the ACL), was also one of the most influential racists of his era; his ideas helped spawn apartheid. Seven species are named after him. So are 80 landmarks from the little-known Agassiz Rock (a bouldering venue in Edinburgh), a glacier in Aotearoa-New Zealand, to features on the Moon and Mars.

Huber's artworks often focus on physical interventions at sites named after Agassiz, recorded as photographs or film. A powerful video installation at the gallery showed a Maori resetting ceremony or *karakia* at the Agassiz glacier, Aotearoa. Also on show were striking portraits, part of the 'Tailoring Freedom' series, based on Agassiz's commissioned slave daguerreotypes but then embellished by metal staples to add back garments (the original pictures were nude or semi-nude). A further portrait in this series shown at Autograph that called attention to historically under-represented figures was of Matthew Henson, the African-American explorer and companion of Peary, whose claim to be the first to reach thc North Polc has long been subject to debate and whose treatment of the Inughuit was at times exploitative.

Although the exhibition has now moved to Turku Art Museum, Finland, an excellent catalogue is available: *Sasha Huber: You Name It*. Whilst not suggesting culture wars need be declared at Charlotte Road, the issues Huber covers are now at the forefront of modern museum practice and perhaps need to be considered in relation to the AC's collections.

Andy Tickle

Alpine Club Library

New librarian Emma McDonald. *(Adam Butterworth)*

People and Events

Following the easing of Covid-related closures and restrictions, the demand for in-person library services started to increase during 2021 but never recovered to pre-Covid levels. The same has been true for 2022, with visitor numbers remaining low relative to historical levels. It is also interesting to note that visits by non-members are now starting to equal or even exceed visits by AC members. It seems that Club members have become used to accessing material online via the website and via email enquiries. While this is seemingly efficient, I remain convinced that the gleaning of important details often requires a visit and first-hand perusal of relevant documents.

Having only joined us on a part-time basis in April 2021, our librarian, Beth Hodgett, resigned her post in May 2022 in order to pursue a career in academia. This threw us into a bit of a tailspin and I would like to go on record in thanking **Barbara Grigor-Taylor** and **Glyn Hughes** for their efforts in managing the Library for several days each week, dealing with visitors and enquiries, whilst we sought a new librarian. The post was advertised widely on various platforms over the summer and we were pleased to receive a large number of applications from people with a wide range of experience, qualifications and geographical locations. A selection panel agreed on a shortlist and, after a series of face-to-face interviews, the panel was unanimous in offering the position to **Emma McDonald**. Emma graduated with an MA in library and information management from Loughborough University in 2007 and has worked in a variety of public and academic libraries since then. She joins us from the Aldrich Library at the University of Brighton where she supported a wide range of subjects including geography and geology. Emma commenced work in the AC Library in January 2023 and was faced with a daunting backlog of work resulting from our hiatus. This did not seem to faze her at all, and I am pleased to say that her very methodical and professional approach has already got the Library back operating on an even keel.

Newly appointed keeper of the pictures, William Mitchell.

Also, during most of the year, Janet Johnson and Richard Nadin kindly acted as joint, interim keepers of pictures while a permanent replacement was sought. I am delighted to report that **William Mitchell** enthusiastically agreed to take on that role and was appointed at the end of 2022. William is a third-generation art dealer and a specialist in alpine paintings. Most recently, he co-curated a major exhibition on the life and works of the pioneering *peintre-alpiniste* Gabriel Loppé at the Forte di Bard in the Aosta valley entitled **'Gabriel Loppé, Painter, Climber and Traveller'**. The exhibition brings together more than 90 of Loppé's paintings drawings and photographs, exhibited alongside a selection of his climbing equipment, and runs until January 2024. Before joining the family business in the late 1990s William worked in the art trade in Paris. This kindled his interest in alpinism and he has returned to climb in the Alps almost every year since. He has a longstanding association with the Club's art collection, having held a major exhibition of Club pictures at his gallery in 2001 and hosted a party to celebrate the AC's 150th anniversary in 2007. William's primary interest centres on the *peintre-alpinistes* who both painted and climbed, such as Loppé and the Comptons and their more recent disciples. Nevertheless, he has promised to raise the profile of some of the more neglected artists represented in the AC Collection. We welcome William and wish him well in this endeavour.

Library trustees now have a fixed term of office of three years, so it is necessary to appoint or re-appoint several trustees each year. At the 2022 AGM, **Robin Ashcroft** was re-appointed as the trustee nominated by the RGS and **Kimball Morrison** was re-appointed as the trustee nominated by the BMC. The Library and the keepers continue their active participation in the AC's wide-ranging and on-going ICT review. Significant progress is being made towards our goal of streamlining and integrating detailed information about all the collections in order to be able to provide a better and more easily accessible service to members. More specifically, the Club's digital and social media officer **Adam Butterworth** has put great effort into developing our social media presence, and the Library pages of the website have been updated and now include a page to highlight newly published books written by AC members. As I have noted previously, collections inevitably increase in size over time. This not only puts continual pressure on space, but also on the work required to organise and manage the holdings. We are therefore always looking for volunteers to help out with the collections. If you are interested in helping out or would like more information about volunteering opportunities, please contact me (***p.meredith@ucl.ac.uk***) or any of the keepers. Not only can the work itself be very rewarding, but it also provides access to a truly wondrous world of mountaineering heritage.

'Party Passing a Crevasse' by John Auldjo, 1828

'The Dent du Géant and Glacier des Périades from the Aiguille du Tacul', by William Frederick Donkin, 1882.

Exhibitions

After a period of necessarily reduced activity over the past few years, it was exciting to return to a full schedule of exhibitions in the Lecture Hall for 2022. The year started with the **'Glaciers'** exhibition, curated by **Janet Johnson**, our assistant keeper of pictures, which ran from January to March. The exhibition was designed both to showcase rarely seen paintings of glaciers from the Club's collection and to highlight our relationship with our digital partners **Art UK** and **Watercolour World** that allows us to widen access and thus increase awareness of the breadth of the collection. Due to continuing Covid-19 restrictions during the period leading up to the opening of the exhibition, promotion had been limited and this was reflected in initial visitor numbers. However, it was pleasing to see that visitor numbers picked up as the exhibition period progressed. This may have been helped by a video in which Janet selected a number of images to discuss in detail produced by

François Durafour lands his biplane at the Dôme du Goûter in a Caudron G3 aircraft on 30 July 1921.

Adam Butterworth and designed to entice members and outside visitors to come to see the paintings in person. The new glass exhibition cases, purchased the previous year, proved to be a real asset in allowing fragile and delicate supporting material for the exhibition to be displayed. In this case they were used to display the collection of very long unframed watercolour panoramas of glaciers, the work of **Gottlieb Studer**.

The Club owns a fine collection of very large 19th and early 20th century photographs, including works by W F Donkin, Edward Whymper and Fanny Bullock Workman. These had previously been stored for many years in the

Charlotte Road basement where they cluttered up the space and had accumulated damage. It was therefore decided that they should be renovated and eventually displayed on the walls of the Clubhouse. **Richard Nadin** took on this task and did a fantastic job in returning these stunning images to their former glory. We therefore took the opportunity over the summer period to display **'Historic Photographic Treasures of the 19th and Early 20th Century'** in the Lecture Hall, curated by Bernie Ingrams and Richard Nadin, before they were due to be hung in their permanent locations around the Clubhouse.

In the autumn, Polly Townsend, an associate member of the Club, curated **'A Wider Landscape: Examining Mountains through the Female Gaze'**. In addition to displaying paintings by a group of contemporary female artists, Polly and Janet Johnson combed through the AC Collection to find other supporting paintings by earlier female artists. In addition to finding prints by **Una Cameron**, used in past issues of the *Alpine Journal*, that were displayed in the glass cabinets, a framed etching of the 'Bernese Oberland: Eiger, Mönch and Jungfrau' by M Dicker was discovered. In a happy coincidence, her daughter, who had previously been in touch with the Library researching artworks by her mother, was able to come and see it on the opening night.

Our final exhibition of the year was **'The British Alps'**, exploring the Cuillin of Skye, which ran from November 2022 to January 2023. The exhibition comprised striking images of experiences on the ridge drawn and painted by **Helen G S Forde** in a variety of media: watercolours, gouaches, charcoal drawings and oil paintings. Again, supporting images and entries from the Club journal that matched some of Helen's artwork and graphics were found and displayed to enhance the exhibition.

The Everest centenary exhibition **'Everest By Those Who Were There: 1921, 1922 and 1924'**, which was mounted at Charlotte Road in 2021, continues to generate interest. Facsimiles of items from the exhibition were displayed at the Planinski Muzej In Slovenia from October 2022. The British ambassador opened the exhibition and the embassy provided support for honorary secretary **Sherry Macliver** to attend and represent the Club. Following the opening ceremony, a day of activities was arranged, including a mountain with Slovenian climbing legends **Andrej** and **Marija Štremfelj**, the ambassador, embassy and museum staff, and Sherry.

Collections

A Swiss friend of the Library, **Marcel Fischli**, kindly donated a copy of the *Alpine Club Register of Members 1857-1890*, published in three volumes between 1923 and 1928 and providing an invaluable and detailed record of each member's climbs. Marcel also donated a copy of his own publication ***Himalayan Pioneers in Zermatt*** describing ascents in the Himalaya by climbers from Zermatt in the Himalaya in the 19th century.

'Save the Day' (Oil on Panel) by Polly Townsend.

Left to right: British ambassador to Slovenia Tiffany Sadler, Marija Štremfeljs, Sherry Macliver and Andrej Štremfeljs. *(Tina Horvat)*

Eagle-eyed Richard Nadin spotted a large album of previously unknown watercolours by one of the AC's original members, Frederic Elliott Blackstone, for sale at auction. While the Club does not normally purchase items to enhance the AC Collections, the history and provenance of this album was deemed an exception and it was purchased. The album contains 70 highly accomplished paintings of the English Lake District and the Italian Alps. Although Blackstone's climbs are fully recorded in *Mumm's Register*, his talents as an artist are not mentioned, and his paintings have not been found in other UK collections.

The book collection of **J H Emlyn Jones** (AC president 1979-82) was donated to the Library by his widow Louise. It includes a first French edition of John Hunt's ***Ascent of Everest*** signed by all members of the 1953 team, along with Hunt's handwritten notes on finding the route to the summit of Kangchenjunga in 1954 while he was chair of the Kangchenjunga Committee. The collection also included a group of finely bound first editions of mountaineering classics from the library of **Humphrey Owen Jones** (AC 1910). The entire Emlyn Jones collection will feature under his name in the online Library catalogue.

Admirers of Jan Morris (1926-2020), whose coverage in *The Times* of the first ascent of Everest in 1953 was a world exclusive, may be interested in the first biography of the admired author of *Venice* and *Pax Britannica* written by Paul Clements and published by Scribe. This portrait of Jan, titled 'Jan Adre/Jan At Home', was painted by Annie Morgan-Suganami and featured in an exhibition curated by Welsh artist Iwan Bala to celebrate Jan's 90th birthday.

While identifying books requiring repair and conservation a surprising discovery was made on the basement bookshelves by Barbara: a folio volume labelled ***Sketches of Switzerland 1929-1930 by F.R.B.*** This turned out to be a series of original pen and pencil sketches, mostly of scenery, towns and peaks viewed from the north shore of Lake Geneva. After removing a shabby, torn cloth covering the original binding, a finely executed watercolour panorama was found folded and tucked inside the cloth; possibly the first time it had been revealed in a century or more. The panorama is presented in six panels totalling 219cm in length and shows peaks and ranges from Mont Tendre, past Lausanne and the Diablerets to Mont Jaman.

AC member **Peter Berg** has kindly donated a set glass lantern slides by **Edward Whymper**. These have all been scanned at high resolution and most have been retouched using Photoshop. AC member **Roy Lindsay** has been bequeathed all of the mountaineering photos of the late **Rick Allen**. Roy has loaned these to the AC for copying before they are eventually deposited into the archives of the Scottish Mountaineering Club and the Scottish National Library. So far, the lecture slides from six carousels have been scanned by Bernie Ingrams and **Peter Payne**, who are also going through boxes of other slides and multiple USB sticks to identify images that are worth archiving.

Photographic images from the AC Collection have been provided for the ***Histoire de l'Alpinisme*** from French publisher Glénat. Photographs have also been provided for window and shop-floor displays at The North Face and Peak Performance in Covent Garden and Stockholm respectively. Projected images of **A F Mummery** and **Isabella Charlet-Stratton** from the AC Collection have been used to illuminate the English Church in Chamonix.

Interest in the pictures from the AC Collection displayed on Art UK continues to increase. Images by John Ruskin, Gabriel Loppé and A Gos continue to be the most popular. A recently uploaded painting of Everest Base Camp by **Philippa Stephenson** (1858-1941) was selected for the feature on 1000 Women Artists by Art UK. Our presence there now provides a small but steady income stream that is used to pay for conservation of the picture collection. We have therefore upped our participation level allowing us to display up to 250 images rather than the previous 100. Janet Johnson has been engaged in selection the extra images to display. We also now have 617 images from the collection scanned and uploaded onto the website of Watercolour World. This includes all the watercolours from the recently purchased Blackstone album described above.

There have been some notable acquisitions to the Archives during the year. These include: the transcripts of **Peter Lloyd's** diaries from the 1936 and 1938 Nanda Devi expeditions; letters sent home by **Peter Oliver** from Everest in 1936; Emlyn Jones' diaries from the Annapurna Himalaya expedition in 1950 and the Ama Dablam expedition in 1959; and copies and transcripts of letters sent to **Douglas Freshfield** by the guide Devouassoud. Research visits and email enquiries to the Archives are increasing, but remain below pre-Covid levels. The most popular topics for study remain Mallory and Irvine, and women climbers. The most studied women climbers include Katharine Richardson, Emmeline Lewis Lloyd and Victoria Maude Biddlecombe; all little known names but with strong climbing records. Conservation work is continuing on archive material; and in particular, a further tranche of AC membership application has been bound, bringing us up to 2020.

Thanks to the prolonged efforts and diplomatic skills of **Charlie Burbridge** and **Victor Saunders** there has been some progress at last on the movement of the Mathews Monument in Chamonix. Charlie reports that the Chamonix authorities have approved a site in the Parc Couttet and also agreed to fund its removal from outside the old Couttet Hotel and to lift it over the moraine ridge into the park by crane. In response, the Club has offered to pay for its cleaning and restoration of the inscription. It is anticipated that the monument will be installed in its new home by summer 2023.

Endnote

As always, I end this report by expressing my deep gratitude to everyone in the Library team, librarian, trustees, keepers, members and volunteers, who again gave their time so generously and ungrudgingly throughout the year. Thanks also to everyone who supplied we with the details of activities needed to compile this report.

Philip Meredith

Boardman Tasker Prize 2022

Last year's recovery in submissions continued with 40 books entered from around the world. The depth was also maintained with several notable books not making the short list, including Hamish MacInnes' well published *The Fox of Glencoe*, Jonathan Howland's widely praised novel *Native Air* and former *Alpinist* editor Katie Ives' *Imaginary Peaks*. Canadian author and editor Marni Jackson was chair of judges and delivered her speech from Toronto. Her co-judges were UKClimbing editor Natalie Berry and Matt Fry, director of international sales at Quarto Books. Part of Joe Tasker's extended family, Fry grew up with a passion for mountaineering literature and attended Boardman-Tasker award ceremonies as a child. The short-listed titles, with comments from Jackson's awards speech, are as follows:

Kieran Cunningham for *Climbing the Walls*, 'a highly engaging account of how he spent the pandemic in the Italian Alps, in lockdown, forbidden to climb his favourite peaks and what that did to his mental health. *Climbing the Walls* is a reminder of the healing power of mountains and why they matter.'

Robert Charles Lee for *Through Dangerous Doors*. Lee, a retired risk scientist who went from adventuring with psychedelics to climbing on rock and ice, often with his equally adventurous partner Linda, Lee has written 'an unfiltered, unpredictable memoir that's a pleasure to read.'

Anna Fleming for *Time on Rock*. This book 'captures the intimate relationship between climber and rock, whether it's the gritstone of the Peak District or the granite of the Cairngorms. Her elegant, muscular writing puts us right there on the route with her, creating a peripatetic meditation on how "we shape the rock and the rock shapes us".'

Paul Pritchard for *The Mountain Path*. A previous Boardman Tasker winner, Pritchard 'has gone even deeper into the spiritual rewards of a life in the mountains. *The Mountain Path* is a devastatingly honest and inspirational account of choosing to live. It's also great fun to read.'

Helen Mort for *A Line Above the Sky*. Poet Helen Mort 'draws a line between the risks and terrors of new motherhood and a more untethered life in the mountains. Shadowing the story of Alison Hargreaves, who refused to give up alpinism when she became a mother, Helen brilliantly captures the soul-forging power of two extreme experiences: climbing mountains and giving birth.',

Brian Hall for *High Risk*. Hall grew up 'with the radical climbers who would come to define a wild and glorious chapter of mountaineering in the 1970s and 1980s. He partied with them, climbed with them and grieved them. Full of humour, affection and respect, *High Risk* takes the reader to the heart and soul of the golden age of UK climbing.

In a unanimous decision, the jury also took a risk and drew a line. The 2022 Boardman Tasker Award for Mountain Literature was shared between Brian Hall for *High Risk* and to Helen Mort for *A Line Above The Sky*. More details on the Boardman Tasker Award at ***www.boardmantasker.com***

Ed Douglas

Peter Hillary and Jamling Norgay speak under an image of their fathers.

Everest at 70

Celebrations for the first ascent of Everest were held worldwide in remembrance of the achievement itself as well as a remarkable and enduring legacy that is still very much alive and kicking.

In London, two charities that sprang directly from the 1953 expedition – the Mount Everest Foundation and the Himalayan Trust UK – came together to organise a celebration at the Royal Geographical Society on Tuesday 13 June. The only living member of the 1953 expedition, Kanchha Sherpa, was sadly unable to attend but the next generation were there in full force. Some 35 members of Hillary and Tenzing's family travelled from around the world to attend the event, including Ed Hillary's son, Peter, and Tenzing Norgay's son, Jamling, who spoke alongside Col John Hunt's daughter, Sue Leyden, Stephen Venables, Kenton Cool and, just back from Everest, Hari Budha Magar: the first double above-the-knee amputee to climb to the summit.

In the afternoon, an event to inspire young people to 'go out and explore' included bushcraft legend Ray Mears, Everest climber and physicist Melanie Windridge, high-altitude mountaineer and endurance athlete Adriana Brownlee and world-class rock climber and mountaineer Leo Houlding, all bringing their magic to what was a remarkable and memorable day.

Contributors

ELAINE ASTILL brought her enthusiasm for the Alps and their social history to this year's *Alpine Journal*, her contribution inspired entirely by the discovery of some remarkable illustrations. A previous contribution to the *Alpine Journal*, and also to that of the Italian Alpine Club, focused on the early Alpine Club artist Elijah Walton.

ROBIN CAMPBELL has held every office in the Scottish Mountaineering Club for which administrative competence is not required, including a long stint as editor in the 1960s and 1970s, and as archivist since 1997. Retired from a desultory career as an academic child psychologist, he now wastes his time and money in collecting and studying old drawings and watercolours, particularly those depicting mountains before they were trampled into familiarity by the boots of mountaineers.

JACOB COOK is a mathematics professor originally from London now living in British Colombia. An elite rock climber, his greatest passion is free climbing on the world's biggest rock faces. Highlights include the first free ascent of *Disco 2000* (5.13c) on Blamman in Norway with Dave Macleod and a free ascent of El Niño (5.13c) on Yosemite's El Capitan over six days with Robbie Phillips.

JOHN CLEARE has been a freelance professional photographer for over 50 years but a climber for rather longer. Business and many expeditions have taken him all over the world, while he has several dozen books, several films and live TV broadcasts, more than a few new routes and several virgin summits to his credit. An ex-vice president of the AC and an ex-president of the Alpine Ski Club, he lives in remote Wiltshire.

ANNIE DARE is head of communications at the International Centre for Integrated Mountain Development (www.icimod.org).

RON DART teaches in the political science, philosophy and religious studies department at the University of the Fraser Valley. He was on the staff of Amnesty International in the 1980s. Dart has published 40 books including *Erasmus: Wild Bird* (Create Space, 2017) and *The North American High Tory Tradition* (American Anglican Press, 2016).

PETER FOSTER is a retired consultant physician. He has been a member of the Alpine Club since 1975.

TERRY GIFFORD was director of the annual International Festival of Mountaineering Literature for 21 years. Former chair of the Mountain Heritage Trust, he is the author of *The Joy of Climbing* (Whittles, 2004) and *Al Otro Lado del Aguilar* (Oversteps Books, 2011). Visiting professor at Bath Spa University's Centre for Writing and Environment and *profesor honorífico* at the University of Alicante, he celebrated his 70th birthday appropriately on *Wreckers' Slab*.

DENNIS GRAY started climbing on Yorkshire gritstone in 1947. Secretary of the ACG, first national officer, then general secretary of the BMC, Dennis has visited over 60 countries, most recently travelling widely in China. He has written two autobiographies, two books of stories, a novel and a volume of poetry, plays the banjo and sings on three CDs of climbing themed songs.

LINDSAY GRIFFIN lives in north Wales, from where he continues to report on developments in world mountaineering. An enthusiastic mind still tries to coax a less than enthusiastic body up pleasant bits of rock and ice, both at home and abroad. He remains the world's leading chronicler of mountaineering achievement.

J G R HARDING, a former Alpine Club vice president, no longer climbs but still writes about mountaineers and mountaineering. The article on Freda du Faur is one of a trilogy featuring some outstanding women climbers. John's mountaineering autobiography *Distant Snows* (Bâton Wicks) was published in 2016.

RACHEL HEWITT is a best-selling, award-winning writer of creative non-fiction, as well as a critic and broadcaster. She writes about the 'great outdoors', running, women and public space, grief and recovery, history and feminism, memoir and biography. She is a fellow of the Royal Society of Literature. Her earlier books were *A Revolution of Feeling: The Decade that Forged the Modern Mind* (Granta, 2017) and *Map of a Nation: A Biography of the Ordnance Survey* (Granta, 2010).

MAREK HOLEČEK is one of the world's leading mountaineers as well as an author and documentary filmmaker. In 2018 he won the Piolet d'Or with Zdeněk Hák for the difficult new route *Satisfaction!* on the south-west face of Gasherbrum I, completed on his fifth attempt having suffered bad frostbite and the loss of a partner on previous expeditions.

JIM LANGLEY is an international mountain leader and co-author of *The Alps: A Natural Companion*. He runs professional development courses for mountain leaders and instructors in Snowdonia and also the Alps. through his educational business Nature's Work.

TOM LIVINGSTONE is a 31-year-old climber and writer originally from the south of England. He has a penchant for trad, winter and alpine climbing; his ascents include a winter ascent of *Rolling Stones* on the Grandes Jorasses, *The Great Game* on Koyo Zom and the *North Ridge Variation* on Latok I, for which he was a Piolet d'Or. In 2020 he founded the Young Alpinist Group.

ADÈLE LONG is a retired medical researcher. Although a latecomer to the world of rock and alpinism, she has been fortunate enough to climb or ski on six of the seven continents, bagging a handful of first ascents along the way. During Covid-19, she has been less active on the hill and more occupied with the Pinnacle Club's centenary heritage project and the Alpine Club's Women Rise Up! project. Normality may, or may not be resumed in 2022.

JOHN MIDDENDORF was born in New York City and studied engineering at Stanford. During the 1980s and 1990s he was among the world's best climbers, particularly on big walls, with a formidable record in Yosemite and the Karakoram. A near-death experience with a portaledge led to him to establish the equipment company A5, and later, D4. He remains deeply interested in the evolution of climbing gear.

DONALD ORR is a member of the Scottish Mountaineering Club and recently retired from a career in theology and fine art, which does beg questions. He now spends his time climbing and writing, and being irresponsible with his grandsons. His writings on mountaineering and the mountain environment have contributed over the years to the *Scottish Mountaineering Club Journal*.

SIMON RICHARDSON lives in Aberdeen. Experience gained in the Alps, Andes, Patagonia, Canada, the Himalaya, Caucasus, Alaska and the Yukon is put to good use most winter weekends whilst exploring and climbing in the Scottish Highlands.

VICTOR SAUNDERS was born in Lossiemouth and grew up in Peninsular Malaysia. He began climbing in the Alps in 1978 and has since climbed in the Andes, Antarctica and across the Himalaya and Karakoram. Formerly an architect in London, he is now an IFMGA guide based in Chamonix. His first book, *Elusive Summits,* won the Boardman Tasker. In 2007 he received an honorary MA from the University of Stirling for services to Scottish mountaineering.

MARCELO SCANU is an Argentine climber who lives in Buenos Aires. He specialises in ascending virgin mountains and volcanoes in the Central Andes. His articles and photographs about alpinism, trekking, and mountain history, archaeology and ecology appear in prominent magazines in Europe and America. When not climbing, he works for a workers' union.

DAVID SEDDON is a physician in Nottingham. He was an indifferent member of both OUMC and CUMC but had more success as a ski-mountaineer under the leadership of John Harding, the late Derek Fordham and Peter Edgerton. He remains enthusiastic about the pictures of TH Somervell.

RODERICK A SMITH began his fascination with mountains following the first ascent of Everest in 1953. He has travelled to the Himalaya, Svalbard, Greenland, Arctic Canada, Japan and the Alps but always returns to his favourites in the Lake District. A lifetime's enjoyment has not been hampered with overweening ambition, but he is proud of his first ascent of a peak in the Stauning Alps and that he can still enjoy climbing and skiing at a modest level, despite the onset of decrepitude

NICHOLAS HURNDALL SMITH is a climber and classical singer based in Cumbria. Having helped reinvigorate the Club's climbing meets, he is currently on the Committee, working on the aspirants' programme to boost the approachability of Alpine and expedition climbing. He loves nothing better than a day at an esoteric crag in Cumbria or the traverse of an Alpine 4,000er.

SUZANNE STRAWTHER is a retired secondary school English teacher and Alpine Club member. In 2021, she co-curated the 'Women with Altitude' exhibition at the AC, celebrating the Ladies' Alpine Club and the centenary of the Pinnacle Club. She 'works' intermittently in the Archives at the Club.

IAN WALL worked at Plas-y-Brenin in the 1960s. Since then he has climbed extensively throughout the UK, the Alps and in Norway. He now lives in Nepal and acts as an advisor to the Kathmandu International Mountain Film Festival, Kathmandu Environmental Education Project and in developing the Nepal Mountain Leader programme working closely with the Nepal Mountaineering Association.

JOHN WILKINSON started climbing aged 28 and was bitten for life. In 1969 he left the oil industry to become a don, marrying Anne Sauvy. In 1977 he became senior member of OUMC and started a new period of mountaineering and expeditions. He kept going until the onset of Covid-19 with friends and an intensive annual three weeks with a guide. He is a member of the ACG and GHM.

NOTES FOR CONTRIBUTORS

The *Alpine Journal* records all aspects of mountains and mountaineering, including expeditions, exploration, art, literature, geography, history, geology, medicine, ethics and the mountain environment.

Articles Contributions in English are invited. They should be sent to the Hon Editor *The Alpine Journal*, Alpine Club, 55 Charlotte Road, London EC2A 3QF, UK. (**social_media@alpine-club.org.uk**) Articles, including images, can be sent as an email attachment, on a disk or memory stick. File-sharing services are also acceptable, by prior arrangement with the editor. With files created in Microsoft Word please confine formatting to italics and bold. A typical article is 2,500 words **and may be edited or shortened at the editor's discretion**. Longer pieces should be discussed with the editor.

The Alpine Journal is unable to offer a fee for articles published, but authors who are not AC members receive a copy of the issue of the *Journal* in which their article appears.

Maps and diagrams These should be well researched, accurate and show the most important place-names mentioned in the text. If submitted electronically, maps and route diagrams should be originated as CMYK ***.eps*** files in Adobe Illustrator, Freehand or similar ensuring embedded images are **300dpi** resolution and CMYK. Fonts must be embedded or converted to curves. Hard copy should be scanned as a **300dpi** ***.tiff*** or ***.jpg*** file at A4 finished size. This can be arranged through the editor if required.

Photographs Image files should have unique names or serial numbers **that correspond to the list of captions** appended to the article, as a separate document, or in an email. They should be large jpgs or tiff files. Captions must include the photographer's name. Colour transparencies should be originals. Pre-scanned images should be **300dpi** Greyscale or RGB, tiffs or maximum quality jpegs at A4 final size or larger.

Copyright It is the author's responsibility to obtain copyright clearance for text, photographs, digital images and maps, to pay any fees involved and to ensure acknowledgements are in the form required by the copyright owner.

Summaries A brief summary, listing team members, dates, objectives attempted and achieved, should be included at the end of expedition articles.

Biographies Authors are asked to provide a short autobiography of about 50 words, listing noteworthy highlights in their climbing career and anything else they wish to mention.

Deadline Copy and photographs should reach the editor by **1 February** of the year of publication.

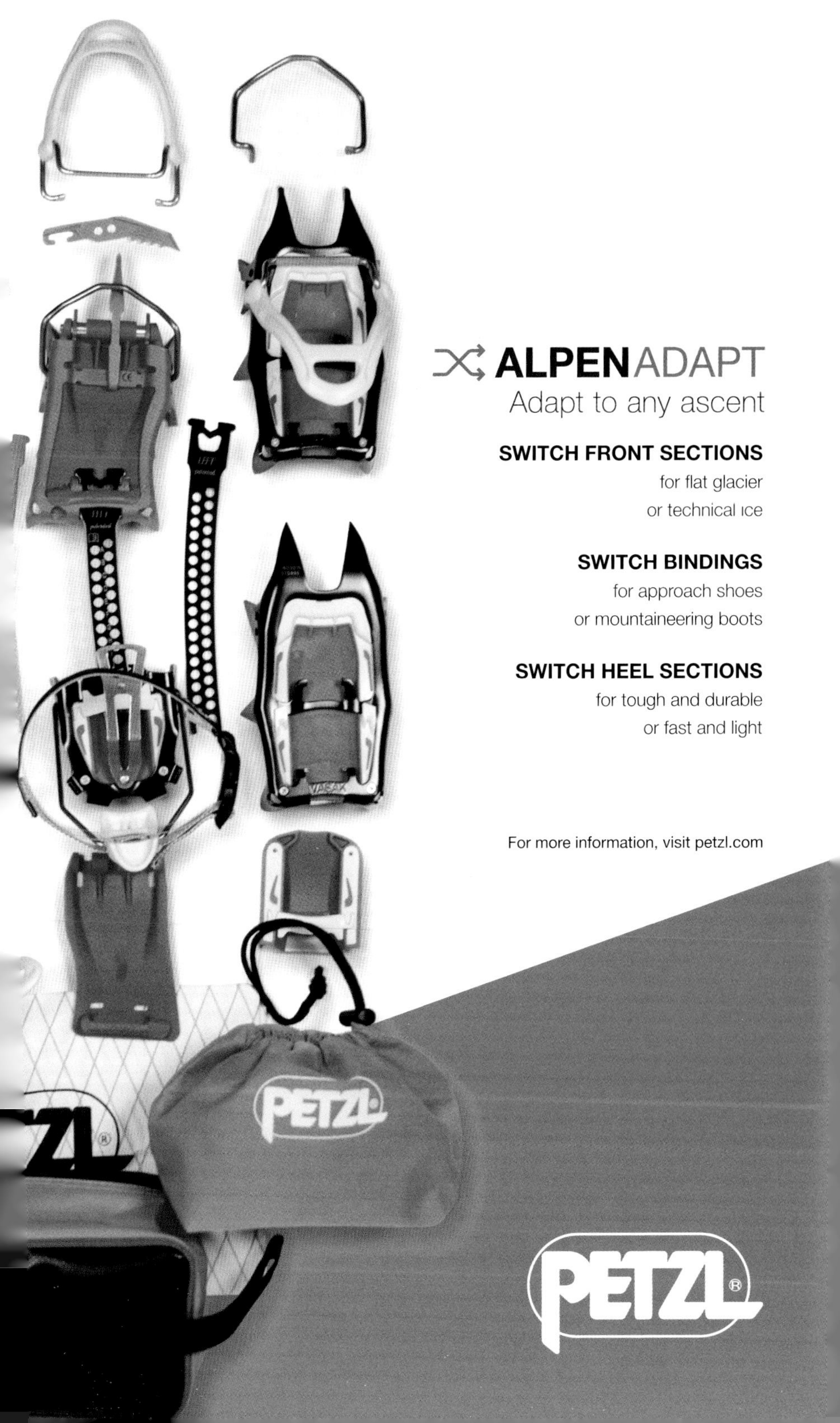
ALPENADAPT
Adapt to any ascent
SWITCH FRONT SECTIONS
for flat glacier
or technical ice
SWITCH BINDINGS
for approach shoes
or mountaineering boots
SWITCH HEEL SECTIONS
for tough and durable
or fast and light
For more information, visit petzl.com
PETZL

Index

'Moonlit Mountain Landscape', Elijah Walton, undated, watercolour touched with white, 13.8cm × 22.4cm. *(British Museum)*

Index 2023

C

D

E

F

G

M

N

Y

Z